TURNING POINT

First published in the UK in 1998 by
Earthscan Publications Ltd
Copyright © Robert U Ayres, 1998

A catalogue record for this book is available from the British Library

ISBN: 1 85383 439 4 (paperback)
ISBN: 1 85383 444 0 (hardback)

Typesetting and page design by Oxprint Design Ltd

Printed and bound by Biddles Ltd, Guildford and Kings Lynn

Cover design by Dan Mercer, Myriad Design

For a full list of publications, please contact
Earthscan Publications Ltd
120 Pentonville Road
London N1 9JN
Tel: 0171 278 0433
Fax: 0171 278 1142
email: earthinfo@earthscan.co.uk
http://www.earthscan.co.uk

Earthscan is an editorially independent subsidiary of Kogan Page Ltd and publishes
in association with WWF-UK and the International Institute for Environment and
Development.

TURNING POINT

AN END TO THE GROWTH PARADIGM

Robert U Ayres

EARTHSCAN
Earthscan Publications Ltd, London

Contents

List of Tables

List of Figures

List of Boxes

List of Acronyms and Abbreviations

AAAS	American Association for the Advancement of Science
ADC	aid to dependent children
APEC	Asia–Pacific economic council
BaP	benz(a)pyrene
BIS	Bank for International Settlements
bps	bits per second
BTU	British Thermal Unit
CEO	chief executive officer
CERCLA	Comprehensive Environmental Response, Compensation and Liability Act
CFC	chlorofluorocarbon
CGE	computable general equilibrium
CH_4	methane
CIS	Council of Independent States
cm	centimeter
CO_2	carbon dioxide
COLA	cost of living adjustment
COMECON	Council for Mutual Economic Aid
CV	contingent evaluation
DASA	Defense Atomic Support Agency
DM	Deutschmark
DRAM	dynamic random access memory (chip)
E/GNP ratio	energy intensity of GNP
EEC	European Economic Community
EFPLS	expected future personal labor surplus
EPA	Environmental Protection Agency (US)
ESP	electrostatic precipitator
EU	European Union
FF	French Franc
FGD	flue gas desulfurization
FY	fiscal year
GATT	General Agreement on Tariffs and Trade
GDP	Gross domestic product
GNP	Gross national product
GPI	Genuine Progress Indicator
GTR	Global 2000 Report
HRS	human resources securitization
H-O	Hecksher-Ohlin
H-O-V	Hecksher-Ohlin-Vanek
HMO	health maintenance organization
IHT	*International Herald Tribune*
IIASA	International Institute of Applied Systems Analysis
INSEAD	The European Institute of Business Administration
IMF	International Monetary Fund
IRA	individual retirement account
IRS	Internal Revenue Service (US)

ISEW	Index of Sustainable Economic Welfare
IT	information technology
K/L	capital–labor ratio
km	kilometer
kWh	kilowatt hour
LAN	local area network
LBO	leveraged buyout
LDC	Less Developed Country
LET	light-emitting diode
MBTU	Million British Thermal Units
MEW	measure of economic welfare
MITI	Ministry of International Trade and Industry (Japan)
MNC	multinational company
MPC	maximal permissible concentration
N_2O	nitrous oxide
NAFTA	North American Free Trade Association
NASA	National Aeronautics and Space Administration
NATO	North Atlantic Treaty Organization
NO_x	nitrogen oxides
OECD	Organization for Economic Cooperation and Development
OPEC	Organization of Petroleum Exporting Countries
PAN	per-acyl nitrate
PC	personal computer
PCDD	poly-chlorinated di-benzo-dioxin
PCE	personal consumption expenditure
PPP	polluter-pays principle
PQLI	physical quality of life index
PV	photovoltaic
R&D	research and development
RCRA	Resource Conservation and Reclamation Act
RFF	Resources For the Future Inc
S&L	savings and loan
SEC	Securities and Exchange Commission
SNA	System of National Accounts (UN)
SO_2	sulfur dioxide
SPRU	Science Policy Research Unit (University of Sussex, UK)
UNCED	United Nations Commission on Environment and Development
UNDP	United Nations Development Program
UNEP	United Nations Environment Program
USSR	Union of Soviet Socialist Republics
VAT	value-added tax
VCR	video cassette recorder
WCED	World Commission on Environment and Development
WTA	willingness to accept
WTO	World Trade Organization
WTP	willingness to pay
WWF	World Wildlife Fund

Preface

Though I am an academic person by temperament and profession, this book is much more informal (and a bit more personal) than the usual academic monograph. I make no apologies for that. In the last few years I have changed my view radically on several important issues, notably economic growth, trade, social progress, and equity. Today I have deep misgivings, both about economic growth, as currently defined and measured, and especially about world trade as an instrument for achieving it.

This turnabout on my part has been mostly triggered by the growing evidence that economic 'growth' today is benefiting only a few of those people now alive, at least in the Western world. I am somewhat less skeptical about the benefits of growth for Asians en masse, although there, too, most of the benefits seem to be appropriated by a very few.

The major part of the statistical 'growth' we now see in the US, and Europe, merely reflects increasingly frantic activity, especially trade. In many respects it amounts to running faster and faster to stay in the same place – 'wheel spinning' – rather than true wealth creation. Meanwhile social life and family life are deteriorating. This is true both in the West and in the developing world. It now seems that economic growth in western countries, as currently measured in terms of gross domestic or gross national product (GDP or GNP),[1] is mostly an illusion. It reflects little or no progress in human welfare in 'real' terms (health, diet, housing, education, leisure, etc).

GNP growth in the past century owes a good deal to the monetization of subsistence agriculture and, more recently, the monetization of household (ie – often – women's) work. This fact alone makes intertemporal comparisons difficult. But an increasing share of GNP growth in recent decades is attributable to expenditures resulting from three other trends:

1) unavoidable transportation, child care and other costs associated with employment outside the home;
2) a growing need for protection against threats to life, health and property due to urbanization, congestion, social malaise and side effects of other human activities (such as highway accidents), together with a growing need to repair or compensate for such damage; and
3) 'living on capital'. This means depletion of natural resource stocks, from minerals to forests and fisheries, without replacement or substitution.

There is also an element of regressive wealth distribution. The principal beneficiaries of GNP growth in the US are few and already prosperous – the top 20 per cent of family incomes. (Let us not argue about who is, or isn't, 'rich'.) The losers are nearly everybody else, especially the poor, the less educated and the politically powerless of this and future generations. A two tier society is being reconstituted, by radicals of the right and former communists alike, from the ashes of burnt out socialist ideals. 'Beggar thy neighbor' is the new watchword. 'Greed is good' say the wealthy, who think that unfettered capitalism won the Cold War.

To future generations, the educated elite in this generation, myself included, is bequeathing a more and more potent technology and a significant investment in productive machinery and equipment and infrastructure. But these benefits may not – almost certainly cannot – compensate for a depleted natural resource base, a gravely damaged environment, and, most important of all, a broken social contract. In consequence, as time passes it will be increasingly difficult to mobilize technology in the service of society as a whole.

The fraying of the social fabric in the Western world – including Japan – is hardly disputable. Virtually all contemporary political discourse today in the West concerns the symptoms themselves (crime, drugs, domestic terrorism), the most immediate threats (unemployment, taxes) or the most visible targets (immigration, 'welfare abuse', 'reverse discrimination', etc). As is usual, the victims are often the principal objects of blame. For instance, illegal immigrants and unmarried single mothers are being singled out for punishment under recent welfare 'reform' legislation in the US.

But, my purpose here is not to denounce today's populist politicians of the right, though I deplore and oppose many of their policies. The leftish populists of the past were equally misguided in blaming bankers, industrialists and landlords for many of the same social problems. In both cases, the politicians were, and are, simply unscrupulous power seekers willing and able to exploit public confusion and unfocussed dissatisfaction by offering convenient scapegoats and equally simple-minded panaceas. (Hitler blamed the Jews, Bolsheviks and the 'evil' Treaty of Versailles for the problems of Germany. Many Germans accepted these false explanations, though without understanding all of their implications.) The fundamental source of confusion, then and now, is inability on the part of the public and politicians alike to distinguish between superficial *symptoms* and underlying *causes*. It is particularly difficult to do so, of course, given the complexity of the problems we face, and the plethora of misinformation and deliberately induced disinformation propagated by the popular media.

No small contribution to the disinformation problem arises from the efforts of honest scholars to compensate for media exaggeration and oversimplification. Scientists are wary of drawing hasty conclusions from incomplete and often confusing evidence. They often feel compelled to emphasize doubts and uncertainties (not infrequently to justify the need for further research). This creates openings for pseudo-scholarly ideologues of the status quo, a species that is always well represented in modern society. In this book I take particular issue with some of these 'Panglossians' or 'Cornucopians' (without, by any means, accepting the neo-Malthusian thesis they so energetically denounce).

I recognize that many – even most – people in the world are materially better off than their ancestors were. I acknowledge that many of the trends that made this material progress possible have been going on for a long time and that, at first glance, there is no compelling reason to suppose that the trends will not continue. I acknowledge that many people have falsely predicted disaster in the past. In most cases this was unintentional; it resulted from an excessively narrow view of the problem – usually by not seeing that natural feedbacks can and do compensate for some perturbing forces. I also acknowledge that some 'doomsayers' may have deliberately exaggerated the problems, either to get publicity or to stimulate action. There is, undoubtedly, a history of crying wolf. This, in itself, seems to convince many people that the wolf is imaginary and will never come.

Yet, having said this, I think the coming of the wolf is now imminent. It is not the prospects for material aspects of welfare or standard of living that concern me; it is social breakdown, and its likely consequences, including environmental deterioration.

Without dwelling prematurely on the matter of cause and effect, I think it sufficiently clear, on reflection, that the symptoms of social breakdown that create so much present anguish are largely consequences of a number of deeply embedded long-term trends. Some of these trends are precisely the ones that drive economic 'growth' and thus encourage the Panglossians.

In particular, the trends that matter are *urbanization, industrialization, materialization, automation* and *communication*, as well as *economic globalization* which is partly a consequence of the other trends. From these trends, taken together, other social phenomena inevitably arise. For instance, *alienation* (loss of cultural identity) results from urbanization and industrialization; *insecurity of employment* results from automation, free movement of capital, and other consequences of 'economic development'; *insecurity of person* results from urbanization, alienation and economic distress; and *environmental deterioration* is a consequence of the material-intensive production of goods and services. But these impersonal social trends are not the whole cause of impending trouble. In addition, I am inclined to put some of the blame on the spread of simplistic economic doctrines, based on oversimplified models and theories that no longer reflect the most important aspects of reality.

The libertarians who are now in the political ascendant in the US and the UK deny that they would dispense with law – only too many laws, and too much enforcement of laws, and regulations they do not personally like, such as laws against private ownership of certain types of lethal weapons. Much of the Republican right in the US advocates more legislation and stronger enforcement of what they see as 'morality' – laws against abortion being the most obvious example. Yet the very same people want to cut off welfare assistance to unmarried mothers in order to force them to go to work, leaving their children even more vulnerable to the slum, drug and crime culture than they already are. The right wingers rant and rail publicly against crime. Yet, in practice, they promote policies which transfer still more wealth from the poor to the rich, and undermine efforts to create more jobs suitable for the less privileged and less educated, and to assist such people to qualify for honest employment. Thus, their actions create conditions where social pathologies are inevitable.

The libertarians do not see the inconsistency of such attitudes, or the downstream consequences of destroying the social safety net. They do not want to see. They are too busy getting richer, or trying to. They are as naive as the Marxists who were sure that the state would wither away once the oppressing capitalists were destroyed. It will be a great tragedy for civilization if the libertarian illusion lasts as long as the Marxist illusion did.

To repeat an earlier remark, economic development along the conventional track – increasing GDP per capita – is not necessarily increasing social welfare. The game is becoming zero-sum, or even negative-sum. The popular phrase 'sustainable economic growth', as it is currently interpreted by the dominant businesses and government institutions of our society, is probably an oxymoron. In other words, I have come to the conclusion, somewhat reluctantly, that economic growth, *as we know it*, is not sustainable. That is the bad news.

The good news is that conventional development (ie GDP growth) is no longer doing much good for most people, at least in the industrial world. This is *not* to suggest that economic growth was not very important to my own generation and, even more so, to all the preceding generations back to the Industrial Revolution. But for the last two decades the tide has no longer been rising for most people in the US, and since 1990, give or take a year or so, it has stopped rising in Europe and Japan too. So, a change of direction need not be very painful to those who have been flattened, rather than floated, by the economic development juggernaut.

Another bit of good news is that an end to the 'growth paradigm' does *not* necessarily imply an end to growth itself. It certainly does not mean (as the Panglossians tend to argue) that we and our descendants need to give up all the good things money can buy and freeze in the dark. There are far better options. However, they will not appear automatically like a *deus ex machina*, nor will they be easily or painlessly achieved. Cutting income taxes for the wealthy or the middle class will not do the trick. In fact, a revenue-neutral tax cut on labor would be desirable, but only if other taxes (on consumption, pollution or resource use) were raised to compensate for the lost revenue. Otherwise tax cutting is likely to make every one of our problems worse.

This seems to contradict much conventional wisdom, so it requires some explanation. Hence this book.

NOTES

1. Gross domestic product (GDP) is defined as the sum total of the output of all goods and services produced for sale, at market prices, by private entities within the national boundaries, plus the sum total of government services produced at cost by government. Gross national product (GNP) includes goods and services produced by national entities outside the country but excludes the goods and services produced by foreign entities within the national boundaries. For the US and other large industrial countries the two measures are nearly the same. In both cases, the sum total of goods and services produced (ie output) must be essentially equal to the sum total of wages, salaries, dividends and interest income to individuals.

Chapter 1

On Possible and Impossible Futures

INTRODUCTION TO FORECASTING

Before plunging headlong into controversy, I want to make some (hopefully) non-controversial remarks about forecasting. It is common for writers who disparage the activity to note that prediction is difficult, 'especially as concerns the future'.[1] Isaac Asimov's *Foundation* novels feature a psychohistorian genius named Hari Seldon, who has developed a probabilistic theory of social systems. An early scene has Seldon demonstrating to a young research assistant that there is a probability of 92.5 per cent that the galactic empire will collapse into anarchy within 500 years (Asimov, 1951). The notion that any such prediction could be made from a set of mathematical symbols has always tickled my funny bone.

Anybody who has wrestled with forecasting models will share my amusement at the *naïveté* of the notion that future history could ever be reduced to a set of equations. We can take it for granted that 100 per cent accuracy in forecasting is impossible. Nevertheless, some important things can be said. One of them is that not all imaginable futures are possible. Some imaginable futures are simply inconsistent with the laws of nature, as far as we know them. (For instance, most of the gadgets and plots of *Star Trek* violate several of these laws. Unfortunately, it is not only on TV that impossible futures are taken seriously by some people.)

Of course, some possible futures are far more plausible than others. It is imaginable, but very implausible, that all the nations and peoples of the earth would decide spontaneously to disarm, live in peace with each other, and decide all disputes by referendum and a world court. There are, however, still a great many plausible but different futures. It is impossible to predict which among the many plausible ones will come to pass. On the other hand, it is the legitimate business of forecasting to select the most plausible among them for consideration, particularly as a guide to policy. In this context, there are two very different types of forecast. For symbolic reasons, I will call them 'alpha' and 'omega'.[2]

The first type is the alpha forecast or *contingent extrapolation*. It is a description of the situation that will arise if present social or demographic trends, or policies, continue as currently. An important point to note is that not all contingent extrapolations lead to desirable outcomes. Some outcomes are flatly impossible. Thus the contingent extrapolation may point to a need for policy or behavioral change. In such a case, the forecast is intended to be self-denying.

An interesting example comes from the history of technology. In the early 1940s a vice-president of Bell Telephone Laboratories extrapolated the growth of demand for telephone services for several decades. Then he extrapolated the need for automated central telephone exchanges. Finally he calculated the amount of electric power needed to serve those exchanges (at the time, telephone exchanges were based on electromechanical switches). According to the story, he then noticed that demand for electric power for electromechanical telephone switching would exceed the then current forecasts of total demand for electric power for all purposes.

This was a self-denying forecast. The Bell Laboratories man saw that continued growth of the telephone system would require a new kind of switching technology that would use much less electric power than the (then) current technology. As luck would have it, there were some young physicists at Bell Laboratories who thought that a strange phenomenon in certain transition metals and alloys called semi-conductivity might point the way. Their names were William Shockley, John Bardeen and Walter Brattain. They were assigned to work on the project. The end result was the invention of the transistor, surely one of the dozen or so most important inventions since the wheel. Needless to say, demand for telecommunications has multiplied hundreds of times since then, but demand for electric power to run the telephone system is now almost unnoticeable.

The second type of forecast (omega) is an attempt to describe a desirable distant future and, working back, to delineate possible pathways to that future. It is sometimes called a 'normative' forecast. Such a forecast also has policy implications. Needless to say, an omega forecast is intended to be self-fulfilling, rather than self-denying. An example might be John Kennedy's 1962 forecast that an American would land on the moon 'before the end of the decade'. Kennedy's forecast was a call to action. It galvanized the Congress to create NASA and to provide the funds needed. The moon landing was achieved, on time, in 1969.

CONTINGENT TREND EXTRAPOLATIONS

With respect to contingent or alpha extrapolations, there is somewhat more to be said. There are three major points:

1) in the absence of a *specific* reason to think otherwise, an historical trend that is well established is much more likely to continue for a while, than not. Hence, trend extrapolations are generally the safest thing for a short-term forecasting practitioner to do.
2) Trends do not always continue; sometimes they cannot. Reversals do occur. (Consider the stock market, for instance.) In fact, trend reversals occur fairly often. Moreover, when trend reversals occur, it is often sudden and surprising, even though the reason for the reversal is usually quite obvious in retrospect.
3) Trend reversals are usually important events, sometimes worthy of headlines, whereas linear extrapolations are like old news. The real non-trivial task of a would-be forecaster is to identify likely future reversals and their implications. Unfortunately, the timing is always a major problem. Whereas it is very easy to extrapolate a trend – all that is needed is graph paper and a ruler – it is extraordinarily difficult to pinpoint the date of a turnaround. One key reason for this is

that the turnaround is usually delayed by institutional inertia. When it finally comes, it is more often than not triggered by a random event. Moreover the turnaround, when it finally occurs, is quite sudden and even catastrophic.

With regard to the issue of timing, consider the 'oil shock' of 1973–1974. It occurred because domestic US oil production peaked in 1969–1970 and began to decline. Imports began to rise sharply, and the strategic importance of the Persian Gulf rose in parallel. But these things, in themselves, might not have caused a crisis. The triggering event that brought the Arab world together was the third Arab–Israeli war in 1973, which prompted the Arab oil embargo. The embargo was effective because of the lack of reserve capacity in the US or elsewhere in the world.

How accurately could the timing of the oil shock have been predicted? The best answer to that is that none of the concerned government agencies, major independent forecasting groups, or the oil companies themselves, did foresee it. Only one major oil company, Shell, considered it to be a plausible future scenario in the sense I have used above. Shell, unlike the others, did some strategic contingency planning based on the possibility of something like the events that actually occurred. Shell gained substantially on its competitors thanks to this coup, and now ranks as the world's most successful oil company. (Curiously, Shell's systematic use of scenario analysis for strategic planning has spawned several successful consultancies. But no other large firm, to my knowledge, has actually attempted to do the same thing.)

Many past forecasters have identified likely turnarounds, but failed to predict the timing accurately. I doubt that I could do better. A predicted turnaround with a date attached (such as the many predictions of the end of the world or the second coming of Christ) is an almost certain failure. But a linear trend extrapolation that fails to foresee a turnaround is a far greater failure, at least in my view. If a predicted event occurs early or late but somewhere near the predicted time, and for the reasons proposed, the forecast should be graded as a qualified success.

CYCLES

Cycles are to be distinguished from discontinuities, but both are important in the forecasting business. A cycle is an oscillatory phenomenon analogous to the pendulum of a clock, the rise and fall of the tides, the waxing and waning of the moon, or the progression of the seasons. In all of these cases, the cyclic motion is driven by gravitational forces (generated by large masses) acting on much smaller masses. Since the masses involved are unchanging, the motion is very predictable. The analogy with economic and other cycles in the social sphere is far from perfect, because the forces involved are much more complex. Nevertheless, some of the economic relationships are orderly enough to produce a quasi-regular behavior. The relationship between retailers' inventories and orders to manufacturers for re-stocking is the classic example. When inventories are high, orders fall, and vice versa. This is the so-called 'business cycle' of four to five years, a well-studied phenomenon in economics.[3]

Some observers have attempted to explain the so-called Kondratieff inflation/deflation cycle of about 50 years. During the rising part of the cycle, economic activity accelerates and commodity prices rise. During the declining part of the cycle, activity slows and commodity prices fall. The cycle has repeated itself several times since 1780 or so (at least in the UK and the US) and the deflationary period tends to end with a war.

Speculation on this topic peaked a few years ago – as the fiftieth anniversary of the Great Depression of 1932 passed, more or less uneventfully – but has since died down. Other observers have gone so far as to try to explain wars in terms of sunspot or climate cycles. However, while there may be some correlation between general economic conditions and/or general climatic conditions and the probability that a local conflict will become violent, such deterministic schemes have never proved to be accurate guides to the future. Given the complexity and uncertainty of the ex post explanations for most macro-economic phenomena, as well as wars, it is not plausible that they should be related to each other in any simple way.

Having said this, however, I should add that there are nevertheless some good reasons for taking the Kondratieff cycle seriously. It is not that the cycle itself is a reliable basis for forecasting. But the mechanisms that drove the cycle – more or less – are probably still operating. Here I acknowledge the existence of a number of competing theories, none of which has dispatched the others. However, my own view of the Kondratieff cycle emphasizes two key features. One is the fact that from the late eighteenth century on, the cycle closely followed the succession of major energy and power technologies. First came the rise of coal and mobile steam power, which peaked in the mid-nineteenth century. Then came the rise of steam-electric power and hydrocarbon fuel based on internal combustion engines. During this period coal was largely displaced by petroleum. Natural gas, in turn, began to take a large share of the energy market in the middle of this century. Nuclear power, of course, entered the picture in the 1960s. These technological shifts had enormous ramifications throughout the economic system.

The other key feature of the past Kondratieff cycles is that the end of the declining phase and the beginning of the rising phase seems to be characterized by a cluster of technological innovations, whereas the period of peak activity and most rapid growth is also a period of relatively sparse technological innovation. The logical explanation for this may be something along the following lines:[4] after a period of innovative activity, investment is attracted into speculative ventures and new products. This period corresponds to the bottom of the cycle. As these new products and services begin to develop momentum in the marketplace, they also attract capital into capacity expansion. The period of rapid capacity expansion is a period of strong growth, easy market entry, high employment and gradually rising commodity prices (as shortages develop). This is the rising phase of the Kondratieff cycle.

While capital is being used profitably for capacity expansion, it is less available for riskier long-run ventures, so the rate of innovation slows down. But eventually, markets become saturated, barriers to entry are high, and the dominant firms merge and consolidate to protect their profits by forming oligopolies or cartels. At this stage of the cycle, economic expansion slows down and unemployment rises. The deflationary period begins. But paradoxically, thanks to disinvestment in older sectors, there are funds available for riskier ventures with higher profit potential. The present appears to be such a time. (However, the new ventures being financed currently are mostly old businesses relocating in East Asia). Thus, as the economy slows down, a new period of innovative activity begins, setting the stage for a new period of growth.

Obviously there is nothing predetermined about the rate of adoption of important technological innovations or the size of the markets created thereby. Some products or services can grow more or less indefinitely, through successive generations of improvements, without exhibiting any apparent market saturation effect. The telephone, the automobile and the airplane would be examples, although the automobile market does appear to be saturated in North America and Western Europe. Other new products or processes may penetrate and saturate their markets within a few years. The transistor did that. Still others, such as Bessemer steel or the fax machine, may be overtaken and displaced before ever reaching their full market potential. Still, it is not unreasonable to view the Kondratieff cycle as an average over a fairly large cluster of innovations arriving at different times, being adopted at different rates and spanning territories of different sizes. Yet the sum total of all these wavelets does not necessarily add up to a slowly but steadily rising tide. The tide does rise, but superimposed on it is a big wave with a long wave length and surprisingly regular behavior.

DISCONTINUITIES

As a simple analog of a cycle is the swinging of a pendulum, a simple analog of a discontinuity is a collapse or crash of some sort. Human history is full of examples.

Earthquakes can cause enormous destruction. The most famous in Western Europe was the earthquake that destroyed Lisbon in 1755, killing 30,000 people in that city alone. The San Francisco earthquake of 1906 resulted from a major slippage of the San Andreas fault which passes through the city; only about 3000 people were killed, but the earthquake was followed by a fire that destroyed the city completely, causing damage valued at US$400,000,000. Recently, destructive earthquakes have hit both Los Angeles and Kobe, in Japan.

Volcanic eruptions occasionally compete with earthquakes in violence. The Cretan civilization was probably destroyed by an explosive volcanic eruption on the island of Santoro in the Aegean and the tidal waves that followed it. The destruction of Pompeii, near Mount Vesuvius, in AD 79 is an example that happens to have left a record. Floods are also not to be neglected; there are several candidates for Noah's legendary flood, one being the flooding of the Red Sea due to rising sea levels from the melting of the ice caps somewhere around 6000 BC. Another scenario, that has recently been supported by independent geological evidence, is that the Black Sea formerly occupied a much smaller area but that rising sea levels from the glacial melt-down filled it up to its present contours in the course of a few hundred years, flooding much valuable coastal land in the process. This would have been enough to start several tribes, possibly including the Magyars, off on a search for new lands.

Asteroids and comets also occasionally penetrate the atmosphere and hit the Earth. An extraterrestrial object of some sort entered the Earth's atmosphere and caused an extremely violent explosion in 1908, in a remote part of Siberia called Tunguska. It left hundreds of square kilometers of forest flattened. The consequences if such an object had hit a major city, or even a heavily populated agricultural area, can only be imagined.[5]

Social catastrophes often have had natural, or partly natural, causes. The Black Death of the fourteenth century is an example of a natural phenomenon with profound social consequences. The population of some parts of Europe was devastated, resulting in labor scarcity, rising wages in towns and more freedom for peasants, at least in the West. The Irish potato blight and famine of the 1840s was accompanied by a typhus epidemic; the population of Ireland was cut in half, while hundreds of thousands of Irish emigrated to the USA and Canada. The 1919 influenza pandemic may have killed as many people as the preceding war, and epidemics, in turn, often influence the outcomes of wars. Typhus has tilted the balance in many a military campaign, not least Napoleon's disastrous invasion of Russia.[6]

In the same way that the news media concentrate on the bad news, such events tend to catch and attract our attention because of the human horror stories associated with them. But the long-term importance of such events is often that they are causes or facilitators of social change. It is the latter aspect of discontinuities that we need to consider more seriously.

I have mentioned a few instances to make a point about the nature of change itself. Forecasters tend to assume that change will be gradual and smooth. Often, probably more often than not, change is sudden and shocking. Apart from truly unpredictable events like asteroidal collisions, most catastrophic events arise from a scenario something like the following: there is an initial balance between some active force, or pressure – like steam in a kettle – and some passive resistance, or frictional force. For instance, two tectonic plates are moving slowly in contact with each other. The balance of forces is inherently unstable. At first, friction prevents all movement. But without relief, the pressure builds up in the rock until it eventually overcomes the friction. When this happens, the plates move suddenly and rapidly until the accumulated pressure is relieved. Everything standing in the way is likely to be crushed or smashed.

Discontinuities in human affairs can often be described in similar language. There is a pressure, or stress. Change that might relieve the stress is blocked, perhaps by an oppressive regime, perhaps by institutional inertia. Eventually the stress becomes too great and there is an explosion, such as a riot, a *coup d'état* or perhaps an armed insurgency. Most insurgencies are eventually repressed, but sometimes they are successful, as in the case of the American Revolution of 1776–1780. Political revolutions differ from insurgencies. They tend to start out as legitimate changes of government, by election or constitutional convention. But when radical changes are proposed by a new government without deep roots, they may be followed by organized coups or counter-revolutions. This happened after the French Revolution was taken over by the Jacobins. A coordinated assault on France was mounted in 1792–1793 by the monarchists of Europe, under Austrian leadership. This invasion, in turn, failed as the French rallied to defend their homeland. Napoleon eventually took power and, temporarily, conquered Europe.

Examples of revolution and counter-revolution in the more recent past include the revolutionary (elected) government of Mohammed Mossadegh in Iran (1950–1953), which nationalized the oil industry and proposed an alliance with its neighbor, the USSR. This alarmed the Anglo-American alliance, which supported a counter-revolution by the Shah, Reza Pahlavi. The Shah's regime, in turn, fell in 1979–1980 to a sort of anti-Western counter-counter-revolution led by Islamic fundamentalists. In Chile, Salvador Allende (1970–1973) was elected President, but with only a third of the national vote. He attempted to implement a radical Marxist program of social programs and nationalizations. His government was overthrown by a military junta, with CIA assistance.

Wars are the most obvious examples of large-scale discontinuities in human affairs. The French Revolution was the end of an age and the Napoleonic Wars began as a national uprising in opposition to an Austro–British-inspired and orchestrated counter-revolution to restore the monarchy. It quickly evolved into something else entirely. But, while the French monarchy was eventually restored in name, the underlying change in the balance of civil powers in France – and in Europe – was permanent.

The Great Crash of 1929 and the Great Depression of 1932–1936 that followed certainly qualify as a major discontinuity. They led to the election of Franklin Roosevelt, the New Deal, and radical (for the time) legislation in a number of fields. It also led to the adoption of federally-sponsored social security in the US. The problem of structural unemployment finally reached the consciousness of political leaders and professional economists. Deficit financing and 'pump priming' to stimulate demand became academically respectable, mainly thanks to John Maynard Keynes. The problem of unaffordable entitlements that plagues governments today arose from small beginnings in the 1930s.

World War II saw Hitler's revanchist Germany eager to regain control of the Saar, Alsace-Lorraine and the corridor to East Prussia that Poland had obtained after World War I, as well as the rich agricultural lands to its east. Japan's program was similar. To create room for the overcrowded Japanese, Japan conquered Taiwan and Korea, rather easily. This success tempted the Japanese into China and finally South East Asia where the remnants of Europe's Asian colonies were nearly undefended.[7]

The Japanese scheme of military conquest ultimately failed, but the war had immense long-term consequences, nevertheless. The communist takeover of Eastern Europe and the construction of the Iron Curtain in Europe were direct results of the circumstances of the war and its aftermath. By the same token, the victory of the British Labour Party in the 1945 election dismissed Winston Churchill into Opposition. The perceived need to contain communism on the march resulted in the Marshall Plan, the Coal and Steel Community (which later became the European Economic Community and still later the European Union) and the North Atlantic Treaty Organization (NATO). Of course, the technology developed for military purposes and the circumstances of the Axis's defeat were also of great importance. Jet aircraft, radar, nuclear weapons (and nuclear power) and electronic digital computers were among those consequences. But the Cold War was undoubtedly the dominant one.

The Soviet Bloc, and the USSR itself, self-destructed in 1989–1990.[8] The USSR quickly broke up into its component pieces, now known as the Commonwealth of Independent States or CIS. Meanwhile, Russia was revealed to be an economic basket-case without stable institutions or constitutional structure. Democracy and free market capitalism have both taken a couple of steps forward, in some places, but not without a step or two back.

The main point of these last few pages on discontinuity is that change in the political and economic arena is much like change in other spheres. Usually it tends to be very slow, due to inertia in the politico-economic system. Pressures build up under the ground or behind the scenes; then some event occurs that releases the pressure, breaks the apparent equilibrium and triggers a much more rapid sort of change. Sometimes it is a natural disaster, like an epidemic; sometimes a war. Sometimes it is an economic crisis. There are a variety of other change mechanisms that operate in different spheres. I have mentioned a few examples. Any alert reader will be able to think of others. Often the enduring changes that result from the crisis are quite unrelated to the proximate cause, or 'trigger'. I will have several occasions to remind the reader of these points hereafter.

Before ending this section I want to raise an important point concerning social learning. It is a constant regret among scholars and thinkers that it is so difficult to make necessary changes in the body politic *without* a crisis or a catastrophe. But there is at least one glimmer of hope. I refer to the nuclear war that has not occurred, despite an arms race lasting decades and a considerable level of hostility between the contending factions. In the 1950s, 1960s and 1970s there were few people who were willing to predict that the world would survive to the end of the century without a nuclear conflict. The prevailing mood of despair was captured in novels like Nevil Shute's *On the Beach* and movies like Stanley Kubrick's *Dr Strangelove*.[9]

Today, few people seem to worry about nuclear war. Yet in some respects the dangers are greater than ever, given the large number of nuclear weapons in Russian stockpiles that are controlled by underpaid and undisciplined soldiers and potentially corrupt officers. However, despite these objective causes for concern, I think there is hope in the fact that most people no longer think that nuclear weapons could ever be used again in war. In effect, the learning has occurred without the catastrophe. Perhaps it can happen again in the context of sustainable development.

ENDURING LONG-TERM TRENDS

The discussion of discontinuities above is not to deny that there are also some orderly and quasi-predictable trends. Population growth is the most obvious and among the most important. Underlying it, however, are a number of determinants that vary less predictably. Among them are fertility, child mortality, age of marriage, social attitudes toward divorce, contraception and abortion, female literacy and years of schooling, and life expectancy.

Economic growth is considerably less certain or predictable. Again, there are important underlying variables. One is the size of the labor force. That, in turn, depends on population, but also on the age at which productive employment begins (which depends on the years of schooling), the age of retirement, female participation in the workforce, and unemployment rates. Gross national product (GNP) is a constructed variable that has acquired great symbolic importance since national account statistics began to be compiled about half a century ago. Capital accumulation, both financial and 'real', is a related economic variable of great importance. Debt, credit and money supply (of various kinds) are others.

Non-economic variables that change slowly but have an important influence on economic growth include education level (literacy, numeracy, years of schooling), urbanization and land use. Land use by category (agriculture, pasture, managed temperate forest, tropical forest, desert, tundra) are also important environmental variables, as are rates of change, especially deforestation and desertification.

Some kinds of economic behavior are quite predictable. For instance, in our everyday lives as individuals we must, and do, prepare and plan, save and invest for the future, notwithstanding a certain irreducible myopia. The rate of saving is an important socio-economic variable. It fluctuates with national circumstances, but the range within which it fluctuates does not change very quickly. Another behavioral variable is the 'discount rate', which is the minimum rate of interest that will induce a person (or a collectivity) to save for the future instead of spending today. Again, this changes with circumstances (income and age, for instance) but the changes themselves are slow and relatively foreseeable.

Other behavioral features that play an important role in economics are known as elasticities. These are essentially logarithmic derivatives (slopes) of one macro-variable plotted against another. One important example is the price elasticity of demand, which is the percentage reduction in demand (for any commodity or service) resulting from a 1 per cent increase in its price. Another example of this kind is the income elasticity of utility, which is the percentage increase in utility resulting from a 1 per cent increase in income. There are quite a number of other quasi-parameters of this sort. They are not quite constants but they do possess a considerable inertia. If they change over time, they change slowly.

Health is a factor related to population growth. But it is an important element of social welfare in its own right. For instance the United Nations Development Program (UNDP)'s Human Development Index combines statistics on literacy and life expectancy with national income statistics. Health statistics of importance include infant mortality rates, undernourishment, average food energy intake, mortality due to infectious disease by age, race and sex, mortality and morbidity due to cancer, by age, race and sex, degenerative disease, and so on. Social pathologies are measurable to a degree. Divorce rates, out-of-wedlock childbirth, single-parent families, crime rates, prison population, drug use, and so on are relevant to the state of society.

Clearly we are willing to bet that some features of our present world are enduring, while others will evolve in certain directions, along clearly defined tracks. Our ability to anticipate cyclic phenomena and possible discontinuities is much less clear. However, the first step in developing long-range forecasts is to identify the continuing, irreversible long-term trends. I return to this in Chapter 2. One can then look for reasonably well-established cyclic phenomena. Finally, it is essential to scan the horizon for possible discontinuities and surprises.

IMPLICATIONS

A lot of people think that forecasting must be done with models. This is understandable, since many short-term economic forecasts are made with the help of complex econometric models. At some risk of giving offense to the practitioners, I think it is safe to characterize these models as very sophisticated trend extrapolation machines. I do not propose to discuss their structure in greater detail, or their record of accuracy, except to say that these models often disagree with one another (sometimes radically), and seldom do better than naive trend extrapolations or panels of experts.[10]

To forecast turning points it is necessary to get away from trend extrapolation. This requires identifying deeper connections and relationships, some of which are not readily quantifiable. Surprisingly, this has also been attempted. The over-ambitious 'world' models of the 1970s, especially *World Dynamics* (Forrester, 1971) and *Limits to Growth* (Meadows et al, 1972) were almost a parody of Asimov's 'psychohistory', except that, unlike Hari Seldon's model, they were avowedly deterministic. Of course, these models were harshly criticized at the time of their introduction for many other failings, including attempting to represent too many complex and non-linear interactions by means of too few macro-variables related by an ultra-simplified set of linear first order differential equations.[11] (A few hundred variables would, of course, still be too few.) We now recognize that deterministic systems can exhibit quasi-random chaotic behaviors under some conditions.[12] But the real world is surely not a simple deterministic mechanism. Among other non-deterministic elements, human choices yet to be made will be based on free will. They are not predetermined. In short, the fore-caster's task is complicated by the fact that there are cyclic, discontinuous and even chaotic behaviors in the world, complicated by conscious but not predetermined human decision-making.

So, what does all this mean with regard to the turning point that I have predicted in the title of this book? It means, I think, that simple quantifiable models will not be very helpful in elucidating timing and other details. Theory can be applied, here and there, but much of the applicable theory is faulty in major or minor respects. Naive intelligence and intuition may be the best available tool for coping with a very complex and non-deterministic future. But, I remain confident that a turning point is inevitable. The critical question is whether it will only come after a major catastrophe or whether the human capacity for anticipation and avoidance of future problems can, for perhaps the second time, achieve a soft landing.

NOTES

1   Comment attributed to Niels Bohr, possibly apocryphal.
2   I used this terminology in an earlier book, *Uncertain Futures* (Ayres, 1979). It still seems apposite.
3   Major investigators include Kuznets (1930, 1953) and Schumpeter (1939). Longer cycles have also been suggested, up to the well-known 50-year Kondratieff cycle (Kondratieff, 1926, 1928).
4   This scheme was especially proposed by Gerhard Mensch (1975).
5   It is now thought that a much larger asteroid – about 10km in diameter – did hit the Earth about 65 million years ago. It landed in the Gulf of Mexico, near Yucatan. Its impact probably caused the demise of dinosaurs and most other large species then alive, and allowed the rise of mammals from which we are descended.
6   For a fascinating account of this and other episodes see Hans Zinsser's *Rats, Lice and History* (1963).
7   This ambitious plan of conquest was euphemistically called the 'Greater East Asian Co-Prosperity Sphere'.
8   The underlying causes of the breakup had been growing for a long time, even though – apart from the Solidarity movement in Poland – many were not visible to most observers in the west. The increasing gap between living standards in the West and the East was a major cause of discontent. The Soviet military occupation of Eastern Europe, in the implausible name of defense, was an increasingly unaffordable burden on the USSR. Morale in the Soviet military was already deeply troubled by the Afghanistan fiasco. The Soviet servicemen stationed in Eastern Europe were ill-housed, ill-paid and very unpopular with the locals. The pressure to withdraw was becoming irresistible. This reduced the credibility of any threat of Soviet military intervention in local affairs as in 1956 (Hungary) and 1968 (Prague). Gorbachev confirmed publicly that the USSR would not use military force in this manner. This left Eastern European regimes unprotected, except by their own security forces whose mood (by then) was more anti- than pro-communist. Thereafter, the timing of the collapse was almost accidental. East German vacationers, many of whom traveled to Hungary (or through Hungary to Yugoslavia or Bulgaria) for holidays, discovered in 1988 that the Hungarian government would not prevent them from escaping to Austria. In 1989 Hungary took the critical step: it tore down the symbolic barbed-wire fence between it and Austria. The USSR looked the other way. The trickle of departures soon became a flood that fatally undermined the East German economy, and thence the keystone regime of Eastern Europe. A transitional regime in East Germany quickly agreed

to rejoin West Germany. The communist rulers of the rest of the countries of Eastern Europe saw how the wind was blowing, renamed their parties, and called elections. Communists (at least under that name) were initially thrown out of power in every single country except Yugoslavia. This resulted in the collapse of the Warsaw Pact and the Council for Mutual Economic Aid (COMECON). It was all over, largely without bloodshed, by the end of 1990.

9 The best indication of this widely shared despair is the cover of the famous *Bulletin of Atomic Scientists*, published at the University of Chicago (where the first successful controlled nuclear chain reaction was demonstrated in 1942). The front cover of the *Bulletin* displays a clock face showing the minute hand a few minutes before midnight. As Cold War tensions fluctuated, the editors moved the hand a little nearer to, or a little farther away from, the zero hour. But until the collapse of the Soviet Union, the threat of nuclear catastrophe never seemed far away.

10 For an interesting discussion of the weaknesses and failures of econometric forecasting models, see Chapter 5 of Paul Ormerod's excellent book *The Death of Economics* (1994).

11 The criticisms were numerous. However, two are worth citing, viz *World Dynamics: Measurement without Data* (Nordhaus, 1973) and *Models of Doom* (Cole et al, 1973).

12 In the language of non-linear dynamics, chaotic behavior tends to be limited to distinct regions, which are characterized as 'strange attractors'. It is the latter which are the proper subject of analysis in non-linear dynamics.

Chapter 2
Drivers of Change

IRREVERSIBLE TRENDS AS CAUSAL AGENTS

At first glance, a driver of change might be thought of as an 'unmoved mover' or a force of nature. But in reality action and reaction operate together. There are no movers that cannot be moved. There are no irresistible forces, nor immovable objects. Our economic system is embedded in the bigger and more inclusive bio-geochemical system of the Earth. This bio-geochemical system is driven by energy from the Sun, which is part of a galaxy (the Milky Way) and so on. Changes at any higher level of this hierarchy can, and do, affect the lower levels. It is convenient to think of them as exogenous to those lower levels. But events at the lower levels sometimes also generate feedback effects at higher levels. Certainly human activity is now affecting the bio-geochemical system. This point is relevant, because the levels are differentiated not only by size and scope, but also by the time-scales of the cross-level influences, namely exogenous influences from higher levels and feedbacks from lower levels.

Having said this, I think it is safe to neglect galactic influences on the solar system, such as possible supernovas or interstellar collisions. I think we may also neglect intra-solar system changes, such as the fact that the Sun is gradually warming as hydrogen is converted into helium and thence into carbon. (Our Sun's radiation intensity has increased 30 per cent during its five-billion-year lifetime). We can safely ignore the fact that the Sun will eventually burn itself out. I think it is also safe to neglect the remote possibility that the Earth may be hit by an asteroid or a comet, or invaded by aliens.

Last, but not least, we can safely ignore very long-term trends at the global bio-geological level. The evolution of life itself is the most obvious of these. Biological activity in the last several hundred million years created the oxygen atmosphere, as well as the carbon, nitrogen and sulfur cycles. It has evolved in several other dimensions. One is the evolution of multicell organisms of increasing complexity. Another trend is in the direction of increasing biodiversity, including the bio-colonization of the land surface. A third important trend is the buildup of terrestrial biomass, especially on land (forests). The trend toward increasing biological complexity is particularly significant.

The first million years of human history involved further evolutionary developments, most notably in the area of communication, language and record keeping. Since recorded history began a few thousand years ago, humans have spread over the

Earth. They have also developed alphabets, mathematics, tools, engineering, libraries, music and literature, art, science, religion and law. Monarchies have declined. Multi-party democracies (in some form) have gained ground. Religious faith is declining. Skepticism and secularism are gaining ground. Technology is becoming more and more potent. Barriers of all kinds are falling. Market-based economics and trade are growing in importance. The world does seem to be on the way to becoming a 'global village' as Marshall McLuhan prophesied many years ago.

In Chapter 1, I briefly touched on some of the long-term trends of importance to us and their underlying driving forces. But it is not enough to observe past trends. The question is: what forces will be important to us in the relatively near future?

DEMOGRAPHIC DRIVERS

Population growth is the first example that comes to mind. One principal driver of demographic change in recent centuries has unquestionably been progress in medical science, and especially public health. Scientific discoveries (such as Harvey's recognition of the role of the blood circulatory system and Pasteur's discovery of the role of micro-organisms as a cause of infection) and simple technologies such as vaccination, chlorination of water supplies, and the segregation and primary treatment of sewage have had a dramatic impact on the propagation of infectious disease. Antiseptics and anesthetics have made childbirth and surgery far safer than they once were. All of these advances have dramatically cut death rates and extended life expectancy everywhere. Unfortunately, from the demographic standpoint, death rates declined without (immediately) affecting birth rates. This happened first in eighteenth- and nineteenth-century Europe. More recently it has happened in the rest of the world. The consequence is an explosive increase in world population, as shown in Figures 2.1 and 2.2.

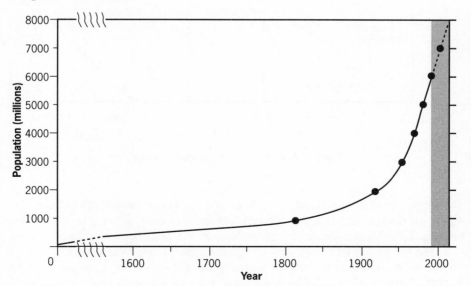

Figure 2.1 World Population Growth

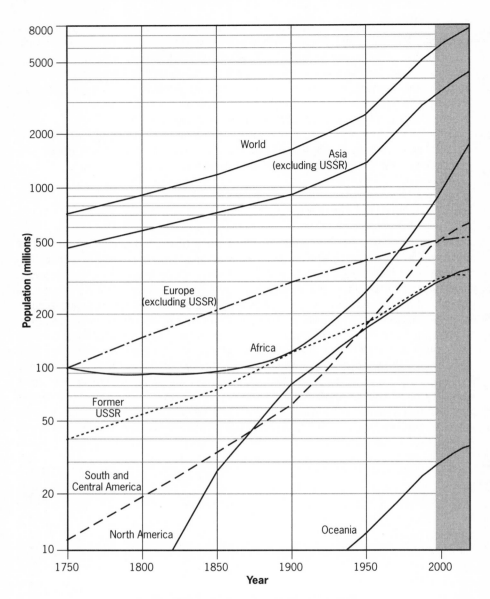

Figure 2.2 Regional Population Growth

The other major current driver of demographic change is urbanization (Table 2.1). Again, the causes are social and economic. In rural societies, in the absence of social security, large families are useful for working on the land. Even very young children can feed animals, plant seeds, pick off insects, harvest vegetables and fruit, and so on. Moreover, in primitive societies surviving and self-supporting adult sons are the traditional source of support for the elderly and incapacitated. Thus desired family size, in rural societies, depends partly on infant mortality and life expectancy.

Table 2.1 Urbanization of World Population

Year	World Population (millions)	Urban Population (millions)	Urban Increase (millions)	Urban Portion (per cent)
1950	2520	737	–	29
1975	4086	1538	801	38
1995	5716	2584	1000	45
2000	6274	3137	1599	50
2025	8294	5065	1928	61

Source: WRI (1996), Tables A.1 and 8.1

But in overcrowded countries, such as Ireland in the early nineteenth century, or Egypt, India and China today, farms are already too small for further subdivision. There is no unoccupied arable land. Hence, surplus younger sons are forced into the status of landless rural laborers. Or they are forced altogether off the land and into urban slums. In nineteenth-century Europe and America, and perhaps in twentieth-century Asia, this forced migration of rural labor into cities has been a powerful driver of industrialization, since these unskilled workers could quickly be absorbed into the burgeoning but unskilled factory workforce. This process has certainly been observable in Japan, Hong Kong and other East Asian 'tigers', where significant immigration from the hinterlands to the big cities has occurred.

Over one or two generations, if all goes well, the newly urbanized workers go to school, learn new skills, and adopt middle class habits and outlooks. Large families are not economically beneficial to middle class urban dwellers, since children must be housed, clothed and fed, and they cannot earn money if they are forced to go to school. In fact, even without social security, children are an expensive luxury, rather than an economic necessity, for city dwellers. Thus, as societies urbanize and industrialize, and as education levels rise – especially among women – net birth rates tend to fall. In the industrialized West populations are aging but no longer growing much (except through immigration). For this reason childbirth is now quite heavily subsidized in Europe and Quebec, where birth rates are actually below the replacement level in most countries.

However, in much of Asia, Africa, and Latin America, the majority of the population is still rural and educational levels remain minimal. Birth rates in Muslim countries, especially, are far above the replacement rate. The average number of surviving children per woman ranges from six to eight in Muslim Africa, and not much less in Muslim Asia, except for Indonesia. In some poor countries populations are already close to, if not beyond, the sustainable level. The migration to cities is in full swing. Urbanization is one of the most important and – for various reasons – stressful trends of our times. Population growth and explosive urbanization, especially in Africa and Asia, create a constellation of problems the world has not yet faced up to. But pressures from religious leaders, especially Roman Catholics and Muslims, interfere with any organized attempt to deal with the problem globally, or even to talk about it sensibly. The number of desperately poor and hopeless people in Africa, mostly under military or theocratic rulers, or warlords, is growing rapidly.

The Middle East and South Asia are demographic trouble spots. Most Muslim countries – along with India's Hindus and Latin Americans – share a set of social attitudes which enforce the subordinate position of women. Most Muslim males in these countries practice bigamy if they can afford it. Hindus in the more remote rural areas of India still practice female infanticide, child marriage, and virtual slavery of married child-women to the family of the husband. It is surely not a coincidence that these countries also share one other thing: a much higher birth rate than the rest of the world.

Lacking any realistic hope for improving their lives where they now live, many of the young men from these poor and overcrowded countries will be drawn more and more easily into revolutionary anarchist and nihilist movements, often with millennial religious trappings. China's 'Proletarian Cultural Revolution' of 1965–1968, Cambodia's murderous Khmer Rouge and today's violent Muslim fundamentalist insurgencies in Afghanistan, Algeria and Egypt are illustrations enough. These movements will interfere increasingly with any possibility of normal economic development. A direct consequence is likely to be more and more desperate waves of refugees, washing across national frontiers to escape civil wars, massacres, pestilence, starvation and – increasingly – all of them together.

One of the most rapidly growing industries in the world today is the relief and care of refugees. Unfortunately, in most cases there is nowhere for them to go. The industrial world does not want them, and cannot realistically open its gates to everybody who would like to escape from poverty or oppression. In 1996 Hong Kong authorities were still trying to repatriate the last 20,000 Vietnamese 'boat people', the remnants of the million refugees who escaped from Vietnam over 20 years ago. In the summer of 1996, a thousand armed French police broke into a church in Paris where a couple of hundred illegal immigrants from Africa were engaging in a hunger strike to persuade the authorities to allow them to stay. Most of them have been or will be sent back to impoverished countries that do not want them. More recently, Germany began repatriating Bosnian orphans to Sarajevo. There are fewer and fewer escape hatches for refugees, no matter how pitiful.

TECHNOLOGICAL DRIVERS

Technological change in the broad sense is essentially a consequence of growing scientific knowledge, together with an accumulation of inventions and improvements built on that knowledge base. The accumulation of knowledge is the nearest thing to an irreversible trend in the social domain. From a broader historical perspective, this accumulation of knowledge began in prehistoric times, but the only mechanism for knowledge transmission and storage, at first, was direct interpersonal communication: teaching and learning, from parent to child, and from tribal elder to youth. The development of language itself was the first great leap. The invention of hieroglyphics was a big step forward, since it permitted some permanent records, albeit crude. The alphabet, which simplified writing, was a far greater invention. Once knowledge could be reduced to writing, books and libraries became possible. We are able to read the writings of Plato and Aristotle today thanks to these inventions.

The linked processes of knowledge accumulation and dissemination have accelerated in relatively recent times. The convergence of paper manufacturing and of mechanical printing technologies around 1500 led to an explosion of book publishing and a rapid spread of knowledge during the sixteenth and seventeenth centuries. This undoubtedly contributed to the emergence of natural science as an intellectual discipline, beginning with astronomy and mechanics. The industrial consequences of this began to emerge in the late seventeenth and eighteenth centuries. Telecommunications, beginning with the electric telegraph in the 1840s but rapidly encompassing the telephone, the radio, television and now the internet, have combined to make the present period the beginning of the 'post-industrial age' or the 'age of information'. Meanwhile the acceleration of knowledge accumulation continues, as information technologies contribute to the growth of knowledge itself.

It is a fact that most of the important technologies in the world today were literally inconceivable two centuries ago, and many of them were undreamed of one century ago. The steamship was not an evolutionary development of the sailing ship; the automobile is not an evolutionary improvement of the horse and buggy; the transistor was not a better kind of vacuum tube, and so on. This is one of the causes of our 'irreducible myopia' noted earlier. Partly because of this history of radical change, science and technology are often regarded (by economists, for example) as inherently unpredictable. The simplistic argument is sometimes advanced that if an invention could be predicted it would have already been invented. The same truism would seem to be applicable to scientific discoveries.

But this argument is naive and demonstrably wrong. It is quite possible to predict some inventions with fairly high confidence while others can be ruled out with even higher confidence. The sociologist of science, S C Gilfillan, demonstrated the first half of this proposition in the 1930s by noting firstly that some invention was needed to permit aircraft to land safely in fog, or at night, and secondly that several alternative means to solve the problem could be envisioned without violating any known physical laws (Gilfillan, 1937). Indeed, Gilfillan identified around a dozen such conceptual possibilities. Ironically, the solution that actually emerged within a few years – radar – was not on his list. But his point was that such a technology was needed, that there were no theoretical barriers, and therefore one could expect a solution to the problem to be developed within a few years. He was right.

By the same token, it is easy to identify a number of technologies that do violate physical laws (insofar as we know them) and that can therefore be ruled out with high confidence, if not absolute certainty. These include time travel, interstellar travel faster than light, anti-gravity, matter transmission and 'tractor fields'. The 'highly improbable' category includes medical rejuvenation, immortality drugs, intelligent robots and the ubiquitous (in science fiction movies) portable laser pistol.

There is also an intermediate category of technologies that are currently regarded as extremely problematic (ie requiring an unknown, but very large, research and development (R&D) effort to realize) but which are clearly not contradicted by any physical principle. It is from these possible but problematic technologies that any future technological revolutions will probably emerge.

Can we make non-trivial forecasts about the future of technology over the next half century or so? The answer is clearly yes. The trick is to identify technological performance trends of a sufficiently aggregated nature to be forecast, or simply extrapolated, without specifying the details of the technical means needed to achieve the performance in question. Here are some straightforward examples:

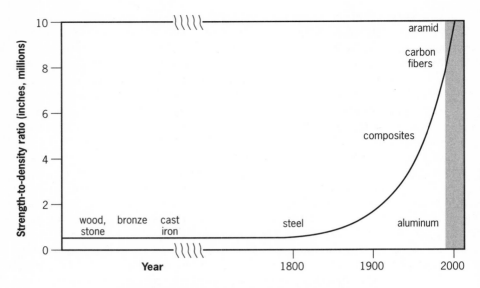

Figure 2.3 Materials Strength-to-Density Ratio

- energy productivity – or output per unit of energy consumed – will increase in most sectors.
- Materials performance will continue to increase in several domains, as illustrated by Figures 2.3 and 2.4. This will make it possible for materials productivity – or 'dematerialization' – (by material and by sector) to continue to increase.
- Industrial process yields (useful materials output per unit of materials input) will continue to increase.
- The hydrogen/carbon ratio of fuels will (probably) increase.
- Electrification (ie electricity consumption as a fraction of final energy use) will continue to increase.
- Information storage, transmission and processing technologies will continue to get faster and cheaper (partly by continuing to dematerialize). For instance, the number of circuit elements per square centimeter of active electronic materials will increase (Figure 2.5), while power consumption per circuit element will decline. The number of bytes per second transmitted by long-distance communications channels will increase (Figure 2.6), while costs will decline, and so on.
- Product complexity will increase along with performance.

There are many possible generic performance measures, and much can be learned from this kind of trend analysis. Broadly speaking, it is safe to say that the information content of materials and products will continue to grow, the functionality of products and services will continue to increase, while the inputs of energy and materials per unit of functionality will tend to decrease. It is also fairly safe to say that the productivity of labor and capital goods will tend to increase, although increasing labor productivity is beginning to be an important cause of social stress. (I return to this point, from several different perspectives, several times in coming chapters.)

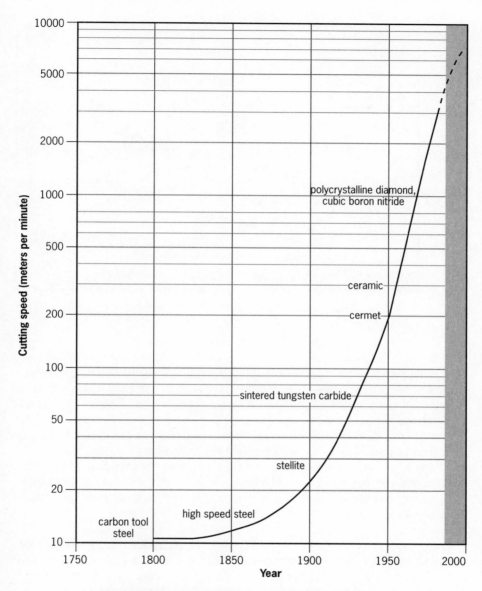

Figure 2.4 Trend in Speeds of Cutting Tool Materials

However, while it is relatively safe to predict that all of the above technological trends will continue, it is much less safe to forecast future rates of increase and, especially, increases or decreases in such rates. In this regard, trend extrapolation (or any of its variants, such as S-curve forecasting) is a slender reed. There are four reasons for this:

1) simple extrapolation presumes that physical limits (eg the speed of light) will not be approached too closely.

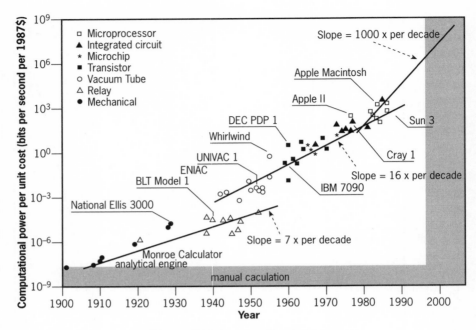

Figure 2.5 Computational Power

2) It presumes that the measure being extrapolated will still be technologically relevant in the distant future. (It is not clear, for instance, that the number of circuit elements per unit area of semiconductor will still be a good measure of electronic functionality 50, or even 20, years hence.)

3) It presumes that whatever economic forces are pushing the technology today will still be pushing it in the same direction in the distant future.

4) There is at least some chance of major and truly surprising scientific breakthroughs, perhaps in the area of biological sciences. For instance, designer organisms may be created to perform specialized functions such as scavenging soil for toxic metals or chemicals.

Speaking of economic forces, it is important to recognize that some of these economic forces may get much stronger, while others may be weakened, as a result of shifting social and environmental priorities. For instance, the current pattern of dependence on virgin raw materials in preference to reclaimed or recycled materials is a consequence of the current pattern of relative prices. Specifically, it is a consequence of the fact that raw material prices are too low, to the extent that they do not reflect environmental externalities associated with extraction, processing, use and ultimate disposal. The price system, however, is an artifact of the social and economic system. As such, it is subject to the possibility of deliberate change through the political process. Again, I return to this topic at several places in future chapters.

All of the important technological trends listed above are essentially direct consequences of the irreversible accumulation of human knowledge. In virtually every case there is also a further, economic argument for irreversibility; namely that no one would ever willingly adopt an inferior technology (in terms of cost effectiveness) given the

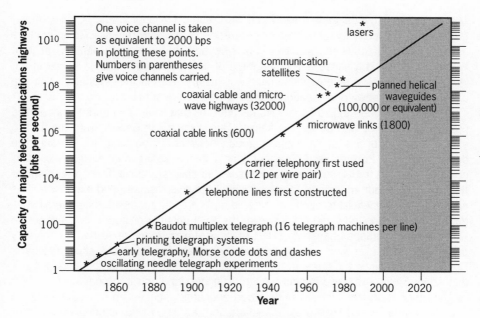

Figure 2.6 Telecommunications Capacity

availability of a better one. There is, of course, one major caveat: that the political and social order does not collapse into anarchy. The Dark Ages which followed the collapse of the Roman Empire were dark, primarily, from the standpoint of knowledge creation and dissemination. For hundreds of years, almost no new knowledge was created. During that time, knowledge of the past was preserved only in ancient manuscripts that survived in odd corners of the world, largely by accident. Much may have been lost.

I do not think we are about to enter a new dark age, but it cannot be absolutely ruled out. The collapse of the western Roman Empire did lead to a period of cultural, scientific, economic and social relapse lasting hundreds of years. A major world war, especially if it involved the use of nuclear weapons, could lead to an extended period of chaos and turmoil in which most of the civilizing and knowledge-creating or -preserving institutions we know might also disappear.

However a more important aspect of increasing technological capability, in the short run, is that it is a facilitator – if not a direct driver – of economic growth. It is important not to confuse the two. Scientific discovery facilitates invention and innovation, but does cause it. Knowledge feeds on itself, and grows potentially without limit, but knowledge alone does not generate wealth. Other factors and mechanisms are needed.

ECONOMIC DRIVERS

Wealth was once thought to be derived entirely from nature, whether from the land (crops, animals), the sea (fish), or from under the Earth, which implies that tangible wealth must either be discovered in nature or appropriated from someone else. This zero-sum view has historically justified the idea of conquest of territory to gain wealth.

The perception that tangible wealth can be created by labor, savings, investment, trade – and especially by technological progress – is relatively recent. Like economics as a discipline, it does not go back much beyond the eighteenth century, even in Western Europe. In a sense, the emergence of *homo economicus* as a power in the world is also a very recent phenomenon in history. It coincides, roughly, with the acceleration of knowledge creation and dissemination described above.

There are two well-studied economic mechanisms that have contributed to increased prosperity. The first was trade. The Italian cities, Venice and Genoa, were the first to exploit the possibilities of exchanging goods between Europe and the Levant. The development by Portugal and Spain of long-distance sailing and navigational technologies enabled traders to carry goods such as spices and silk from places where they were abundant and cheap to places where they were scarce and expensive. This exchange was beneficial to all those involved and certainly increased their overall standard of living, although it did not increase the total quantity of goods available in the world (except, perhaps, marginally). Nevertheless, it was trade per se that most visibly contributed to the growing wealth of Renaissance Italy, the Hanseatic cities, Flanders, Holland and Britain in the fifteenth to eighteenth centuries. It was the benefits of trade that Adam Smith and David Ricardo sought to understand and to propagate by policy.

The other important and well-understood economic mechanism of wealth creation is division of labor and large-scale manufacturing. At first, manufacturing was a mere enhancement of traditional handicrafts, via the introduction of more efficient tools, such as the spinning jenny. But a cluster of technological innovations in eighteenth-century Britain, from the power loom to the boring machine – and, above all, Watt's steam engine – brought about the first Industrial Revolution. The essence of this revolution in manufacturing was that it kicked off a long period of sustained increases in labor productivity (output per unit of labor input) that has continued to the present day. It is this phenomenon, of course, which has created the flood of material goods that we associate with the idea of wealth. Over the past two centuries, manufacturing has contributed vastly more to aggregate wealth than trade; indeed, most trade nowadays is in manufactured items.

A third, less well-understood, prerequisite of wealth creation and economic growth is technological progress. The notion that technological progress is a driver of growth has now been generally accepted and incorporated into economic growth models. But the connections remain obscure. As I have noted above, knowledge per se is not a creator of wealth, so it cannot be a cause of growth. It is merely a facilitator, a necessary but not sufficient condition for growth to occur. The mechanism that converts ideas into wealth – when and where it is allowed to operate – has been described.[1] In brief, risk-taking innovators with a new product or service to offer can gain a temporary advantage over their competitors. This is equivalent to a de facto monopoly and permits them to capture extraordinary (monopoly) profits. These profits, in turn, finance the R and D and investment that generate more new products and services. The feedback effects of economic growth and its accompaniments on technological change itself remain relatively neglected by economists (see Chapter 5). However, in the spirit of the discussion earlier in this chapter, I take technological progress as a given.

There are two more trends with an impact on growth that I think have been inadequately covered by the economic literature. The first of these is the availability of cheap energy from fossil fuels, which has facilitated the substitution of machines for animals and human muscles. I discuss the role of energy briefly below. The growth of output, in this case, has been very large indeed. The problem is that this growth has been largely attributed to the accumulation of produced (man-made) capital rather than – as it arguably should – to the exhaustion of natural capital.

The second trend I want to call attention to is the specialization and monetization of several kinds of formerly unpaid jobs, beginning with the labor of (formerly) self-sufficient farmers and now extending to what has traditionally been the household and child-rearing labor of women. The phenomenon is obvious and hardly needs explanation. The problem, however, is that while specialization can increase efficiency (hence output per unit input), monetization per se only increases money income without increasing real output at all. In the case of the American or European farmer, efficiency has unquestionably increased enormously in the past two centuries. The only question is how much of this increase has been due to mechanization (and the availability of cheap energy) and how much has been due to specialization, and other technological inputs such as fertilizers, pesticides, hybrid seeds, weather forecasting, and so on. One might argue that, in this case, monetization of farm work has not unreasonably distorted the growth picture.

In the case of household labor, the efficiency gains have been much less dramatic. To be sure, the advent of gas heat, washing machines, and other appliances has sharply reduced the number of hours a person need spend each week in order to cook for a family, do the laundry and clean a house. Nowadays these things can be done in a couple of hours per day. But the number of hours spent in child care has fallen mainly because the birthrate has fallen, not because of significant real efficiency gains. The growing shift of child care responsibilities to institutions such as pre-schools, not to mention the practice of leaving young children to unsupervised TV-watching, and feeding the family frozen dinners or pizza, enables many home-makers to work outside the home. This change does not increase the societal output of goods and services, however. What this implies is that apparent economic growth as measured in terms of income and payments is not all real. Some of it is evidently attributable to people paying other people to do what they could do themselves just as well.[2] (In fact, there are deeper problems with the conventional measure. I reconsider these issues from the welfare perspective in Chapter 9.)

But, then, what are the underlying causes of economic growth? Back in the eighteenth century two factors of production were commonly identified, viz labor and land. Labor capacity was assumed to be essentially proportional to the adult population (there being no such thing as unemployment, in practice, from the fourteenth century until the twentieth). For the moment, we can probably accept the idea that the size of the labor force is exogenous; that is, determined primarily by population. However, this is by no means the whole story. Economic as well as socio-political factors are certainly among the reasons why many more women are in the workforce today in the US than in Western Europe or Japan. In any case, the importance of raw labor is obviously declining, while the importance of skills and human capital is increasing.

Land, of course, was the source of all food, animal feed, wood and fuel. As noted above, virtually all tangible wealth, prior to the eighteenth century, was derived from the land. But even when trade and manufacturing began to be significant, it still seemed reasonable to think of fields and forests as being 'outside' the economic system, since production depends on the natural fertility of the soil, the sun and the rain. However, the product of land also depends on the application of labor and capital.

What is capital? It is helpful to distinguish between what it is, and what is conventionally measured. Capital goods are a confusing aggregate of infrastructure (roads, canals, harbors, bridges, tunnels, pipelines, telecommunications systems, etc), machinery, and production equipment and buildings. Capital also includes software, chemical formulae, blueprints, instruction manuals and so on. Some definitions include housing and consumer durables, since the latter provide 'final' services. There is no physical measure of all this. What is measurable is money: savings and investment. Capital, then, is assumed to be the accumulation of savings, less depreciation. Depreciation is loss of value due to age, wear and obsolescence. This is almost as difficult to measure as capital itself. In general, little attempt is made to measure it. Depreciation, at the firm level, is whatever the tax authorities are willing to allow. (It appears in the national accounts as 'capital allowance'.)

Despite the many conceptual difficulties, economists have attempted to estimate the capital stock of the major industrial countries, and its accumulation. It was a major surprise, however, when econometric studies in the 1950s (eg Abramovitz, 1952, 1956; Solow, 1956, 1957) showed convincingly that output per capita had grown very much faster than capital stock per capita. The major engine of growth could not have been savings and investment; it must have been something else. This unexplained residual was quickly labelled as 'technological progress' in some general, and mostly undefined, sense.

In the aggregate, technical progress is typically measured by economists as a modest but continuous increase in 'total factor productivity', or gross output per unit of (weighted) labor and capital input. However, while increased productivity must owe something to technological progress, there is no theoretical reason for supposing that productivity growth is irreversible. The irreversible character of increasing knowledge stock, and of most technological trends, is not *a priori* applicable to productivity trends. This is because technological capabilities per se do not depreciate (at least, not in normal circumstances) whereas productivity depends on fixed investment, demand, capacity, and prices. It can decrease under some conditions. Since productivity can decline, it follows that economic output can also decline. (I could also have stated this the other way round.) Anyhow, economic growth is not irreversible – as the 1930s demonstrated for the West and the 1990s are doing for Eastern Europe and the former USSR.

In fact, aggregate rates of growth can be, and are, quite variable, from time to time. At the sectoral (or lower) levels of aggregation, experience tells us that changes can be radical and – comparatively – discontinuous. Growth in one sector can be accompanied by decline in another. Unfortunately, this variability is not reflected in current economic forecasting models. For instance, it is common for macro-economic models to assume (for convenience) that the economic system grows smoothly and continuously along an optimal path in a perpetual state of competitive supply–demand equilibrium. This implies that there are no non-economic forces at work in the system. It also implies that technological progress is smooth, continuous and exogenous: a sort of continuous manna from heaven.

There is nothing in the conventional model of an economic system to explain why one industrial sector grows faster than another, or why a sector might disappear altogether. Also, the assumptions of constant discount rates and constant rates of productivity increase seriously weaken the long-term predictive power (and credibility) of conventional economic models. This is not the place for a detailed discussion of simplifying economic assumptions and their implications (see Chapter 13). The question still arises whether models based on simplistic assumptions can be of any value for understanding the relatively distant future.

So far I have discussed economic growth in relatively conventional neo-classical language, namely in terms of labor and capital productivity, where capital is taken to refer to something hard to define precisely, but produced by humans. Capital consists of either money or tangible products (of labor and exergy and capital) that can be used (in combination with labor and energy) to help produce other products. The argument for treating capital as an independent factor of production is a pragmatic one; that, once produced, it endures for a significant time. Conceptually, one can treat capital as a given. In a static model, capital pre-exists. It is there, or it isn't. Its origin does not matter. In a dynamic model, of course, capital must be produced in order to accumulate. But there is no conceptual difficulty in producing capital from capital, labor, materials and energy.[3]

As regards raw materials and energy – or, more broadly, natural capital – the key point is simple: energy and other natural resources cannot be produced by human labor, with or without man-made capital. Oil is not 'produced' by drilling an oil well, notwithstanding the sloppy language that is commonly used in discussing these matters. Some wells yield oil or gas (for a while), others are dry from the start. The amount of labor and capital employed in either case may be the same. The oil or gas is either there, or it is not. But the oil and gas were produced by natural processes, not by human actions. The same holds for minerals, forest products and agricultural products. In short, energy from the environment is a truly exogenous factor of production, even though it requires labor and capital to extract.

I emphasize the fact that natural resources should be regarded as an independent factor of production because a large part – possibly the largest part – of the historical increase of labor productivity since the eighteenth century is, in fact, attributable to the vast increase in the energy (exergy) flux, per unit of human labor, from outside the system (see Figure 2.7). In effect, exergy (in combination with machines, ie capital) has been a substitute for human labor in many sectors. A good illustration of this substitution is the US agricultural system (see Figure 2.8).

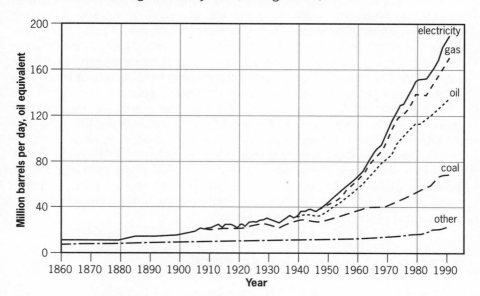

Figure 2.7 World Primary Energy Consumption

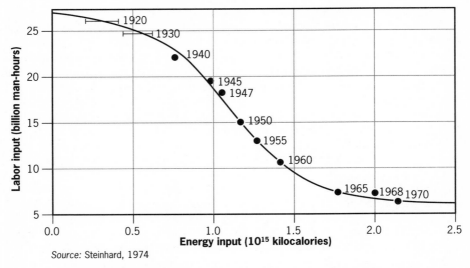

Source: Steinhard, 1974

Figure 2.8 Substitution of Energy for Labor on US Farms

Obviously energy (exergy) alone does not replace labor. But it makes still less intuitive sense to say that capital (machines) alone can replace labor. Allowing for an independent measure of resource or energy productivity, defined as the change in GNP per unit change in resource input, the economic growth (per capita) would have to be reallocated between the two factors, capital and exergy. This allocation would surely explain a much larger fraction of total historical GNP growth per capita. The unexplained statistical residual (hitherto defined as technical progress) would be correspondingly much smaller.

To reformulate the growth problem in this manner would more clearly display the extent to which past economic growth has depended on (increasing) resource inputs. It brings out into the open a very fundamental difficulty: if past growth owes so much to natural resource inputs – especially fossil fuels – how can the economy continue to grow in the future if natural resource inputs are cut sharply, as is being recommended by many environmentalists? This problem needs to be addressed more seriously than it has been. The discussion is continued in chapters 8, 10, and 13.

All things considered, it is not clear whether economic growth and industrialization are an irreversible, continuing worldwide trend. Some of the underlying trends are likely to continue indefinitely. Others, such as the availability of cheap fossil fuels and the monetization of household work, may soon reach natural limits. Undeniably there have been major setbacks in the growth process in the past. In the case of the Great Depression of the 1930s, the economic growth process appears to have stopped spontaneously, due to some failure in the control mechanism. There are many theories to explain the Depression, and little consensus.

GLOBALIZATION: CAUSE OR EFFECT?

Is globalization of economic activity an irreversible long-run trend? This is another crucial question. If so, it is largely a consequence of two priors. One is technological progress in communications and transportation. Marshall McLuhan coined the term 'global village' in the 1960s when the trends were clear to anyone who was paying attention, but the reality was still far in the future. In the 1990s, however, the global village is real. The internet and the world wide web are the hottest business prospects of the age. The number of people using these systems is doubling or trebling each year.

The other causal factor is politico–economic. The Cold War has ended. Almost every country has discarded central planning and adopted market economics in some form. The world is wide open to multinational corporations. And formal barriers to international trade, especially tariffs, have been declining decade by decade, thanks to a series of international trade negotiations, since the creation of the General Agreement on Tariffs and Trade (GATT) under United Nations auspices in the late 1940s. 'Globalization' is the new catchword.

But the long-running argument over free trade would not have occurred if everyone agreed that globalization is such a good idea. There are a lot of influential people who favor it. But there are others – Ross Perot and the late businessman Sir James Goldsmith, to name two – who do not. Business, trade and financial organizations, the World Bank and other international financial institutions, editors and financial writers from the *Wall Street Journal*, *Barrons*, *Fortune*, *Financial Times*, and *The Economist*, among other pillars of the business establishment, backed up by trade theorists from major US universities, have led the charge. They have asserted ad nauseam that global free trade was just the nostrum needed to end recession and unemployment (just as they claimed two years earlier that the single market in Europe would create a burst of new growth).

In fact, the multinational companies (MNCs) are the most direct beneficiaries, and – along with importers and investors – almost the only beneficiaries in the industrialized world. MNCs are increasingly free to move their capital and outsource their manufacturing operations to low wage, low tax countries while selling their finished products profitably in the high wage countries where their owners, managers and customers live. (At least, they can do this as long as their domestic customers are still getting high wages from other organizations that haven't yet moved their operations abroad.) The MNCs can also move their profits from country to country to wherever they pay the least taxes. MNCs have been shifting their less visible medium scale manufacturing and assembly operations away from the high wage countries toward Asia (and Mexico) for several decades. Large-scale manufacturing is now beginning to shift. Engineering, design, and supporting services are likely to follow in due course. This is one of the basic reasons for rising unemployment and economic distress in the West.[4]

I recently encountered a new buzzword: 'human resources securitization' or HRS. This has an appealing sound. It conveys the warm feeling that capitalism is finally ready to recognize the true value of its workers. What it really means is that, thanks to globalization, more and more Western firms are giving up manufacturing operations entirely and concentrating entirely on marketing and design. (A few years ago *Business Week* called this phenomenon the 'hollow corporation'.) Without factories, equipment and inventory, hollow corporations have no hard assets. This gives the accountants problems in making up balance sheets. What is the book value of a company like Nike that makes nothing and owns nothing, but consists only of office workers in a rented building and a logo or a brand name? These are very real and difficult questions for accountants.

The fact that these questions are arising suggests that other more painful ones may soon follow. Is a world of free capital movement but no freedom of movement for labor sustainable? (I take it for granted that free movement of labor – meaning free immigration – is a non-starter.) Is globalization, in its current guise, socially beneficial? These are tough questions. The answers are not as clear as the financial media would have us believe, because the benefits of trade liberalization – however great – are not being widely shared. If the benefits continue to be so one-sided, no one should be surprised to see a sharp increase in protectionist sentiment, with possibly ill-considered reactionary policies to follow. Ross Perot and Sir James Goldsmith may be only the beginning. The reaction might go too far. It often does.

IMPLICATIONS

In this chapter I have discussed irreversible trends as drivers of change. There are (at least) three and perhaps four categories of (quasi-) irreversible trends. The first is population growth and its associated trend toward urbanization. Since a large number of urbanites must be fed by a relatively small number of highly productive agricultural workers, the very possibility of a world of self-sustaining small farms and villages is disappearing.

The second irreversible trend is the accumulation of technological knowledge and know-how. This has led to an enormous increase in technological capability, or functionality. This, in turn, provides the scope for technical progress as a primary driver of economic growth.

The third quasi-irreversible trend is economic growth, in the usual sense. Economic growth, in turn, is also driven by labor supply and capital accumulation. But labor, at least the unskilled variety, is becoming less important as technology becomes more potent. Certainly unemployment is a vexing problem in most of the industrialized countries (the US being an exception, for the moment). There may come a time – whether it will be in the near or distant future is hard to say – when labor is no longer scarce and thus no longer a critical factor of production.

Meanwhile, production per capita is apparently driven by capital accumulation and technical progress. However, technical progress must not be confused with factor productivity, although they are often implicitly assumed to be equivalent. (Indeed, factor productivity is generally taken as a proxy for technical progress, since there is no direct measure of the latter at the aggregate level.) The fact is, factor productivity can and sometimes does decline in the short run, whereas technological capability never does.

Apart from the accumulation of produced capital, there is another factor of production that needs to be taken into account, namely the use of raw materials and energy extracted from the environment. The importance of energy consumption as a driver of economic growth has been underestimated by received economic theory up to now. The issue is discussed at some length later in the book, because of the intimate link between resource consumption and environmental quality.

One final candidate as an irreversible trend and possible driver of change is globalization. This phenomenon is evidently a consequence of technical progress in transportation and communications, coupled with periodic reductions in formal trade barriers, notably tariffs and restrictions on capital flow. The rapid economic growth of the 'Asian Tigers', some of which have become influential proponents of free market economics, has undoubtedly been a contributing factor in recent years. But whether a regime of free capital movement without free movement of labor is socially (or otherwise) sustainable over a long period remains to be seen. I lean toward the skeptical view on this question.

NOTES

1 The basic theory was set forth by the Austrian economist Joseph Schumpeter (in German, 1912; English translation, 1934). It has, of course, been considerably elaborated since then.
2 Sherwin Rosen, an American economist, speaking of Sweden, put it succinctly:
   'A large fraction of women work in the public sector to take care of the parents of the women who are looking after their children.' *The Economist* February 18 1995, p37.
3 I am using the word 'energy' as it is normally used. However it would be technically accurate to use another term, such as available energy, available work, or – simplest of all – exergy. All of these (plus a few others) are to be found in engineering literature. The exact definition is unimportant here; suffice it to say that exergy is the 'useful' part of energy. It is not a conserved quantity; whereas energy is conserved, exergy is actually used up, or consumed, in every production process.
4 The vaunted European social safety net has reduced the immediate pain of job loss by spreading it over all still-employed persons in the form of higher social security taxes. These taxes, in turn, raise labor costs further, making Europe still less competitive. By contrast, the US has a much less generous social security system, which has kept labor costs from rising so fast but has left more and more American workers, especially the least skilled, with declining real living standards.

Chapter 3

The Coming Economic Crisis of the West

BACKGROUND

To anticipate much that will be discussed at greater length in subsequent chapters, I believe that the increasing inequities in our society are creating dangerous stresses. They are partly attributable to increasing unemployment resulting from increasing globalization on the one hand, and to excessive past borrowing to pay for current consumption from future tax revenues on the other. I suspect that most objective observers of the contemporary scene would agree with the above diagnosis, so far as it goes. Unlike most commentators, however, I also foresee a decline in the rate of economic growth of the West. I also question whether increasing globalization of economic activity is either inevitable or desirable. I think it is time for an extended pause for restructuring our domestic economic arrangements.

The underlying reasons for worry are mostly the result of decades of economic mismanagement. (The mismanagement, in turn, is due in large part to fundamental flaws in economic theory with a much longer history. I return to this problem in Chapter 13.) There are two irreconcilable trends like powerful locomotives on the same track, heading for a crash. One is the fact that most governments of the so-called 'rich' countries are now, or are nearly, de facto bankrupt. They do not have the resources to pay their future bills and cannot obtain those resources from future economic growth at current growth rates. The second is that economic growth is more likely to slow down than to accelerate. I say this despite the spate of very good news about the current state of the US economy (at the time of writing in spring 1997).

In fact, there are disturbing premonitions of a major world depression. There are parallels with the late 1920s, albeit some significant differences.[1] One is the fact that wages are stagnating – especially in the US – while profits and capital gains have been increasing spectacularly. The result is a major shift of wealth from the poorest to the most prosperous – especially to the very rich – and a corresponding lag in consumer demand. Exactly the same thing occurred in the years immediately preceding the Great Crash of 1929. Demand in those years had also been beefed up by an expansion in consumer credit, as in recent years. When the crash came, many debtors couldn't pay and many creditors (banks) failed, making the problem worse.[2] By an interesting coincidence, the US banking system was badly weakened by events in the late 1980s from which it has now thankfully recovered. The Japanese banking system is undergoing a similar crisis at present, however, from which it has by no means recovered.

To be sure, most of the 'wise men' of Anglo Saxon economics still believe that standard nostrums (like fiscal and monetary discipline, balanced budgets, lower taxes, increased private savings, open markets, deregulation, privatization, and greater labor market flexibility) will solve the problem by simultaneously reducing claims on government and 'unfettering' the private sector. Belief in the power of the competitive free market to adjust automatically to perturbations is as irrationally strong today (at least in the Anglo Saxon world) as it was in the 1920s.

I think they are wrong about this, for several reasons.

DEBTS AND DEFICITS

Debts – mostly invisible – are one primary problem. An ominous long-term trend that has contributed greatly to the debt crisis is the seemingly irreversible rise in the costs of health care, pensions, education and other government services such as policing. A greater and greater proportion of the workforce is employed in these sectors, where productivity is not increasing significantly, if it is increasing at all. In 1970, 7.2 per cent of US GDP went into the health care system; by 1992 it was 13.5 per cent – despite the fact that some 30 million Americans were essentially left out of the system. Figures for other major OECD countries are somewhat lower (see Table 3.1), reflecting different approaches to the delivery of health services.

Table 3.1 Total Health Care Expenditures as a Percentage of GDP

	1970	1975	1980	1985	1990	1995
US	7.2	8.1	9.3	10.5	12.3	13.5
Canada	6.9	7.1	7.4	8.4	9.3	9.9
Japan	4.6	5.5	6.7	6.5	6.9	7.1
Germany	6.0	7.9	8.7	8.5	8.6	9.1
France	5.9	6.8	7.7	8.2	8.9	9.2
Italy	5.3	5.9	7.1	6.9	8.2	8.4
UK	4.4	5.4	5.9	5.8	6.3	6.7
EEC	4.9	6.2	7.0	6.9	7.3	7.5

Data Source: OECD. In the US administrative paperwork (form filling) consumes 1 per cent of GDP not including the time spent by patients themselves (which is 'free').

Two observations are unavoidable.

1) The most 'privatized' health care system in the world (in the US) is also by far the most expensive. On the other hand, notwithstanding self-serving claims by the US medical fraternity, there is no reason at all to accept the dogma that US health care services are the best in the world. On the contrary, a number of indicators, ranging from life expectancy to infant mortality, suggest that the US system is actually among the least effective. This contradiction should be kept in mind in discussions of the efficiency gains of privatizing government services.
2) The *rate of increase* of health care costs is similar everywhere. For the European Union (EU) as a whole, the 1970 expenditures were 4.9 per cent of GDP; by 1992 the EU figure was 7.5 percent.

Extrapolating into the future, unfunded Medicare liabilities (as of the end of 1991) amounted to approximately US$6 trillion (1991 dollars), and that applies only to the health care needs of pensioners.[3] Considering the population as a whole, economist William Baumol projected that the percentage of GDP needed for health care alone in the US will reach 35 per cent by the year 2040, with education accounting for another 25 per cent.[4] The reason he gives is that the services in question require high levels of personal inputs by highly educated people, and that little can be done to change these personal input requirements. Baumol calls this the 'cost disease of personal services'. It is evident that such services tend to require ever-increasing subsidies and thus tend to migrate into the public sector. (Needless to say, Baumol's forecast was intended to be self-denying.)

Social security and government pensions are also underfunded. Unfunded liabilities for US social security and government employee pensions at the end of 1991 amounted to about US$8 trillion according to one estimate. While most retirees think they are only getting back the money they paid in (or their employers paid in for them) this is not so. Each retiree in the system up to now has or will get back more than was paid in, depending on when he or she retired. People who retired in the mid-1980s will get back two-thirds more than they contributed. Retirees on Medicare currently each receive US$100,000 more in services than they paid in. But current benefits are being paid for by current contributions, which are approximately 4 per cent of US GDP. On the other hand, those born after 1960 (baby boomers) will have a different experience. Based on current policies (and one set of pessimistic assumptions) expenditures will outrun contributions after 2005, and will reach 7 per cent of GDP by 2035. Either US social security taxes must rise sharply (by around 75 per cent) or benefits will have to be cut sharply.

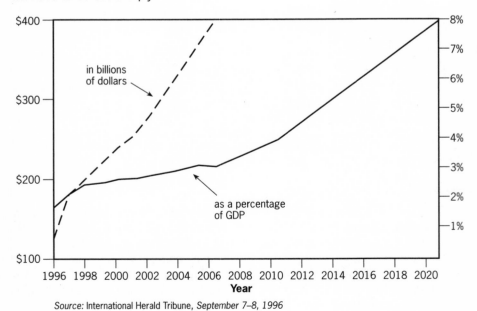

Source: International Herald Tribune, *September 7–8, 1996*

Figure 3.1 Congressional Budget Office Projections of Annual US Budget Deficit

Part of the deeper problem, of course, is that life expectancies have been getting longer, while retirement ages have been getting younger. As a result, the number of years during which a retiree can expect to collect social security has risen significantly. Sharp increases in social security taxes have been imposed since 1980 (up 32 per cent in the US, for instance) but the increases have not kept pace with the promises. The annual federal budget deficit in the US is rising inexorably, despite remarkable improvements in the last four years (1994–1997). US presidential candidate Bob Dole's proposed tax cut would have made it far worse (see Figure 3.1). Since the number of retirees is increasing, and they live longer, the financing of the system is increasingly shaky. In fact, the projected net tax rate for those in the post-baby-boom work force who have to pay the bills – if current spending and entitlements remain unchanged – could be 84 per cent.[5] Based on more optimistic assumptions about these policies, the net tax rate on future workers might be as low as 59 per cent. But, since such rates are clearly unfeasible, we face an impossible situation. Something must give.

The major cause of public sector deficits is the growing cost of pension and health services. In the US there were 3.3 active workers to finance each retiree in 1995. Their ratio is expected to fall to 2.0 by 2020. In Germany today, there are 2.2 employed persons to finance social security costs out of current income for one retired person. By the year 2035 this ratio will drop to 1:1, unless retirement ages are drastically extended.[6] This problem is equally severe elsewhere in Western Europe (see Figure 3.2).

The official debt of the US federal government at the end of 1991 was US$3.6 trillion, or 64 per cent of GDP. But the unofficial federal debt at that time, including US$14.4 trillion of unfunded liabilities for 'entitlements', was US$17.9 trillion, as against only US$2.4 trillion in financial assets on the books. In effect the 'hidden' unofficial debt was four times as big as the 'official' debt. As the years go by, unfunded entitlements are converted into actual debts, as current budget deficits grow. In the US case, for instance, the federal debt had grown to US$4.96 trillion by the end of 1995, despite significant debt reduction efforts by the Clinton administration. More significantly, except for the past two years, the debt has grown faster than the economy. From 64 per cent of GDP at the end of 1991, it reached 70.6 per cent just four years later. The so-called balanced budget deal of spring 1997 between congressional Republicans and President Clinton has been structured to make most of the savings in unlikely ways in future times, without touching the sacred entitlements.

Japan, despite its permanent trade surplus, and recent signs of economic recovery, is not exempt. For six years, from 1987 through 1992, Japan enjoyed a growth rate of more than 4 per cent (over 6 per cent in 1990, 5 per cent in 1991) and a public sector surplus of more than 2 per cent of GDP in 1989–1991. However, since 1991, the growth rate dropped to 1 per cent in 1992, virtually zero in 1993, and less than 1 per cent in 1994 and 1995. Some recovery (to 3 per cent or so) was expected in 1996, although this now appears to have been too optimistic. As growth slowed, the Japanese public sector budget surplus has shrunk rapidly, becoming negative in 1992 and more negative every year since. Japan's deficit was 2 per cent in 1993, 4 per cent of GDP in 1995 and is expected to be 4.8 per cent of GDP in 1996. Accumulated national and local government debt in Japan now amounts to 90 per cent of GDP, not including some 'special discounts' such as the outstanding US$270 billion debt load of the formerly state-owned Japanese railways.

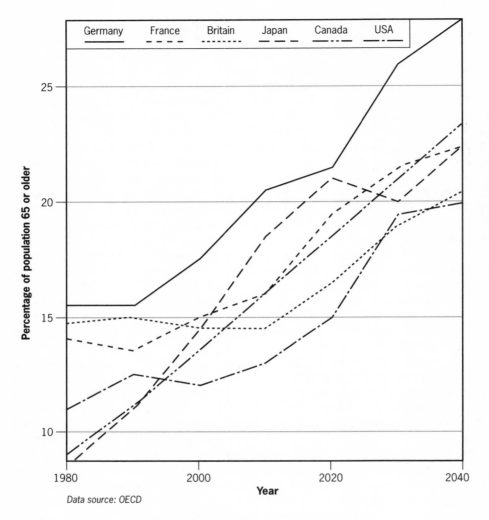

Figure 3.2 Soaring Demand for Pensions

Japan's public sector deficit problem was compounded by a persistent recession brought on by the collapse of the bubble economy of the late 1980s, and especially in Tokyo real estate prices.[7] In the early 1990s, the market value of the land in one Japanese city, Tokyo, was several times the value of all the land in the US and greater than the entire US national debt. This was, of course, based on marginal values based on relatively few exchange transactions. This land nevertheless constituted the security for a mountain of private sector debt. Five years later the land values in Tokyo are a fraction of what they were in 1987,[8] and many Japanese banks are still in deep trouble. (The government has kept the banks afloat by lending them money from the treasury at virtually zero interest rate.)[9] Nevertheless, as of mid-1996 the Japanese banking system was faced with at least US$400 billion in bad debts (according to the Ministry of Finance), and knowledgeable outside observers think the real number is considerably higher. Business has started to recover, but the end of the bubble economy has left the entire Japanese financial system seriously weakened. Meanwhile, Japanese savers have suffered a very painful loss of interest income that has caused great distress among savers and retirees.

In 1996, Japanese expenditures on pensions were 20 per cent of the national government budget and close to 5 per cent of GDP, while contributions were a little over 6 per cent. However, Japan also has one of the world's oldest populations. By 2020 one-quarter of the Japanese population will be over the age of 65. So expenditures on pensions and health care are rising very rapidly as the population ages. They will probably double (to 10 per cent of GDP) by 2010 and triple (to 15 per cent of GDP) by 2050.[10] Increasing public debt will follow, as the night follows the day.

The growing debt burden of virtually every nation on Earth is a fact. In most European countries (except the UK), and in Japan, the situation is actually considerably worse than it is in the US. In most of Europe, 1995 government budget deficits significantly exceeded the criteria established by the Maastricht Treaty for a common EU currency (3 per cent). The 1995 German budget deficit was about 3.5 per cent of GDP, not quite within the allowed range. Greece (9 per cent), Sweden (8 per cent), Italy (7 per cent), Austria, Spain and the UK (more than 6 per cent), and Finland, Portugal and France (more than 5 per cent) were far outside the Maastricht limit. Only Ireland, Denmark and Luxembourg met the criteria. Of course, most countries have forecast significant improvements. By 1998, most members of the EU are expected to make the target, or the target will be moved. But in a number of cases this will be done by creative accounting gimmicks or single-year tax increases (as in Italy), not by long-term reforms.

The European social security system is already essentially bankrupt. For instance, in Germany pensions already account for more than 10 per cent of GDP, and rising. Social charges for pensions currently amount to 7 per cent of GNP. Based on existing policies, demographics and growth assumptions, pension costs in Germany will continue to creep up to about 12 per cent of GDP by 2020, and then leap to nearly 18 per cent of GDP by 2035. Germany's public debt is still slightly lower than that of the US as a percentage of GDP (57 per cent in 1995, estimated), but it is rising much faster – having jumped from barely 40 per cent in 1991.

WHY GROWTH WILL (ALMOST CERTAINLY) LAG

As I have noted, the projections in the previous paragraphs are based on current standard assumptions about economic growth. Some of these assumptions may turn out to be too optimistic. In fact, many government spending commitments, including retirement benefits, were made at times when the economy was growing faster than it is growing now.

In fact, during the years from 1950–1970 the 16 richest countries in the world grew at an average rate of about 3.6 per cent per year. This was by far the fastest in history. It was almost three times as fast as during the period 1870–1950, when annual growth rates averaged about 1.3 per cent per year. But since 1970, average economic growth in these countries has slowed down significantly (to about 2.2 per cent per year). Major conferences have been held, and books have been written, to try to explain this slowdown. Hypothetical explanations abound. They include the suggestion that the previous postwar high growth rate was really 'catch up', or 'convergence', that the slowdown was due to the impact of the oil price rise of the 1970s, and the seductive suggestion that the problem is really a statistical illusion (ie that the difficulty lies with an underestimation of productivity growth in the service sector). Only a few people have suggested that the observed decline in growth might actually reflect a continuing shift of resources away from productive investment into social security and increased consumption by the elderly and unwell.

But the fact remains that real growth, insofar as we can measure it, has slowed since the early 1970s. Yet many government policies are still really predicated on the notion that earlier (1960s) rates of economic growth are the norm. When actual growth slows below the assumed rate, deficits tend to increase sharply. This is happening now in many countries. If the current growth assumptions prove to be too optimistic, the budget crisis will be even more acute than I have suggested above.

Why should we anticipate further decline? Many economists and financial writers attribute declining growth rates with declining savings rates. Personal savings in the US, (as a percentage of disposable income) ranged between 6 per cent and 7 per cent from 1950 through 1967, then rose sporadically to a high of 9 per cent in 1974 – a very bad year for the stock market – and then declined more or less continuously to 4 per cent, where they have hovered since 1987 (with a brief spurt to 5 per cent in 1992 and another in late 1996). The decline corresponds very closely to the rise in stock prices, and a bolder spirit than I might try to explain it by arguing that a declining stock market encourages saving while a rising stock market discourages it.[11] I do suggest, however, that the personal savings rate is not easily changed by policy measures now on the table. For example, I doubt that relief from capital gains taxes will make much difference.

Incidentally, Japanese household savings – once the wonder of the world – are also declining. The Japanese savings rate was 20.8 per cent in 1978. In 1997 it will probably be below 13 per cent. The total pool of Japanese household savings is still huge, US$9.7 trillion. But the Japanese government has the legal power to utilize a significant part of this pool to finance its own growing deficit. Worse, by forcing bank interest rates down to protect the banks from failure, the Japanese government has effectively confiscated much of this savings pool already.

The declining personal savings rate (not only in the US) is probably due, in some degree, to the expansion of government-sponsored social security programs, which most people think of – mistakenly – as a kind of saving. Certainly social security taxes cut into disposable income that might otherwise be saved. A part of the decline in savings is probably attributable to demographics. The population of the rich countries is aging. Middle aged people do most of the saving (after the house and the car and the college bills are paid for). But earlier retirement – not to mention layoffs – force many people in their forties and fifties to save less than they would like and spend more of their savings as they move from good jobs to less good jobs[12] or from the work-force into involuntary retirement. Once retired, of course, they also live longer. In the future, as I have already noted, the number of younger workers to pay the taxes to support each retiree will be smaller. And those younger workers will have less disposable income with which to save because they will have to pay much more in taxes to support the older generation in retirement.

I should say here that I don't believe that the slowdown in personal savings is the primary reason for slower growth, though more savings would help. This is because business investment is mainly financed from profits and allowable depreciation;

personal savings go first into housing and durables, and then into life insurance. The relevant part is what goes into pension funds such as individual retirement accounts (IRAs). Much of this money buys government bonds, which pay for highways, bridges, water and sewage treatment plants, schools, and so forth (including the federal deficit). Of course, it is also true that private savings that (partly) finance the federal deficit are not available for other investments. Thus increasing government debt cuts the potential for private investment. This topic comes up again in Chapter 13.

The next problem for growth is too-high taxes, although this is not so much of a problem in the US as in Europe. In general the taxes supporting the social security systems of all countries, including health services, are levied directly on wages. In Europe these taxes are much higher than in the US. (For instance, I pay 18 per cent of my salary, directly, and my employer pays an additional 57 per cent of my salary into this pot. Social security tax is in addition to income tax and value added tax or VAT.) In Europe taxes on labor, both direct and indirect, are already so high that the total cost of an average employee is roughly double the direct wage cost. For this reason, job creation in Europe (outside the public sector) has been essentially nil for many years. And the ratio of beneficiaries to taxpayers keeps rising.

Employment opportunities for the young and inexperienced are drying up; illegal immigrants in the 'black' economy take many of the low wage unskilled jobs, especially seasonal labor. Young school leavers, even with college degrees (and even with more advanced training) are not finding real jobs with career potential and employment benefits. It is not unusual for young people in Europe, including the UK, to be without jobs (except for temporary short-term positions) several years after graduating from university. Employers have learned to hire a series of young people for three-month, six-month or one-year contracts to avoid giving them the full rights and benefits of regular jobs. Even these temporary posts are very scarce.

There is a heated debate with regard to the causes of wage stagnation and the growing youth unemployment problem. Some blame immigration. Some blame globalization and the increasing tendency of big multinational firms to subcontract their manufacturing to firms in countries – mainly in Asia – where the wages are much lower. Stories appear daily in the financial sections of the press about some big firm or other closing its American or European operation and moving production offshore. The economists who defend free trade, in turn, blame technological change for the unemployment problem. In this instance I tend to agree with the latter. I think both trade liberalization and the rapid spread of information technology are to blame, but primarily the latter. Information technology, in practice, is destroying far more jobs than it creates. These topics are considered further in Chapters 5 and 6, and again in Chapter 14.

But whatever the root cause, the problem of unemployment and underemployment is clearly getting worse, at least in Europe. When unemployment gets worse, more and more people are unable to support themselves. They still need education, health-care and income support. If these things are denied, other social problems, including crime, will soon get worse too. Either way, the taxpayers who still have jobs will have to carry the load, thus adding to their tax burdens and reducing their ability to save and invest. (Even though, as I noted above, personal savings are not as important for growth as the financial press keeps insisting.) Or the government budget deficits will accelerate. Or, most probably, both.

Economic growth rates will almost certainly fall for other reasons, too. One of them is that a larger and larger share of total investment must go into replacing depreciated capital, especially infrastructure. This is an automatic consequence of having invested so much in past years to substitute capital for labor. Our Western economic system is now very capital intensive. But capital, including infrastructure, wears out and must eventually be replaced. Not only that, the *rate* of capital depreciation seems to be rising. In the early part of this century it was apparently around 3 per cent, meaning that the average item of capital equipment or infrastructure had a lifetime of 30–35 years. By mid-century the depreciation rate had risen to 5 per cent or so, corresponding to a 20-year lifetime. The difference probably reflects the fact that motor vehicles, trucks and buses (with a 12-year lifetime, on average) constituted an increasing share of the capital stock. Today, the capital depreciation rate is certainly higher still, if only because computers, computer equipment and software, with a four-year lifetime, now constitute the biggest single share of business capital investment. (The basis for these estimates is discussed in Chapter 13.) I have not seen a good recent study of this issue, but it seems unlikely that the true rate of capital depreciation today is less than 6 per cent. It could be more like 8 per cent.

A final reason to expect the rate of economic growth to fall in future is very simple. In the past two centuries, the substitution of machines and mechanical equipment for human labor has accounted for a lot of the growth in every major country. This substitution has been encouraged and accelerated by cheap fossil energy, starting with coal-burning steam engines in the nineteenth century and continuing with petroleum, gas and electric power (mostly from burning coal, gas or oil). The cost of fossil fuels and other natural resources has been falling in real terms for all of this time. This trend of falling resource prices may not end immediately. But the stocks of high quality natural resources are finite, and rapid economic growth in Asia, for instance, will surely accelerate global demand for these resources. At the same time, the environmental impact of fossil fuel use is already creating new sorts of economic burdens, including emission control costs and the even greater health and other costs associated with uncontrolled emissions.

Eventually, non-renewable energy sources must be phased out. One possibility is to use less energy (by using it much more efficiently). Increasing electrification of the economy is a step in this direction. The other possibility is to replace non-renewable sources by renewable sources, such as biomass or solar power (or, conceivably, nuclear power). But all of these alternative technologies are, or will be, more capital intensive than the current ones. This massive investment in alternative energy technologies will absorb much of the available investable capital in the world over the next half century. And there is every reason to expect the price of fossil energy (and other resources) to begin to increase within the next decade or two, after its long decline. The turning point for petroleum and gas prices could come at any time. This will surely have a negative impact on the rate of economic growth.

One thing that could ameliorate this part of the problem would be to accelerate R&D on renewable energy sources. After all, technological progress, in general, has always been the dominant source of economic growth (see Chapter 13). Yet, because of the long-term governmental budgetary squeeze, together with pressure from the established energy industry, the tiny amount of government support for research in this field is actually being cut rather than growing. But the sort of increase in renewable energy R&D that is really needed – a massive program analogous to the space program of the Kennedy era – seems visionary, to say the least.

THE SQUEEZE

Unemployment in Europe in the 1990s is more than double the US level (below 5 per cent in early 1997), and rising ominously. At this time (spring 1997): unemployment in Spain remains over 20 per cent; in France it hovers around 12.8 per cent; and it is over 12 per cent in Italy. In Eastern Germany unemployment is at 16 per cent, and it is over 11 per cent for Germany as a whole. Only the UK is moving in the right direction – down from just over 10 per cent at the end of 1992 to just under 6 per cent today. While most of the 36 million additional jobs created in the US from 1973 through 1991 may not be 'good' jobs (sufficient to support a family without a second income), at least some 31 million private sector jobs were added, as against only 5 million in the public sector. This is often taken as an excuse for bragging by American politicians, financial writers, and economists. The Europeans, they say, should follow our wonderful example, mainly by decreasing 'inflexibility' in the labor market. What this means, of course, is reducing the barriers against massive American-style layoffs. Should these barriers fall, incidentally, most large European firms would soon cut their employment by 50 per cent or more – as AT&T, GE, IBM and quite a few others have done in the US.

By contrast, in the same period the European Union (EU) added the same number of public sector jobs (5 million), but only 4 million were added in the private sector (*The Economist*, 1993). It has been aptly remarked that, in Europe, economic gains were mostly passed on as higher wages and benefits to those with jobs already. In Europe, a 2 per cent economic growth rate is required just to keep employment levels constant. But growth since 1979 has averaged only 2.4 per cent. Job creation in the industrial countries is weak partly because of inflexibility in the labor market but mainly because labor as a factor of production is just too expensive. This is due, primarily, to the high cost of social security taxes which pay for unemployment benefits, child benefits, health and retirement.

The almost continuous increase in unemployment in France – fairly typical of Western Europe – since the 1970s is charted in Figure 3.3. Each ratchet upward in the unemployment level was accompanied by a new jobs program of some kind. None of these programs has had any permanent impact on the unemployment level. What they have done, of course, is to increase the budget deficit and the national debt of France. To an American, the French social security system is almost unbelievably generous (see Box 3.1) Sadly, it operates at an annual deficit of US$50 billion – equivalent to $250 billion in the US which has a population five times as large – despite the highest taxes in the world.

Only late in 1995 did the Chirac government finally try to come to grip with the realities by introducing some comparatively mild reforms. The result was a five-week convulsion of strikes by workers in the public sector that essentially forced the then Prime Minister Alain Juppé to back down. The 'austerity' plan now in effect is so watered down that it will have essentially no effect on the French deficit. For instance, though the salaries bill of the bloated (5 million strong) French Civil Service accounts for 40 per cent of the national budget (US$120 billion per year out of a US$300 billion budget), the only saving Juppé was able to extract from a reluctant Assemblée Nationale was to eliminate the jobs of about one in ten civil servants through attrition.

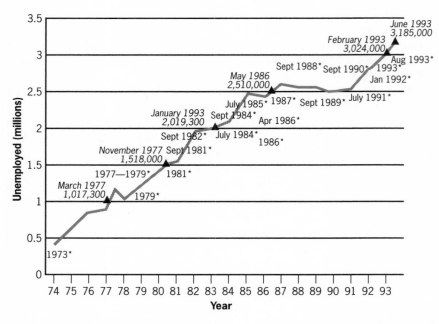

1973 First oil crisis (October).

1977–1979* Raymond Barre launches three national pacts:
1) Exemption of social security charges when under-25 is employed.

2) Creation of a retraining fund.

3) Exemption of social security charges for single women and for long-term unemployed.

1979* Second oil crisis.

1981* Election of François Mitterand.

Sept 1981* Maurois plan: contracts between state and firms, development of employment pools, help to employ the young.

Sept 1982* Launch of employment-training contracts.

July 1984* Firm training for the young and integration help.

Sept 1984* TUC (Collective Utility Contracts).

July 1985* Creation of retraining periods.

1986* Chirac elected Prime Minister.

April 1986* Chirac-Séguin plan: exemption of social security charges for employing the young.

1987* PIL: Program for Local Integration (for long-term unemployed). More TUC.

Sept 1988* Re-election of François Mitterrand.

Sept 1988* First Rocard plan: reduction of firms' costs and of wealth tax; measures for local employment.

Sept 1989* CES (Contract for Employment and Solidarity). TUC become PIL. CRE (Contract to Return to Employment) for long-term unemployed.

Sept 1990* Third Rocard plan: exemption of costs for first employee. Loans to small firms.

July 1991* Cresson plan: Reduction of costs, help to small firms, increase in help to partially unemployed, reduction of tax for employment in a family.

Jan 1992* Second Cresson plan: extended in April 1992 by Bérégovoy. Inclusive and permanent abatement of social contributions for employers on a part-time basis.

1993* Balladur elected Prime Minister.

Aug 1993* Balladur plan.

Figure 3.3 Unemployment in France

> **Box 3.1** Summary of French Social Services
>
> - 39-hour working week.
> - 50 per cent overtime pay for extra hours worked.
> - Minimum five weeks paid vacation.
> - Unemployment insurance providing 57 per cent of regular wages for the first 12 months
> - Minimum wage of US$1200 per month.
> - Pension payments up to 70 per cent of final wage for blue collar and 80 per cent of final salary for white collar workers, depending on length of service.
> - Maternity leave on full pay for at least six months.
> - Job protection for working mothers.
> - Free day care, nursery and kindergarten facilities.
> - Free schooling through university.
> - Lump sum payment of US$2400 to mothers upon giving birth.
> - Monthly allowance of US$120 per child for second and subsequent children.
> - Comprehensive medical and dental service with most costs reimbursed.
>
> In addition, many sectors of society receive additional benefits at public expense. For instance, paid retirement at age 50 for train drivers and truck drivers, and at age 55 for automobile workers. Civil servants (of which there are 5 million in France) retire at age 60. French farmers are, of course, heavily subsidized.
>
> *Source:* International Herald Tribune, *June 25, 1996.*

In early 1997 there was another series of strikes, mainly by truck and transport workers. The outcome of the truckers' strike was another blow to French fiscal austerity. The result was an agreement to allow truck drivers to retire at 55 with full pay (chargeable to the central government). If a conservative government with an enormous majority in the Assemblée Nationale is unable to resist such demands, a socialist government is hardly likely to do better. The new socialist Prime Minister Lionel Jospin has promised to reduce the official work-week from 39 hours to 35 hours at full pay, among other budget-breakers.

DEBT AND PUBLIC POLICY

How sustainable is a policy of public sector borrowing to pay for rising public sector deficits? Keynes and his disciples could argue in the 1930s that deficits were not only sustainable, but necessary growth stimulants. It is true that, when there are significant under-utilized resources (of labor or capital) and real economic growth is rapid enough, government debts do not necessarily increase in relation to the size of the economy. Under such conditions deficit financing is a free lunch for politicians.

In any case, there is no good economic argument for actually balancing the government budget. This is rhetoric for the unsophisticated. It is based on a false analogy between government debt and personal debt. The personal debt is owed to an outside institution or another person. The government debt, on the other hand, is owed mostly to its own citizens.[13] While it is true that taxes are collected to finance the debt service, the interest payments flow (mostly) back into the same economy. In many cases, those who pay the taxes are the same as those who (directly or indirectly) receive the interest payments on the bonds. These same interest payments finance many (if not most) pensions and annuities. So the money flows around in a closed circular path, from citizen-taxpayer back again to citizen-taxpayer.

A balanced budget sounds like prudent common sense, which is what it would be in the case of a family budget. However, for a nation borrowing from itself, there is no need to balance revenues and spending *if* the public debt is stabilized as a fraction of GNP. In general, a bit of deficit spending is indeed beneficial, both in terms of stimulating demand, and in terms of the benefits achieved by the spending per se. I disagree with those doctrinaire libertarians who argue that all government is bad and that, anyhow, people can always decide better how to spend their own money than the government can. In the first place, private individuals cannot afford to run a permanent deficit, whereas the government can do exactly that. A sustainable deficit is stimulative, which is good for everybody if there are un-utilized resources (such as unemployed people). Secondly, there are areas where private individuals will not (or cannot) step in on the required scale. Public health, public education, public housing, public safety and environmental protection are all examples.

But nowadays, when economic growth slows, public debt accelerates. Certainly there are limits to tolerable debt. At the end of 1980, when Ronald Reagan took office, the US national debt was a modest 26 per cent of GDP. By the end of Reagan's second term in 1988 it had reached 50 per cent of GDP. Eight years later in 1996, the US national debt is equivalent to 70 per cent of GDP and debt service accounts for 15 per cent of the US federal budget (or a fraction over 4 per cent of GDP). State and local debt adds another 1 per cent or so. This is significant, but not (yet) actually crippling to the US economy. And there has been some improvement since 1994.

Some countries in Europe (notably Greece) have debt burdens that are twice as large in relation to GDP, which implies that debt service in Greece could easily account for 8 to 10 per cent of GDP, or as much as 25 per cent of government revenues, depending on the market rate of interest.

Still, there must be a limit. Can these trends be extrapolated to 2020, or 2030? It seems obvious to anyone familiar with the facts that, given declining economic growth rates together with aging populations and accelerating entitlements, national debt burdens in many countries will sooner or later become unsustainable – probably sooner rather than later. They are close to this point now in Belgium, Greece, Italy and Spain, for instance. Clearly, the share of national (federal) government tax revenues allocated to debt service in any country cannot soak up 100 per cent of the revenues. After all, other essential activities must continue. Tax revenues to pay for the social services and service the debt *cannot* increase faster than gross output except by raising tax rates. But, there must be a point where declining returns set in, beyond which rising rates will reduce output and, thus, reduce total revenues.[14] Nobody can say with confidence what rates will yield the maximum tax revenues.

However, thanks to the barrage of anti-tax propaganda, voters in the US, at least, are fiercely opposed to any increase in taxes. In fact, in 1996 Bob Dole ran for the Presidency on a platform of major tax cuts 'to stimulate growth', despite an unemployment rate of only 5.5 per cent, as compared to 7.3 per cent in 1981 when Reagan enacted his massive supply-side tax cuts. The Reagan deficits doubled the

US national debt in eight years. To repeat this electoral tactic today is surely a recipe for inflation, not growth. Fortunately, Dole lost.

Deficits have grown because governments want to spend more than they collect in taxes, hoping to finance the deficits from future economic growth, in the traditional sense of the word. But economic growth in the West can no longer be assured. It is not possible to finance current spending, that continues to accelerate, from decelerating future growth. It doesn't compute. Western society cannot continue on this track indefinitely. *There is no way the next generation of retirees can be given the panoply of services and benefits now enjoyed by most Americans, Europeans and Japanese and paid for by the present generation of taxpayers.* Government expenditures for social security and debt service, based on current entitlements, will inevitably grow faster than tax revenues. There are several interrelated reasons for this.

1) Populations are aging while life expectancy is increasing, thanks to medical progress. This will result in rising costs for health services, especially in later years of life. These costs will push up government deficits.
2) Increasing labor productivity – thanks partly to advancing technology and partly to deregulation and trade liberalization – will continue to cause ever-higher domestic unemployment. This, in turn, reduces the number of working people paying taxes while increasing both unemployment compensation costs and earlier retirements, resulting in rising social security costs. These costs will push up the deficit further.
3) The rising tax burden will fall on fewer and fewer people (those still employed) and fewer businesses. This will reduce economic growth still further, increase unemployment still more and inevitably result in accelerated job export, capital export, and tax evasion. Eventually government revenues will fall – as in Russia today – and the system will change or collapse.

In short, governments of most OECD countries are faced with a superficially simple choice between three strategies:

1) Raise tax revenues by raising tax rates, despite the negative immediate impact on growth.
2) Cut government spending, especially entitlements, to reduce the deficit, but at the cost of both jobs and services (not to mention long-term investments such as education, R&D, etc).
3) Borrow as much as possible to put off the evil day when the choice is reduced to 1 or 2. Hope for a miraculous revival of economic growth – thanks to trade liberalization or divine intervention – that will somehow come to the rescue. But, failing a miracle, the day will eventually arrive when debt service consumes too large a proportion of the available revenues.

It need hardly be said that both policies 1 and 2 would be recessionary. They would make the problems even worse, at least for a while. Thus all Western democracies have chosen, and continue to choose, strategy 3, although Western Europe has also adopted 1 to some extent, while the US has opted for 2. So far, 2 looks like the better bet. In Europe, no miraculous economic recovery has occurred and none is on the horizon. Trade liberalization has not helped, as I discuss in more detail in Chapters 6 and Chapter 14. All the evidence suggests the contrary – that trade deficits and job exports are at least part of the problem.

In fact, the economic recovery in the US since 1991 would have been a modest cyclic uptick if it had not been for sharply falling interest rates. (Interest rates fell largely because they had been kept artificially high by the Federal Reserve for several years due to the Savings and Loan crisis which was finally being sorted out by the early 1990s.) This was helpful as a stimulant to personal borrowing and spending. But while many new jobs were created in the service sectors, they were not as good as the manufacturing jobs previously lost. Incomes have not risen (except, as noted, for the well-to-do). Resistance to taxes has, if anything, increased.

In Japan, interest rates have hovered around zero for two years, with only modest indications of economic recovery as of spring 1997. Domestic demand in Japan continues to be weak, probably because expectations have declined and the aging Japanese population is ever more concerned with stretching its savings – badly dented by the real estate collapse – as long as possible. Of course low interest rates to borrowers also mean low interest on savings accounts, which depresses demand.

Europe is in a far worse situation. Germany, the leading economic power, suffers from an overvalued currency and increasing unemployment. The Deutschmark (DM) is overvalued in terms of buying power because Germany has a large and persistent export surplus.[15] Meanwhile the Bundesbank has been slow to cut interest rates because of fears of inflation resulting from politically imposed increases in wages – and hence labor costs – in the former East Germany that are not compensated by productivity increases. The rest of the countries of Northern Europe, including France, are so closely linked to Germany that they are unable to reduce domestic interest rates faster than the Germans without triggering a capital flight. As I have mentioned, all of Western Europe except the UK is burdened by a very costly social security system, paid for (in part) by extremely high social security tax rates.

Every European government is hanging on, hoping for a miracle, perhaps a surge of growth triggered by the long-heralded (but repeatedly delayed) European single currency. A single currency would help, of course, by reducing the complexity and exchange costs of trade across internal EU borders. Big businesses want it. However, the common currency would also hurt the big banks, which get significant income from 'taxing' monetary exchanges. This frictional cost alone might account for as much as 0.5 per cent of European GDP. Major worries have begun to surface with respect to the eventual exchange rate between the Euro, as the European currency is to be called, and the US Dollar, not to mention the possibility of the 'stability pact' proposed by Germany. Elements of both the left and the right in European politics are now campaigning against the common currency, on the grounds that it would be kept too strong (by the Germans), thus encouraging imports and discouraging exports. These worries are serious enough to look threatening to the whole system. Anyhow, a real acceleration of growth in Europe is highly unlikely as long as taxes on labor remain as high as they are to support a range of unaffordable entitlements. In other words, the combination of strategy 3 and strategy 1 is inconsistent.

Given a common monetary policy in Europe (which is still not a certainty) some relief *might* be achievable by forcing short-term interest rates down still further (as the US Federal Reserve Board did in 1991–1992). This policy would be moderately expansionary. When short-term rates are low enough, medium and even long-term rates may also drop for a while – as they did in the US – enabling the government (along with other borrowers) to refinance some of their short- and medium-term debts. Many Americans were able to refinance mortgages during the 1992–1994 period. This freed money for current consumption, and for business loans. However, thanks to the Bundesbank, European interest rates and bond yields have already fallen from the 10 per cent range in 1992 to the 6–7 per cent range as of spring 1997, with no significant stimulative effect outside of Germany. In fact, French unemployment actually increased over this period from 9 per cent in 1991 to over 12 per cent in 1994, and after a slight dip in 1995, the upward trend resumed in 1996 and continues.

Labor market rigidities in Europe are surely part of the problem, as financial writers and economists continually point out. This is due to both labor legislation and – especially – powerful unions such as the German Metalgesellschaft (metalworkers) and the French public sector (eg transport) unions. Some of these rigidities, such as the restrictive store opening hours in Germany, can probably be reduced further. But the unions are likely to fight every inch of the way. The result is a Hobson's choice. With any resurgence of economic growth, unions – long frustrated by stagnating wages and declining membership – will demand sharp increases both in wages and benefits.

In fact, some German and French unions are already demanding shorter workweeks for the same pay – in the name of job sharing – and earlier retirement (at age 55 or even 50) on the fallacious grounds that this will cut unemployment. The Metalgesellschaft in Germany wants to cut the workweek in Germany from 35 hours to 32 hours (in South Korea the standard work-week is still 49 hours!). The French unions are not far behind. What this will do, instead, is increase both costs and government deficits. There will be strong pressures to devalue European currencies vis-à-vis the US Dollar; in fact, the dollar began a strong rise in 1996. Inflation then becomes an immediate threat, due to rising import costs. It can only be kept in check by administrative or other indirect constraints on commercial lending – in other words, by artificially depressing liquidity.

Nobody can say with confidence how long this policy of postponement – refusal to face reality – can continue, but it seems unlikely that it can last much longer. There are indications that strategy 3 is nearly out of gas – or should I say it is bankrupt? In the US both the Republicans and the Clinton administration publicly – albeit briefly – agreed in 1995 that strategy 2 should be attempted in some form. Unfortunately, since the budgetary standoff in the winter of 1995–1996 both sides have partially recanted. As I write, a budget deal is said to be in the works in which the Republicans give up most of their middle class tax cut and the Democrats agree to a reduction in the inflation adjustment formula. But Clinton may renege on this, and nothing more is being said about even modest cuts in entitlements. The devil is in the missing details. None of the plans being debated in public so far will solve the problem. It will get worse.

In the UK, the situation is somewhat less critical. Thatcherism (strategy 2) came along in time to reform the pension system in Britain, starting in 1979. In Britain the welfare system has been held in check and partially privatized – albeit piecemeal – and social security costs to provide current levels of benefit are now rising at only 2 per cent per year. Optimists think that the UK economy will grow faster than this. According to another set of calculations, expenditures are expected to exceed contributions for the next 50 years, but only by about 1 per cent of GDP. After 2035 expenditures are expected to decline gradually. In either case, the UK is in the best shape, even though the value of the basic state pension in the year 2035 is expected to be only 8 per cent of the basic (male) wage, as compared to 15 per cent now and 20 per cent in the late 1970s, when Margaret Thatcher came to power.

This explains, in part, why the British initially opted out of the Maastricht Social Chapter which attempted to standardize workers' rights and benefits throughout Europe – although the new Labour Prime Minister Tony Blair has promised to reverse this. The British still hope to encourage domestic economic growth by devaluing their currency against the DM (or the Euro) while retaining full access to European export markets. In this respect, explicit British policy amounts to 'beggar thy neighbor'. This policy has succeeded for the moment, which puts a heavy strain on the tolerance of the rest of the EU. However, it seems likely that if the rest of Europe moderates its social policies (which it will have to do, sooner or later) Britain will eventually see the light and rejoin the European Union in more than name.

European governments are now talking about austerity (strategy 2), as the Swedish Conservatives under Carl Bildt tried to do in the early 1990s,[16] Lamberto Dini tried to do in Italy before losing office at the end of 1995, and Alain Juppé tried to do in France at the end of 1995. The re-elected social democratic government of Austria has promised to cut the Austrian deficit by half in two years. A newly elected conservative coalition in Spain has made similar promises, though follow-through remains in doubt. Chancellor Kohl's government in Germany finally realized in 1996 that entitlements must be cut. A package has been presented to the parliament that would cut unemployment benefits, raise retirement ages, cut vacation pay and reduce job protection guarantees for small companies with less than ten employees. If approved, it would save DM70 billion (US$46 billion), or 2 per cent of Germany's GDP. But approval of the plan is very doubtful. Germans are no less unwilling than the French to give up the perks of a generous welfare society.

There is another negative feedback in operation here: as the inability of governments to pay the interest on their debts and/or fulfill their obligations becomes more and more obvious, private sector savers will become increasingly reluctant to buy government debt instruments (bonds). If money supply is kept in check by central bankers, long-term interest rates will then be forced up by market forces. High long-term interest rates will increase the prices of many goods and services, thus accelerating inflation. This will slow economic growth even more, or stop it altogether, further increasing the current deficit.[17] There is no pot of gold at the end of this rainbow.

In all industrialized countries the imperative of cutting future costs is in conflict with the present political imperative of cutting unemployment. The outcome so far has been a stalemate, at least in Europe; there has been no progress in either area.

THE FINAL SOLUTION – INFLATION?

Entitlement cuts would be the most responsible, but also by far the most difficult, thing to do. It seems more than likely to me that politicians – following the electorate – will continue to opt for 3 (no action) until the whole house of cards falls down. At that point, debt-ridden, functionally bankrupt governments will have no real choice, in practice, except to renege on government debts to their own people by allowing the currency to inflate. It is the only way to pay the current bills, finance the budget deficit and devalue the debt 'painlessly'. This will not be done openly, of course. It will be done by some backdoor scheme, such as devaluing the Euro against the Dollar, creating new money via new forms of cheap credit, or exchanging real assets (such as infrastructure) for paper. But the net effect will be accelerated inflation and negative real interest rates. The end result will be to penalize small savers and bond holders (banks and insurers), causing chaos in financial markets and poverty for many pensioners. This would probably have happened before now in Europe but for conservative central bankers, the Bundesbank in particular.

To be sure, inflation is not a choice any political leader or party will make openly, but it may nevertheless be *politically* preferable to openly dismantling a luxurious but unaffordable social security system. For Europe, this choice seems increasingly unavoidable. If the inflationary solution is to be avoided, the bitter pill will have to be swallowed soon. When inflation is allowed (it need not be actively encouraged) by any government, private money leaves that country for safer havens. Nowadays this occurs virtually instantaneously. Money moves around the world electronically in the blink of an eye.

The failure of the simple money-printing approach to coping with debt and deficits has been an all too recent and obvious failure in Latin America, Russia and many other countries. Hyper-inflation destroys credit and becomes a direct cause of stagnation and even decline (as happened in Argentina, once a wealthy country). Thus, a little inflation may be tolerable but too much inflation is as much of an impediment to growth as is deflation. Nevertheless, inflation of the currency is often the least painful path, in the short term, for politicians facing a growing deficit.

In the short term, however, continental Europe is still ruled by conservatives who fear inflation more than unemployment. But, even if they did not, they have no tools for job creation. The unions argue for phony non-solutions, such as cuts in the work-week with no cut in pay, as a way of spreading the work. The real problem is that taxes are too high. But the political leadership is unwilling to cut value-added taxes or social security taxes (which fall on labor) because the revenue is apparently needed to pay for the unaffordable subsidies and entitlements that politicians haven't the courage to cut back. The current path leads to increasing stagnation, recession and, quite possibly, a major depression. Barring radical changes in tax policy (see Chapter 11), only the timing and the severity of the next downturn are in doubt.

An upsurge of 'Fortress Europe' protectionism is a likely accompaniment to any extended deep recession. The trend toward trade liberalization and globalization has gone too far, too fast. New policies are needed in this domain. One of the most promising, I think, would be a North Atlantic Trade Association, linking the North American Free Trade Association (NAFTA) with the EU. Baroness Thatcher has been very much in favor of this idea. But it would be very difficult to achieve because of conflicting agricultural policies and disputes about protecting national cultural values by restricting imports of movies and TV programs. In any case, transatlantic free trade – by itself – would not solve the basic problems facing most of the industrial countries.

Conventional protectionism, at least in the traditional form of high tariffs, would be both depressing and inflationary. It would raise prices and cut consumption. It would protect some manufacturing jobs in high cost Europe, especially at the expense of Japan and Asia. But, as the free traders point out, it would also raise the prices of imported consumer goods and thus the cost of living. Unions would then demand wage increases to compensate. Unemployment would restrain this trend, for a while, but if interest rates stay low enough, long enough, a recovery would eventually begin, and the inflationary spiral would follow. It would then continue until the overhanging debt burden is devalued to a tolerable level.[18] The difficult part would be to stop the spiral, once it started.

All of these pressures, together with the growing inequity of income (see Chapter 9), are creating forces that are undermining the social cohesion of Western societies. If present trends continue, our society will be more and more bifurcated into two classes. The upper class will continue to be well-educated, secure, employed, mobile, healthy and wealthy – or at least comfortably well-off. The lower class will be under-educated, under-employed, insecure, unhealthy, immobile, and poor. It will also be crime-ridden. Worst of all, the upper class will begin to grow smaller over time, while the lower class will grow larger as marginal people from well-to-do backgrounds fall back into poverty for various reasons. The middle class bridge from poverty into the comfort zone is falling into disrepair, largely due to the disappearance of well-paid blue collar jobs. Far from having a reasonable hope that their children will be better off than they were, more and more middle class people will see their children failing to 'make it' and falling back into poverty and hopelessness.

One of the unhappiest side-effects of the decline of the middle class, combined with technological breakthroughs in communications, is that the asset owners are able to move and manage their assets anywhere. They are not only able to abandon the central city – as the wealthy began to do in the nineteenth century – but also the parent country itself. Already, we see a number of 'tax haven' mini-countries where the rich can take their money and live in luxury and safety without paying any dues to the larger society. Switzerland is the original haven for the irresponsible rich of other countries, but its example has been followed in varying degrees by Andorra, the Bahamas, Belize, Bermuda, the Channel Islands, Cyprus, Liechtenstein, Monaco and several small Caribbean republics.

In the years 1994–1995 alone, several hundred extremely wealthy Americans left their country *and renounced their citizenship*, simply to avoid paying their fair share of taxes. They did this even though the US is among the least heavily taxed of the industrial countries. When the rich are able to renege on moral obligations in this manner, the burden on those who are unable to leave jobs and dependent relatives becomes that much greater.

SUMMARY AND IMPLICATIONS

Governments in the rich democracies have mortgaged their future. They have done this by committing future growth dividends to current consumption by, and subsidies to, all sorts of politically well-connected groups, including government employees themselves. Health services and pension costs are increasing inexorably. Rising health costs reflect the fact that health service costs have long been rising faster than GDP. This is fundamentally because, on the one hand, new and expensive forms of therapy are constantly being discovered and, on the other hand, productivity is not increasing significantly in the service sector. Rising pension and social security costs per worker are due to the aging of the population, the fact that fewer people of working age are supporting ever more people no longer in the workforce.

If governments are not to renege on past promises by cutting entitlements (strategy 2), these social costs must be financed somehow. This can only be done by increasing taxes on those presently employed (strategy 1), or by adding to government budget deficits (which must be financed by future taxes), while hoping for a miraculous surge in growth to pay for it. I have called this strategy 3. In practice, strategy 2 is 'budget cutting' and the first cuts are made in long-term programs such as health, education and scientific research – not entitlements. Either of the other alternatives, 1 or 3, reduces the funds available for job-creating investment and, thus, cuts economic growth as compared to what it would otherwise be. The investment deficit, along with the national government budget deficits of most rich countries, is becoming critical. A day of reckoning is fast approaching.

The economic growth that was supposed to finance those entitlements painlessly has been taken for granted. It was assumed to be an automatic consequence of technological progress which has, in turn, been assumed to be a kind of manna from heaven – or more accurately, perhaps, a gift from the invisible hand of free competitive markets. (Economic theorists have contributed greatly to the defense and justification of this blind assumption of inevitable growth.) The real drivers of long-term growth, R&D and investment in both physical capital and human resources, have been comparatively neglected for many years. But, to make matters worse, the leading edge of technological change today is information technology (IT). Although this technology is currently very much in the limelight with much talk of an 'information superhighway', 'surfing the internet', and the 'world wide web', the major impact of the technology appears to be destroying more jobs – in other businesses – than are being created in IT itself. This is, after all, what increasing labor productivity means.

In summary, there are several strong reasons to expect that real economic growth in the West will continue to slow down. It may even become negative in the near future. I have already mentioned most of the key points:

- entitlements in most Western countries are clearly out of control. To finance them by taxation soaks up potential savings directly. To finance them by deficit spending also soaks up potential investment capital that might otherwise sustain growth. In this context, R&D spending and education should both be considered as forms of investment. And these types of investments, having very distant payoffs, are particularly vulnerable to cuts by short-sighted vote-counting politicians.
- Economic growth in the past two centuries has been driven, at least partly, by economies of scale in manufacturing. But economies of scale in manufacturing depend on economies of scale in capital equipment. Bigger is normally more efficient. Thus, economic growth is strongly linked to increasing capital intensity. The more capital-intensive the economy, the more capital is needed to replace that which depreciates. Replacing depreciated fixed capital investments (including infrastructure) soaks up funds that might otherwise finance new projects. Depreciation is one of the causes of declining marginal productivity of capital.
- Technological progress in information technologies tends to increase the rate of depreciation of both fixed and human capital through obsolescence, in some sectors at least. The need to replace obsolescent human capital (eg obsolescent skills) obviously diverts capital away from new investment.
- Fossil energy has been a form of 'natural capital' that could be easily substituted for human labor, either directly as a prime mover or indirectly via electrification. For the past 200 years, the price of fossil energy in usable forms has consistently declined, partly as a consequence of technological progress, and partly thanks to discoveries. The role of discoveries is almost certain to decline in the future, and environmental constraints are bound to restrict future growth of fossil fuel use.

I have not even mentioned the export of capital from the rich industrial countries to developing countries with cheap labor. In this case, the loss of potential growth in one area of the world is presumably compensated by faster growth elsewhere. Nevertheless, this trend to export capital to places with cheap labor exacerbates unemployment in Europe and America and the accompanying social problems.

To return to the title of the book, then, it is not economic growth itself that must end; indeed, it must not! But existing patterns of growth and government policies, economic incentives and institutional mechanisms are driving economic growth along unsustainable and ever more harmful paths. These policies, inconsistent as they are, are based partly on history and partly – as will be seen – on faulty economic theory. The history is relevant to where we are, but it will not help us to make the U-turn in policy that is necessary. The economic theory that supports present policies is faulty and misleading in several ways. The standard economic models and their underlying assumptions must, therefore, be challenged and reconsidered, insofar as they apply to economic growth. In short, the growth paradigm must change.

Looking ahead, I do think there is a possible way forward other than choosing between strategies 1, 2 or 3. This is the subject of Chapters 10–11. However, before getting to that point, there is a good deal of groundwork to cover.

NOTES

1   One important difference is that in the 1920s the US was the world's creditor of last resort. The German economy, in particular, depended on US loans which were largely funnelled back to France and the UK as war reparations. The US Congress had been trying (without much success) to recapture some of this money to repay French and British debts to the US. The German reparations bill, fixed under a 1921 settlement, amounted to 150 per cent of German GNP as of 1929. The British wartime debt to the US was 50 per cent of British GNP; the French debt to the US amounted to 67 per cent of French GNP. In the 1930s all further US lending to Germany was stopped – resulting in a crisis for the Weimar Republic – and all war-related repayments to the US stopped in 1932. The financial house of cards collapsed. See Hobsbawm, 1994, p98.

2   Luckily, at least one of the factors that exacerbated the stock market crash of 1929 is no longer a problem, namely the large-scale purchase of stocks on margin.

3   This number and some others used in the following paragraphs come from Peter G Peterson's book *Facing Up: How to Rescue the Economy from the Burden of Crushing Debt and Restore the American Dream* (1993).

4   Paper delivered at the Annual Meeting of the American Philosophical Society, May 1993, by William Baumol. Cited by J K Glassman in the *Washington Post*, August 20, 1993.

5   This figure was calculated by Lawrence Kotlikoff of Boston University, Alan Auerbach of the University of California and Jagadeesh Gokhale of the Federal Reserve Bank of Cleveland, in a paper prepared for the US Office of Management and Budget. It was intended for inclusion in the 1995 Budget but was left out, apparently for political reasons. Reported by James K Glassman in the *Washington Post*, February, 1995.

6   As mentioned earlier, the French railroad system, SNCF, currently has 350,000 retired workers as compared to only 180,000 active ones, a ratio of 1:2. Obviously this imbalance (a direct consequence of productivity gains) is too extreme. Consequently the railroad pensions are now subsidized by the rest of the nation. But what happens when the same sort of ratio holds for the whole manufacturing sector?

7   There are good reasons for blaming the 'asset bubble' on a convergence of interest between Japanese exporters, banks, and – above all – the Ministry of Finance, in response to the Plaza accord of the G7 countries in September 1985 which led to a sharp devaluation of the Dollar vis-à-vis the Yen. The Ministry wanted to keep capital costs low for industry and encouraged high share prices, both to allow companies to raise capital cheaply and to maximize revenues from the privatization of government assets (such as NTT and Japan National Railways). Japanese banks were allowed by the Ministry and the Bank of Japan to speculate on their own accounts without incurring capital gains liabilities on their historic shareholdings. Higher share prices allowed the banks to satisfy capital adequacy requirements. Exporters, finding it more difficult to profit from exports, began to engage in financial engineering (*zaitech*) as an alternative. Corrupt politicians got in on the game through distributions of shares in Recruit Cosmos and other vehicles. (See Murphy, 1994).

8   A vignette from the *Japan Times* of March 27, 1996, is instructive. The Japan National Railway was privatized in 1987 and a trust was created to sell off its surplus properties in order to reduce its large debt load. One parcel of land (a former freight terminal on the waterfront of Tokyo) was valued at ¥4 trillion (about US$25 billion) in 1989 at the peak of the bubble economy. By 1996 the appraised value had fallen to ¥750 billion (about US$7 billion), and there were no bidders. According to the article, Tokyo property values were still falling at 15–20 per cent per annum.

9   This created an opportunity for Japanese banks – and others – to borrow money in Japan and buy foreign bonds yielding higher interest rates. This is an opportunity denied to the general public however. Ordinary Japanese citizens will not be allowed to invest outside Japan until 1998 according to current plans.

10 Figures in this paragraph are taken from *The Economist* April 27 1996, p45.

11 At any rate, the usual explanation of savings behavior – the so-called 'life cycle' model – does not seem to explain what has been happening. According to this theory the baby-boomers should be saving for their retirement years. In fact, they are not doing so.

12 A recent survey by the US Department of Labor found that only 33 per cent of people who have been laid off are able to find other jobs at equal or higher pay. Two-thirds suffer a loss of income.

13 The problem of foreign debt is another matter. But this is not a major issue for the rich countries. It is true that the US is the world's biggest debtor, with foreign debts amounting to roughly half a trillion dollars. However, these only constitute about 10 per cent of the US national debt.

14 This was the point of the famous 'Laffer curve', allegedly drawn on a paper napkin in a Washington restaurant by Arthur Laffer, a Reaganite economics professor from the University of Southern California, during Reagan's 1980 presidential campaign. Laffer argued, on the basis of this hypothetical curve, that taxes were already too high and, therefore, tax cuts would increase revenues. This became (and remains) central to Republican ideology, despite the total absence of empirical support for the assertion that taxes are already above the point of declining returns.

15 This looks like a contradiction in terms. However, as in Japan's case, the surplus is largely built-in by long-standing business relationships and monopolies. It is also, to some extent, driven by capital exports. (Remember the accounting balance: capital exports must flow back. In the German case, they flow back as purchases of German cars and industrial goods.)

16 Bildt's conservatives cut the public sector in Sweden from 70 per cent to 60 per cent of the economy, but lost the next election to the Social Democrats. However, the Social Democrats have now realized that further cuts are imperative.

17 There have been several doomsday books predicting imminent collapse of the US economy based on similar arguments. For instance, *Bankruptcy 1995* by Harry Figgie (1992). The fact that it has not happened yet does not mean the arguments were entirely wrong, merely that Figgie over-estimated the rate at which the US deficit would grow. Obviously, one of the purposes of writing such books is to create alarm and motivate appropriate responses. To some extent, this has happened in the deficit reduction budget of President Clinton and the Republican Congress.

18 The inflationary devaluation of debt in the industrialized world is unlikely to occur as a 'big bang' as it did in Germany in 1921–1922. In the first place, restraining monetary institutions (central banks), having learned from past disasters such as the German example, may be able to keep inflation within bounds. Secondly, indexing of some entitlements is a moderating factor. In the third place, governments today have more sophisticated regulatory tools at their disposal, many developed in response to past economic catastrophes.

Chapter 4
Wild Cards: Russia, China, India and Islam

INTRODUCTION

A brief digression at this point seems appropriate, if only because of the recent controversy instigated by Harvard's Samuel Huntington.[1] Huntington's book ends with a scenario for war between the US and China in 2010. Huntington explains that such a conflict is plausible, if not necessarily probable. The claim of plausibility rests on a number of assumptions, of which the most important is that the West has begun an inevitable decline while Sinic civilization is on the rise, and that the two will inevitably clash, if not necessarily violently.

At any rate, the future of Russia, China, India and the Muslim world is important to the West. On the one hand, we have much to gain from trade with increasingly prosperous and stable neighbors, if that is the way things develop. Let us fervently hope that they do. On the other hand, we have much at stake and much to lose – major investments included, but global security more importantly – if things turn sour.

The first two countries on my list are former great powers that aspire to regain this status. Russia formerly (ie until 1989) had a great empire known as the Union of Soviet Socialist Republics (USSR), which some Russian nationalists want to reconstitute, at least in part, via the Commonwealth of Independent States (CIS). Russia, China and India all have nuclear weapons (as may Pakistan). None of them, except India, has any tradition of democracy. Russia and China were ruled by doctrinaire communists for a long time – seven decades in Russia, four decades and counting in China. Both have undergone periods of catastrophic economic mismanagement – which still continues in Russia and most of the Islamic world.

Let us discuss these countries individually.

RUSSIA

At the moment, Russia is an economic basket case and an environmental disaster. Economic output is down about 50 per cent from the late 1980s. No economic recovery has occurred as yet and none is in sight, though the rate of deterioration may have slowed. The situation changes month by month. Most of the reformers who might have made a difference are now out of office, though one or two may have regained influence. President Yeltsin involved himself, for obscure reasons, in a civil

Table 4.1 Russia's Ethnic Republics

	Income Per Person ($, Nov 1994)	Population ('000 Jan 1995)	Percentage of Russians 1989
Ethnic trouble spots			
Chechnya	na	1,006	22.0
Chuvashia	36.3	1,361	26.7
Dagestan	49.1	2,009	9.2
Ingushetia	na	228	23.0
Kabardino-Balkaria	35.7	787	32.0
Karachevo-Cherkassia	35.7	435	42.4
North Ossetia	40.5	664	29.9
Tuva	57.4	308	32.0
Resource-rich republics			
Karelia	116.2	789	73.6
Komi	98.7	1,203	57.7
Yakutia (Sakha)	142.6	1,035	50.3
Volga republics			
Bashkotorstan	51.8	4,077	39.3
Kalmykia	36.4	320	37.7
Mari-El	41.7	767	47.5
Mordovia	37.0	959	60.8
Tatarstan	48.7	3,754	43.3
Udmurtia	47.9	1,641	58.9
Others			
Adygeya	36.2	450	68.0
Altai	70.6	200	60.4
Buryatia	45.2	1,052	70.0
Khakassia	56.9	583	79.5
All Russia	**89.9**	**148,200**	**81.5**

Source: The Economist, *January 14 1995, p23*

war in Chechnya that his generals were incapable of winning cleanly and that finally stalled in a ceasefire that was really a defeat.

The reasons Russia was so unwilling to allow Chechnya to secede are clearly evident from Table 4.1. It is the old domino theory. If Chechnya had been allowed to secede painlessly, how could the rest of the 21 ethnic republics in the Caucasus, along the Volga and in Siberia, some of which are rich in resources and half of which are populated mostly by non-Russians, be prevented from seceding also? The problem of unassimilated ethnic minorities will be Russia's Achilles' heel for decades to come.

Russia in the 1990s is a classic illustration of how not to run a country economically. The two biggest problems of the communist era were inefficient agriculture and inadequate housing. China's example should have suggested beginning with agricultural land reform to increase the food supply, thus simultaneously enriching the dissatisfied peasants and creating a base of political support. It would also have made sense to allow apartment dwellers to buy their own apartments, and/or build their own houses in rural areas, thus soaking up the accumulated savings that otherwise would surely go to buy imported cars, TVs and so forth. This, too would have created political support for the regime among the urban middle class. It would also have released those savings and made them available for infrastructure investment, which was badly needed and which could have soaked up some of the surplus labor (and steel production) that was released by downsizing the armed forces and the military–industrial complex.

Regrettably, the Yeltsin government ignored these opportunities. In short, the post-communist leadership has done almost everything possible wrong. It began privatization not with housing and agricultural land, but with the biggest and most profitable companies, mainly oil and gas producers. Worse, it allowed the former communist managers to acquire controlling interests in these enterprises through banks and holding companies at nominal prices. This has created a new class of super-wealthy capitalists, from among whom Yeltsin has drawn his political support and campaign financing. The inner circle of new tycoons includes: Prime Minister Chernomyrdin, formerly head of the giant gas monopoly Gazpro; Boris Berezovski, deputy chief of the Kremlin Security Council and head of the holding company Logovaz; Vladimir Potanin, Deputy Prime Minister for Economic Affairs and former head of Oneximbank; Vladimir Gusinsky, a media tycoon; Mikhail Khodorovsky of The Menatap Group; and a number of powerful bankers.

On the other hand, the majority of money-losing enterprises have remained in government hands. For several years they were allowed to continue operating under the old rules, simply borrowing money from the national treasury, which in turn simply printed more money. This policy caused a roaring hyperinflation that wiped out the savings of most Russians and has left many millions of the old and infirm in utter destitution without the means to buy food. Too late for Russian savers, the Yeltsin government has finally reined in the central bank.

But, now the inefficient money-losing companies have little business. They do not pay their workers or suppliers, for whom there is no social safety net and no other employment (because most large enterprises are concentrated in 'company towns'). Yeltsin's communist opponent in the recent election, Zyuganov, proposed to re-open the central bank's credit line to the inefficient enterprises, while simultaneously raising the pay of government workers, farmers, pensioners and everybody else. Yeltsin, who trailed at first in the polls, was forced to make similar unkeepable promises. The very least consequence of all this mendacity must be the further discrediting of government, and democracy, in Russia.

Yeltsin, who survived the election, walks a razor's edge. If he gives in to all the demands for money the resurgence of roaring hyperinflation is an immediate threat. His immediate hope is increased tax collections from the prosperous. This may not work. If it does not, having no better ideas, Russian leaders in the post-Yeltsin era are likely to resort once again to renationalization, authoritarian government, central planning and still more inflationary finance. Finally, they will probably blame the West for pushing for NATO expansion, conspiring to break up the USSR and to impoverish Russia. Conceivably, there may be an attempt to revive the Soviet Union – especially reunion with the Ukraine and Byelorussia – 'voluntarily'. The parallel with Serbian behavior since 1991 is hard to miss. I see an unstable Russia, which is still a major nuclear power, as the most likely trigger for a new global conflict.

Financial mismanagement is not the only problem for Russia. Public health is a disaster, and not only because of a breakdown in public services. Deaths in Russia have risen 50 per cent since 1986, from 1.5 million to 2.3 million in 1994; meanwhile births have declined almost as much, from 2.5 million in 1986 to 1.4 million in 1994. Deaths have outrun births since 1991 and the gap, nearly 900,000 in 1994, is still widening. Life expectancy for Russian women is down from 75 years to 71 years. For men, it has fallen from 65 years to 57 years (1994). If the present trend continues, male life expectancy will fall to a shocking 53 years by the year 2000.

The reasons for this demographic disaster are not well understood. Some attribute it to an epidemic of alcoholism and smoking. The murder and suicide rates are extraordinarily high. Stress-related illnesses, such as heart attacks, are on the rise. Industrial accidents take a significant toll. Environmental pollution in Russia has become a major killer. By some estimates, toxic pollution accounts for an estimated 20 to 30 per cent of all deaths. Here are some other disturbing statistics.[2]

The military–industrial complex accounted for as much as 50 per cent of the GDP (Glazovsky's figures, not mine). Industrial development was deliberately natural-resource intensive. Mining activities in the former USSR generated twice the amount of solid waste per unit of output as compared to Western countries. Losses in timber extraction were estimated at 20 per cent. Oil and gas extraction and transport were very inefficient; the coefficient of oil extraction is estimated to be only 30 per cent. Consumption of fresh water is extremely wasteful. Water use per unit of GDP was five times the US level and ten times the British, French or Japanese level in the late 1980s.

In every one of the 570 cities of the former USSR where air pollution was monitored in the 1980s, maximal permissible concentrations (MPCs) of air pollutants were exceeded for phenols, carbon disulfide, benzo-a-pyrene and ammonia. MPCs for NO_x were exceeded in 90 per cent of the cities and for carbon monoxide in 78 per cent of the cities. At least 5.5 million people lived in areas where MPCs were exceeded on more than 50 days per year. Over 120 million people, or 40 per cent of the population of the USSR, lived in areas classified as degraded, ecologically disturbed or compromised by erosion, flooding, deforestation or forest damage, mining damage or radioactive contamination. This area, totalling 3.63 million km^2, is about 17 per cent of the land area of the former USSR and six times the total area of France. Of this area, 2 million km^2 was classified as 'critical' by the Institute of Geography. The supposedly banned insecticide DDT was found in 16 per cent of the areas surveyed for contamination. Informal estimates suggest that between 20 and 50 per cent of all foods contain excessive amounts of weed killers or toxic heavy metals. Water pollution by chemicals is widespread. In some places infant mortality exceeds 10 per cent of live births.

In short, I am not optimistic about the near-term future of Russia. If Yeltsin fails, the most likely extrapolation of current trends is an upsurge of aggressive nationalism, followed by a program of remilitarization similar to that of the Nazis in the 1930s. While reconstitution of the USSR seems unlikely, a semi-voluntary merger of Russia with the Ukraine and Belarus is already in the works. The Baltic states are also especially vulnerable, since they have large Russian minorities. On the other hand, the current problems in Chechnya could spread to neighboring Ingushetia and other ethnic enclaves. Of course, I hope events will prove me to be quite wrong. The Russians, on balance, are extraordinarily nice people. They deserve a little luck, for a change.

CHINA

By contrast, China had its worst economic disasters under Mao Zhe Dong in the 1950s and 1960s. Impatient with a conservative peasantry and eager to achieve faster progress, Mao conceived the 'Great Leap Forward' in the late 1950s. The objective was to abolish the 'division of labor' – especially between intellectual and physical labor, and between city and countryside. In practice, it was a brutally enforced top–down attempt to industrialize the Chinese countryside by building millions of small-scale foundries and factories in the villages, in which everyone was forced to work. All land was confiscated from landowners and turned over to collective farms administered by party officials. Agriculture suffered; in fact, 30 million people died of starvation. The whole effort was very costly in every way. After four years, the industrialization scheme had to be given up, although agricultural collectivization was retained.

In 1965 the aging Mao (influenced through his wife) was induced to pronounce the so-called 'cultural revolution', spearheaded by the radical 'Red Guard'. Again, the object was to abolish distinctions between urban and rural work. Intellectuals and universities were particular targets.[3] Hundreds of thousands of Chinese professionals were disgraced, demoted, and sent out into the villages to do manual work. For three years of turmoil, economic progress again came to a halt.

After 1968, Maoist ideology was increasingly discredited, especially with the trials and convictions of Mao's wife and the 'gang of four'. When Mao died, orthodox communists remained in charge for another decade. But by 1979 the leadership was firmly in the hands of Deng Xiaoping, another reformer with better ideas then Mao. Under Deng, collective farming was gradually abolished. Though the land itself remained in the hands of the state, privatization of agriculture began to gain momentum during the early 1980s. Food production jumped and by 1984 China had a record harvest; per capita production of rice in China was up to 90 per cent of Japan's level and the country was self-sufficient. In 1985 China exported grain. Diets continued to improve. In 1990 another record harvest was achieved, 10 per cent above the 1984 level. Production in 1995 was 465 million metric tons, according to Prime Minister Li Peng's latest report to the National People's Congress. The target for 2000 is 500 million metric tons.

There is no doubt at all that China's remarkable economic progress since 1980 could not have occurred without this agricultural revolution. It has been the growth pole of the world in the 1990s, as Japan was in the 1960s and 1970s and the 'Four Tigers' were in the 1980s. However, the details are elusive.[4] The first year for which Chinese GNP was estimated on a consistent basis was 1978, when gross output was 373 renminbi (now Yuan) per capita, rising to 453 in 1980, 816 in 1985 and 1558 in 1990. When adjusted for inflation, the figures (in 1980 rmb) were 391, 453, 733 and 1061 – still a healthy 270 per cent increase over 12 years. However, when converted to 1980 US dollars at the official exchange rate, there was no apparent growth at all! The dollar equivalents were $261, 292, 200 and 215. It is perfectly clear that the exchange rate was both unrealistic and subject to arbitrary official adjustments to tax imports and subsidize exports.

To obtain a more realistic estimate, one might use something like The Economist's well-known 'hamburger standard' for comparing costs of living in various places. The Chinese equivalent would be based on the price of rice, pork and cooking oil. On this basis, Smil calculated that the purchasing power of the rmb (Yuan) in 1988 was 3.7 times its official exchange value. This would put the real GNP per capita of China in 1988 at US$1300 in 1988 dollars or just about US$1000 in constant 1980 US dollars.[5] This sets the Chinese economy in 1988 at roughly US$1.5 trillion (in real 1988 US dollars), give or take US$100 billion or so. The Chinese economy is big, but not nearly as big as the inflated World Bank estimates.[6]

Thus, since Deng came to power, GDP has quadrupled. Despite significant budget deficits and inflation (21.7 per cent in 1994 and 14.8 per cent in 1995) real growth has been extraordinary, up 76 per cent in the 1991–1995 period, and 10.2 per cent in 1995 alone. Is there any reason to think fast growth will not continue for many more years? The government thinks not. Prime Minister Li Peng expects 8 per cent annual growth in real terms for each of the next five years, at a reduced rate of inflation.

There is also no doubt that China's double digit growth in the 1990s has been partly fueled by direct foreign investment. Cumulative investment increased eightfold, to US$114.4 billion, in that time. Most of the investment in China, so far, has come from overseas Chinese, in Taiwan, Hong Kong and Singapore. Japanese investment in China in 1990 was only US$349 million. For the year 1995–1996 it is expected to be ten times as great or around US$3.5 billion, partly driven up by the rising Yen.

China's overall current account balance with the world was positive for 1995, over US$15 billion for the year. At the same time, China is the recipient of large direct investments from abroad: US$27 billion in 1993, US$34 billion in 1994, and US$37 billion in 1995 (figures from the World Bank). The capital inflow increased eightfold during the 1991–1995 period to US$114.4 billion, according to China's State Statistical Bureau. Thus, China appears to have a net capital inflow together with a net surplus in the trade account adding up to something like $150 billion during the 1990s.

Trade theorist Paul Krugman points out that this combination is impossible because of the accounting balance rule (see Chapter 14). How can China have a trade surplus and also a net capital inflow? According to the balance rule, it can't. Yet the discrepancy is quite large ($150 billion over five years) and there is no obvious explanation.

A plausible possibility is that China's elites are secretly exporting black capital, in much the same way that corrupt Latin American and African regimes do. Certainly it is entirely plausible to suppose that, despite rigorous controls on foreign exchange, rich Chinese are smuggling liquid (foreign currency) assets out of the country, mainly via Hong Kong. Some returns as 'legitimate' foreign investment, which is thus double counted. Some goes elsewhere to safer havens. If this is so, China is probably a much riskier investment than most people in the financial community seem to believe.

The extent of the irrationality involved in this Chinese investment boom has recently been highlighted by data compiled by the US Commerce Department. Comparing investments in ten Asian countries, average returns for the year 1996 are lowest in China (5 per cent) and South Korea (7.5 per cent). Next was Taiwan (16 per cent) followed by India, Thailand, the Philippines. Hong Kong and Singapore (20 per cent more or less) with Malaysia (32 per cent) and Indonesia (36 per cent) at the top of the list. Averages over the last five years are roughly parallel, although slightly lower. What makes this astonishing is that independent analysis of investment risk (by the Economist Intelligence Unit) put China at the top (risk factor 4.1), followed by India (risk factor 3.4) and Indonesia (risk factor 3.2) on a scale where the US would be rated 1.0.

What is occurring in China now is *not* growth based mainly on indigenous techno-logical development and local investment (as was the case in Europe, America and Japan). It is growth driven by overseas Chinese and Western investment (while Chinese capital leaks away into safer havens). The Western investment is partly based on bubble psychology. Western businessmen have convinced themselves that they cannot afford not to be represented in the gigantic (according to the World Bank) Chinese market. Much of the rush to invest in China is a Pied Piper phenomenon. It will continue only until it stops, at which point a lot of unwise foreign investments – especially in the auto industry – will have to be written off. In short, I'm skeptical of the standard growth model, as it applies to China, to say the least.

A further point can be made here: if China really wants to import capital (as it does) then it should not try so hard to maintain a trade surplus. On the contrary, bearing in mind the accounting balance referred to above, in order to assure a net capital inflow, China should be running a trade deficit, and a budgetary surplus. The larger the trade deficit, the more capital will necessarily flow back into the country, and a balanced budget would ensure that the funds were investable and not used to subsidize consumption (as in Thailand). The major role for the government would be to minimize imports of consumer goods and divert as much as possible of the capital inflows to long-term infrastructure projects. Needless to say, the Chinese government, with its trade surplus and budgetary deficit, is making matters worse.

The industrialization of Asia will not and cannot be a quasi-smooth labor displace-ment process like the industrialization of Europe and America. Europe and America industrialized at a time when manufacturing technology was primitive and labor-intensive, so displaced rural people could soon find employment in the cities. This is no longer the case.

Yet, there is one similarity between past Western industrialization and what is going on now in China, India, Indonesia and elsewhere: Asian industrialization does concen-trate employment in urban areas. This is for logistical reasons. The more sophisticated the product, the more complex the process. Sophisticated products entail a wide variety of specialized suppliers and labor skills. This means big cities.

Export orientation also favors big cities with direct access to deep water ports, especially Shanghai and the Pearl River delta. Factories are being set up with Hong Kong and Taiwanese money to make goods for re-export to the US. (The clothing sold in the US today is largely produced in China.) This process has resulted in a great acceleration of economic activity in the coastal provinces of China. Real estate speculation is rampant, and the construction industry is booming. Construction equipment and machinery for the small factories are imported, of course, largely from Japan. New Chinese millionaires buy Mercedes Benz cars to drive on the new highways. China is already an oil importer, and demand for petroleum is rising rapidly.

In China, urban population in 1950 was 61 million; currently it is around 330 million; by 2050 it is expected to be around 1 billion, according to the UN's population projec-tions. The situation in India is, of course, comparable. This urbanization will, among other things, remove very significant amounts of land from cultivation. In China, for instance, cities, towns, and infrastructure took 324,000 km^2 of land in 1994, as compared to 1,364,000 km^2 that was cultivated.[7] If population increases as projected and the density of cities does not increase, urban area would have to increase by a factor of 3, ie to about 1 million km^2, mostly at the expense of nearby land which is mostly cultivated at present. So the potential loss of cultivated land could be as much as 650,000 km^2 or *close to half of the current total.* Concerns about China's ability to feed itself in the future have recently received a great deal of publicity, with associated controversy.[8]

A closely related problem associated with urbanization and economic development is groundwater shortages. The cause of the water shortages now plaguing much of Northern China is debatable, but the most likely cause is too many wells and too much intensive pumping of groundwater for industrial and municipal purposes. Wet rice cultivation and fish farming have both been abandoned in this region of China. The Heaven River no longer exists, and canals that formerly brought water to Beijing are now dry. In late 1993, the water resources minister of China (Niu Maosheng) said that 82 million rural Chinese were suffering water shortages, along with 300 Chinese cities, in 100 of which the shortages were 'extreme' (Tyler, 1993).

China is also facing a transportation crisis. A few years ago many Chinese cities were initiating infrastructure projects. For instance, the city of Qingdao was planning a ten-mile bridge and a subway tunnel to connect the two sides of its great harbor. Now these projects, like numerous others, are on hold for lack of financing. Another example is a project to build an enormous canal to transport water from the headwaters of the Yangtze River to the dry North East. It will, if built, absorb an enormous amount of capital and cause considerable environmental harm.

One of the problems is that public transport in China is unprofitable. Fares are low and fixed and the system is overloaded and inefficient. As public transit competes with private vehicles for road space, service inevitably deteriorates further. Congestion and pollution are already acute. Yet Prime Minister Li Peng and the State Council, backed by the Ministry of Machine Building Industry (and its 2 million workers), wants to make automobile manufacturing the 'pillar industry' for the new China. The government intends to create half a dozen giant automotive manufacturing joint ventures with foreign partners such as Daimler Benz, GM, Ford and Toyota. Yet this would require huge investments in roads and bridges by national and local governments. The road network of China is particularly underdeveloped. Even India, a significantly poorer country, boasts twice as many miles of road per capita as China. Apart from funds, a vast highway-building program would take hundreds of thousands of hectares of China's most productive farmland and divert it to transportation purposes.

Apart from loss of farmland and sources of food supply, urbanization of this magnitude brings with it enormous problems of water treatment, sewage treatment, air pollution and waste disposal. As it happens, these local problems are the ones most likely to have a direct impact on human health and welfare in the industrializing (and urbanizing) countries. Sewage treatment and air pollution are already extremely serious problems in most developing countries; these problems can only get much worse. In fact, several different estimates have set the monetary cost of pollution (in health terms), deforestation, erosion and other kinds of damage at between 8.5 and 10 per cent of GNP.[9] If these estimates are accurate, as I think them likely to be, then the Chinese economy is not growing in real terms at all. Increased GNP is being paid for by destruction of the natural environment and health of the population.

What is the effect of industrialization and urbanization on the Chinese hinterlands? Farmers can now sell their food products, to some extent, on open markets for higher prices than before. The hinterlands are facing rising inflation and heavier taxation, to pay for subsidies to inefficient nationalized companies and urban infrastructure. Rural incomes have been declining for several years. Farmers (who still do not own the land) are being squeezed both by local Communist Party officials and by rising prices. When land is sold by communes to politically well-connected speculators the lease-holders receive little or no compensation, leaving them homeless and jobless. This squeeze forces tens of millions of people to move to the cities.

Already, displaced or simply dissatisfied agricultural workers are flocking from the interior to the coastal provinces, seeking work, in huge numbers. In Asia, there is absolutely no hope of employing billions of displaced agricultural workers in factories. Manufacturing today simply does not require very many workers. Machines do almost everything better and faster than humans. (Assembly is the single – and temporary – exception.)

In China alone, it is variously estimated that anywhere from 100 million to 180 million peasants have already migrated from the hinterlands to the coastal provinces. The next stage can already be seen around Johannesburg, Rio de Janeiro, Sao Paulo, Bombay, Calcutta, Manila and Djakarta. Most of the migrants cannot be employed. Hence they cannot be taxed, provided with basic housing, utility or health services. Foreign investments are not intended or available for providing social services to the poor. But the local government cannot finance these services either. It is the responsibility of the central government, and one the central government is unprepared for.

The problem of social and financial instability in China is compounded by the fact that a large number of Chinese enterprises are still state-owned, inefficient, and losing massive amounts of money. Of 13,000–17,000 large and medium state-owned firms, one-third to two-thirds are operating at a loss.[10] As in Russia, the regime has allowed this to continue by means of state subsidies. On the one hand, the central government has major problems in collecting taxes, which means that the subsidies are increasingly funded by debt. This accelerates inflation. But, on the other hand, the central government has been unwilling, or unable, to privatize these dinosaurs, for fear of throwing more scores of millions of workers onto the streets.

It is claimed that long-delayed structural changes – ie privatization – to inefficient state-owned industries are imminent. But this would result in massive layoffs, despite the fact that unemployment is already projected to reach 268 million by the year 2001 (*New York Times*, 1995). The costs of providing a social safety net for these workers must be met either by taxation on those still employed or by heavy borrowing from abroad. The choice is analogous to that faced by Western governments. The first possibility, taxation (strategy 1) would stifle growth even if it were administratively and politically feasible, which it is not. The second option (borrowing) is very limited. Domestic borrowing potential is simply inadequate, not to mention inhibiting domestic investment.

China's infrastructure needs during the period 1996–2000 alone have been estimated by the World Bank at US$300 billion. The money has to come from abroad. But foreign borrowing on this scale can only be sustained by a growing trade deficit, as pointed out in Chapter 14. Such a deficit would be welcome to the hard-pressed West. However, it is unlikely to occur, given that the principal motive for foreign investment until now has been the search for cheap labor to manufacture consumer goods for export. Thus China has a trade surplus it does not need and which causes continuing trade friction with Western governments, especially the US.

In short, I believe the present pattern of double-digit growth in mainland Asia is not sustainable. China is not attractive to long-term infrastructure investors from the private sector. The Chinese government, still influenced by communist ideology, wants to limit rates of return, restricts the convertibility of currency and continues to force employers to pad their payrolls in various ways. But acute environmental problems, energy and food shortages will also come into play very soon to slow the seemingly invincible Chinese growth juggernaut.

The third option for the Chinese government – postponement (strategy 3) – is the most likely. But, in the long run, it will almost certainly threaten the stability of the current regime. Not only is the core of communist doctrine – public ownership of the means of production – essentially discredited, but the Communist Party is now so corrupt and sclerotic that collapse, followed by regional breakaway, seems more and more likely. The only remaining unifying power is the army (which accounts for Chinese military muscle-flexing and nationalist claims in, for example, Taiwan).

Most observers still discount the possibility of a breakup of China. However, the stresses in China today are extreme. The consequences of the inevitable slowdown and possible outright collapse of the Chinese economic bubble are unfathomable, except that – as with the collapse of the Soviet empire in 1989 – local ethnic conflicts are likely to become more violent. Any one of them could spread, especially with the piecemeal withdrawal of American military security from the Western Pacific.

Social instability on the scale envisaged is incompatible with continued double digit growth for another reason: that growth is being fed by direct foreign investment, mainly by overseas Chinese in Taiwan, Hong Kong and Singapore. This flow of money can – and probably will – cease abruptly at the first hint of civil unrest (as it has in Russia). This means Chinese growth is likely to slow down drastically as soon as the economic and administrative incompetence and/or instability of the central government is fully revealed, causing a major economic downturn in East Asia when the bubble bursts.

A possible scenario which becomes more probable and more dangerous with every passing year is that China, Japan, Korea and Taiwan will delay making major reforms in their trading policies. This could result in a world trade war triggered by some hasty and ill-conceived US attempt to force a change overnight, leading to retaliation and quickly resulting (as in the 1930s) in a cataclysmic global depression.

INDIA

India is the second most populous country in the world. Although it is currently poorer than China, and growing less rapidly, there are indications of change in the offing. Despite troubles, India is a relatively successful multi-party, multi-ethnic and multilingual democracy. However, the Congress Party, which dominated Indian politics since independence in 1947, was finally defeated decisively in the elections of spring 1996. Hindu nationalists became the leading (but not majority) party, ushering in an era of political uncertainty. The major threat to stability is Hindu fundamentalism. This is extremely threatening both to Muslims (of whom there are 130 million in India) and to Sikhs. Sikhs are the majority in North Central India, especially the Punjab (India's grain belt). Hindu extremism could lead to Sikh separatism, of which there have been ominous signs already. Tamil separatism in the South, not currently a problem, could easily follow. The quarrel between India and Pakistan over Kashmir is also getting worse. Kashmir itself is the principal victim. Broader conflict between India and Pakistan continues to be a possibility.

India also shares many of the problems faced by China, including environmental degradation and a massive influx of displaced agricultural workers to the overcrowded cities. However, as a functioning democracy, these problems are more likely to be discussed openly and addressed fairly than in China.

Nevertheless, I think India will survive these various threats (which, to some extent, cancel each other out) and continue to prosper as a secular democracy. By the mid-twenty-first century India will be a growing, if not great, industrial power in its own right, and will increasingly dominate its own sphere of influence – ie the countries bordering the Indian Ocean, including East Africa and the Persian Gulf.

ISLAM

The chief rival influence around the Indian Ocean (as well as in Central Asia and North Africa) are the Muslim countries. However, while Islam is the dominant religion of the world today, there is no other basis for unity among Muslim countries. In the first place, the split between Sunnis and Shiites is very deep. It is analogous to the split between Roman and Eastern Orthodox Catholics, or even Protestants. The Arabs are mostly Sunnis; Iran is dominated by Shiites. They despise and persecute each other.

In the second place, the Ottoman Empire which dominated the Muslim world until it was finally destroyed by World War I, left no metropolitan successor states except Turkey, which is now secular, industrializing, and Europe-oriented. The Turks have ethnic and linguistic links with some of the Central Asian countries, but Turkey has ancient grievances with neighboring Greece, especially over Cyprus. Turkey also has a long-term problem with its separatist minority Kurds (who also occupy parts of Northern Iraq and Western Iran). The Arab countries to the south – including Syria, Iraq, Lebanon, Egypt and the Arabian peninsula – have no fond memories of past Turkish military occupation. These frictions prevent Turkey from becoming a future leader of the Muslim world.

The other conceivable candidates for bloc leadership are Indonesia, Pakistan, Iran and Egypt. Indonesia is the most populous Muslim country, with nearly 200 million people. Its first post-independence president, Sukarno, attempted to make himself a leader of the non-aligned countries, but not specifically of Muslim countries. Since Sukarno was deposed three decades ago by the current president, Suharto, the country has avoided international entanglements and concentrated (quite successfully) on economic development. It now has very strong economic relationships with the Pacific Rim countries (of which it is one) and virtually no links with the rest of the Muslim world. Muslim fundamentalism is apparently a minor influence in Indonesia. But in the summer of 1996 the first signs of serious political dissatisfaction appeared in the form of a political party led by Sukarno's daughter. The Suharto government is not yet seriously threatened, but the President is aging and has no anointed successor. Despite an easy victory in the 1997 election, trouble will almost certainly erupt when Suharto dies or falls ill.

Pakistan is the second most populous Muslim country. For a long time Pakistan was a US ally in the Cold War, and a logistical base of operations against the USSR's occupation of neighboring Afghanistan. This has left a nasty residue of refugee camps, drug trafficking and arms smuggling. But today Pakistan is almost exclusively concerned with domestic politics and with neighboring India (and Kashmir). It has no language in common with other Muslim countries. Fundamentalism is increasing, but is not (yet) a dominant force.

Iran is the country where Muslim fundamentalism first took power. Under the Ayatollah Khomeini, Iran became a proselytizer for Muslim governance elsewhere. The political consequences are visible in a number of other countries, especially in North Africa. But the results for Iran have been economically disastrous. Despite its oil-based wealth Iran has, if anything, de-industrialized since the Shah was deposed in 1980. The inconclusive seven-year war with Iraq is over, but Iran's post-revolutionary ambitions to dominate the Persian Gulf have been checkmated. Its support for the Hezbollah (Hesb-Allah) in Lebanon is virtually its only current influence in other Muslim areas. An interesting trend towards internal division of power between religious and secular authorities has begun to emerge.

Egypt is the most populous Arab country. Under Gamal Abdel Nasser it tried to play off the US against the USSR. Nasser attempted to unite the Arabs under his leadership. A merger with Syria was briefly attempted, but failed. In more recent years Egypt has been preoccupied by conflicts with Israel. A secular regime, supported by the US, is currently in power, but there is a growing fundamentalist underground that is doing its utmost to undermine the government by destroying the economy. If the secular regime survives, Egypt will continue to try to industrialize along present lines. If not, it will probably relapse into chaos. The chances of leading a unified Arab (or Muslim) entity of any kind seem remote.

I should also mention the Persian Gulf, if only because of its importance as the world's major reservoir of exportable petroleum. The chances of regional domination by Iran seem minimal today, and Iraq's attempt at regional domination also seems to have failed. Nevertheless, the possibility of a home-grown revolt in Saudi Arabia cannot be ignored. The ruling family is fairly solidly entrenched, but Saudi Arabia is no democracy. The two bloody attacks against US military targets in 1995–1996 were probably carried out by homegrown fundamentalist militants, though outside support cannot be ruled out. (The second, more deadly bombing has not yet been attributed to any group, as of early 1997.)

Dissatisfied younger army officers not belonging to the ruling family (tribe) could be another source of trouble. This group would appear to be more likely to be secular and modernist than orthodox, but a fundamentalist underground within the military is not totally implausible. Iranian or Iraqi sponsorship of terrorist undergrounds remains possible. As the US withdraws increasingly into isolationism, a secular or fundamentalist coup d'état in Saudi Arabia – which could rapidly spread to the nearby Emirates – would have an unpredictable but enormous impact on the balance of power in the world.

The very least of the likely consequences of a belated and ineffective Western response in defense of the status quo would be a repetition of the 1973–1974 Arab oil boycott on a larger scale. Anyone with an active imagination can construct a number of horrific scenarios based on such an event. However, I do not think the worst will happen. US influence in the region is simply too overwhelming.

SUMMARY AND IMPLICATIONS

Despite a number of possible scenarios leading to disaster, my best guess at this point is that Russia will neither collapse nor quickly regain its former superpower status. China will suffer a sharp slowdown – perhaps some internal conflict – due to indigestion from the recent rapid investment-driven growth spurt. Foreign adventures are unlikely to be appealing, given that they are very costly and there are no under-populated lands nearer than Australia – which is inaccessible to China. On the other hand, the central government will not lose control altogether and a slower, more sustainable growth pattern will duly emerge. The modernization trend in China has a great deal of forward momentum now, and it will not go into reverse.

India, too, is on a growth trajectory that may, if anything, accelerate. Market mechanisms are well established in India and the major restraint on growth is excessive regulation and bureaucracy. However environmental degradation is a potentially limiting factor, as in China. The major problems, of course, remain: the large number of ethnic groups and languages; the heavy burden of the Hindu caste system; the high birth rate; and the large number of small villages that are isolated, barely self-sufficient and play no part in the larger economy or society.

The 'Muslim world' is a misnomer. Muslim countries are united only by a common religious faith, Islam, and only in the most general sense. North Africa will be, as in the past, a social problem for Europe (due to immigration pressures and incompatible religious practices) and for Israel, and thus for the US. Muslim countries, taken as a group, control most of the world's remaining petroleum deposits and could – in principle – hold the West to ransom. OPEC was an attempt to do just that. But the Persian Gulf countries have most of these reserves and except for Iraq and Iran – who are bitter enemies – they are militarily impotent. Barring some extremely unlikely combination of circumstances, the Islamic world will not unite against the West in the next few decades.

In short, there are risks, but none of the wild cards are likely to be jokers.

NOTES

1   Huntington's article 'The Clash of Civilizations' in *Foreign Affairs* began the firestorm. His recent book *The Clash of Civilizations and the Remaking of World Order* has added fuel. (Huntington, 1993, 1996.)
2   During the glasnost era statistics began to be gathered and published, albeit somewhat haphazardly. The source for most of the following data is Nikita Fedorovich Glazovsky, who was Deputy Minister for Ecology and Natural Resources for the Russian Republic in the early 1990s. In summer 1992 he participated with me (and others) as a lecturer in a short course on environmental issues for senior managers, sponsored by the European Commission and held in Finland. He contributed a typewritten document, and a copy of a chapter (by him) in a published book, in English, entitled *Toward Sustainable Societies*. It was evidently written before the breakup of the USSR. I have xerox copies of both documents, but the xerox copies do not identify the editor or publisher of the book. Other published and reliable sources of data on the catastrophic environment and health situation in the former USSR are Feshbach and Friendly, 1992 and Feshbach, 1994; 1995a; 1995b.

3 The Khmer Rouge in Cambodia had essentially the same idea: to eliminate the distinction between city and village. When the Khmer Rouge under Pol Pot captured Phnom Penh in 1972, they carried out their program by forcing all city and town residents to leave their homes and ruthlessly killing everyone with 'soft hands'. The death toll was in the millions.

4 For a good discussion, from which I have extensively borrowed, see Chapter 3 of Vaclav Smil's book *China's Environmental Crisis* (1993).

5 See Smil, 1993, p73. Smil also cites, as confirmation, a Rand Corporation estimate (based on earlier CIA estimates of purchasing power parities) that put the Chinese GNP for 1988 at US$1.2 trillion in 1986 dollars, or US$1200 per capita in 1988 dollars.

6 The realism of Smil's estimate as compared to the other two extremes is confirmed by calculating energy/GDP ratios by the three methods of GDP calculation. Using the official exchange rate (for 1985), China's E/GDP would have been by far the world's highest (1.7 kg oil equivalent per $ of GDP). Using the Summers-Heston PPP, on the other hand, China would have been the world's most efficient energy consumer, only 0.14 kg/$, despite the fact that China is known to be a very inefficient energy user. The Smil estimate, however, puts Chinese energy intensity at 0.55 kg/$, roughly on a par with Poland and the former USSR and double that of Japan. This is plausible.

7 Data in this paragraph are taken from Gerhard Heilig (1995), Table 3 and Table 4.

8 See books by Vaclav Smil and Lester Brown of Worldwatch Institute, followed by an article in *Scientific American* (Smil, 1993; 1995; 1996; Brown, 1995; Prosterman et al, 1996).

9 The 10 per cent figure was derived in a detailed study at the East-West Center by Vaclav Smil (1996). Smil notes that his own study was inspired by reports of a Chinese study, carried out by the Academy of Social Sciences, which set the overall cost of environmental damage at 8.5 per cent of GNP, but did not include the background data or methodology by which the estimate was obtained. As a further confirmation, Smil commissioned a group of Chinese scholars to do their own estimate, the results of which were comparable.

10 Sources differ. David Shambaugh (1995) reported from 'sources' that two-thirds of 13,000 firms were loss-making. Zhang Sai, director of the State Statistical Bureau, put the loss-making fraction at one-third of 17,000 firms (*International Herald Tribune*, 1996c). More recently, *The Economist* reset the unprofitable fraction at one-half.

Chapter 5

Technology, Progress and Economic Growth

WHAT IS PROGRESS?

The topic of technological progress as a driver of change, and its role in economic growth, was introduced briefly in Chapter 2 but not discussed in depth. I want to revisit this topic now because of its vital importance for what follows. Specifically, I address four questions in this chapter:

1) to what extent is increasing human welfare attributable to science and technological progress rather than to economic growth?
2) To what extent is technological progress currently a driver of economic growth, and to what extent is the relationship the other way around?
3) Does technological progress in some domains have a negative impact on economic growth?
4) What kind of technology is needed for a truly sustainable future? This last question turns out to be rather subtle but also crucial.

There is a potential for confusion here between technological progress and 'progress' in the more general, even more undefined sense. Along with many others, I have long tended to carelessly *equate* economic growth with that undefined kind of progress. Though aware of the difference, I nevertheless assumed for convenience that the one is virtually a surrogate for the other. The time has come to try to sort out this confusion.

In a certain simplistic sense the difference between growth and progress is all too obvious: it is the difference between quantity and quality, between 'more' and 'better'. In challenging the growth paradigm itself I am not assuming that growth necessarily means more physical goods. Far from it: the true measure of economic output is clearly not the quantity of goods produced, but the quality and value of final services provided to the consumer. What is most wrong about the growth syndrome is not its tendency to consume material resources (as Barry Commoner (1971, 1976), for instance, assumed in the 1970s). Resource consumption is not entirely benign, as I have had occasion to note later; but it is not the major problem either. What is wrong with it is that growth of the kind now occurring in the US and Europe is no longer making most people happier or improving their real standard of living.

In fact, it is theoretically possible to have economic growth – in the sense of providing better *and more valuable* services to ultimate consumers – without necessarily consuming more physical resources. This follows from the fact that consumers are ultimately not interested in goods per se but in the services those goods can provide. The possibility of de-linking economic activity from energy and materials (dematerialization) has been one of the major themes of my professional career. (See, for example, Ayres and Kneese, 1969; Ayres, 1978; Ayres and Kneese, 1989; Ayres, 1989b.)

Many people instinctively doubt that services can be provided in the absence of material goods. It seems intuitively obvious that there must be a lower limit to the material content of any service. For instance, it is impossible to conceive of a house without walls. Yet, while I agree that most services do require materials, it seems fairly straightforward to dematerialize by building more and more value (and even 'intelligence') into materials. Why shouldn't the walls, or wall-panel, of the house be modular? Why shouldn't a variety of other kinds of services, from heating and cooling to illumination and information display, be built in? Why shouldn't these panels also be designed for easy disassembly, removal, remanufacturing and upgrading to incorporate technological improvements?

There is really no definable upper limit to the amount of services a given material object can deliver, especially given the possibility of indefinitely long life. Dematerialization is really a misnomer. It is, fundamentally, a strategy for achieving economic growth by continuously increasing the productivity of natural resources, in contrast to the present strategy of achieving growth by increasing the productivity of labor through the use of material capital and energy.

Ideally, then, it would be helpful to start by asking what are some of the indicators of progress in the general sense? To what extent was economic growth the source of that progress? To what extent does technological progress drive economic growth? Finally, I want to ask to what extent progress – in the broader sense – may, to the contrary, be inhibited by growth? And where is technological progress taking us now?

As to the first question, I think there is convincing evidence of progress in the world since the eighteenth century. Here are some specifics that hardly anyone could argue with.

- Inhabitants of industrial countries are much healthier than our ancestors. Diets are better (except for the poorest). Vitamin deficiency diseases like scurvy and pellagra are virtually unknown today. Childbirth is routine and safe in most cases. Clean water is nearly universally available in the West. We live more than twice as long, on average, as our ancestors two centuries ago. Most of us can live all of our lives – at least until the final days, weeks, or months – without serious pain or physical disabilities.
- Work is less exhausting and requires less time, and is generally less routine. In the eighteenth century most men's work was farm labor, the work-day was ten hours or more (especially in the summer), and the work-week was six days. Farm work was diversified but physically exhausting. For women in the servant category, the days were equally long and tiring. Child labor has been abolished, at least in the Western world. The conditions of work in offices and factories are vastly improved in terms of physical strain, safety, fatigue and monotony.[1]

- Again in the West, people have more leisure time – meaning disposable time for activities of choice – than in the past. In the early nineteenth century children started work at 14 and worked 12-hour days, six days a week, until they died in their 30s or 40s. Actually, in the worst period of the early industrial revolution, children worked in textile mills from the age of eight or nine (as children working in the carpet-weaving industry of India and Pakistan still do today). Leisure was unknown, except for the landowners and rentiers. As late as 1890, the average working year in Western Europe was 2800 hours, or 55 hours a week, 51 weeks a year. Today the work year is 2000 hours in Japan, 1900 hours in the US and less than 1700 hours in Western Europe.[2] People also have more disposable income than they did two centuries ago. The conditions for enjoying leisure are vastly improved (see below).
- Life in the developed world is much more comfortable (and convenient) in the physical sense. The major contributors to this increase in comfort are electric light, ventilation, central heating, better quality windows, better insulation, better quality clothes, a variety of electrical appliances, and so on.
- Communication and transportation are far cheaper and vastly improved. Books are cheap and easily available. Tens of thousands of titles are in print and millions have been printed in the past. Telephones and TV bring immediate contact with people and events from around the world at very low cost. Most people have immediate physical access (within an hour or two) to a large town or city, with all its services and shops. Within a day it is possible for most people in the West to reach almost any city in the world, at a price comparable to an average wage for a few weeks at most. Roads are mostly free to use and good to excellent in quality.

In each of these respects, and some others, life is easier and better now, for most people in the industrialized countries – and many people in other countries – than it was two centuries ago.[3] David Morris of Brown University has compiled some data on the physical quality of life index (PQLI). The PQLI is a composite based on three factors: infant mortality, life expectancy at age one, and literacy. Data comparing 1960 and 1990 show dramatic progress in virtually every part of the world, including Sub-Saharan Africa. In 1960 most of Africa, Saudi Arabia, the Persian Gulf Emirates, the Indian subcontinent, Laos and Papua New Guinea all had a PQLI of less than 30, with Gambia in West Africa being the lowest of all (6.3). In South and East Asia, only Sri Lanka, Thailand, Malaysia and The Philippines had scores above 50. All of Latin America except Argentina and Uruguay had scores below 70. In 1990, by contrast, only Afghanistan and two small West African countries fell into the below 30 category, while substantial parts of Africa, India and Indonesia had scores above 50, and Sri Lanka (despite the Tamil rebellion) achieved a score of 85 in 1993. The highest score of all (94) was Japan.

Of course, other indices could be compiled, taking into account other qualitative aspects of life. Some statisticians tend to stress ownership of such things as telephones, TVs, automobiles and single-family dwellings. In all of these areas, not surprisingly, the US tends to lead the pack, though Western Europe is not far behind. On the other hand, in terms of access to museums, symphony orchestras, theaters, architectural monuments and so on, as well as public transportation and leisure hours to enjoy cultural assets, it is Europe that leads by far.

CAUSES AND EFFECTS

Most economists tend to stop thinking at this point and say, in effect, 'These are the benefits of economic growth. QED.' But it really isn't that simple. The question was: how important was economic growth (ie increasing production and consumption of materials goods) in bringing about this admittedly significant degree of secular progress?

It must be conceded from the outset that shorter working weeks and increased leisure time are directly related to rising labor productivity. The same is true of increased income. Economic growth did make a contribution, in every period, in the sense that more leisure, more income and buying power are generally better than less. But, these improvements were a long time in reaching beyond the (small) middle and upper classes. In fact, from the 1770s to the 1840s or so, things got worse for many, Britons included. The accumulation of wealth only began to benefit the factory workers significantly toward the end of the nineteenth century and through the twentieth. By that time mass production had brought prices down and a few hesitant labor laws and union organizations had brought wages up to the point that consumer goods were becoming available to far more people. To this extent, economic growth was directly responsible for progress, at least in one of its multiple dimensions.

Since then, however, continued economic expansion has added less and less to the standard of living of ordinary people, at least in the advanced industrial countries. In recent times, indeed, the benefits of economic growth have been distributed among fewer and fewer people, especially in the richest country of all, the US. This is not the place for an extended review of the evidence of increasing inequality (see Chapter 7) but there can be no real doubt that it is a fact.

If progress is not primarily due to economic growth, then what are its sources? Here the situation is much murkier. Many of the most notable improvements in quality of life cited above arose almost directly from scientific progress and invention. Science was never a child of economic growth, even though the latter owes much to the former. Science as a continuing activity emerged in Europe from the Renaissance, the Reformation, and the Enlightenment. The details of that intellectual history are fascinating but somewhat beside the point.

To me, the pre-eminent contributors to progress in the broad sense are science and education. For instance, consider health: once the causes of infectious disease were understood (eg thanks to the discoveries of Pasteur, Koch and others), many causes of infectious disease and death became controllable at very low cost. Even modern water and sewage treatment can be provided without enormous investment, although the cost of retrofitting a large city in the developing world is not trivial.

Most of the requisites of public health are now available in many parts of the developing world, and their availability is largely a question of social organization rather than industrial production. In short, it is doubtful both that more economic growth is a necessary precondition to improve the health of the people still living in primitive conditions, and that more rapid growth would necessarily lead to that result.[4]

To pursue the same point further, conditions of work, domestic comfort, and possible uses of leisure time have improved almost as much for middle class people in the cities of the poor countries as in the West. Consider the benefits of electric light, and other electrical appliances. These services are available to all today at real prices far less than the wealthy paid for vastly inferior services a century ago and that the poor could not afford at all.

An educated middle-class Indian or Chinese living in an apartment in Bombay or Shanghai is not significantly worse off in terms of life expectancy, comfort, leisure, or culture than a lower-middle-class apartment dweller in the UK or the US. If he or she has a disadvantage, it is in terms of the ability to buy manufactured goods, especially automobiles.

In the two centuries since the industrial revolution, the middle class has progressed, by most of the above measures, almost everywhere. It has also grown as a fraction of the whole population. It is in the rural villages and the urban slums of Asia, Africa and Latin America that life still goes on much as it did 200 years ago. In fact, for many of these people, conditions (except health) are surely worse. They lack land, housing, family relationships, social status in the village, and access to common property resources that once were the norm for their ancestors. They are also surrounded by evidence of opulence they cannot share. Unfortunately, there are more of these people than ever before, and – thanks to public health – their numbers are now rising rapidly.

In short, one can very reasonably ask: could we not have had many – even most – of the benefits of these scientific and technological improvements without having had such enormous economic growth in terms of production of goods (and pollution)? I think the answer is an emphatic 'yes'. Science, technology and education were the source of most of the real benefits. Growth contributed relatively little, except to the extent that it permitted goods prices to fall, thanks to economies of scale in manufacturing.

OTHER SOURCES OF TECHNICAL PROGRESS

In seeking the sources of progress, consider too the enormous social and economic value of some of the major inventions and innovations of the past. Just a few examples should suffice: the steam engine (James Watt), the steam railway (George and Robert Stevenson), vulcanized rubber (Charles Goodyear), low cost steel (Henry Bessemer). Such people were major creators of wealth in the nineteenth century and the first half of the twentieth. It would be easy to make a much longer list. In recent years the inventors and scientists are less well-known (perhaps because most of them worked in teams) but one would have to add outstanding inventions like FM radio (Edwin Armstrong), the transistor (Shockley, Bardeen and Brattain, Bell Laboratories), the 'pill' (Carl Djerassi, Syntex), and the user-friendly personal computer (PC) operating system (Steve Jobs, Apple). Some of these inventions created fortunes for their inventors, some created fortunes that were subsequently appropriated by others. But it is these inventions, and hundreds of less famous ones, that have made life better – to the extent that it is better – for many people living today.

It is possible to argue that some technological innovations in the past caused hardship and loss to many and gain for only a few. This might well be true of some early labor-saving machines, such as the power loom, which caused a great deal of unemployment and destitution among cottage weavers. But in the long run it brought down the price of cotton cloth and made it available to vastly more people than before. Railroads undoubtedly resulted in hardships for carters and canal barge men. Electric lights may have put some candle-makers out of work and saved the lives of some whales. But most of the inventions I have listed did much more than displace one technology and its workers by another. These technologies created whole new capabilities, new products, new services, and new industries. Most of them created employment and jobs for many, not just wealth for a few.

On reflection, I'd have to say that the answer to my first question at the beginning of this chapter – whether increasing welfare is attributable more to science and technology, or to increasing prosperity from economic growth – is that science and technology were primary and economic growth was secondary, at best.

To the second question I raised at the outset, namely whether growth drives technology or vice versa, the answer is equally clear. It wasn't economic growth that generated scientific and technological progress, but actually the contrary. Having said this, it must also be acknowledged that technology created an efficient engine of production that contributed further to the kinds of progress that I sketched above. For instance, the fact that conditions of work are easier and people have more leisure time is largely due to the use of labor-saving machinery. No doubt the increased level of comfort is partly due to the availability of products and appliances that did not even exist two centuries ago. And the crowning achievement of the industrial system is, of course, the large-scale production of automobiles, which has brought personal transport within reach of most people in the industrialized countries.

Clearly economies of scale and mass production have played an important part. But it is nevertheless more accurate to say that economic growth sprang from technological innovation, than the other way around.

Nevertheless, scientific and technological progress are not self-creating or self-generating (endogenous, in economic jargon). If they were, science and technology would thrive everywhere, rather than in a very few countries and – remarkably – in a very few enclaves in those few countries. Here it is important to understand that technological progress comes in two varieties: radical and discontinuous, and incremental.

The most important kind of change, in the long run, is 'radical' innovation. The steam engine, Bessemer steel, and the internal combustion engine are examples. (There are many more, of course.) Radical innovations create new products and services, new industries, new kinds of jobs, and new social structures. They are the primary drivers of long-term economic growth.

But each radical innovation also admits of a vast number of subsequent improvements and refinements. One need only compare the electric light and telephone of today with the electric light or telephone of 1880;[5] or compare the automobile of today with the Ford Model T (not to mention its predecessors). Big corporations are typically very good at incremental improvement. Radical innovations are more likely to be created by individuals or small teams in start-up ventures.

The first prerequisite for successful incremental improvement is an educational system that produces large numbers of young people trained not only to read and write, but also to use numbers and to think quantitatively. Second, there must be adequate sources of financial support, and public support for science and engineering activities. Virtually all of the industrialized countries, including some of the developing countries, meet these two requirements, at least to some degree. The success of the East Asian economies in recent decades is commonly attributed to their high level of investment in education.

There are four additional prerequisites for successful radical *technological* innovation in the present world.

1) There must be a strong underlying science base, including educational and research institutions working at the frontiers of knowledge. This may include support for engineering projects with very long-term payoffs (such as the space program). Also, the prevailing culture must be compatible with the methods of science, notably skepticism, hypothesis formulation and testing by experiment. (A theocracy such as Iran, for instance, could not meet this requirement.)
2) The general culture must also encourage and reward originality, creativity, individual excellence and innovation. Since skepticism and original thinking do not fit well with religious faith and doctrinal purity, a technologically competent society is almost certain to be secular or – at least – exceptionally tolerant of diversity.
3) There must be a breakthrough culture, in which scientific discoveries are quickly translated into ideas for practical products and services. This means there must be a market for innovative but risky business ideas, including sources of venture capital.
4) There must be a regulatory environment that accommodates the special requirements of small, innovative enterprises.

WHY THE US IS THE TECHNOLOGY LEADER

The only country in the world that has provided three of the four conditions mentioned above consistently in recent decades is the US. It is the unique ability to spawn and nurture successful and innovative small companies, a few of which later grow into giants, that has kept the US economy moving ahead despite excessive regulation and a number of other weaknesses.[6] Northern Europe is strong in the first two areas, but it is weak in the third (support for risky enterprises) and especially the fourth (flexible regulation). The UK, France, Germany and Sweden were once hotbeds of technological innovation, but this is no longer true. Europe – despite a recent wave of privatization – is dominated by nationalized industries, cartels and oligopolies in industry, finance and labor. Prices and wages are largely fixed by cartels and labor law, in particular, is notoriously inflexible and hard on small employers. The lack of financial support for small risky enterprises in Europe is also noteworthy, though European firms often participate in American venture capital funds.

Japan is comparatively weak in the second area (individualism), and also the third (risk taking), though perhaps less so in the fourth area (an accommodating regulatory environment). The Japanese themselves have begun to recognize that their educational system, and their culture itself, promotes consensus rather than individualism or originality. Children in Japan are trained to fit in, not to stand out. Partly for this reason, and partly for other historical reasons, Japan is also comparatively weak in basic science. Finally, there is no venture capital market in Japan, though Japanese firms often go shopping around the world for innovative technologies they can buy or imitate. Japan was and still is, in fact, extraordinarily good at assimilating technologies from outside. This has been a major source of its competitive strength. The USSR had a very strong science base, much of which still remains. But the communist state did not encourage original thinking among its citizens, nor did it reward risk takers. (In fact, it was more inclined to punish them.) Central planning, communism and/or socialism, fundamentalist religion and excessive emphasis on doctrinal purity or consensus are not conducive to innovation.

In short, it is important, but extraordinarily difficult, to sustain a socio-economic system that regularly generates radical innovations. Clearly, the government plays a central role in the system. It provides most of the financial support for education in general, and science/engineering education in particular. It supports the basic research that underlies the entire superstructure. It provides an initial market for the products of many start-up 'high-tech' firms. Finally, it provides the regulatory framework within which the innovation system operates. This includes a range of diverse elements. They include anti-trust law, which restricts the extent to which oligopolies can use their financial and market power to impede competitors. They also include financial market regulation that permits small start-up firms to go to the financial markets for equity capital, but protects investors by requiring very full disclosure of all relevant information about potential risks.

The 1994 libertarian-inspired lurch to the right in the US seriously threatens two of the four 'legs' of the innovation system. It threatens to starve the science base and the human resource base of funds in the name of budget reform. Even before the recent cutbacks, job opportunities for young scientists were painfully scarce. The Republican Congressional majority also threatens the regulatory framework that has successfully enforced a modicum of competition and created a viable market for risky investments in new ventures. By weakening anti-trust enforcement and securities regulation, for example, the new libertarians are creating the conditions for more and easier mergers, on the one hand, and for more scandals and frauds (victimizing small investors) on the other.

GROWTH CONTRA TECHNOLOGICAL PROGRESS?

The third question I raised at the beginning of this chapter was whether (or how much) economic growth along present lines might actually hinder either economic growth or technological progress. This question seems almost perverse, at first sight, since the conventional assumption is that profits from economic growth finance R&D, which drives technological progress, which is the engine of growth. But, while there is some validity to this, it is not the whole story. In fact, I think that one of the most important economic growth mechanisms actually tends to hinder technological progress.

The growth mechanism in question is a consequence of relationships between demand and price on one hand, and between cost, experience and scale of production on the other. The first of these relationships states that declining prices will result in increased demand for the product or service. (Stated in reverse, higher prices imply lower demand, which is perhaps a more familiar idea.)

The second relationship is known to economists as 'increasing returns' to experience and to scale. Costs tend to fall with cumulative production experience, due to institutional learning. Also, for any given investment in plant and equipment, the least cost per unit of output – which also permits the lowest prices – is the one that corresponds to maximum utilization of fixed capital. Increasing returns drive the production system towards the largest possible scale. Large scale typically also requires a high level of investment in fixed capital. But increasing returns-to-scale (and closely related phenomena, such as increasing returns-to-adoption) have an undesirable side-effect: they tend to reduce the rate of innovation. They can also 'lock out' a superior technology.[7]

Box 5.1 The Lockout Mechanism: An Example

Suppose a clever inventor designs a superior type of automobile engine (on paper), that would theoretically perform 10 per cent better in terms of fuel economy and also achieve a 10 per cent production cost saving, if it could be mass-produced. The inventor must first produce a prototype. The unit cost of a single one-of-a-kind engine of conventional design made by standard machine tools would be of the order of US$500,000 to US$1 million.

The same engine, mass-produced at a typical volume of 250,000 per year, might cost only US$2500 to US$5000. The differential cost factor is roughly 200:1. Such an inventor has no chance of going into direct competition with the established auto-industry. S/he cannot start small and hope to grow, because nobody will buy engines costing US$500,000 each, even if they perform slightly better than existing ones. S/he cannot expect to raise large amounts of capital based on the theoretical design, since s/he still has only one small part of the technology needed for building engines, and there is no plausible means of acquiring the rest. Thus s/he is 'locked out'.

Nor does the established auto-industry have much motivation to innovate, unless the innovation offers a major advantage over the competition. Even then, there is a certainty of enormous capital commitments to the new technology over a period of years. Yet there is always a significant and irreducible risk that the projected performance gains and/or manufacturing cost savings might not be realized due to 'scale up' problems that cannot be completely anticipated in advance. (The highly touted Wankel engine failed for similar reasons.) For these reasons, there is an excellent chance that the improved technology will never be adopted. The greater the returns-to-scale of the existing technology, the smaller the chance that a superior one could overtake it except under extraordinary conditions (most likely due to government invervention).

In fact, the technology 'lockout' problem and the so-called 'productivity dilemma' illustrated above apply quite generally to small firms in competition with large firms. The argument is virtually a straightforward extension. In practice, large firms can buy raw materials at lower cost than small ones. They can borrow money at lower cost. They can spread R&D, design and marketing costs over a larger base. It is an everyday empirical observation that, once an industry has become established, the number of viable (ie profitable) competitors tends to shrink because high barriers prevent new entries, whereas bad luck or bad management occasionally forces one of the competitors to the wall. The usual outcome is a forced merger. Sometimes it occurs rapidly; when this happens it is called a 'shakeout'. The end result is that a competitive market gradually evolves into an informal oligopoly, if not a formal cartel. Oligopolies and cartels offer benefits. They stabilize markets and employment. But cartels have every incentive to resist rapid innovation, and especially radical innovation, precisely because innovation accelerates the rate of depreciation of invested capital. In short, they exemplify the productivity dilemma mentioned above. John Kenneth Galbraith characterized the kind of industrial organization that results in his influential book *The New Industrial State* (Galbraith, 1968). He described a world in which technological progress is carefully matched by corporate planners to correspond to the planned rate of capital depreciation and replacement. The catch phrase for this was 'planned obsolescence'.

Unfortunately, the insights of Galbraith and others have been largely forgotten in recent years. This was because the trend toward cartelization and planned obsolescence that was clearly evident in the American economy during the postwar years was interrupted in the late 1970s and 1980s. The cause of the interruption was trade liberalization, which opened the formerly insulated American market to Japanese competitors. The liberalization was good for consumers, but it devastated most of the oligopolies that had dominated markets in steel, machine tools, automobiles, white goods and electrical equipment, not to mention watches, cameras and computers. But the end result was simply another shakeout, with a new set of dominant corporate players emerging. History reversed itself for a while. Now many of the old competitors are out of business (or swallowed up) and these industries are again visibly becoming oligopolistic.

Economic growth may be unkind to technological innovation in other subtler ways as well. In recent years, investment in science and technology has declined in relative terms. This is because the private sector is more and more oligopolistic and short-term oriented. On the other hand, Western governments have been increasingly squeezed for funds. Major cuts in government support for R&D seem to be inevitable in the US. (This follows partly from the prevailing free market doctrine, but mainly from inability to control costly entitlements.) There is no reason to expect the private sector to make up the gap. The cuts in R&D investment will have an adverse long-term impact on economic growth.

IS TECHNOLOGICAL CHANGE NECESSARILY GROWTH FRIENDLY?

Here I come to the core issue. The fourth of my original questions was: does technological progress (especially the current version) have a negative impact on economic growth, and – most particularly – on job creation? In particular, what are the contributions of economic growth, international trade, and technological progress respectively, to job creation? The long-term decline in agricultural and manufacturing employment in the West is an established fact. The erosion of jobs in services is a newer phenomenon, less well-established in statistics.

Indeed, the whole issue is troublesome to professional economists. There are several levels of problems. The first of them is that, according to standard neoclassical economic doctrine, the real economy behaves as if it were in an idealized competitive equilibrium. But in a true competitive equilibrium there is no such thing as unemployment. This is because the competitive equilibrium is a situation in which all markets clear. In other words, prices are such that the supply of every product and service is exactly equal to demand for that product or service. The labor market must satisfy this condition too. It follows that the existence of unemployment is actually a measure of economic *dis*equilibrium.

Any well-trained economist whose education has presupposed the existence of competitive equilibrium is almost forced to conclude that employment problems are primarily due to labor market problems, especially inflexibility. For instance, a highly-publicized report by the McKinsey Global Institute concluded that the unemployment problem in Europe – in contrast to the US – is primarily attributable to the difference in labor market flexibility. This means the mobility of European labor is too low and the price (ie wages, benefits and taxes) is too high. Inflexibility means, in practical terms, job protection for those who have jobs. In Europe a high percentage of the workforce is unionized and labor laws make it very difficult for companies to 'down-size' or to shift jobs to low-wage countries to cut costs. But the other side of the coin, of course, is that firms are very reluctant to take on new employees they will not be able to lay off if market conditions change for the worse. Thus the jobs and wages of currently employed workers are being protected at the expense of opportunities for the young and the inexperienced.

On the other hand, the majority of economists who believe in the competitive equilibrium are skeptical of any suggestion that trade deficits could be the source of the wage stagnation and unemployment problem that is getting worse year by year in most of the OECD countries. In fact, leading trade theorists, taking up the cudgels, have made an interesting case that the decline in real wages for unskilled manu-facturing workers in the US since 1973 is *not* primarily attributable to the effects of trade.[8] The argument is somewhat indirect, but the core of it is as follows:

> *The share of manufacturing in GDP is declining because people are buying relatively fewer goods; manufacturing employment is falling because companies are replacing workers with machines and making more effi-cient use of those they retain. Wages have stagnated because the rate of productivity growth in the economy as a whole has slowed, and less skilled workers in particular are suffering because a high technology economy has less and less demand for their services. Our trade with the rest of the world plays at best a small role in each case.*
>
> (Krugman and Lawrence, 1994, p49).

As to why the manufacturing share has fallen, the explanation is that prices of manu-factured goods have fallen more than prices of services (which are mainly wages). Or, putting it another way, the labor productivity of the manufacturing sector has increased faster than the labor productivity of the service sector. Nobel Laureate Robert Solow has called attention to the fact that even very large investments in computer tech-nology had little apparent impact on productivity in the service sector, at least until recently. This became known as the 'Solow paradox'.[9] From a different perspective, William Baumol has called this phenomenon the 'cost disease of personal services' (Baumol, 1993).

The slow growth of productivity in services has an important implication in terms of the argument I made earlier (Chapter 3) for slower growth: *as the manufacturing share declines, the overall economic growth rate must also decline.* Growth rates of GNP in the industrial world have, indeed, declined significantly, especially since the early 1970s.

What about stagnating or declining wages? Again, the trade theorists deny that competition with low-wage countries (ie the trade deficit) is to blame. As hinted in the above quotation, they point the finger, instead, at technology as the job-destroyer. The main argument here is somewhat theoretical, but perhaps worth recapitulating. In effect, they say that free trade will tend to equalize the wages of high-skill workers in poor countries (where skills are scarce) with wages in rich countries (where skills are less scarce). From this premise – actually a theorem based on some arguable assump-tions – they conclude that, if competition with low-wage countries had been the cause of the decline in jobs, then two things would have followed. First, the US would be preferentially importing goods from those countries in sectors with a high percentage of unskilled labor. At the same time, it would be exporting more goods from sectors requiring a high percentage of skilled labor. Second, in a free and flexible labor market with full employment, this would increase the wage differential between skilled and unskilled workers in the US. This would push the wages of unskilled workers in the US down and the wages of skilled US workers up. In response, employers would then find ways of using fewer skilled workers and more unskilled workers, to redress the balance.

Hence the net result of trade-driven competition should be a small increase in the wage differential between skilled and unskilled. For this reason, according to theory, the ratio of skilled to unskilled workers should have declined in all sectors, but total employment in more skill-intensive (exporting) sectors should have increased due to increased exports. (NB: it is not clear how the ratio of skilled to unskilled could decline in all sectors in a full employment economy without either unemployment among the skilled or de-skilling.)

Contrary to this theoretical prediction, however, it seems that employment of skilled (white collar) workers actually increased across the board in all sectors, but total employment in the more skill-intensive sectors increased scarcely at all. This fact is taken to be evidence that US trade with low-wage countries had little if any impact on wages, at least through 1993. The authors pronounce, rather magisterially: 'We have examined the case for the havoc supposedly wrought by foreign competition and found it wanting' (Krugman and Lawrence, 1994).

I do not find the line of argument summarized above as convincing as the authors do. It could be taken as another confirmation of the obvious fact that the labor market is not free and flexible, which we already inferred from the existence of unemployment. In fact, I think trade liberalization is indeed a significant cause of declining manufacturing employment. However, I also think they are right that technological progress is the bigger part of the current problem.

Yet, coming from academic economists of such high repute, the Krugman–Lawrence diagnosis of the US unemployment problem is just a bit surprising. When challenged on the subject by non-economists, most professional economists have always maintained that technical progress always creates more jobs than it costs. Social critics who question the rate of introduction of labor-saving technology are usually denounced as Luddite, which is a term of opprobrium in academic economic circles almost as scathing as 'protectionist'.[10]

The classic debate about technology and job creation has been revived once again by the well-known technophobe Jeremy Rifkin in *The End of Work* (1994). Rifkin predicts boldly that information technology, in particular, can and will displace three of every four workers in industrialized countries. By the end of the next century, he believes, the industrialized countries will be so automated as to have virtually no need of either factory or office workers. Actually, this is not a particularly surprising forecast. In effect, it says that manufacturing will follow the same pattern as agriculture. Whereas a century ago, most workers in the US – indeed in every country except the UK and Germany – were employed on farms, today barely 3 per cent of US workers work on the land. Based on much the same argument, I made essentially the same prediction myself several years ago, in a study of the impact of computers on manufacturing. However, unlike Rifkin, at the time I viewed the distant prospect of unmanned factories without alarm.[11] Today I am less sanguine.

Rifkin's arguments do smack somewhat of Luddism. As such, they prompted a strong and prompt response from *The Economist*, which reflexively counter-claimed that:

such evidence as does exist bears out few of the 'doomsters'' claims.
There is also a strong theoretical reason for doubting them.
                                                    The Economist, 1995, p22.

Consider now the evidence for this position. First and foremost is the fact that the US is by far the world's leader in IT investment, with 28 computers per 100 people in 1993 against 19 for the next highest country (Australia). Yet unemployment in the US was only 5.5 per cent at the time, no worse than in the early 1960s. By contrast, Western Europe was (and is) suffering from 12 per cent unemployment.

As *The Economist* says, 'This is hardly a persuasive sign that IT is a big cause of unemployment'. But there are other factors influencing the current unemployment situation in the US vis-à-vis Europe, notably the major differences in unionization and labor market flexibility mentioned a few paragraphs above. Also IT, including software, is a major US export, thus accounting for at least a small part of the unemployment differential between the US and Europe.

The fact that Japan has the highest rate of robot usage but the lowest unemployment rate of any industrial economy (in 1993) was also cited by *The Economist* as empirical evidence that there is no link between computers and unemployment. On the other hand, I would attribute Japan's low unemployment partly to its barriers to employment of married women and partly to its domination of certain export markets, due to well-documented predatory trade practices in the past. Thanks to this, Japan now employs twice the percentage of its total workforce in manufacturing as compared to the US. Also, while Japan leads the world in robot usage, the number of employees directly replaced by robots in Japan is only a few hundred thousand, at most. That is a fraction of 1 per cent of the Japanese workforce.

The only other evidence offered by *The Economist* was a report by the OECD which concluded that IT is, if anything, 'modestly beneficial for jobs'. This is the canonical view. It seems to have been substantiated largely on the basis of a survey of employers. The survey compared the number of employees made redundant by IT with the number newly recruited to work in areas involving IT (OECD, 1994). According to the survey, the latter number far exceeded the former, allegedly proving that IT creates more jobs than it destroys. If this is true, of course, Krugman and Lawrence must be wrong in their analysis. I don't personally think the OECD survey proves what *The Economist* claims it does. To mention one problem, there is no good way to measure redundancy. But even if the survey methodology was impeccable, my worries are not much assuaged.

Table 5.1 gives some disturbing numbers from a recent multi-client study (Coates, 1996) by Coates and Jarrett Inc, a well-known futures think-tank. The second and third columns reflect the favorable unemployment picture that existed in 1995. The fourth, fifth and sixth columns reflect two possible scenarios for the year 2005.

Case (a) in Table 5.1 for the year 2005 simply extrapolates 1995 percentages of the workforce (columns 2 and 3) to the larger 2005 workforce, but assumes that total employment will rise in proportion to the number of people wanting jobs. This scenario amounts to a labor market version of Say's law: 'supply creates its own demand'. This seems far-fetched. Case (b), on the contrary, makes explicit assumptions about each sector. For example, it assumes employment in agriculture will actually increase from 2.8 million to 3.1 million, in proportion to population. It assumes that manufacturing jobs will fall from 21 million to 16.6 million – a 21 per cent decline, but plausible in

Table 5.1 Employment and Unemployment in 1995 and 2005, US

Year	1995		2005 (a)	2005 (b)	
Distribution of Work by Sector	Percentage of Workforce	Number of Workers (Millions)	Number of Workers (Millions)	Assumed Per Cent Job Loss (Gain)	Number of Workers (Millions)
Agriculture	2	2.8	3.1	11	3.1
Manufacture	16	21	23.1	−21	16.6
Information	60	78.8	86.6	−12	69.2
All Other	22	28.9	31.8	−1	28.6
Employed		131.5	144.6		117.5
Unemployed		7.6 (5.5%)	8.4 (5.5%)		35.5 (23%)
Workforce		139.1	153		153

view of recent trends. It assumes the number of jobs in services other than information will remain almost constant (down 1 per cent). Finally, it assumes that the number of jobs in the information sector will fall, for the first time, by 12 per cent from the 1995 level.

In fact, a number of clerical job categories, such as stenographers and typists, have already been largely taken over by machines. Whole job categories are disappearing. Data entry of all kinds is being automated, thanks to devices like electronic counters, sensors, optical scanners capable of reading print, and local area networks (LANs) that permit direct communications between computers. Telephone and switchboard operators are fast being replaced by voice mail. Whole layers of middle management are now being eliminated as information is being passed back and forth between functions (eg sales, finance, manufacturing, purchasing) with less and less need for human interfaces. The devastating impact of these IT innovations on employment up to now has been masked by the growth in personal service jobs, such as pre-school child care.

A further comment is warranted. The 1990s situation of rather low unemployment in the US was predicted long ago, simply on the basis of demographics. It marks the entry into the job market of the 'baby bust' generation that followed the 'baby boom' of the 1950s. Thus the employment statistics are somewhat deceptive. The number of unemployed adults will soon rise as the children of the baby boomers enter the job market in the next few years.

Several reasons for special concern about IT are worthy of mention. First and foremost, it is ubiquitous. Whereas most labor-saving technologies in the past (for instance spinning jennies, harvesters or numerically-controlled machine tools) affected only a small part of the economy, IT affects everybody, including the service sector, where all the employment growth in the Western world has occurred for the last two or three decades.

Apart from being ubiquitous, IT is also penetrating new markets more rapidly than new technologies have done in the past. But its markets are mostly in business, not household consumers. Certainly, the service sector – at least in the US – is now being deeply penetrated by computers and IT. Because of this fact the service sector, defined broadly, is no longer readily absorbing workers made redundant by automation in manufacturing.

Finally, IT makes work more portable. This means, for instance, that more people can work at home by 'telecommuting' – already a significant trend. It means, of course, that telecommuters may live in other countries where wages are lower. In other words, telecommuting can be a way of exporting jobs. There is already some evidence of this, too.[12]

TECHNOLOGY AND GROWTH: STANDARD THEORY

The canonical theory that technological innovation creates more jobs than it costs is based squarely on the old growth paradigm. The assumed mechanism is that technological progress translates into labor productivity gains that enable a given amount of capital and labor to produce more goods and services. The economic engine then starts to crank in a virtuous circle. More goods for the same capital and labor input result in lower prices. Lower prices mean that the consumers (who are just the same as the workers when they get home and take off their white or blue collars) can buy more goods or services with the same income. This creates a potential demand either for more of the same goods and services, or for something else – new products or services – which clever entrepreneurs will then rush to offer. (See Chapter 13 for a more detailed discussion.)

Of course the consumers (who are workers when they put their blue or white collars back on) may want more leisure time. That is, they may want to translate their productivity gains into less work. No problem! If they work less, but produce just as much as before, they can have more leisure time with no sacrifice in pay or in the consumption of other goods and services. Ski resorts and beachwear manufacturers will prosper.

Either way, the standard (growth) theory says that the economy automatically creates new jobs to soak up the labor that is no longer needed to produce the original set of goods and services. *The Economist* (1995) noted that it is a fallacy (known to textbook writers as 'the lump of labor') to believe that there is only a fixed amount of output, or work, to go around. In other words, growing incomes should create new demand for goods and services, resulting in the creation of new jobs.

In the face of the empirical analysis by Krugman and Lawrence quoted in the last section (and others like it) such an answer seems too facile. It is based on historical evidence of questionable relevance and on a theory with little empirical support. In short, I am convinced that Rifkin is right about the employment impact of IT, namely that this technology now destroys more jobs than it creates.

What, however, could be wrong with the neat textbook explanation of how job destruction through increasing labor productivity is really job creation through increasing demand? There are several flaws in the logic. In the first place, technological innovation does not always increase demand by increasing wealth through direct productivity gains. On the contrary, the major employment-generating radical innovations in the past – such as electric light, telephones, automobiles and TVs – had nothing to do with increasing labor productivity. They offered truly new goods and services, which stimulated demand *without* destroying jobs. At first, perhaps, only the rich could afford to try the new product, but as the technology improved the product became more attractive to consumers, the scale of production increased, costs and prices dropped, and the market grew.

On the other hand, some technological innovations really have no other purpose than to displace workers. Automatic machine tools are intended to displace machine operators, and they do so. Automatic elevators do not provide better service; they simply make elevator operators unnecessary. Word processors reduce employment for stenographers and typists. Industrial robots replace human workers. Only a few of those displaced by a robot can hope to find jobs doing robot maintenance or robot manufacturing, as was blatantly advertised a few years ago. They must hope for new job creation in totally different fields.

It may be a fallacy to believe that the number of jobs to go round is fixed. But it is also an empirical fact that economic growth in the West isn't producing many more new jobs than are being lost. For each 1 per cent in GDP growth in the West, employment goes up by a meager 0.1 per cent. The fact is that a few years ago lots of new jobs were being created in the service sector but now nearly as many jobs are being lost to automation. The problem is that when jobs are lost to automation in the service sector there is no other sector to absorb the unemployed.

I pointed out earlier (Chapter 2) that capital intensity tends to slow down innovation because firms are reluctant to replace capital equipment that is still productive. But exactly the same argument also works in reverse. Rapid technological change driven from outside the firm can accelerate the depreciation of invested capital. Suppose a new product technology arrives on the scene before it is expected, in a truly competitive dynamic market. The manufacturer would prefer to wait until his factories are fully depreciated, but he cannot afford to be left behind in the competitive race. The new technology must be introduced into the next generation of products. This may well mean scrapping an expensive automated plant before its time. Or it may mean adopting more costly flexible manufacturing systems capable of being reprogrammed to deal with new designs. Either way there is a productivity penalty to pay. In short, faster technological change can accelerate capital depreciation. What this means is that more investment is needed to replace each generation of depreciated capital goods. In short, less net growth is delivered per unit of invested capital.

The major hope of new manufacturing jobs in the industrialized countries would be a new product like the electric light or the automobile – better yet, a new class of products – that provides new and previously unavailable services to consumers and also:

- embodies a large amount of sophisticated design (but not a large amount of material);
- *must* be produced near the consumer by skilled technicians, rather than unskilled assembly-line workers; and
- does not displace an existing product or service that employs much labor.

This is a difficult set of conditions to meet. I doubt that there are any major new consumer products in the pipeline that will grow into large manufacturing enterprises employing large numbers of people. Today's hottest high tech fields – computer software, multimedia applications and biotechnology – employ few people. Indeed, Microsoft is already a giant in financial terms, comparable with IBM on recent stock market valuations. But Microsoft and other software firms are very minor employers of labor. The prospects for large-scale new job creation in new industries in the West are not favorable.

But even if such a miracle product were developed, it might not help the employment situation in the industrialized countries much. In the past, a firm with a new product had time to develop its product design, its manufacturing technology and its marketing strategy – in short to mature – before expanding outside the borders of the host country. This gave the innovating firm a long-term advantage in scale and experience, which enabled it to go on producing for export in the home country before building new production facilities abroad and becoming truly multinational.

But this historical pattern no longer holds. A firm can separate its R&D from its manufacturing operations, retaining one set of functions in high-cost countries and another set of functions in low-cost countries. Manufacturing technology is based on standard programmable modules developed at the same time as the product (known as 'simultaneous engineering') and production need not take place next door to the R&D lab where the product was developed. In fact, if the product is electrical or mechanical, the chances are strong that it will be produced from the very beginning in some low-wage country. Nowadays product introduction, at least by multinational firms, is likely to be virtually simultaneous and worldwide. The firm itself can go anywhere. It is stateless and rootless.

SUMMARY AND IMPLICATIONS

Four questions were addressed in this chapter. The first was: to what extent is human welfare due to progress in science and technology directly, rather than to economic growth? The conclusion was that growth takes second place. Much of the improvement that has occurred in real human welfare is attributable to education, public health and some core innovations such as public water supply, sewage treatment and the telephone. These did not require dramatic increases in the production of consumer goods. They are available even in some low-income countries.

The next two questions concerned the relationship between technological progress and economic growth. It was concluded that technical progress normally drives growth, and has done so in the past, but that it need not. The link is not forged in iron. For example, growth based on increasing returns to scale or to experience can actually inhibit innovation by locking out more favorable processes that are developed later but do not offer immediate cost benefits.

This brings us to the last and hardest question. Is technological progress growth-friendly or not? In the past, it has usually been so. In the first century and a half of the Industrial Revolution technological change generally created more jobs than it cost. New industries were created to produce new products and services. Even though technological change made labor more productive, the increased output of goods and services more than compensated by forcing prices down and thus stimulating increased consumption.

Economists have tended to argue that this synergy between technological innovation and job creation is automatic. Information technology appears to be different, however. Technological improvements and declining costs in information technology have undoubtedly caused prices of information services to fall and demand for them to rise. In this respect the mechanism has operated according to classical economic theory. But, unfortunately, unlike previous technological revolutions, information technology has not yet resulted in economically significant new products or services to final consumers. In short, IT has not created any service for which consumers are willing to pay a lot more money, thus creating a lot of new jobs to produce it. (Personal computers and computer games don't qualify: they are too cheap.) Instead, IT has displaced enormous numbers of jobs in other industries, both in manufacturing and in services. Thus technological change, for the first time in history, has become a major contributor to overall unemployment.

Many of the labor-saving innovations of recent years are just that: they merely displace human labor to reduce costs. IT, in particular, is reducing the market value of human capital by making many skills obsolete. Nothing new or better is created thereby. Whole categories of jobs are disappearing. The only gainers are the employers, mainly the stockholders and top managers. Increased wealth for a few is created at the expense of many who are less well-off.

Only the fact that the lower costs of information processing have sharply increased the demand for information keeps the employment picture from being much worse than it is. All the evidence suggests that we can expect continued job losses in absolute terms, not just in manufacturing, but also in services, including information services. In fact, the very plausible scenario described by the study quoted in Table 5.1 points to a possible US unemployment rate of something like 23 per cent within a decade. Of course, the scenario may be too pessimistic. I hope it is. On the other hand, if there is a major world recession, which is certainly possible given the other factors at play, unemployment could be even higher.

The core question raised earlier (Chapter 3) was: will technological progress deliver the needed burst of job creation? For all the reasons sketched in this chapter, I doubt it. I no longer believe that economic growth via traditional labor-saving technology will generate enough new jobs, via the traditional demand mechanism alone, to compensate for the job losses that are now snowballing.

NOTES

1   There is, however, a recognized new physical disorder called 'carpal tunnel syndrome', that is associated with working long hours at computer keyboards.
2   But strange things are happening. The US led the world in cutting average working hours in manufacturing from 70 per week in 1850 to 40 per week in the 1930s. But the workweek stabilized and began to creep up again in the 1980s. It is currently 42 hours per week in the US; US manufacturing workers now work longer hours than even the Japanese and 15 per cent longer hours than the Germans and most other Western Europeans (*The Economist*, October 22, 1994). Possible explanations abound. One, often cited, is union weakness. Another is the strong preference of large-scale manufacturers to pay overtime rather than take on new employees with associated unemployment insurance and other overhead costs. Job insecurity is another possibility. Stagnant or declining real wages, combined with lower marginal tax rates, may have shifted the point of indifference. Lack of attractive leisure time options (or lack of money to pay for them) may also be a factor.
3   For a rather rose-colored but interesting review of the evidence, see for instance, Julian Simon et al *The State of Humanity* (1995).
4   The best evidence for this statement may be Cuba under Castro, which enjoys excellent public health together with a very low economic standard of living.

5 To be more specific, Edison's first carbon-filament lamp produced 2.6 lumens per watt and had a relatively short lifetime (tens of hours). Light from this lamp cost 9.23 cents per 1000 lumen-hours. Today's comparable tungsten filament lamp produces over 14 lumens per watt – and lasts hundreds of hours. Light from it costs 0.6 cents per 1000 lumen hours. Newly introduced compact fluorescent lamps produce much more light – 68.3 lumen hours per watt and light costs only 0.124 cents per 1000 lumen hours (Nordhaus, 1994).

6 This statement contradicts the conventional wisdom that the US is rich because of its natural resource heritage. The fact that many people believe in this notion does not make it true. One need only compare the economic circumstances of resource-poor countries such as Israel, Sweden, The Netherlands and Japan with resource-rich countries like Brazil and Venezuela to see the falsity of the argument.

7 The inhibiting effect of capital-intensive 'hard automation' used in large-scale manufacturing was discussed very thoroughly by the late James Abernathy of Harvard Business School in an important book, *The Productivity Dilemma* (1978). The lock-out mechanism has been discussed by Brian Arthur (1988).

8 See, for instance, Paul Krugman and Robert Z Lawrence (1994). The argument is elaborated in Chapter 14.

9 An OECD conference was held in 1989 to explore the reasons for this phenomenon (see OECD, 1992).

10 The reference goes back to the early days of the Industrial Revolution, when some angry unemployed weavers acting in the name of a fictitious revolutionary, 'Nick Ludd', attacked and burned cotton mills in the north of England. They were caught, tried and hanged for their offense against property.

11 This was in the context of a major study of the subject carried out under my direction at the International Institute of Applied Systems Analysis (IIASA), Laxenburg, Austria. The final report consisted of four volumes, of which I wrote the first (Ayres, 1991; Ayres et al, 1991a,b,c).

12 In fact Swissair has moved its entire reservation service to Bangalore, India; Lufthansa has announced that it intends to do the same.

Chapter 6
More on Jobs

INTRODUCTION

The last chapter suggested that information technology, at least, is no panacea. But is it fair to put all the blame for job losses in Europe and the US – and more recently, Japan – on technology? I think not. In trade debates the first question that arises is whether trade between a high-wage country and a low-wage country creates more new jobs in the high-wage country than it costs. The canonical answer offered by trade theorists is, again, 'yes'.[1] It is invariably argued by the free trade lobby (as by the productivity lobby) that the job gains will outweigh the job losses.

In fact, the economic theory supporting this position is almost identical to the theory of job creation by increasing labor productivity through technological innovation. It goes roughly like this: suppose imported goods are cheaper than domestic ones (because of lower wages in exporting countries). Domestic consumers are happy about this – at least while they are shopping and still employed. They spend less on necessities than they would otherwise, or they buy more luxuries, or both. The idea is that, if they spend less they will save more and invest in domestic industrial expansion. If they buy more, the increased demand will enable the domestic manufacturer to expand. Either way, it is argued, jobs are created.

WHAT DOES THE EVIDENCE SHOW?

The creation of a unified single market in Europe in 1992 was supposed to generate huge numbers of new jobs by reducing trade barriers. Demonstrably, it didn't happen. Europe suffered an unexpected recession instead. The same promotional hype was trotted out, by the same people (who have no shame), to support the case for creating a new international World Trade Organization (WTO). In 1992 the World Bank estimated the potential global benefits of freer trade to be US$300 billion per year in accelerated GNP growth. Two years later GATT published a new, higher estimate of US$500 billion per year.

The basis for both estimates is the idea that trade increases market size, which permits greater economies of scale, which permit lower cost, which increases demand and justifies more growth. (This virtuous circle mechanism is discussed again in Chapter 13.) GATT modelers apparently assumed more radical economies of scale than the World Bank modelers. Unfortunately, the modelers are not paid on the basis of accuracy of their forecasts.

The same thing has happened in the case of NAFTA. In November 1993 President Clinton, lobbying for the passage of NAFTA legislation, said: 'If this trade agreement passes. . . we estimate America will add another 200,000 jobs by 1995 alone'.[2] President Clinton said in the fall of 1994, in justifying his support for the Asia–Pacific Economic Council (APEC) meeting, that exports to Asia 'would employ 3 million Americans by the year 2000'. These new jobs are supposed to be created in export sectors: according to the standard government rule of thumb, 19,000 jobs are supported in the US for each billion dollars of exports,

Clinton failed to mention the job loss consequences of imports, however. If each billion dollars of US exports creates 19,000 jobs in the US, it is only reasonable to assume that the same rule, or something close to it, holds true for other exporting countries, including Japan, Germany or China.[3] Actually, there is a slight (7 per cent) difference in average wages between US exporting and importing sectors. Exporters do pay slightly better. Politicians and economists always stress this point. But it also means that importing sectors lose more jobs (over 20,000) per billion dollars of imports. In other words, a billion dollars of manufactured imports means that 20,000 jobs – more or less – were gained by other exporting countries and lost to the US. The problem is that the US imports far more goods than it exports.

The US merchandise trade deficit for 1994 was US$166 billion, and the overall US balance of payments deficit for the year was US$108 billion – both records. The trade deficit for 1995 was only slightly lower at US$153 billion. The Chinese trade surplus with the US for 1994 was US $29 billion. In 1995 it was US$36 billion. So, a merchandise trade deficit of US$153 billion corresponds to a job deficit of 3.1 million jobs, more or less. Those displaced range from farm workers to electronic assemblers. What if the trade deficit goes to US$300 billion?

The reality of NAFTA turned out to be rather different than the expectations. The US enjoyed a US$1.3 billion trade surplus with Mexico in 1994 (the first year of the pact) but this turned into a US$15.4 billion deficit in 1995 as imports from Mexico rose 25 per cent and exports to Mexico declined 9 per cent. Republican presidential aspirant Patrick Buchanan used these figures, along with the rule of thumb (19,000 jobs per billion dollars) mentioned above, to assert that 300,000 jobs had been lost to Mexico alone. Whatever the true number might be, evidence of job gains in the US attributable to NAFTA is non-existent.

Ralph Nader's organization Public Citizen has compared the pre-NAFTA promises of a number of firms that lobbied in favor of NAFTA with their post-NAFTA performance. The list included Allied Signal Corp, General Electric, Mattel Inc, Procter & Gamble, Scott Paper and Zenith. All promised that freer trade would be beneficial to domestic employment. In almost every case examined, however, the reverse happened. The toy manufacturer Mattel is an egregious example. The firm had 2000 employees in the US at the time of the NAFTA legislation in late 1993. Within two years it had laid off 520 workers from one facility because of increased toy imports from Mexico. Another example is JVC, a unit of Matsushita, which recently closed its US operation, laying off 200 people. JVC has simply moved lock, stock and barrel to Tijuana, Mexico. Why? The Mexican workers of JVC get US$50 per week, compared to US$350 per week for its former US workers.

Another unplanned consequence of NAFTA is that new investments by Asian companies that had planned to invest in the US moved their investments to Mexico instead. Sony, Hitachi, Samsung and Daewoo have all shifted major planned investments (mainly in electronic assembly and TV tube production) from the US to Mexico. Samsung alone invested US$212 million in Tijuana, where it now employs 2300 workers to manufacture 1.5 million color TV sets, of which 90 per cent are exported to the US. Thanks to NAFTA and unrestricted access to the US market, Samsung plans to invest US$581 million in Mexico over four years (1995–1999) and increase its Mexican workforce from 2300 to 9300. Those jobs would otherwise have been created in the US.

The US Department of Labor has formally certified that, as of August 1995, over 38,000 US workers had lost their jobs directly because of NAFTA. As of January 1996, the number was up to 60,000. This figure obviously does not include the loss of potential jobs, such as those mentioned above, that would otherwise have been created in the US. Given the bureaucratic process involved and the narrow definition of eligibility for certification, it is virtually certain that the true figures are much higher. Even during NAFTA's first full year, before the disastrous devaluation of the Mexican Peso (which occurred in the winter of 1994–1995), real hourly wages for production workers in the US dropped by 3 per cent – the greatest single-year decline in history. This was almost certainly a direct consequence of the downward pressure on manufacturing wages due to competition from Mexico and Canada.

In fact, as of early 1997, the big (and only) winner in NAFTA is Canada, mainly because the US auto companies that formerly assembled only Canadian models in Canada have now shifted much of their production across the border because of the lower wages and favorable exchange rate. This has happened to a lesser extent in several other sectors.

The downward pressure on wages is being felt strongly in Europe, too. In the UK, executives of the textile industry have argued that a minimum wage, promised by the Labour Government, would eliminate a third of the 450,000 textile workers' jobs in that country. Under the circumstances, their argument is likely to be convincing to some. A survey published by *Financial Times* (1995) reported on a growing number of European companies that are moving production to low wage countries. As the article says, the benefits are mouth watering (to the owners and investors, of course, not to the workers). Workers at a new plant in Vietnam are paid 30 cents a day, compared to Japanese workers in the same industry who get US$31 per hour. Labor costs per car are only US$145 in Mexico, compared to US$705 in the US. Ford and GM continue to move production of auto parts, including engines, outside the US. Mercedes Benz is moving production away from Germany to Brazil, India and China. Philips, the loss-making electronics and appliance giant, is also moving production abroad, as are many other companies.

Is this job exodus some kind of anomaly? Of course not. Every firm that lobbied for NAFTA (and WTO) and made rosy promises about more domestic jobs was privately thinking along the following lines. Suppose a factory employing 400 workers, each costing US$12.50 per hour, or US$25,000 a year (the average in 1995) – a payroll of US$10 million – closes in the US and re-opens in Mexico. The immediate Mexican gain of 400 jobs is essentially equal to the US loss of 400 jobs. Actually, since newly hired and untrained Mexican workers are likely to be less productive than their US counterparts, even with the same equipment, the 400 US workers might be replaced by 500 or even 600 Mexican workers.

But the Mexican workers cost a lot less: on the average, US$2.30 per hour or US$18.40 per day or US$3700 per year each. So the first-order annual loss for the

US economy is US$10 million, while the Mexican gain is roughly US$2 million. The US$8 million saving in payroll costs goes to the owners of the business. They may use part of it to pay the interest on the loan that financed the new factory, part of it to cut prices so as to increase sales, and part of it to increase profits. Let us assume the interest on the loan swallows up half the payroll savings, or US$4 million per year. Assuming a low interest rate (8.25 per cent), this implies a capital outlay of roughly US$50 million,[4] of which perhaps US$30 million goes for construction costs (spent in Mexico), and the rest (US$20 million) is used to pay for capital equipment. In general it can be assumed that capital equipment will be partly produced in Mexico itself, while part would come from the US and other countries, including Germany and Japan.[5] The US share might realistically be as much as US$10 million, but hardly more and probably less. This would be a one-time boost to US exports. Still, this one-time export bonanza of US$10 million for capital goods is the same order of magnitude as the annual loss of US factory payroll.

Of course, in the above scenario, the 400 Mexican workers now have US$2 million more money to spend each year. But some will be taxed by the Mexican government and the first priorities of the consumers are likely to be housing, food, clothing, medical care, and other necessities purchased from the Mexican economy. It would be very surprising if as much as a quarter of the new money was used for imports from the US, but let us assume it for purposes of argument. Altogether, the postulated annual loss of US$10 million in US payrolls is compensated by US$10 million in capital equipment exports (once only) and less than US$0.4 million annually in possible exports of US consumer goods to the Mexican workers.[6]

Up to this point I have implicitly equated US Dollars with the equivalent value in Mexican Pesos, the currency in which the Mexican workers are to be paid. The products of the factory, no longer made in the US, will be imported instead. One can make various assumptions about indirect and overhead costs, but the minimum annual cost of the imports from Mexico will be US$2 million (labor) plus US$4 million (capital) making US$6 million per year. This money now circulates through the Mexican economy.

As trade theorists point out, these dollars should eventually flow back to the US in the capital accounts if not in the trade accounts (see also Chapter 14). If money flows alone are considered, the factory's move to Mexico does not reduce the size of the US economy. It may actually increase it slightly. But the return flow of dollars does not necessarily go back via the trade sector to purchase either goods or services produced in the US by US workers. In fact, there is good reason to believe that much of it does not. It returns via the financial sector, where it finances asset purchases (including government bonds) and speculative investments. The bond purchases do support employment, to a degree, but the speculative investment in stocks and land does not.

INDIRECT WAGE IMPACTS OF TRADE

There are other indirect effects of trade on jobs that I haven't yet counted. One of them is the increased profits of the US owners (which is why they lobbied for NAFTA in the first place), and the consumer savings in lower prices for the goods produced by the factory, assuming they are all sold back to the US market. By assumption, however, these amount to only half of the payroll savings, or US$4 million (since the other half of the payroll savings went to finance the factory construction). Thus, taking everything into consideration, the loss of US$10 million to the US economy is counterbalanced by exports of US$10.4 million in the first year and less than US$0.4 million annually thereafter, plus domestic consumer savings and dividends to investors combined, amounting to US$4 million per year. So, after the first year, the annual loss to the manufacturing sector of the US economy is something like US$5.6 million, which corresponds to roughly 220 new US manufacturing jobs at the same wage level, or perhaps 200 jobs at higher-skilled wage levels (recalling the 7 per cent wage differential between exporters and importers).

Thus, by any reasonable calculation, when factories move from the US (or Europe), to a low-wage country, the losers in the high-wage economy far outnumber the winners. A 3:1 ratio would be my best guess for an average. In other words, for every 100 low-wage manufacturing jobs lost in the US perhaps 30 or 35 new manufacturing jobs are created in the US.

Of course, factories don't necessarily move in exactly the way I suggested above. More commonly, some existing businesses in low-wage countries gain markets at the expense of competitors in high-wage countries. (Recall the Samsung example cited above.) But the net effect on US workers is exactly the same as if a factory moved from one place to the other. The workers in the recipient countries don't necessarily gain very much either. The chief gainers are the owners. Sir James Goldsmith characterized the situation as the poor in the developed countries subsidizing the rich in the developing world. Fred Iklé calls it 'xenophilia'; that is, favoring people far away over one's family, friends, neighbors and fellow-citizens. Very altruistic, no doubt, but hardly the real motivation of the financiers and tycoons behind the free trade lobby.

Let me digress a bit further on trade. Countries like Japan and the four Asian Tigers with investable capital (resulting from many years of trade surpluses) can – and do – send it to countries with even cheaper labor, like China, Indonesia, Vietnam and Bangladesh. Ditto, technology. There is no longer any reason to manufacture anything in a country with high labor costs. There is nothing in the theory of trade to rule out the possibility that the hard-working people in East Asia, or just in China, could produce all the world's manufactured goods.

Ridiculous? Perhaps; but this is exactly what some Asian political leaders really expect. Let us take the idea seriously for just a moment. If all the world's manufacturing finally moves to Asia, Europeans and Americans would all presumably be employed selling services to each other – 'taking in each other's laundry', as the saying goes – and selling services, raw materials and assets to the Asians. Is there anything to prevent this scenario from coming true?

Of course there is. The problem is that the rest of the West (counting Japan as Asian) can't sell enough services or raw materials to Asia to pay for the imported manufactured goods. If the Asians don't buy Western products, what happens? In this scenario, Asians will have more Dollars or Deutschmarks than they need and the West will not have as many Yen or Yuan as it needs. The classic result is that the price of Dollars and Deutschmarks falls in terms of Yen per Yuan and conversely. In other words, in the long run the Dollar per Deutschmark exchange rate vis-à-vis the Yen per Yuan must fall.[7]

Countries with big trade deficits are automatically faced with a difficult problem. If the currency is allowed to fall, imports become more expensive. This is inflationary. The bigger the import flow, the greater the inflationary impact. To prop up a devalued currency (eg the Dollar) the Federal Reserve or Bundesbank can raise domestic interest rates. This attracts Asian buyers of government bonds, and (temporarily) preserves the buying power of the currency, thus holding inflation at bay. But it raises the cost of money (ie credit) to domestic consumers and similarly penalizes small businesses. Thus, inflation is counteracted by deflation: a downward economic spiral ensues.

The only other alternatives to monetary devaluation are to restrict imports, or to raise the price of exports. The former is theoretically prevented by free trade rules. The latter is difficult, since higher export prices would presumably reduce demand for the products in question, thus countering the desired effect. Besides, Western governments do not control export prices. The exception to this rule is agricultural products, which are still, to some extent, regulated (certainly in Europe). However it is not feasible to finance manufacturing imports from Asia only by means of agricultural exports.[8] At least, not with the price of food as low as it is now.

So, what happens next is more or less fore-ordained. The Federal Reserve, the Bank of England and/or the Bundesbank try to hold the fort against devaluation by raising interest rates and other gimmicks such as the use of foreign exchange reserves to buy the Dollar/Deutschmark in the open market, in the hope that currency traders will follow the leader and allow the central banks to bail out again. (Assuming the fundamentals point toward devaluation, this tactic fails more often than not. Currency traders have become sophisticated enough to anticipate it.) Higher interest rates do support the currency, but only by choking off the economy. Sooner or later that policy becomes too painful to continue. In the end the devaluation occurs; often the adjustment is quite large, having been delayed for too long.

The impact of devaluation/revaluation is superficially similar to that of a wage equalization between the countries. However, for the exporting country, the effect is that imports are cheaper but exports are more expensive, thus reducing demand for those exports. Workers in the country with the trade surplus are better off to the extent that they can buy more imported goods for their money. Conversely, workers in the country with the trade deficit are worse off for the same reason.

However, the currency adjustment process between two developed countries is not comparable to the case where a very low-wage country is involved. An upward revaluation of the Chinese Yuan against the Dollar is not equivalent to a raise in wages for Chinese workers. The reason is that the average Chinese worker, whose wage is only 4 per cent of their Western counterpart, is still not able to buy Western luxury imports (except possibly cigarettes). The factory owner is in a higher-income bracket and is more likely to buy an imported BMW or Mercedes; but there are very few factory owners in that income bracket. The ordinary worker spends his/her money on food, clothing and housing. None of these – except some marginal food imports and cigarettes, as mentioned – compete with foreign goods, hence none will fall in price as foreign currencies fall in value. On top of that, if higher export prices mean reduced unit demand, the Chinese worker could actually be out of a job. In summary, the bigger the trade deficit the faster the devaluation. The winners from devaluation (apart from financial speculators) are consumers in the importing country and factory owners in the exporting country.

According to standard trade theory (see Chapter 14), Europe, the US and Japan – the high wage economies – will continue to make and export goods where they have an inherent comparative advantage. These areas are, supposedly, high-tech products like microprocessors, advanced weaponry, chemicals and pharmaceuticals. But there are snags. In the first place, the high-wage countries may have more engineers per capita, but they have no inherent advantage in high-tech. Already the Asian Tigers produce computers and cars and have announced their intention of producing civilian airliners. This happened within a few days of Daimler-Benz's abandonment of financial support for the troubled Dutch aircraft manufacturer, Fokker. Fokker declared bankruptcy a few weeks later, only to be rescued by a Korean conglomerate seeking a foothold in Europe. Another Korean conglomerate was trying to buy the French civil electronics firm, Thomson. The French government has thrown up barriers, largely out of a well-founded suspicion that the Koreans will move production and technology out of France. Indeed, in many of these high-tech areas the Japanese have deeply penetrated Western markets while successfully protecting their own markets. R&D can be, and is being, done in Asia, and the Asians have no intention of being perpetually dependent on Europe and America for advanced technology.

There is another glitch in the standard theory. It is impossible to imagine an economy that produces only at the top of the value-added chain. In other words, it is inconceivable to make high-value products like supercomputers for export entirely from imported materials and components. Do the free trade theorists really think that China will agree to sell Boeing and IBM the components – computer chips, turbine blades and gear wheels – at low prices and buy back the finished products at high prices?

Such a situation can exist only for a few years, if ever. It will last only as long as big 'systems integrators' who live at the top of the value-added chain (eg Boeing, Daimler-Benz, GE, IBM, Siemens, etc) keep their headquarters and engineering in the West, buy cheap components from Korea or China or Vietnam, and retain a monopoly on the design technology. But such a monopoly is unsustainable. Both common sense and recent experience with Japan suggest that if the Asians can make the component parts more efficiently than we can – which is increasingly the case – they can certainly put the pieces together. (In fact, much of the final assembly for personal computers is being done in Taiwan or South East Asia right now.) If the US and Europe can't also make most, if not all, of the critical components for these sophisticated goods, at competitive prices, we are not going to be able to manufacture the goods themselves, let alone be able to export them.[9]

The conventional view is that the Asian labor cost advantage will disappear because Asian wages will soon rise in Asia to Western levels. If this cheerful view were valid the outcome would be the creation of a large Asian market for Western goods. History does not always repeat itself. In this case, it won't. In the nineteenth century, displaced agricultural workers in Europe and the US moved to the cities and took factory jobs. The social stresses caused by this migration were enormous – Marxism was one of the consequences – but widespread unemployment was rarely significant until the aftermath of World War I and the Great Depression. The explanation is that manufacturing in the nineteenth century was extremely labor-intensive. Today it is not. As late as the 1950s over 40 per cent of US workers were employed in manufacturing. The figures for Japan and Germany reached comparable levels even a decade later. The percentage of workers in manufacturing reached 60 per cent in some of the centrally-planned economies where services were deliberately neglected. But today, the manufacturing sector employs less than 20 per cent of the labor force in the US and the productivity trends in this sector suggest that in three or four decades as little as 5 per cent might suffice. This is plausible because it is already true for some high-tech firms.

In short, manufacturing no longer requires large numbers of workers. Since a small fraction of the labor force can produce all the goods consumed, even by a rich country, there is no conceivable need for a billion or so Asian factory workers, even if one assumes a large increase in demand within Asia itself. No labor scarcity means no rise in wages. This bedrock fact, in turn, means that manufacturing wages in China and India cannot rise very much. Instead, labor will be increasingly surplus in the West, and wages in the West will have to fall. This process has already started, at least in the US. (See also Chapter 9 for more details.)

Will the Chinese buy McDonald's hamburgers, Gillette razor blades, Unilever detergents and Coca Cola? Surely they will. But virtually all of these products will be made locally in Asia, not exported from America or Europe. Worse, many products like CDs are already being made in counterfeit versions, by pirate factories that don't even pay royalties. If China can be persuaded to enforce the copyright laws it has agreed to, the parent multinational corporations (MNCs) will receive some profits or royalties, which will make the stockholders happy.[10] But no new jobs will be created back in Birmingham, Chicago, Milan, or Stuttgart by the 'China Trade'. On the contrary, more and more jobs will be lost.

What, if anything, can European and US factories hope to export to Asia to pay for the products Asia wants to export that Western MNCs and consumers want to buy? The list of plausible long-term export possibilities is shockingly short. Apart from armaments and high-tech capital equipment, the list consists mainly of tourism and agricultural or food products.

There is another reason why exchange rate adjustments cannot be relied on to take care of the problem. Experience with Japan is revealing. In 1985 the US Dollar was worth 236 Japanese Yen. As of mid-June 1995 the exchange rate was 83 Yen to the Dollar. By spring 1997 it had rebounded all the way back to 126. But this is a reflection of the continuing troubles in the Japanese banking system – a consequence of the collapse of the bubble economy of 1987–1989 – rather than the long-term strength of the Dollar. When the Japanese banking system sorts itself out, the next major move of the Dollar against the Yen is likely to be down once again.[11] Yet, despite the over-valued Yen, the Japanese trade surplus for 1990–1994 (US$396 billion) equaled the entire Japanese surplus for 1980–1989 inclusive. It continued high in 1995, dropped a bit in 1996, but began rising again in spring 1997.

HOW TO PRESERVE A TRADE SURPLUS WITHOUT REALLY COMPETING

Why didn't the rising Yen (before 1995) depress Japanese exports? It did, to some degree, but not nearly enough to eliminate the persistent Japanese surplus. The reason is 'linkage'. The Japanese have become effectively world monopolists in a number of crucial industrial sectors, thanks to predatory past trade practices – mostly utilizing administrative rather than tariff barriers – which allowed them to prevent foreign competition in their home markets and even in world markets. Now that they have wiped out the competition, it doesn't matter whether a rising Yen raises prices to foreign consumers. There are no (or very few) alternative suppliers for many consumer and industrial products. For instance, though color TV was a US innovation (RCA), there is no longer any TV producer in the US. Similarly, tape recorders were a

US innovation; there is no US producer today. There are no longer any significant US producers of bicycles, sewing machines, watches or cameras either.

In the 1970s Japanese conglomerates invested heavily in mass production facilities for dynamic random access memory chips (DRAMs) and cut export prices while maintaining domestic prices at a high level. Investigations by the International Trade Commission, as a result of complaints, concluded that the Japanese were exporting memory chips to the US at prices well below the cost of production. By 1986 most US producers, unable to sustain the losses, had dropped out of the market, and the US world market share dropped below 20 per cent. At this point, the US government intervened and the US–Japan semiconductor agreement was signed. This agreement effectively created a cartel. It ended the predatory pricing policy of the Japanese, and (eventually) stabilized market shares. But the agreement left the Japanese and Koreans in control of the DRAM market. At this point the Ministry of International Trade and Industry (MITI) issued production and export guidelines and, in the second quarter of 1989, prices of 256-kilobit DRAMs rose by over 50 per cent. (See, for example, Tyson, 1992.)

Such practices are normal in Japan. They permit the Japanese exporters, operating as government-sanctioned cartels, to make high monopoly profits in their home markets which they use to subsidize exports, especially to the US. In a number of instances, this has finally enabled them to drive US competitors out of business altogether. Japan is now the world's monopoly – or near monopoly – producer of a long list of important products and equipment, including;

- computer-controlled production equipment for automobile manufacturing;
- microchip manufacturing equipment;
- high performance wire for engine valves;
- carbon fiber for the aviation industry;
- liquid crystal displays for laptop computers;
- lasers for laser printers and CD-ROM recorders and players;
- engines for ships;
- shipbuilding (with South Korea);
- DRAM computer memory chips (with South Korea);
- fax machines;
- VCRs and TVs (except for Philips);
- cameras;
- hi-fi equipment;
- watches; and
- sewing machines (with Taiwan and South Korea).

It is true that one could also make shorter but similar lists of effective monopolies for the US and Western Europe. For example, US or European firms dominate world markets for communications satellites, large civil airliners, and many industrial chemicals and pharmaceuticals. However, whereas the Europeans have been working hard to defend their most threatened industries, the Japanese invasion of US markets was positively welcomed by successive US administrations as a boon to consumers. Only recently has it been noticed that the declining Dollar makes Japanese imports more expensive, and that once the Japanese have taken control of an industry, they raise export prices. But this comes far too late to help domestic producers in areas such as consumer electronics, where there are no significant domestic producers remaining in the US.

Yet it follows, from being perceived as the sole remaining superpower, that the US, having sponsored the seemingly endless GATT negotiations since the 1950s, must now be the godfather of the WTO. As seen by virtually everyone not living in the US, this means that the US has a unique responsibility to obey the rules it proposed and agreed to, regardless of what any other country does. When the Brazilians, French, Spanish, Japanese and Chinese behave in their own best interests (ie against the rules) the world looks the other way. But if the US tries to use its own laws to enforce minimal reciprocity on the part of its trading partners, the world castigates the US as a bully. In short, the US is expected not to use its alleged power to defend its own economic interests. It is the price of superpowerdom.

In trade, the US is expected to accept unlimited Asian imports without complaint and to accept Asian restrictions on US exports also without complaint. If it must complain, for example about piracy, it must do so by taking its case to its supposed creature, the WTO. The most that could possibly be expected from a US complaint, no matter how well-documented, would be a gentle reprimand to the sinner with no effective enforcement. More likely, the US complaint would be nullified by a counter-complaint and a noisy propaganda barrage. The Japanese have perfected this tactic. The offender would claim, as usual, that their markets are not really closed at all, that the victims are just lazy or incompetent, and that, in any case, the government is not responsible for decisions in the private sector.

Meanwhile, the US is also expected by the rest of the world to protect the value of its currency (in which most of the world's reserves are denominated) not by protecting its industry but by intervening in capital markets and raising short-term domestic interest rates. The effect of this policy – especially advocated by the Germans – would, of course, raise capital costs for US industry and credit costs for US consumers. This, in turn, would raise prices and depress domestic demand, thus slashing profits and increasing the need for even more domestic downsizing and restructuring. Unemployment would rise sharply, and wages would fall. The impact of a monetary policy of raising interest rates to protect a strong Dollar would be to create a recession – just the opposite of what happened when the Federal Reserve Board began cutting US interest rates (to fight recession) in 1991-1992.

When the US (inevitably, in my view) fails to live up to the unrealistic expectations of the rest of the world with respect to both security and trade, it will almost certainly slip more and more into economic nationalism and isolationism. The first lurch in this direction began after the 1994 Congressional elections, which brought Republicans into power in both Houses of Congress for the first time since the Truman adminis-tration. The irony of the situation is that the best inoculation against the isolationist virus would be an open and honest admission that free trade at the world level (ie the objective of WTO) is premature by many decades. This should have been obvious long ago. It has taken four decades to approach a true common market in Europe, and the end of the road – a common currency – is by no means a sure thing, despite having been promised for 1999. 'Euroskeptics' are growing in number and influence almost everywhere in Europe, including Germany. (Germans are beginning to fear that their beloved strong Deutschmark would be weakened and diluted.) Yet the common market for Europe is a far more feasible undertaking than a global version could ever be.

Unfortunately trade liberalization also means moving manufacturing jobs from high-wage countries to low-wage countries. It is jobs export insofar as Europe and the US are concerned. I doubt that the West, especially Europe, can afford much more of it. As soon as Asian universities start producing enough scientists, engineers, designers, and MBAs, the basic reason for retaining any functions (except marketing and distribution) in the West will have vanished. But before the implications of this trend have penetrated to the decision-making levels of our society, it may be too late to do anything to stop the rot. If this makes me a doomster and a neo-Luddite as well as a protectionist, so be it.

Economists defending free trade and free markets point at the number of new jobs created by the service sector in the US. With a work force of 150 million, the 4.9 per cent (official) unemployment rate as of spring 1997 still means that 7.4 million people who are looking for jobs don't have jobs. But the official rate is somewhat deceptive, as all economists know very well. There are many millions who were downsized in their 50s and who have given up the search, millions more who are under-employed, and many more millions in 'McJobs' like fast-food hamburger cooks with no health benefits, no insurance, no prospects and no security. Lawrence Mishel, research director of the Economic Policy Institute, is a pessimist on this issue. He points out that jobs paying wages too low to support a family above the poverty level had actually increased from 24 per cent of the workforce in 1979 to 30 per cent in the mid-1990s. Of course, the continuing high level of under-employment is the reason why low official unemployment has not yet generated any inflationary pressures on wages.

IS JOB TRAINING THE PANACEA?

Many mainstream economists believe that in a competitive free market equilibrium there would be no unemployment, since labor markets – like other markets – would automatically clear. This means that everyone wanting a job would find one – at some wage. (There is nothing in the theory to guarantee that the market-clearing wage is one that would support a family, or even an individual, above the poverty level.)

The problem, in the mainstream view, is inadequate flexibility of labor markets, both on the part of individual workers and labor unions. Some experts blame labor inflexibility on inadequate skills, which can only be overcome by improving education and training. It is important to distinguish advanced education in engineering and science as an essential input to technological change vis-à-vis primary and secondary education as a prerequisite to upgrading job skills by training. It is the latter I am talking about here. Robert Reich, President Clinton's first-term Secretary of Labor, has particularly emphasized education and training as the key to job creation, as have the new Labour Government in the UK. Is this really plausible?

While the more highly-skilled workers have enjoyed some wage gains, real wages of low-skill workers in the US have actually declined in the past two decades (see Chapter 9). If all of these low-skilled workers were as skilled as their more skilled brethren, would their wages rise to match? Or would the result be still fewer jobs? What would it cost? James Heckman, a University of Chicago economist, has estimated the cost at US$400 billion just to upgrade low-skilled workers enough to raise their real wages to equivalent 1970s levels.

But there is another important question that needs to be addressed. After all, training programs, albeit somewhat haphazard, have been in existence for a long time. How effective have they been? Here the balance of the evidence seems to be quite negative; training programs (at least the ones operated by governments) have a very poor record of success. Almost invariably, when the results of a funded program such as Job Training Partnership or Job Corps (in the US) or Youth Training (in the UK) are assessed retroactively, it is found that the participants do no better than equivalent non-participants, either in terms of increased wages or increased employability. A number of studies in the US, the UK, Australia, Germany and Sweden, and by the OECD, have arrived at virtually identical conclusions; the programs for low-skilled unemployed adults, unrelated to specific firms and industries, are almost totally ineffective for men, and only very slightly beneficial for women.

The partial exception to this rule is Germany's famous 'dual education system' in which 16-year-olds sign an apprentice contract with a local industry and work part time for several years at reduced wages, while going to vocational school for formal job-related training. At one time, more than half of all 16-year-olds joined this program. The system has undoubtedly raised the skill levels of German workers significantly above other countries. For a long time, while Germany enjoyed full employment and even imported 'guest-workers' from Turkey and elsewhere, this system was regarded as a great success.

Today, however, the evidence is growing that the main benefit of the dual system now is that it provides industry with cheap labor – for a few years. Many former apprentices find themselves redundant when they reach the age when adult wages are supposed to be paid. For instance, 90,000 well-trained German construction workers were idle in the summer of 1996, while 180,000 less well-trained workers from other countries had construction jobs, at lower wages, in Germany. Almost half of the 4 million unemployed in Germany are graduates of the apprenticeship system. But, it seems they are over-priced for the job market.

What the available evidence seems to show quite clearly is that basic education for literacy and numeracy does help make people employable, and that these things can be taught in state schools, preferably early. It appears that more specific job-related skills can best be taught by employers or by schools working very closely with employers. It also appears that employers (at least large ones) find it worthwhile to provide such training, provided employees are willing to share the cost. But there is no evidence at all that upgrading the unskilled – many of whom are also illiterate – through adult job-training programs will raise wages, stimulate economic growth or reduce unemployment, at least in the West.

SUMMARY AND IMPLICATIONS

The main conclusions of this chapter can be summarized very concisely. First, free trade (the WTO version) is not necessarily beneficial for everybody. It is certainly beneficial for consumers, as long as they are still employed. But I think the evidence is overwhelming that jobs in high-wage countries are being lost in significant numbers. The major gainers are the multinational firms that can move their manufacturing operations to low-wage countries, thus cutting costs and increasing profits. Both statistical and anecdotal evidence supports the conclusion that manufacturing wages in the US have already been suppressed, especially for the less skilled. In Europe, the impact has been less on wages than on employment. This has initiated a long-term trend to increase returns to capital (profits), at the expense of returns to labor (wages).

Trade deficits generate return flows of funds but they need not be expenditures for goods and services. In the case of the US, return flows are more likely to finance government deficits (thus becoming a claim on future tax revenues) or asset sales. The enormous appreciation of the US stock market in the last few years is surely a reflection of the increased profitability of industry. It has probably been accelerated by foreign investment (financed from the trade deficit) seeking higher returns in the financial markets than can be extracted from conventional investments in bricks and mortar.

One popular policy response to the wage lag in the US and the unemployment problem in Europe is more job training. However, available evidence suggests that training that starts after adolescence will accomplish very little. A better system of basic education may be much more effective, but it will also require sustained long-term investment by government. This is very unlikely to happen in the present period of budget deficits and budget-cutting.

In conclusion, the US trade deficit is hardly 'benign' in jobs terms, as two eminent trade theorists have pronounced (Krugman and Lawrence, 1994). In fact, it is driving down wages in the US and employment in Europe. It is also one of the engines driving a stock market bubble that is already historically unprecedented and is virtually sure to collapse eventually, as bubbles are wont to do. The collapse will hurt small investors first, but if it is followed by a depression it will hurt everyone, in developed and developing countries alike. As usual, the least skilled and least secure will be hurt the most. It seems to me that there is a disturbing parallel with the events leading up to the 1929 stock market crash and the subsequent Great Depression. I hope I am wrong about this.

NOTES

1   Krugman and Lawrence (1994) are more circumspect. They merely argue that very few jobs are lost!
2   It seems that this estimate was taken from a 1993 paper by Gary Hufbauer and Jeffrey Schott of the Institute for International Economics in Washington DC. Hufbauer has been quoted as saying, 'In retrospect, it was a big mistake ... The purpose of the calculation was to show the number is pretty small, and that point was missed by everyone' (cited by Paul Blustein, *Washington Post*). In fact, the Hufbauer-Schott paper did say that NAFTA's employment impact 'will be lost as noise in the background of macroeconomic events'.
3   The 19,000 jobs per billion dollars rule-of-thumb is a bit outdated. Due to productivity increases, the current number for the US is somewhat smaller. But the argument is unaffected.
4   A 10 per cent interest rate would correspond to a capital outlay of only US$30 million.
5   Germany and Japan together dominate world export markets for machine tools and heavy electrical equipment, for instance.
6   In fact, my calculation is conservative. For instance, if the wage differential were greater than I have assumed, as in the case of jobs moving to China or Vietnam, the increased buying power would generate significantly less compensating export income in the US than I have assumed.

7 Of course, the Dollar can rise or fall against the Deutschmark, but that is another issue entirely.

8 Manufacturing now accounts for around 30 per cent of GDP in the OECD countries, whereas agriculture accounts for only 5 per cent or so. To produce and sell enough agricultural products abroad to finance imports of all the manufactured goods would necessitate a price increase of the order of 600 per cent.

9 There are no more Western comparative advantages in manufacturing. What the Chinese can't make themselves, they can buy from Japan or Korea. Both countries can make virtually anything the US or Europe can make, better and cheaper. This is because the Japanese have consistently violated the basic principles of free trade in the GATT sense: they have preferred to learn how to make things domestically, even at a loss, rather than import them from Western countries. In the end, learning-by-doing makes them competitive.

10 Within weeks of the highly touted settlement with China, wherein China agreed to enforce its own laws with respect to piracy and protection of intellectual property, the biggest pirate factory – which had briefly ceased operations – was openly back in business. The US government, having won its pyrrhic victory in the war of words, is now once again looking the other way.

11 This rebound apparently began in May 1997. The Dollar dropped 10 per cent during the month.

Chapter 7

The Growth Illusion

INTRODUCTION

During his 1996 presidential election campaign, Bob Dole put forward an economic plan beginning with the words: 'Growth must be the central goal of US economic policy'. This probably reflected a dawning recognition that growth is the only plausible escape from the debt/entitlements trap discussed earlier (Chapter 3). Plausible, that is, to convinced 'supply siders', of whom a few remain in influential circles.

But I want to address a different question: is economic growth, meaning GNP (more precisely GDP) growth, really beneficial to the average American, European or Japanese citizen today? Economic growth is obviously beneficial to all when everybody is poor (in terms of goods) and when exploitable resources that can be converted into goods are readily available. However, does it make sense to assume that quantitative increase is equally socially beneficial regardless of the wealth already accumulated by society? At the individual level we normally assume that increasing wealth or income has declining marginal utility. Should this not apply also to societies?

Unlimited growth is certainly not good for higher animals or plants. Growth is an important biological process, but it normally slows down, and finally ceases at maturity. A fetus grows into an infant, then into a child and finally into an adult. Each species has a natural range of sizes. Uncontrolled growth at the cellular level is cancer. Cancer destroys the organism.

Of course, the economic system is not a biological organism, and analogies such as the above must not be stretched too far. But the analogy is still valuable for one lesson it teaches; that growth is *not* necessarily an inevitable or permanent natural process. True, some dreamers like to imagine that human society can eventually escape the confines of Earth, leap into space and expand throughout the galaxy. This notion makes for interesting (if usually implausible) science fiction. I am sympathetic to the idea of expanding gradually beyond the earth. There are exploitable resources out there, if only of high-quality energy from the sun. But for the foreseeable future, human society will develop mainly on one small planet, and it must adapt to planetary limits.

THE GROWTH DEBATE REVISITED

Economic growth per se has been criticized by a number of voices in the past for a variety of reasons. The first economist to tackle the issue directly was E J Mishan of the London School of Economics in *The Cost of Economic Growth* (1967, revised edition 1993). Another particularly challenging critique of the growth paradigm was E F Schumacher's book *Small is Beautiful* (1973). Schumacher was, in effect, a follower of Gandhian economics.[1] As the title suggests, he found many negative aspects to large-scale enterprise and, conversely, many virtues in small-scale individual enterprise.

The most common basis for criticism of the growth paradigm, however, has been the Malthusian argument: that the earth's resource base is finite and *ipso facto* inadequate to sustain unlimited growth.[2] *The Limits to Growth*, a report by the Club of Rome (Meadows et al, 1972), was probably the best-known of these criticisms. A few others had contributed to the resource/environment debate as early as the 1960s, notably Kenneth Boulding, a very great (if controversial) economist himself, who has said:

> *Anyone who thinks that exponential growth can go on forever in a finite world is either a madman or an economist.*[3]
> Source: cited by Richard Douthwaite, 1993, p1.

However, other economists of note also recognized potential limits to growth. Apart from Boulding and Mishan, they include Nicolas Georgescu-Roegen, who wrote *The Entropy Law and The Economic Process* (1971), Herman Daly, author of *Toward a Steady-State Economy* and (with John Cobb) *For the Common Good* (Daly, 1973; Daly and Cobb, 1989), and Richard Douthwaite, whose book *The Growth Illusion* (1993) particularly impressed me when I started to write this chapter.

This debate has recurred at intervals since Malthus' time, with increasing heat but little progress toward consensus. On one side are the neo-Malthusians, of whom the most pessimistic and best-known (apart from the Club of Rome) are probably Paul and Anne Ehrlich of Stanford University, Lester Brown of the Worldwatch Institute in Washington DC, and Herman Daly, now at the University of Maryland. This group tends to be rather pessimistic about the carrying capacity of the earth.

On the other side are the 'cornucopians' or 'Panglossians': Herman Kahn and his colleagues in *The Next 200 Years* and Kahn and Julian Simon in *The Resourceful Earth* (Kahn et al, 1976; Kahn, 1984). Simon also wrote *The Ultimate Resource* in defense of population growth, and co-edited *The State of Humanity* (Simon, 1980; Simon et al, 1995). These were and are the most extreme exemplars. Wilfred Beckerman, author of *In Defense of Growth* and *Small is Stupid* (1974; 1995) is not far behind. In fact, many mainstream economists and businessmen, as well as political leaders of developing countries, are also more or less in this camp. They believe, first, that the limits to growth are very distant or non-existent. They also believe that free markets and free technology can (and would) solve all remaining problems, if only big government and 'doomsters' would get out of the way.

GROWTH ADDICTION

I am skeptical about economic growth, as conventionally envisaged, but *not* for neo-Malthusian reasons of physical resource scarcity. I think there are potentially practical ways of obtaining energy from the sun and (if need be) scarce metals from space. There is another, much deeper, problem associated with economic growth, however.

It is a structural problem that underlies the more obvious challenges of physical resource exhaustion and toxic pollution. Stated briefly, the problem is that one of the main mechanisms that drives economic growth in manufacturing is growth itself. I don't mean that growth is self-driven in any metaphorical sense.

The growth mechanism I refer to – sometimes called the Salter cycle – was sketched briefly in Chapter 2 as a 'virtuous circle'. It is described more fully in Chapter 13. What happens, in effect, is that increased demand for goods and services drives production to larger scale. Economies of experience and scale in manufacturing then result in lower costs. In a competitive market, lower costs will be translated into lower prices to consumers. Lower prices, in turn, generate increased demand for those goods and services because people can afford to buy more. The cycle is driven by price elasticity of demand and economies of experience and scale in manufacturing.

The other drivers of growth are population, savings and investment, exogenous energy flux, and technological progress. I certainly have no quarrel with technological progress, even though it gives us the means to produce weapons of mass destruction. However, the fact that economic growth depends so much on growth itself is very worrying indeed.

The fact that economic growth is a self-sustaining feedback process influences the behavior of individuals, corporations and governments. All have come to assume it and to depend upon it. Most macro-economic models assume that growth can, and will, continue indefinitely. The standard practice of discounting the future, which is built into virtually all financial models and calculations, is really a statement of faith; that our children will be wealthier than we are. Pleas for resource conservation are met with comments like the following (from Julian Simon): 'asking us to refrain from using resources so that future generations can have them is like asking the poor to make gifts to the rich' (Simon, 1980, p15).

In effect, growth is as addictive to Western society as cocaine and nicotine are to individuals. When firms can make profits from growth they are seldom content to finance expansion from current and past profits. Instead, they sell shares or borrow money to finance expansion. The practice of financing growth by increasing debt is encouraged by government policies of taxing profits and treating interest payments on debt as untaxable costs. The loans can only be repaid out of future profits, of course. To carry the debt-service load, future profits must be larger than present ones. Thus, by borrowing money at fixed rates of interest, a firm stakes its actual survival on its future growth.

The engine of growth must go on turning, however, even when markets are largely saturated. Consumption beyond the natural or comfortable level must be encouraged (by advertising) to keep the engine turning. If markets are not growing, then firms seek growth (at the expense of other firms) by trying to increase their market share. This situation, which characterizes the present period in Europe and the US, leads to more and more ruthless cost-cutting, mergers and takeovers ('rationalization'), raiding of pension funds, cutting back on employee welfare, reduction or elimination of R&D ('restructuring', 're-engineering'), and so on. The weaker firms fall by the wayside. The winners in this game of corporate survival are likely to be the ones that downsize most radically in terms of employment. However, as global markets saturate, the game is becoming zero-sum. That is, we are approaching the point where, for every winner, there must be a loser. When Toyota gains market share, Ford or GM must lose. If Sony wins, Philips must lose. The small producers are already gone.

Despite recent good news in the US, unemployment has been rising in industrialized countries since the early 1970s (Figure 7.1). The common reaction among European left-wing thinkers of past generations was usually to blame capitalism per se and to advocate social ownership of the means of production. Failing that, they advocated highly progressive taxation of income. Marginal tax rates in the UK and Sweden in the late 1950s exceeded 95 per cent. The election of Mitterand in France (1981) and Gonzalez in Spain (1982) was perhaps the last time nationalization of large-scale industry was deliberately used as a strategy to create and protect jobs. Yet unemployment in France rose more or less continuously throughout the 14 years of Mitterand's presidency to its present intractable level of more than 12 per cent. The record in Spain, where unemployment is now 20 per cent, has been even worse.

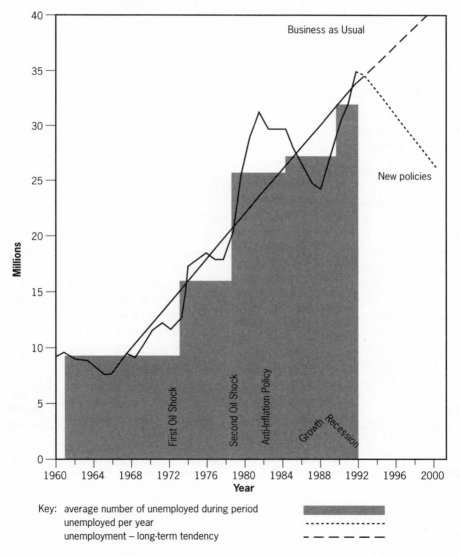

Figure 7.1 Unemployment in OECD Countries, 1960–1993

In the US the socialist solution to unemployment and poverty was never seriously considered. Instead, the US opted in the 1960s for a mixed strategy ('The Great Society') utilizing private enterprise but using tax revenues to tackle social problems through a host of ambitious programs managed by federal and state government agencies. A few of these programs were noteworthy successes (for example the pre-school program 'Head Start' is often cited) but most of them created more jobs for bureaucrats than for the unemployed. The top–down interventionist approach to solving social problems has been largely discredited in the US as a result.

Governments are just as addicted to economic growth as is the private sector. All western countries, without any exceptions, have made financial commitments to their present citizens – mainly social security and pensions – that can only be met out of future growth. As I pointed out in some detail, in Chapter 3, there is now an increasing gap between the need for future government revenues to meet these entitlements and the funds that can reasonably be expected to be available from tax revenues – even assuming the continuation of present rates of growth – to pay for them. In short, most Western governments are functionally, if not legally, bankrupt. Of course, this crisis makes growth even more necessary as the growth engine slows down.

For both firms and governments, growth of output, sales, profits and tax revenues is necessary for financial survival. To unhook the economy from its growth fixation will be a difficult undertaking indeed. But before facing these difficulties, it is important to distinguish growth in the above sense from growth in personal disposable income, or from growth in welfare. Some ideas need to be clarified.

GROWTH OR WELFARE?

The primary muddle is a confusion of economic growth (ie, more money and the things money can buy) with increasing welfare (ie greater utility or a better way of life). What is a better way of life is, of course, mainly a matter of personal values.[3] But the question is; do we as a society need to have, produce and trade more goods in order to live better? Here we come nearer to the nub of the problem. Macro-economic modelers tend to avoid the difficulty by equating welfare with consumption, or income, or GDP per capita. They do this for convenience in model-building, notwithstanding the fact that the economic profession has long recognized – whenever challenged on the point – that welfare is not actually the same thing as gross consumption, either at the individual or national level.

A point that would be raised by many social scientists is that welfare presumably equates more or less with perceived happiness. It is interesting to note that 'happiness' surveys carried out in many countries do not appear to show any significant correlation with wealth or income. On a subjective scale of well-being, most people in most countries score themselves between six and eight on a scale of ten. This has not changed significantly over time although personal incomes have increased markedly. According to these surveys the principal personal factors correlated with happiness are:

1) high self-esteem
2) a high degree of perceived control over the circumstances of life
3) optimism and
4) extroversion.[4]

The major differential social factor appears to be marriage. Married people are significantly happier, statistically speaking, than those who never married.

The fact that income and wealth can contribute to self-esteem, control over one's life and even optimism would seem to imply that happiness should be correlated with income, at least to some degree. Yet, according to many survey results, low-income groups are not significantly less happy than the average, and the very rich are not significantly more happy than the average. Indeed, there seems to be virtually no correlation between happiness and income within countries. However, there is a slight correlation between happiness and wealth when countries are compared. The Portuguese seem to be somewhat less happy than the Dutch, for instance. (But the low-income Irish professed themselves to be happier in the 1980s than the high-income Germans.)

However, the observed correlation between national wealth and perceived happiness is probably mostly due to the fact that wealthy countries are more likely than poor ones to practice democracy, protect civil rights, secure public health, and increase literacy. These attributes tend to increase people's control over their own lives. They also tend to promote optimism. Though I do not want to stress the point unduly, this chain of linkages implies that governments have much more to contribute to welfare than merely providing an arena in which laissez faire capitalism may thrive.

Twenty years ago, Herman Daly raised a very important question, which was then ignored or brushed aside by most economists as too bizarre to be taken seriously. As Mishan had done earlier, Daly pointed out that GDP growth has costs as well as benefits, and that marginal costs may well be rising, while marginal benefits (ie welfare) are probably declining.[5] (After all, economists assume that increasing marginal costs and decreasing marginal benefits are characteristic of *every* product or service. Why shouldn't this be true of GDP?) But Daly went further and suggested that – as far as the Western world is concerned – the optimum may already have been reached in the 1970s, if not exceeded.

I should add a personal comment here: I now think that economic growth still has some way to go before an optimum GDP level is reached. In other words, I do not advocate 'no growth' at this point in time. This is because I am somewhat more optimistic about the potential for technological progress than Daly. But I nevertheless think that Daly's insight is correct in principle, just as Malthus's was. It should be taken very seriously. I also want to emphasize here that the optimum level of GDP is almost certainly *not* determined by Malthusian resource constraints on the input side. It is determined, on the contrary, by the balance between the benefits of economic activity itself, as a function of the intensity of that activity, and the accompanying loss of unpriced – but nevertheless scarce – social and environmental services.

THE PROBLEM OF MEASUREMENT

In order to address this fundamental issue more quantitatively, one must first face the question of measurement. Economic growth in the West, as measured by GDP, is now largely a statistical illusion. What it measures is trading activity or money and goods in motion.[6] But GDP is the kind of measure that is most appropriate to a society consisting of many small, independent producers and consumers – farmers, artisans, tradesmen – interacting with each other only through buying and selling goods and services (including labor) in a truly free market. In biological terms, GDP is a measure appropriate to a society of diverse micro-organisms, like a pond.

However, GDP is increasingly limited as a measure of welfare in a complex inter-active society where many important relationships are not reflected in markets. For instance, GDP counts money income and/or expenditure, whether it merely reflects the monetization of, for example, farmer's work, or the growth of real output. But, it treats discretionary and non-discretionary (defensive) expenditures alike. It neglects most of the real costs associated with urban living, organized production and taking paid (rather than self-) employment. It also neglects the growth in non-monetary costs of social decline and environmental deterioration, not to mention the real monetary costs of environmental damage control and repair.

The confusion between GDP and welfare is compounded by a deep-seated confu-sion between discretionary and non-discretionary expenditure by households. The latter refers to items that are necessities of (urban) life and cannot be avoided. By general agreement, it includes taxes, rent or mortgage payments, utilities, interest charges, insurance and medical costs. There is also a minimum requirement for purchased food, clothing and transportation (at least commuting to and from work), including food, clothing and transportation for children to attend school. Discretionary items, on the other hand, include entertainment, travel, most furniture and furnishings, most clothing, restaurant meals, alcoholic beverages and many food items, especially prepared foods.

There is obviously a grey area between the two categories. For instance, mortgage and interest payments are non-discretionary once the initial home or other purchase decision was made, but the latter has a large discretionary element. (Many people commit themselves to buy houses that they cannot really afford, or they abuse credit cards or suffer reverses that reduce their ability to repay previous debts.) The cost of child care may be non-discretionary for a single working parent, but discretionary for higher-earning couples. An office worker needs more expensive clothing than a construction worker. A significant portion of health care costs go to the treatment of imaginary or psychosomatic ailments.[7] And so on.

But these ambiguities cannot disguise a basic point, namely that – while precise measurement is problematic – a significant fraction of all household expenditure is not really discretionary. An important, but hidden, assumption underlying the use of GDP as a welfare measure is that *an increment added to household income is mostly avail-able for increasing discretionary purchases.* If this were really true, it would be hard to argue that people with more money to spend are not better off than before. I think that, stripped of confusing side issues, this is the reason why most economists still believe that GDP is a valid welfare measure.

However, by exactly the same line of reasoning, if the non-discretionary fraction of household expenditure is growing faster than the discretionary fraction, one would have to reconsider. In such a case the marginal increase in income would have been pre-committed to non-discretionary items like social security taxes, health insurance or school fees. As it happens, there is quite a bit of evidence pointing in this direc-tion. To take one instance, it is a fact that US social security taxes have risen 32 per cent (adjusted for inflation) since 1980 alone, while the average wage has scarcely changed. Similarly, it would be very hard to argue that a car is a luxury in a US city today, given the fact that for most people there is virtually no alternative means of transport to and from work. The cost of owning and operating a car has increased sharply in recent decades. Parking charges and insurance rates, in particular, are up.

Similarly, in the US, medical costs paid ultimately by households, regardless of intermediary arrangements (ie Medicare, Medicaid, Blue Cross/Blue Shield, or private health insurance), are effectively non-discretionary. In the US the quasi-private insurance-based system covers only 80 per cent of the population, yet health care absorbs 14 per cent of GNP.[8] Moreover, this category of expenditure is the fastest growing of all (except possibly the cost of college/university education).

Taxes are a non-discretionary item. Taxes pay for a variety of public services, including public safety and social security. But the costs of these services appear to be rising rapidly without any improvement in the quality of the service delivered. For instance, the quality of postal service has deteriorated even as postage stamp prices rose many-fold. Fear of crime leads to enormous and largely ineffective expenditures on security guards (now more private than public, at least in the US), locks, prisons, and so on. California will soon spend more on prisons than on schools. (Yet it costs $50,000 per year to keep a man in prison; public schools only cost US$5000–$6000 per student per year.) Litigation in the US absorbs enormous resources, resulting in excessive insurance rates for every kind of potential liability, especially medical malpractice. The high cost of insurance, in turn, is one of the reasons medical and health care expenses in the US are at least 50 per cent higher than any other country.

In this context, it can be argued that US economic growth and prosperity in the future is most threatened by the unchecked expansion of parasitic activities, and their associated costs.[9] Excessive litigation is perhaps the most obvious example of such activities, but hardly the only one. Private security and insurance are other examples. Indeed, it is hard to see what real services the prosperous financial sector provides to the public, given the mediocre performance of investment advisory services, most of which perform no better (and often worse) than the market averages. In addition, one must credit the financial sector with a good deal of collateral damage resulting from programmed trading, derivatives, leveraged buyouts, junk bonds, insider trading by savings bank executives, hostile takeovers resulting in huge layoffs, spectacular bankruptcies[10] and other financial fun and games in recent years.[11]

The GNP/GDP measure especially overvalues expenditures to repair damage to the environment or to health caused by other human actions. For example, increased expenditures for health services resulting from automobile accidents, which in turn result from increasing dependence on cars, can hardly be counted as increased welfare. In much of the developing world, Eastern Europe, the former USSR, and notoriously in China today, there is strong evidence that GNP growth was achieved – or is being achieved – largely by cashing in natural capital assets like forests, fisheries and fertile topsoil. Worse, if possible, some of these countries are industrializing at the cost of the health and life expectancy of their citizens and workers. In the case of China alone, several independent studies have concluded that health and environmental damage each year amount to roughly 10 per cent of the GNP (see Chapter 9 and Chapter 15).

Here there are differences between most economists, on the one hand, and social critics on the other. The guru of modern welfare economics was A C Pigou of Cambridge University, who wrote *The Economics of Welfare* in 1920. It was reprinted many times, and has been the bible of welfare economics (eg Pigou, 1952). By and large, mainstream economists accept Pigou's arguments that income and/or expenditure is a reasonably good measure of welfare, and that what is omitted is relatively small, or (a subtler point) that what is omitted tends to be proportional to what is included. Social scientists tend to believe the contrary.

The arguments against the mainstream economists' view are, more or less, as follows. First, to measure only money income certainly undervalues the welfare produced by many kinds of unpaid work, both in the home (raising children, housekeeping, food preparation) and outside the home (growing or gathering food and other materials for direct consumption).

The errors of omission may not be too serious in terms of comparing one industrialized country with another, although even in this case the distortions are sometimes significant.[12] However, the omission of informal work and workers tends to make national accounts statistics virtually meaningless for rural parts of Asia, Latin America and especially Africa, for instance, where up to 80 per cent of all agricultural work is unpaid and is done by women.

Equally clearly, the monetary measure incorporates – and thus overvalues – unavoidable and defensive expenditures, from subsistence-level expenditures for food, clothing, housing, transportation and health care to insurance and taxes. To measure progress (or welfare) in monetary terms also neglects the welfare contributions of non-monetizable social and environmental services, from parents, neighbors and friends, from communities, and from the sun, the air, the climate, the scenery, and the biosphere. As people move to cities they lose those things. They also have to pay rent, whereas in rural areas they could often build their own houses on their own land from local materials – if only mud bricks and palm thatch.

Mainstream economists are not unaware of these criticisms. They have even attempted to address them. The most influential such attempt was made in the 1970s by William Nordhaus and Arthur Tobin of Yale University (Nordhaus and Tobin, 1972; Tobin and Nordhaus, 1972; see also Anderson, 1991). They constructed a new index, called the measure of economic welfare (MEW) by making some corrections to the GDP. Basically, they subtracted from the total everything that could not be considered current consumption, including depreciation, investment and 'regrettable necessities' – ie non-discretionary expenditures – such as the cost of travelling to work and even the higher cost of living in cities. They counted health and education costs as investments in human capital. They then added back benefits from the (imputed) national capital stock, including health and education. They made an explicit assumption that omitted items like environmental and health damages from pollution would roughly balance out against omitted income items like the fruits of unpaid labor.

The MEW was calculated for the 36-year period between 1929 and 1965. During that period, they found that the MEW grew slightly less fast than GDP (1.1 per cent per year as compared to 1.7 per cent per year) but that it did grow. From this result, Nordhaus and Tobin concluded that

> *The progress indicated by conventional national accounts is not just a myth that evaporates when a welfare-oriented measure is substituted.*
>
> Source: Tobin and Nordhaus, 1972, p13

In other words, Nordhaus and Tobin argued that the GDP measure is OK because it *correlates* closely enough with a more precise welfare measure. One immediate problem with this conclusion, however, is that their core assumption (that uncounted income from unpaid work and uncounted costs from environmental pollution roughly offset each other) cannot be extrapolated over time. The reason is that the former is declining – as more and more work is monetized – while the latter is probably increasing as urbanization, traffic congestion and industrial production keep growing.

Actually, however, the Nordhaus-Tobin study did not even show a very close correlation in terms of numbers. For instance, from 1935 to 1945 GDP rose 90 per cent but MEW rose only 13 per cent. From 1947 to 1965 GDP rose 48 per cent but MEW only rose 7.5 per cent. Even that small increase may be overstated, since it assumes that the productivity of unpaid housework increased as fast as the productivity of paid work. The most that they could claim (if they were to argue the point today) is that there is some correlation between GDP and MEW in terms of direction. But the correlation is no longer very close.

Moreover, Nordhaus and Tobin did not consider the depreciation of natural capital, such as forests, topsoil or groundwater, at all. (This is a fundamental problem with the UN's System of National Accounts, or SNA. The 'Green Accounts' exercise now under way at the UN's Statistical Office and in several countries is an effort to compensate for this omission in the standard accounting system. See Chapter 9 for more on this issue). The sun, fresh air, clean water, the climate and the services of the biosphere are also scarce but essential resources.

Natural capital cannot be measured in absolute terms. But it surely has economic value – which is likely to increase with scarcity.[13] In a lightly-populated rural society in a wilderness, where everyone possesses his or her own manual labor but land, pasture and building materials are free for the taking, the most valuable assets may well be the tradeable ones with monetary value (tools, guns, clothing, domestic animals, etc). In the wilderness, the natural environment is, at times, an inconvenience. It may be a threat. Under these circumstances the monetary measure of income (or GDP) may be an adequate surrogate for human welfare. But in a more complex urban society based largely on brain labor and specialized skills, where environmental services are palpably scarce and becoming scarcer, the ability to buy the things money can buy may be a much less satisfactory measure of welfare.

Conventional GNP or GDP measures are potentially very misleading for international comparisons, since they measure only monetizable components, and count all such transactions regardless of whether or not they are voluntary or unavoidable. If unavoidable expenditures were subtracted and if the undervalued components (such as unpaid work and unpaid environmental services) were added – which nobody yet knows how to do properly – the true welfare differences between countries would be far less than the GDP differences. Moreover, welfare growth in the Western world in recent years has been far less than GDP growth. Thus, comparative GDP figures grossly exaggerate the welfare gains that industrialized countries have made relative to developing countries.

Worse, from a policy perspective, the omission of many unquantifiable elements of environmental and social welfare opens up the possibility for governments to increase GDP – but not real welfare – by sacrificing those non-quantifiables. Detailed case studies at the national level by Robert Repetto (1985, 1989) and his colleagues at the World Resources Institute in Washington DC have already demonstrated that this is not just a theoretical possibility (see Chapter 9). By allowing the consumption of natural resource stocks (like forests and fisheries) to be treated as current income without making any compensating provision for the loss of corresponding natural capital assets, GDP measures have implicitly encouraged developing countries, like Indonesia and Malaysia, to achieve misleadingly high growth rates by selling long-term capital assets. The bankers and MNCs looking at GDP growth rates don't notice or don't care that this kind of growth is unsustainable and that the country may already be growing poorer rather than richer.

The 'Genuine Progress Indicator', or GPI, developed by Daly and Cobb, is a step in the right direction. It differs from Nordhaus and Tobin's MEW in several ways. First, it makes some allowance for the depreciation of natural resource stocks, which Nordhaus and Tobin neglected. It rejects the Nordhaus-Tobin thesis that health and education costs are really investments in human capital, which in turn provide a consumable service. (The problem with that assumption is that health care costs have been rising far more rapidly than health; the same is almost certainly true for educa-tion.) Nevertheless, the GPI (also called the Index of Sustainable Economic Welfare, or ISEW) is still seriously inadequate because of unavoidable remaining omissions.

Comparisons between GDP and the adjusted indices are shown for the US, UK and Germany in Figure 7.2.[14] The main point of these graphic displays, as far as I am concerned, is to demonstrate the growing importance of defensive expenditures, both for social and environmental purposes but mainly the former. Even if no allowance is made for non-monetizable environmental damages, the ISEW trend began to depart significantly from the GDP in the early- or mid-1970s. This happens for all three countries. During the 1980s GDP rose quite sharply in the US whereas ISEW remained virtually constant or declined. In the UK case there was an absolute decline in ISEW beginning in 1974. In the German case ISEW declined from 1978 to 1984, but has recovered somewhat since then.

I am somewhat skeptical of any simple scalar statistical measure of welfare, whether it be GDP or a substitute. My objection can be summed up in the phrase 'statistics don't lie, but liars use statistics'. (I'm not even sure about the first part of that proverb, only the second.) The point is that a sophisticated economist with a political agenda can fairly easily dream up a set of adjustments that will support that agenda. I tend to have more faith – other things being equal – in a measure constructed rather mechanically by middle-level civil servants with no particular axe to grind than I do in a measure constructed by a smart ideologue like … (take your pick).

In a rational world, the best solution would be for economists and statisticians to stop using GDP as a measure of welfare, a purpose for which it was not originally designed. To quote one shrewd commentator:

> *The apparent illogicality of the current misinterpretation of the GDP cannot justify criticism of the GDP itself. The GDP in fact deserves its high status; it is an ingenious creation, on which many good minds have worked over the course of half a century, as useful an indicator as it is accurate … To avoid all the contemporary criticism, and so that it may retain its high status, we have to recognize that the GDP in its very nature is best suited to measuring the* commercial *economy, estimating the net outcome of all the movements of currency units that change hands in the production of goods passing through the market. As such, it is an indispensable guide to tax and monetary policy in the public sector and to marketing in the private sector*[17]

Source: L Keyfitz, 1993, p373.

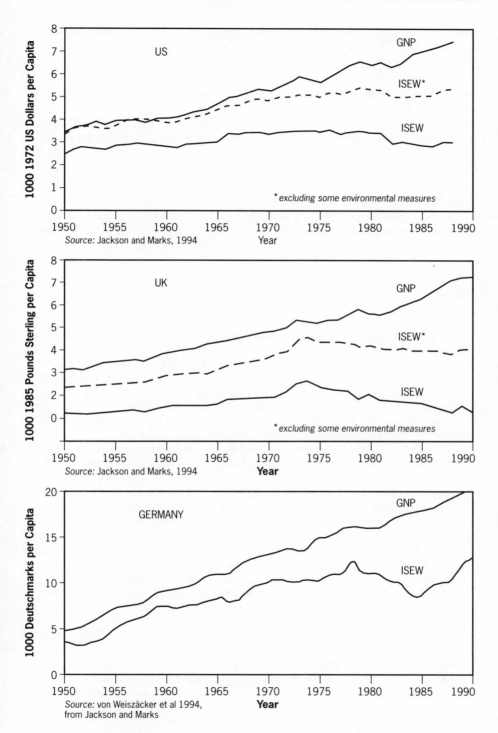

Figure 7.2 Indices of Sustainable Economic Welfare

This book is not the place for a serious critique of the pros and cons of alternative measures or any given alternative measure of welfare. Nevertheless, recognizing that any alternative to the GDP as a measure of welfare can and will be criticized by another expert, I am nevertheless bound to say that I think the alternatives like ISEW now being discussed – however imperfect – are better than the original MEW and certainly better than using GDP.

I note, however, that the ISEW, like the GDP, does not reflect equity (or inequity), which surely is an element of social welfare. It clearly undervalues environmental depreciation. Whatever else can be concluded from Figures 7.1 and 7.2, it should be clear that the conventional wisdom – that rising GDP per capita is equivalent to rising prosperity – must not be accepted uncritically. Quality of life in a crowded, urbanized, industrialized society – 'Spaceship Earth' to use Barbara Ward's (1966) metaphor – is *not* measured simply by the intensity of economic activity. While anecdotal evidence is inherently inadequate, what there is of it suggests rather clearly that *more* is no longer necessarily *better*. In many respects, it may be worse.

NOTES

1   Gandhian ideas have been fundamental to the New Economics Foundation; see eg Robertson, 1988. However they have been very harshly criticized by mainstreamers; see Beckerman, 1995.

2   The neo-Malthusians were so-named after the eighteenth century economist Thomas Malthus (Malthus 1798, (1946)), who warned that population was growing exponentially, whereas the amount of arable land for food production was limited. As it turned out, Malthus' pessimism was premature, insofar as he under-estimated the potential for increasing agricultural productivity. However, it takes a great leap of faith to extrapolate past increases in agricultural productivity into the indefinite future.

3   For instance, priests and theologians of monotheistic religions tend to measure it in terms of morality or in terms of the number of souls who accept the teachings of the founding prophet or of the religious system that deified a prophet.

4   See, for instance, Myers and Diener, 1996.

5   This idea was set forth in Daly, 1977 (revised 1991), especially Chapter 5. Daly was not alone. Others proposed similar ideas, such as Roefie Hueting (1980).

6   Within its domain, it is a perfectly good measure. It has been seriously suggested, in fact, that GDP should be confined and applied to the commercial sector alone (Keyfitz, 1993).

7   Over half of all visits to physicians in all countries for which statistics are available (including non-Western) are not for 'diseases' with a single pathogenic trigger, but for 'illness' consisting of any one of several malaises with multiple causes usually involving stress of one sort or another, from childbirth to wartime horrors. See Herbert Weiner (1992).

8   In Europe, by contrast, government-financed systems cover 100 per cent of the population and cost only 6 to 9 per cent of GNP. Opponents of health care reform like to claim that US medical care is the best in the world, but this claim is thoroughly specious. It is true that if you want a heart transplant you should go to Houston and if you want a liver transplant, you should probably go to Pittsburgh. For people in need of these costly services, living in the US is arguably a good thing. But the US ranks very low among industrialized countries on most indices of public health, from infant mortality to life expectancy. It is these more everyday measures that count for most people.

9   See, for example, Hamish McRae (1994).

10 President Clinton's indirect and murky connection with James MacDougal and the bankrupt Madison National Bank has received the most negative publicity. But one of President Bush's sons, currently in politics himself, presided over the bankruptcy of a much bigger bank that cost the taxpayers over US$60 million.

11 Anyone who thinks I am exaggerating should read *Liar's Poker* by Michael Lewis (1989).

12 The fact that child care is a government-paid occupation in Sweden, but unpaid in most other countries of Europe, tends to exaggerate the apparent profligacy of government in that country vis-à-vis others.

13 Robert Repetto and colleagues at the World Resources Institute in Washington DC have pioneered the monetization of natural capital, with detailed case studies of Indonesia, Costa Rica and the Philippines (eg Repetto, 1985; Solórzano et al, 1991; Cruz and Repetto, 1992). Typically, between 4 and 10 per cent of GDP in each of these cases was attributable to depreciation of natural capital, based on very conservative economic measures. The Chinese case has been analyzed in detail by Vaclav Smil of the University of Manitoba. Health costs have been explicitly included in Smil's work, although at a minimal level. See Smil, 1992; 1993; 1996.

14 The methodology used to construct the three cases shown is discussed in detail in Daly and Cobb, 1989, which was also the source of the original US ISEW. A revised version, including responses to critiques, is discussed in Cobb and Cobb, 1994. The British case can be found in Jackson and Marks, 1994. The German case is taken from von Weizsäcker et al, 1994, where it is attributed to Jackson and Marks.

Chapter 8

Equity, Poverty and the Coming Social Crisis

EQUITY VERSUS EFFICIENCY

I have been guilty, in the past, of arguing that equity should not be named as a criterion for long-term sustainability, since very inequitable governments – the Roman empire, for instance – have managed to last for a long time. It is also commonplace for economists to exclude the problem of social equity by saying 'economics is concerned only with efficiency', leaving everything else in the domain of politics and government. Yet even some economists don't agree that the two objectives are completely independent. Keynesians advocated stimulating consumer demand as a legitimate policy to overcome recessions, on the grounds that providing more income for poor and unemployed people creates jobs. Many conservatives take the contrary view that too much government – including government intervention through social programs to compensate for inequity – interferes with efficiency.

The efficiency-first argument is that 'a rising tide lifts all ships'. But inequity in our society is already extreme. Is it justifiable on efficiency grounds to further impoverish the poor in order to further enrich the prosperous, either within a country, between nations, or between generations? More to the point, what about the relationship between equity and economic growth? Is there a tradeoff? Must we sacrifice growth to improve equity? I used to think so, and many of my professional colleagues still do. The logic behind this position is that redistribution requires government intervention in the operation of the free market and, therefore, inevitably reduces efficiency. Less efficiency means lower growth. QED.

However, this is probably not pure economic logic so much as the disappointing experience of post-World War II egalitarian 'soak the rich' socialism as it functioned for three decades in the UK, Sweden, Australia and India that has had the most influence on recent Anglo Saxon economic thought. Economists in other European countries where taxes were less progressive (though not significantly lower) are much less inclined to see a conflict between equity and growth. I think they are right. The empirical evidence also favors this viewpoint. A study of 56 countries (Persson and Tabellini, 1994) found a strong negative relationship between income inequality and growth in GDP per capita. To put it plainly, countries with less inequality have better growth records than countries with greater inequality. Similar results have been found by other studies. How can this be explained?

There are two possibilities. One is that the supposed efficiency benefits of less government intervention on markets are illusory. For instance, it is possible, even likely, that the observed inequalities in outcomes are not due to the operations of free markets at all, but due to market *failures*. To put it another way, success in the employment and income marketplace is not necessarily determined by competitive merit. 'Equal opportunity for all' is an attractive ideal, but not a reality. It needs to be assured by government intervention. The reality is that in the US, and the other more unequal countries, favored groups have been able to use their positions to protect their wealth, as they have used their wealth to secure favored positions. This occurs through superior access to education, the legal machinery, and the machinery of government (ie political influence) as well as other means. It is no accident that 'less government' invariably means less restraint on the influence of the rich.

This influence takes many forms, of which the well-known abuses (eg campaign finance) are not necessarily the most important. Consider the role of lawyers in writing the laws. In the US, lawyers in legislatures have been in a position to write many laws that encourage litigation, especially in the product liability area. This was not necessarily a deliberate conspiracy. But the result has been to keep a large number of trial lawyers busy, and to raise the operating costs of many businesses. Trial lawyers were the biggest contributors to President Clinton's political campaign, and this was surely no accident.

The other possible explanation for the superior performance of more egalitarian societies is quite basic. It is the Keynesian idea, mentioned above, that redistributing income from the rich to the lower-income groups increases domestic consumption, although it does also tend to decrease savings and investment. Mainstream economic doctrine tends to oppose redistribution in principle. This is because of the neo-classical textbook emphasis on savings and investment as the primary policy lever for growth, which predates Keynes. Even the recognition that technological progress is more quantitatively important does not affect the policy implication, since governments can do little to accelerate technological change in the short term. It would follow that increased demand for goods and services from the lower-income segment of society would merely increase inflationary pressures.

There is some validity to this argument, at least in the short run, especially when the depressing effect of higher taxes on business and the administrative costs (ie the salaries of bureaucrats) are added. I can only say in response that, nevertheless, there must be a point where more inflation is less harmful than greater inequity. I think we have passed that point.

WHO BENEFITS FROM GROWTH?

The idea that 'a rising tide lifts all ships', mentioned a few paragraphs back, is a cliché that has been very widely accepted. GDP per capita (but not real income per worker) has been rising steadily in the US, albeit at a modest pace, for the past several decades. Are people better off? If the comparison is made between 1950 and 1990, the answer is surely 'yes' for almost everybody. But if we look at the last two decades the answer is much less clear. In the US, only the wealthy and the upper middle class – the top 20 per cent of earners – have seen their disposable incomes grow significantly since the early 1970s.

Here are some interesting statistics.[1] In 1967 approximately 1 million US families

(2 per cent) had gross incomes greater than US$100,000 (in 1993 US$). Today, the top 2 per cent of US families has an income above US$200,000, just about double the 1967 number. Meanwhile, there are now 5.7 million US families – roughly 10 per cent – in the US$100,000-plus category. These people can (and do) buy bigger cars, bigger houses, vacation condos, more restaurant meals, and so forth. Adjusted for inflation, the average household income in the US rose 10 per cent from 1979 through 1994.[2] But nearly all – 97 per cent – of this gain went to the top 20 per cent of earners.

Meanwhile, for the rest of the population, the experience of the last two decades has been very different. The median wage in 1994 was 3 per cent less, in constant dollars, than it was in 1979. The poorest and less well-educated Americans are considerably worse off. The average hourly earnings of a non-college-educated US worker in 1979 were US$11.23. By 1993 the average hourly inflation-adjusted earnings of a non-college educated worker had fallen to US$9.92. This is an effective drop of over 11 percent. For college-educated Americans, the corresponding 1979 figures were US$15.52 and US$15.71, an increase of just 2 per cent.

Income inequality in the US generally decreased from 1929 to 1969. In that year (1969), the top 20 per cent of US households received 7.5 times as much income as the bottom 20 per cent. Since then, the egalitarian trend has reversed. By 1992 the US multiple had increased to 11 (as compared to about 4.5 for Japan, 5 for Sweden and Belgium, 5.5 for Holland and Germany, and around 6 for Italy and France). Again, the poorest group of Americans are actually worse off. Between 1973 and 1992 the bottom 10 per cent of households saw an 11 per cent drop in real income, while the top 10 per cent saw an 18 per cent increase. The per capita income of the poorest 20 per cent of the US was only one-quarter of the average for all Americans. However, in many countries, including Japan, the Netherlands, France, Germany and Scandinavia, the differential is only about half as great. Still, it is not only in America that income inequalities are increasing.[3] Everywhere in the West, despite social safety nets, the youngest, poorest and least educated are significantly worse off than their counterparts were 20 years ago.[4]

Meanwhile, the people at the very top are raking in the megabucks. According to a survey of 424 large US firms, the compensation of chief executives was 40 times average workers' earnings 20 years ago. The multiple in 1995 is 190, nearly five times higher. According to another survey, the CEOs of corporate America enjoyed a 23 per cent rise in total compensation during the year 1995 alone – their reward for downsizing their companies.[5] For 35 firms with average revenues of US$21 billion, CEOs' average salaries in 1995 were US$991,300 (up 4 per cent for the year) while bonuses for the year averaged US$1.22 million (up 39 per cent) and stock options averaged US$1.52 million (up 45 per cent). Incomes for sports stars, movie stars, top lawyers and even best-selling authors have followed the same pattern.

The US is the leader in this regrettable trend. In most other western countries, even the poorest people have enjoyed an actual increase in prosperity since the 1970s, although the richest still gained the most. For instance, in the UK, the poorest gained 10 per cent while the richest gained 55 per cent. A graphic index of inequality of income distribution for the UK from 1950 through 1990 is shown in Figure 8.1.[6] It is especially noteworthy that the index remained roughly constant from 1950 through 1965, and then actually declined 10 per cent from 1965 through 1976. Since then, the trend of inequality has been steadily upward.

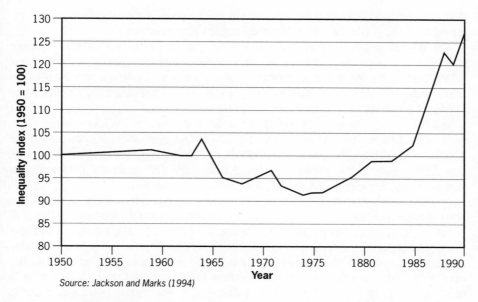

Source: Jackson and Marks (1994)

Figure 8.1 Index of Inequality: Income Distribution in the UK

CAUSES AND EXCUSES

Why has inequality increased so much in the last quarter century? There were multiple causes. Several academic studies suggest that – contrary to some perceptions – fiscal policy and lower marginal tax rates were not the main cause. Rather, deregulation of markets seems to have been the biggest reason for the changes that occurred mainly in the US and the UK (also Australia, New Zealand and Canada), but much less so in continental Europe.

The second major reason for increasing inequality was weakening of the labor movement, especially in the Anglo Saxon countries. Since 1970 union membership fell from 30 per cent of the workforce to 12 per cent in the US, and wage differentials increased sharply. In West Germany, by contrast, union membership remained at 40 per cent, and wage differentials have actually decreased slightly. In fact, it has been shown that income inequality in OECD countries is inversely correlated with union membership.

A third reason for increasing inequality is almost certainly the anti-inflationary policy of rising real interest rates that was in effect from about 1980 through 1991. During the inflationary period that began in the US with the Vietnam War and accelerated during the Arab oil boycott in the early 1970s, real interest rates were low and sometimes even negative. This environment was very negative for profits and the stock market, whereas it strongly encouraged borrowing. The declining stock market of the early 1970s led many small investors to transfer their savings into fixed income accounts. But the negative real interest rates, in effect, transferred wealth from lenders – people with savings – to borrowers. Among the net borrowers were many younger home owners who 'traded up', taking on larger mortgages and relying on inflationary growth in real estate prices to deliver increased equity values. The poorest, unable to take advantage of the real estate price escalator, did not benefit. But a great deal of wealth was drained in the 1970s from older savers, such as retirees, and transferred to younger middle and upper middle class home owners.

The US real estate escalator stopped moving up in 1979–1980 when mortgage interest rates began their sharp rise. Thus began a long and painful decline in real estate prices, except in a few favored locations such as California and Washington (both State and DC). Japan has experienced an even more dramatic decline since 1989, as noted earlier (Chapter 3).

In 1980 the US Federal Reserve Board under Chairman Paul Volcker raised short-term interest rates very suddenly to an unprecedented level (about 23 per cent at the maximum, in spring 1981), in an effort to kill inflationary expectations. Since that time, until 1991, savers and investors enjoyed both high (but gradually declining) real interest rates, increasing real profits, and rising stock markets.

Since the early 1980s the share of national income going to owners of capital has risen sharply, whereas the share going to labor has dropped. One indicator of this shift is the rising value of stocks and other financial instruments, relative to the replacement cost of their underlying assets.[7] Since the 1920s financial security values have averaged around 0.7 of replacement costs, albeit with significant fluctuations. But from 1985 on, the value of securities relative to replacement value has soared. It reached a level of 0.8 in 1990, 1.0 in 1991, 1.7 by the end of 1995 and exceeds 1.8 as I write (June 1997); see Figure 8.2. As a matter of interest, as of July 1996 US stock market capitalization amounted to US$6.8 trillion, or about 93 per cent of US GNP. The UK was the leader in this particular measure, at 120 per cent of GNP. By comparison, stock markets in France, Germany and Italy were capitalized at only about 38 per cent, 25 per cent and 22 per cent of GNP respectively (*The Economist*, 1996).

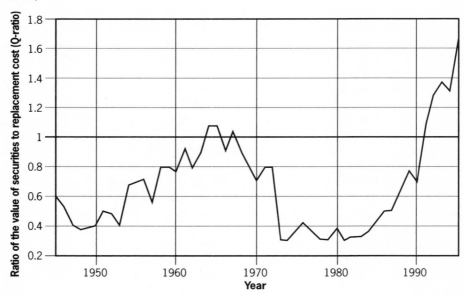

Figure 8.2 The Q-Ratio

There are only two possible explanations of the boom in security prices. Either we are currently enjoying (and probably approaching the end of) the biggest stock market bubble in history, or something has changed fundamentally in the economic system. In fact, both may be true. Specifically, the ability of companies to make profits seems to have increased radically since the 1970s. According to McKinsey Global Institute the return on capital for US firms between 1974 and 1993 was 9 per cent. Return on shareholders' capital (equity) in the US had risen to nearly 15 per cent by 1994, and – since profits continue to surge – even higher levels were reached by early 1997. This naturally increased the market value of the shares of those firms. For German firms, by comparison, the average return on capital from 1974 through 1993 was only 7 per cent; returns on stockholders' equity were 7.4 per cent in 1994. The canonical view from the financial world is simplistic:

> But whatever the social merits of the two systems, in an open trading environment both have to be judged on their long run ability to produce decent returns on investment. Europe is failing this test.
> Source: *The Economist*, 1996 pp19–21.

But, of course, higher profits for the private sector as a whole mean lower wages. In effect, the returns to capital at the national level have increased quite sharply, while the returns to labor have decreased correspondingly. This shift has been plotted (for Germany) in Figure 8.3. In view of Europe's laggardly failure to imitate US business practices, it would seem that the rise in the fortunes of capitalists and the corresponding decline in the fortunes of labor must have been considerably greater in the US. As might be expected, the financial community finds this shift admirable. I do not.

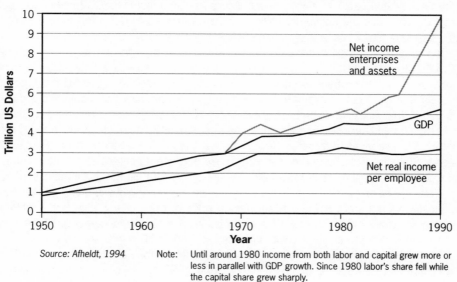

Source: Afheldt, 1994   Note: Until around 1980 income from both labor and capital grew more or less in parallel with GDP growth. Since 1980 labor's share fell while the capital share grew sharply.

Figure 8.3 Changing Shares of Labor and Capital

It is probably important to confront the defenders of the status quo directly. Some of them are fairly sophisticated. Some conservative economists have tried to explain away these embarrassing numbers with three arguments:

1) that when non-wage benefits (such as employer-paid health insurance) are added, total average private sector worker compensation is still rising, albeit very slowly;
2) that broader measures like GDP per capita still show a rise; and
3) that the cost of living adjustment (COLA) for inflation is excessive, because it under-estimates some of the benefits of technological improvement. This third point means that 'constant dollars' are not actually constant, being worth a little more today than 20 years ago because of improvements in the quality of some products and services.

I think these three arguments need to be answered, since (as usual) there is a grain of truth in each of them. The first point is statistically correct. But it applies to the average worker, not the bottom quarter or third. The increasing non-wage benefits go mainly to well-paid industrial union members and white collar employees (with bene-fits) and more part-timers and temporary workers without. They haven't risen much at all for the lower-paid workers, especially the non-union workers and part-timers. Now employers are trying hard to reverse the trend towards increasing non-wage benefits by hiring fewer full-time employees. Union membership is declining sharply.

As regards the second point, it is also statistically correct, but quite misleading. In fact, as I argued at some length in Chapter 7, GDP is a very inappropriate measure of welfare, and rising GDP per capita does *not* necessarily imply increasing welfare. On the contrary, when so-called defensive expenditures – expenditures on things that are unavoidable (such as taxes, health insurance, auto insurance and child care) but that do not leave the consumer better off than before – are deducted from the GDP, the resulting index has actually been declining since the 1970s in the US.

As regards the third point, there is some validity in the criticism of the use of the COLA index for adjusting social security payments. This is because the COLA index – inflation rate – is probably somewhat overstated. However, the main justification for saying that the index is exaggerated (ie that it underestimates real economic growth) is that it does not give enough weight to technological progress as reflected in quality of products and services. For instance, the prices of all kinds of electronic goods, and information services in general, have really declined much faster than the Bureau of Labor Statistics has allowed for because consumers are getting more for their money. It follows that consumers of these services are better off than the COLA index implies.

This criticism is valid, as I said. But, once again, the lower-paid, non-college educated workers are *not* significant beneficiaries of most of these very real techno-logical improvements. The major beneficiaries are the better educated and especially those who work professionally with information. People, in short, like myself.

Michael Novak, of the American Enterprise Institute for Public Policy Research in Washington DC, takes a different view (Novak, 1995). He cites certain statistics regarding the number of poor people in the US (as officially defined by the Census Bureau)[8] at various times. He then offers his own explanations for the figures. For instance, he notes that the number of poor people in 1995 was 6.9 million more than in the last year of the Reagan administration (1988), and was higher than at any time since 1962. In percentage terms, the poverty rate rose from 13.1 per cent to

15.1 per cent of the population over this period. An even sharper rise – also 7 million – took place during the four-year Carter administration. To his credit, Novak did not insist on the obvious (but fallacious) implication, namely that Democrats were actually responsible for these fluctuations. Obviously, the more recent rise in poverty occurred mostly under Bush.

Novak's real point is that the composition of the 'poverty' group has changed significantly in the last 30 years. For instance, there are a lot more elderly and retired people in the poorest group, simply because life expectancies have increased. The fastest-growing age group in the US is those over 85 years of age. Some of these elderly are not truly poor, but have low expenses (such as fully-paid mortgages) and draw on savings. Some other 'non-poor' categories, like graduate students, also fall into the official definition. There are more graduate students now than 30 years ago. As compared with 30 years ago, too, many of the poor have understated incomes, by virtue of benefitting from in-kind subsidies such as food stamps and Medicare.

But the big difference in the composition of the poverty group today is the sharp rise in the number of unemployed, unmarried mothers with dependent children, and homeless people. Here are some other statistics: only one in five of the bottom 20 per cent of households is headed by a married couple (and, of those who are married, many are elderly and retired). By contrast, three in five of this category are unmarried or absent-husband females. As regards dependent children, the number born out of wedlock has risen 600 per cent since 1970, and the number without resident fathers is growing faster still. As regards employment, in 1960 nearly two out of three households in the bottom 20 per cent of incomes were headed by a person with a job. Currently, only 11 per cent of the bottom 20 per cent of households are headed by a full-time worker.

Novak's points add an important dimension to the picture. The social changes he cites are real. But the rhetoric of the right tends to blame the poor for their predicament. The assumption is that long-term unemployment is voluntary; that some people would rather live on welfare handouts than do honest work. The assumption is that if welfare benefits for children were denied, single women would go out and find jobs. The same conservative groups oppose optional abortion.

There is an obvious response to this position; there aren't that many jobs available, especially where the neediest people are living (in central cities). Also, many of the low-skill jobs available today pay too little to support a family even at the poverty level (see Chapter 6). And the decline in the number of decent jobs for ordinary people seems unavoidably linked to the massive transfers of wealth away from ordinary middle class citizens, employees and pensioners of corporations for the benefit of the CEOs, stock manipulators, corporate raiders, bankruptcy lawyers and their ilk. It is hard to understand why the Republicans propose further transfers of wealth, via tax cuts mainly for the middle class and the wealthy, to be financed out of cuts in government social and other programs (that will incidentally create more unemployment). As a rule of thumb, income tax cuts give 80 per cent of their benefits to the top 20 per cent of income earners. In other words, it will help mainly the people who don't need help and who should pay more, not less.

For today's rich, which includes all the people who own and manage large enterprises, the gaining of further wealth is simply the name of the game. These people do not need more wealth for themselves; they scarcely have time to spend the money they already have. They compete for rankings in *Forbes* magazine's annual list of the wealthiest or highest paid. This is all very well for the CEOs of the multinational corporations (MNCs) and the investment bankers of Wall Street and its counterparts. Yet, it must be said that the fierceness of this competitive game for growth and market share has been extremely traumatic for many of the workers who are lower in the corporate hierarchy.

The leveraged buyouts (LBOs) and restructuring of businesses since 1980 has been very profitable to some financial buccaneers. Some of their names – Belzberg, Boesky, Bond, Clore, Fuqua, Hurwitz, Icahn, Kohlberg, Kravis and Roberts (KKR), Maxwell, Milken, Posner, Rowland, Schneider, Sigoloff, Simon, Vesco, Wasserstein and Perella – are well-known.[9] A number of these men have effectively destroyed healthy or save-able corporations by saddling them with excessive debt, raiding pension funds, and leaving personal devastation for tens of thousands of employees in their wake. A few buccaneers have gone to jail for insider trading (Boesky, Milken), or to off-shore exile (Rich, Schneider, Vesco). Others (notably Goldsmith) devastated the environment for personal gain by converting irreplaceable natural resource assets into instant cash to finance a takeover. Goldsmith used his gains to finance his dubious political career in Europe.

The Reagan decade and its aftermath has been extraordinarily painful to those of average or less than average education and skills in the US, as the Thatcher era was for the same category of people in the UK. Europe is now beginning to experience a comparable phenomenon. First the factory and clerical workers, and then the middle managers, and higher managers too, have progressively lost status, promotion prospects, health insurance coverage, pension rights, job security, and even employment itself. In the last seven years 85 per cent of the Fortune 1000 non-financial companies downsized. Six million jobs disappeared in the process. A 1992 survey by the American Management Association reported that 43 per cent of surveyed companies had at least two major downsizings in five years, and 24 per cent had three or more, while 65 per cent of those firms that had layoffs in 1992 did so again in 1993. Privatization of a number of large European firms that were government owned and/or controlled surely presages a similar process in other countries.

Academic economists (protected by tenure) still argue about whether this massive dislocation has been beneficial in terms of increasing competitiveness or not. On that point, the returns are not all in, although business-school professors lean toward the favorable view. However, it seems to me that nobody is asking the more important question: why is competitiveness so important? I have the heretical suspicion that perhaps the world is getting to be *too* competitive; for long-term survival more cooperation seems to be needed.

The answer to this question is, at first sight, so obvious that nobody seems to think it worthy of discussion. It is globalization of trade. If globalization is an unavoidable fact of life, then one must be competitive to survive, whatever the cost in human terms. They say it is necessary to break some eggs to make an omelet. But is the omelet worth eating? Is it digestible? Is rapid globalization truly necessary, or is it a matter of choice? Is it even a good idea? Is the emperor wearing any clothes? I am beginning to doubt it.

STATISTICS ON WEALTH

The trend toward capital appreciation (and labor depreciation) has reversed the previous (1970s) modest shift in wealth away from the older generation to the younger generation. Indeed, it has over-compensated and then some. But the beneficiaries of inflation-driven capital gains from borrowing in the late 1960s and 1970s were able to invest those capital gains in stocks during the 1980s and ride another escalator. Those now approaching retirement age in the US (myself included) have done quite well for themselves, as a generation, just by being in the right age group at the right time. The baby boom generation, by contrast, is in deep trouble.

Some data recently published (1995) put this age-related disparity into quantitative terms. Households with incomes of US$30,000 or more (roughly median) have an average net worth of US$66,000 if the head of household is in the age bracket 35–44, including real estate assets. Net financial assets for this group are less than US$8000. Households with the same income, but headed by a person in the age group 65–74, have an average net worth of US$222,000, of which US$77,000 consists of financial assets. Yet the older group receives social security and Medicare benefits that must be paid for by the younger group or by increasing the federal debt.

Recent survey data from the US Federal Reserve Board (published in 1995) are even more shocking. In 1992 the top 1 per cent of US wealth owners accounted for 30.4 per cent of the nation's total net worth (real tangible assets plus financial assets), while the next 9 per cent had 36.8 per cent and all the rest had 32.8 per cent. This lower group (90 per cent of the population) had an average net worth of US$67,000 per household. The middle 9 per cent averaged US$750,000 each while the top 1 per cent, by contrast, averaged US$5.6 million each. Of course, this is peanuts for Bill Gates and the other members of the Forbes list of the really rich.

Another defender of the status quo, Robert Rector of the Heritage Foundation, cites statistics that seem to prove that the poor in the US are not really poor at all (Rector, 1995). For instance, according to the 1987 *American Housing Survey* US census, 38 per cent of officially poor households owned their own homes, the median value of which was US$39,205. Half a million of these poor households owned homes worth more than US$100,000. The average poor American family's living quarters consisted of 405 square feet of space per capita, compared to 200 square feet per capita for the average Japanese and only 97 square feet for the average Russian. Only 1.8 per cent of housing units occupied by poor households lacked a flush toilet and only 2.7 per cent lacked a shower or bath.

The above statistics prove only that statistics can be extremely misleading. Not that they are wrong. The problem is in the fine print. First of all, the housing data apply only to the poor *who own homes*, a minority of the poor. Those are mostly elderly retirees living on small unproductive farms or in Florida, on social security and savings. The other category – renters and homeless – live in crime-ridden urban slums, a great many of whose occupants are 'unofficial' and who do not respond to census surveys. In other words, room occupancy is seriously under-stated.

Using the same official government statistics, James Smith, a senior economist at RAND Corp, presented the situation from a different perspective (*International Herald Tribune*, 1995). The top 5 per cent of white families with one spouse over age 70 have assets of US$655,000. This is seven times the level of the median white family (with assets of US$90,000). The bottom 10 per cent of white families have assets worth less than US$800. But even that is more than the 'typical' black or Hispanic family, which has total net assets of under US$500. The bottom 40 per cent of blacks and Hispanics have no assets at all. Many of these people are the homeless who live in subways or alleys and live by begging or charity. An estimated 700,000 persons in the US are homeless. From all indications, their number is growing.

SOCIAL PATHOLOGY

It has been reported that 3 per cent of all US citizens are either in prison or on parole. That is 8 million individuals, mostly young and disproportionately black or Hispanic. The state of California now spends more on prisons than on education. Anyone with a prison record for theft or violence is, of course, virtually excluded from consideration for most kinds of employment, except for unskilled manual labor for which there is less demand each year.

Life in the crime-ridden urban slums is difficult for comfortably-off middle class college graduates (who live far away in well-protected high-rises or suburban enclaves) to appreciate. Certainly these realities have not been recognized or addressed by the conservative ideologues. I believe, however, that these very social pathologies are due, at least to some degree, to the declining availability of well-paid work for the uneducated and unskilled. Having no realistic hope for a better life in the future, people from the urban ghettos are more likely than others to grasp momentary relief from stress through drugs, sex or violence.

The middle class in America has discovered that two incomes are needed to achieve a standard of living that one wage-earner could formerly aspire to. Home ownership is falling. Educational achievement levels are falling. Drug abuse and criminal behavior by children are rising. Social mobility is at risk. Working mothers cannot give the same attention to young children that stay-at-home moms once did. The real gain to working women's self-respect is often balanced by guilt feelings.

'Supermom', who can be top executive, doctor, or lawyer for eight hours a day[10] and also be a successful wife-and-mother the rest of the time is not entirely unknown. But she is as rare as a sweepstake winner, and almost always the beneficiary of special circumstances, notably a partner or parent willing and able to stay at home, or at least to be at home on a reliable schedule. The existence of an occasional househusband is a good thing, but not a panacea. However, on the broader stage, society has provided no substitute for stay-at-home parents except the TV, the video game and the frozen dinner.[11] On the domestic scene, rising GDP fails to reflect the adverse social effects of the very real sense of insecurity that seems to accompany increasing competitiveness. I return to some of these issues once more in Chapter 9.

RICH AND POOR IN THE DEVELOPING WORLD

What of the so-called developing countries? Surely they have been gaining, at least in Asia, even if some of their gains have been at the expense of US and European manufacturing workers, especially the less skilled and less well-paid?

The World Bank says so. It crows that the rapidly growing economies of Asia 'have actually increased the equality of income distribution and dramatically reduced poverty'.[12] However, global statistics, scarce as they are, are not too encouraging in this regard. Whereas 36 years ago in 1960 the world's richest 20 per cent were 30 times richer than the poorest 20 per cent, the multiple in 1991 was 61. According to the UN Development Report, the world's top 20 per cent had 70 per cent of global income in 1960; in 1991 they had 85 per cent. The share of the lower 80 per cent had been cut in half. In 1960, the bottom 20 per cent had 2.3 per cent of global income. By 1991, their share of the pie has fallen by 40 per cent, to just 1.4 per cent of the total. The absolute gap in per capita income between the industrial countries and the developing world has increased from US$5700 in 1960 to US$15,400 today.

One particularly outrageous statistic is worth framing: 'Today's net worth of the world's 358 richest people is equal to the combined income of the poorest 45 per cent of the world's population – 2.3 billion people' (Speth, 1996). To be sure, it is slightly unfair to compare income with net worth. On the other hand, the world's 2.3 billion poorest people have essentially no net worth at all. Certainly, their total net worth is far less than that of the world's 358 or so billionaires.

As regards trade in manufactured goods, the 102 poorest countries accounted for 7.9 per cent of exports and 9 per cent of imports in 1960. These shares had declined to 1.4 per cent (exports) and 4.9 per cent (imports) by 1990. To pay for these imports, debt in the developing world is now US$1.8 trillion. Clearly trade liberalization has not helped most of the people in the world's poorest countries.

What of the fast-growing countries of East Asia? World Bank data show some equalization between the richest 20 per cent and the poorest 20 per cent in those countries between the period 1965–1989 and the more recent period 1988–1993. In Malaysia the multiple (of the richest to the poorest quintile) dropped from 15 to 11; in The Philippines it fell from 11 to 7; in Indonesia it fell from 7 to a little less than 5. In the case of Thailand, the multiple remained at 8. However, in the Thai case, more detailed data from a Japanese economist, Yukio Ikemoto, show that the ratio of the household income of the top 10 per cent to the bottom 10 per cent rose from about 17 in 1981 to 38 in 1992. Part of the reason for this is that all of the wealth is in the big cities. Average income per head in Bangkok is 15 times that in the poorest province of Thailand. Similar discrepancies between city and countryside exist in all of the other fast-growing economies.

Some recent data from a Chinese business weekly (*International Herald Tribune*, 1996) are disquieting. The income distribution of urban Chinese families is as follows: the poorest group, with incomes below 5000 Yuan per year, accounted for 3.8 per cent of households; 36 per cent were in the next group (5000–10,000 Yuan); just over 50 per cent fell into the middle group (10,000–20,000 Yuan), 8 per cent belong to the next highest category (20,000–100,000 Yuan), leaving 2 per cent in the highest income category. Most of the people in the top two categories live in the coastal cities.

But these statistics apply to the cities, and it is not clear whether the rural immigrants living in illegal squatter communities on the outskirts have been taken into account. Be this as it may, the average annual income in Chinese cities was said to be 5059 Yuan, compared to only 1578 Yuan for farmers.[13] The most distressing news was that the income disparity between the bottom 10 per cent and the top 10 per cent reportedly quadrupled in 1995. No explanation was given, but it would seem that the beneficiaries of the new prosperity are very few, and probably far fewer than the victims, such as small farmers forced to vacate their land without adequate (if any) compensation and the insecure employees of the 70,000 state-owned enterprises in China that are losing money.

In short, a totally disproportionate share of the economic gains in the developing world goes to the rich and politically well-connected. They do it largely by monopolizing access to foreign aid and foreign investment, government contracts, insider loans from government controlled banks, and – especially – permits to exploit stocks of natural resources, such as forests, that should belong to all the people. In fact, many of the big hydroelectric dams and natural resource concessions result in displacing tens of thousands of peasants. It is invariably the top generals, or the 'president for life', and their brothers, cousins and in-laws, who accumulate the serious wealth.

Consider the past President of Mexico, Carlos Salinas de Gortari, who persuaded the Clinton administration that Mexico was ready to join NAFTA and the OECD. While in office from 1988 through 1994, the Salinas administration privatized 251 companies worth US$23 billion and accounting for a significant fraction of the nationalized sector in Mexico. This program was praised in the US as a 'model'. Somehow it incidentally created a number of instant Mexican billionaires. According to *Forbes* magazine's annual survey of the world's wealthiest people, Mexico had one billionaire in 1987 and 24 billionaires seven years later in 1994 at the end of the Salinas term of office. Meanwhile, thanks to devaluation and economic turmoil, the average Mexican worker lost 52 per cent of his real income. A third of all Mexican households now live in extreme poverty. The peasant uprising in Chiapas is a reflection of these facts.

Thanks to the criminal investigations, a number of interesting details have come to light. Curiously, virtually all of the new Mexican billionaires were personal cronies of the President's brother, and most participated in the privatization program. Think of the new Russian millionaires, mostly former communist *priviligentsia* who were allowed to buy (through banks and holding companies) factories and natural resources at give-away prices. Meanwhile 90 per cent of the Russian population has lost its savings, its job security and its social security. At the end of the communist regime in 1989 the biggest economic problem facing the country was the 'savings overhang'. There being nothing worth buying, and nothing worth investing in, people had trustingly put their money in the banks. When Yeltsin came to power, all this changed.

Privatization should have started with housing and the land. People could have used their accumulated savings to acquire real property – and the incentives that go with it – with no inflationary consequences for the state. Meanwhile, the state would have received investable funds. Instead, the government gave away its most valuable assets to insiders. For example, the former head of the communist gas monopoly, Viktor Chernomyrdin, together with some cronies, was allowed to buy a controlling interest in the privatized successor firm GAZPRO for peanuts (financed by a bank, to be paid out of future profits). Given the size of the Russian gas reserves, Chernomyrdin is now one of the richest men in the world – certainly a multi-billionaire. He is also Yeltsin's Prime Minister and likely successor. It can hardly be doubted that Yeltsin's inner circle supporters include quite a number of other instant millionaires of the same ilk. As for the small savers and pensioners, they have all been pauperized by inflation.

Think of the murderous clique of generals who run Nigeria for private profit, while the slums of Lagos grow and fester. Think of the Saudi sheikhs and Persian Gulf emirs whose families connived with Western oil interests a few decades ago to sell off their national patrimony. Consider Marcos, Mobutu, Suharto and dozens of other less well-known developing world billionaires. Consider where they send their money. Consider the state of their countries.

The educated urban middle classes, the manufacturers and the most efficient farmers (who can afford to buy fertilizer and hybrid seed) are also getting a little bit richer. Everywhere, the rural poor, especially the native tribes and villagers, are being ruthlessly dispossessed and displaced. The building of the Three Gorges Dam in China will impoverish millions of formerly self-sufficient farmers. The evils of the eighteenth century enclosure movement in Britain are being repeated today in much of the world. Much of this activity is being financed by the World Bank (with the best of intentions, to be sure). See Box 8.1.

Box 8.1 Equity in Development Funding

In practice, when the calculated gains (benefits) of a project exceed the losses (costs), economists normally consider that the project is justified, regardless of the distributional consequences – that is, who wins and who loses. In principle, the winners could compensate the losers. Whether they actually do so or not is not thought to be within the economists' proper domain. However, in recent years there have been a number of truly horrific examples of development projects, especially environmentally destructive dams and mining or forestry enterprises in developing countries, in which the gainers are wealthy individuals or big firms and their shareholders, while the losers are poor farmers and indigenous peoples who are displaced permanently from their traditional lands (to which they often have no legal title) and are offered little or nothing in compensation. Examples of such inequitable projects have recently been publicized – and properly criticized – in India, Brazil, Venezuela, Guyana, Indonesia, Cambodia, and elsewhere. The Three Gorges project in China is likely to become one of the most contentious examples in coming years.

The answer, of course, is not to stop all economic development schemes. However, it seems to me that governments, international agencies and multinational corporations – and professional economists – need to reconsider their criteria for justifying a project proposal. It is not enough to show that winners could, in principle, compensate losers. It is time for equity considerations to receive as much attention as efficiency considerations. Economist Scott Farrow has made a very useful suggestion in this regard: he proposes that formal project proposals should include not only benefit cost analysis but also explicit plans for compensation, especially where the likely losers are already very poor people.

Even when developing countries gain export markets for manufactured goods, the benefits don't always go to the workers. In fact, businesses in the developing world often mistreat workers and persecute union organizers, not to mention damaging the environment.

Of course, it can be argued that any job is better than no job and what looks like exploitation to an American or European might not look so bad to a Salvadoran, Indonesian or Vietnamese woman with a family to support. But the big winners are the factory owners and the various middlemen that siphon off the profits along the way from factory to retail store, not the actual workers. It seems particularly outrageous to many that Nike pays sports superstars like Michael Jordan and Tiger Woods tens of millions of dollars annually to advertise its product, while its hapless workers earn only a few dollars a week.

Box 8.2 Child Labor

The Gap, a well-known retail clothing chain in the US, buys clothing from factories in Central America including one firm called Mandarin International in El Salvador. These factories are said to be notorious sweatshops, illegally employing children sometimes with forced shifts as long as 20 hours during peak production periods. Mandarin recently crushed an attempt to unionize its workers, firing all those workers involved. Thanks to recent newspaper publicity and resulting consumer pressure (and a threat by two Jewish Rabbis to declare that wearing Gap clothing would be contrary to Jewish ethical laws), The Gap has agreed to undertake active monitoring of its suppliers. In particular, it has agreed to cease doing business with Mandarin International if the latter does not reinstate the fired workers and comply with other conditions spelled out in its 'Sourcing Principles and Guidelines'. A very similar story appeared a few months ago, describing conditions in an Indonesian factory that manufactures running shoes for Nike. Again, a timid attempt by some employees to get Nike's contractor to abide by Indonesian laws with regard to working conditions and pay was crushed and offending workers were fired. The retail price of a single pair of Nike shoes would pay the wages of one of its factory workers for more than a month.

Nathan Gardels, editor of *New Perspective Quarterly*, writing about the likely effects of then-pending international trade negotiations in consolidating the primacy of the Pacific Rim countries in world commerce, has stated my concerns more eloquently than I could:

> *The outlook for the ROW (rest of world) is bleak. For countries outside the G–7 led system, Mobutu-style military socialism, as the economist Robert Heilbroner fears, may be the shape of things to come. Only the archipelago of the connected classes that reside in every mega-city from Bombay to Sao Paulo, will prosper from the new capitalist order.*
>
> *The rest of the ever-swelling ranks of the lumpen-planeten face a fate worse than colonialism: economic irrelevance. From the standpoint of the market the hundreds of millions of people now merely surviving in places like Bangladesh and across vast stretches of Africa are superfluous. By and large we don't need what they have; they can't buy what we sell.*
>
> *Under the emerging economic order that excludes them will there be any alternative to this squalor without end? There will surely be much imposition of order by force, the doling out of subsistence by the state and the now routine humanitarian rescue efforts to salve the western conscience. Egalitarian development seems far less likely.*
>
> *Source: Gardels, 1993.*

INTERGENERATIONAL EQUITY

So much for horizontal equity. Before passing on, I should say a few words about intergenerational equity. This is a much stickier question for two reasons. First, there are a number of different moral perspectives on just what intergenerational equity means, especially given the differential population growth rates in the world. Should all the members of future generations in poor countries with high population growth rates and socially or environmentally 'unacceptable' cultural practices and religious beliefs be treated the same as (ie subsidized by) future generations of countries that protect the environment and share Western social values? There will be no unanimity on this issue and I cannot offer any easy answer.

The other difficulty is that future generations are not here to defend their interests in our courts and have no votes in our legislatures. They are not identifiable individuals with identifiable interests at stake. What rights they have are only granted voluntarily by us, the present generation. It is worthwhile to bear in mind that some human cultures give great weight to the interests of future generations. Others do not. Thomas Jefferson believed that the living must hold the environment 'in usufruct for the unborn'. In effect, he believed that the environment is only on loan, and that we have a duty to return it to its true owners (our descendants) intact. In 1987 the UN's World Commission on Environment and Development introduced the notion of 'sustainability' in terms of not compromising the essential resource base (undefined) needed by, and available to, future generations (Brundtland et al, 1987). But many still believe that nature is an enemy to be conquered, and that the earth and all its resources are ours to exploit or abuse, as we will.

It is certain that our descendants have no legal or constitutional rights before an impartial tribunal. They cannot choose their counsel, or their arguments. They are in the position of an indigent plaintiff dependent on pro bono counsel chosen by the court or, worse, by the defendant (us). Lacking legal status or constitutional definition, it is doubly difficult to ascertain in detail what is, or is not, equitable in a given case.

I do not propose to explore this murky subject very much further. There is no hope of resolution. However I have one comment on the approach conventionally chosen by economists, which is to combine present and future into a seamless whole by maximizing the discounted present value of 'utility'. Utility, at the national level, is equated with the entire future consumption stream, defined as total economic output (GDP) less savings, extending to infinity. The discounting procedure keeps the total finite rather than infinite, and it is used largely for this reason. Professional economists and accountants use the procedure routinely without much thought. However a full explanation and justification in simple words for readers unfamiliar with the idea is likely to be far from convincing. (See Box 8.3.)

But I have a serious point to make about the practice of discounting. Normally economists only consider positive or zero rates of discount. Yet it is perfectly logical to suppose that there are circumstances where income (or other benefits) received in the future will be worth more in utility terms than income received now. This is actually the case for people approaching retirement, for instance, who know that their income from working will decline and eventually disappear and who must therefore save for a rainy day. Most economists assume without question that people in the future will be richer than people living today, because of continuing and perpetual economic growth. On this basis, one could possibly agree with people like Julian Simon who say that protecting the environment or conserving resources for future use is like asking the poor to give to the rich. I think, however, that it is appropriate to consider seriously the possibility that growth is not inevitable, especially if we in the present squander our natural and environmental resource base. It follows that *people in the future may not necessarily be richer than people in the present*. In that case, it is the richer present that should be sharing with the poorer people of future generations. In this case, the discount rate should not be positive, or even zero, but negative.

> ### Box 8.3 The Discount Rate
>
> The discount rate is thought to be something like the minimum rate of interest that the average person (or society) would accept to save money for future use, rather than spending it now. Economists generally believe that the rate should not be set at zero for the future, if only because discounting seems to be an empirical fact of life. However, an enormous and acrimonious debate has arisen among theoreticians over the appropriate rate of discount. The debate is highly artificial, if only because a zero discount rate (which a number of environmentalists and others prefer on moral grounds) yields an infinite welfare function, whereas any finite rate, no matter how small, leads to finite welfare functions. How can an infinitesimal parametric difference yield an infinite difference in the results?
>
> But the choice of discount rate is extremely important for benefit/cost analysis, because it permits present benefits to be weighed against future costs and, of course, vice versa. This is important, in turn, because protecting the environment for future use means giving up present benefits, whereas exploiting natural resources in the present means giving up future benefits that would otherwise be enjoyed by our descendants. The problems of quantification are obviously enormous, but that is a techinical detail that need not concern us here. The point is that any non-zero discount rate at all values future welfare less than our own. This seems morally intolerable to some people and perfectly natural to others.

All this implies that if we act rationally on the basis of any choice of discount rate, whether positive or negative, the outcome is likely to falsify the assumption we started with. If we assume growth and conserve too little, the future will be poorer than we originally assumed. If, on the other hand, we assume future poverty, we will save and conserve more and the future will be richer than we have assumed after all. From a policy perspective, the second choice seems preferable.

SOCIAL CRISIS

Financial crisis is not the only reason for concern about the future of the West. Another is that social pressures in Europe and the US are becoming intolerable. Apart from racial and religious incompatibilities with Europe's white secular-Christian society, the refugees from surrounding poor countries are becoming a financial burden on governments with declining resources. Since unemployment is already high, and few jobs are being created, newcomers either take jobs from natives or they go on the dole (at least until they are identified, processed and deported). Since the collapse of the USSR and especially since the civil wars in Bosnia and Algeria, waves of refugees and would-be immigrants from Eastern Europe, the Middle East and North Africa especially, have been arriving at the borders of Western Europe. Most are now turned back, despite objections from humanitarians. But Europe cannot totally insulate itself from this pressure, and the number of unwanted, unwelcome and hard-to-assimilate refugees finding their way to its shores cannot help but grow. This, in turn, will feed the fears of the segments of European society that are already feeling left out, ignored, frustrated and paranoid – the under-educated and the unemployed – who are also mostly young men. These are the breeding grounds of skinheads and neo-Nazis. It is also the political soil tilled by the far right, such as Jorg Haider in Austria and Jean-Marie Le Pen in France.

In Europe the safety net has kept this pot from boiling over so far, but all the sources of present discontent are likely to grow, not abate.

In North America the situation is very similar, if not quite as bad. The pool of potential immigrants from nearby lands, mainly Central America and the Caribbean, is not quite so large as the Eastern European/African pool. Nor are the Christian Latinos (and increasing numbers of Asians) nearly so difficult to assimilate into the heterogeneous US culture as the Muslim Arab or even Christian African refugees are in the 'Europe of nationalities'. But the US social safety net is much weaker, the tradition of personal (if not communal) violence is stronger and the system of government is much more decentralized. The US political system is consequently less able to make hard decisions to accommodate major changes (short of reacting to an event like Pearl Harbor). Thus, government in the US has been increasingly unable to solve social or economic problems, especially since the Vietnam War. Not surprisingly, central government itself has become increasingly discredited.

Lyndon Johnson's 'War on Poverty' was well-intentioned, but not well-conceptualized or well-executed. It was drawn up far too hastily. It was also undoubtedly sabotaged by the very same right-wing groups that now proclaim it a failure. Smarter bureaucrats (Eurocrats?) might conceivably have done better, as they have in some countries of Europe. But the most successful European social programs, such as the Swedish, Dutch, German and French, are also running into financial trouble. In any case, the US experiment in poverty eradication by government program was not successful, notwithstanding some successful bits and pieces. Something radically different must be tried. Government, by its very nature, must interfere with private activities in many spheres. There is a moral imperative for society to intervene when intervention is unavoidable, primarily on the side of the poor, the weak and the powerless. Surely a society that claims to be Christian – as many US conservatives do claim – ought to try to practise some of the most elementary Christian virtues.

There is a false, but widely believed, idea that intervention on the side of equity means a 'Great Society' program run from the center by faceless bureaucrats. This, in turn, raises the specter of big government in the sense of Orwell's 'Big Brother': an intrusive Soviet-style (or Austro-Hungarian style) state that forbids everything that is not explicitly permitted.[14] But this idea of big government, which Americans have never experienced, has little to do with equity. There is a good case for reducing government in some areas. Curbing bureaucracy need not, and should not, equate automatically with the deliberate use of legislative power to help the rich get richer at the expense of the needy. But that is exactly what has been happening in America since 1980, if not longer.

Yet government has been discredited just when it is most needed. Poverty is increasing even in the richest countries. The urban public educational system is in a downward spiral, losing its best teachers and its best students to private schools. Increasingly, the public system is a last resort for those who have no other choice. In fact, central cities themselves are in shambles. Housing is deteriorating, schools are ineffective, crime is rampant, the jails are full and overcrowded. Drugs are one of the major causes of all this. The drug problem gets worse year by year, but in the US the only politically-acceptable position is hard-line enforcement – more cops, more jails, tougher penalties – and silly exhortation ('Just say no!').

The future of the West may well be (to quote Gibbon) 'decline and fall'. I would not be surprised at all if historians looking back from the year 2050 concluded that

1969–1989 was the apogee of Western power and prosperity and that 1989 – celebrated briefly as the end of the Cold War, if not the end of history (ie the final triumph of democracy over totalitarianism) – marked the beginning of the long decline. The current boom in the US could end at any moment. The time has come to re-examine many of our basic assumptions, especially with regard to the growth and competitiveness imperatives, the supreme virtues of free trade and unregulated market economics, and the associated philosophy that 'greed is good'.

Of course there is always hope that far-sighted and courageous leaders will emerge and that radical new policies will be implemented before it is too late. My own modest ideas along these lines are described in Chapters 10 and 11.

NOTES

1 Data taken from Cassidy, 1995. These data were also cited by Pfaff, 1995. Also from Uchitelle and Kleinfeld, 1996.
2 These figures are adjusted for inflation by means of the COLA index that is compiled by the Department of Labor based on a market basket of typical goods and services.
3 Data in the following two paragraphs are taken mainly from *The Economist*, 1994, pp19–21.
4 In the first quarter of 1997, with US unemployment at 4.9 per cent – a 23-year low – there was a very slight increase in wages at the very bottom of the scale, relative to higher-paid workers, for the first time in many years. This is good news, but not enough to engender complacency.
5 The survey was carried out by Pearl Meyer, a management consultant. Reported by the Associated Press, March 6, 1996.
6 Inequality in the UK decreased very sharply between 1938 and 1948, due partly to progressive taxation to pay for the war, and partly to the measures introduced by the Labour Government under Clement Attlee in the immediate postwar years. The figures below are taken from Tawney, 1952. During the 1938–1948 period the proportion of national income after tax received as (hourly) wages increased from 39 per cent to 48 per cent, that received as salaries declined from 25 per cent to 21 per cent while that received as profits, dividends, rents and professional earnings decreased from 34 per cent to 28 per cent. Allowing for indirect taxes, which are reflected in prices and therefore in purchasing power, the purchasing power of wages rose 22 per cent while the purchasing power of profits, dividends, rents and professional earnings declined 23 per cent. Upper incomes fell sharply. The ratio of average post-tax incomes in the highest income group vis-à-vis the lowest was 28 in 1938 as compared to 13 in 1948. The highest-income group was defined as people with pretax incomes of over £10,000 in both years, of whom there were 8000 in 1938 and 11,000 in 1948; the lowest income group was defined as those with pretax incomes in the range £250–£500 in both years. There were 2,000,000 in this range in 1939 and 8,650,000 in 1948. However, those with incomes still lower than £250 per annum were not included in the statistics; there were about 10,000,000 of them in 1948 and more like 13,000,000 in the earlier year. Thus, the real degree of prewar inequality was actually far greater than Tawney's statistics suggest.
7 This measure, known as the Q-ratio, was first developed by Yale economist James Tobin, who got a Nobel Prize for his work.
8 The official definition of the poverty threshold is indexed for inflation and other factors. In 1994 it was defined as an income of US$15,141 for a non-farm family of four, and correspondingly less for couples and single people.

9 For a detailed account of the activities of many of these men and others, see Barlett and Steele, 1992.

10 But this is nearly impossible on the face of it, since highly-paid executives and other professionals routinely work much longer hours, and even boast of it.

11 The laissez-faire family policy of the US is not the only possible approach. I rather deplore the German slogan Kinder, Kuchen, Kirche (children, kitchen, church) which has been used to justify a number of family-oriented laws that discourage divorce and make it difficult for married mothers to have careers. The Swedish approach (generous child support and child care facilities) is certainly more liberal, albeit expensive – almost certainly unaffordable. This approach tends to create still more jobs for women, thus driving up the GNP further. (Recall the discussion on monetization of household work in Chapter 2 and again in Chapter 7.) However, it is a fact that both family life and social life in Europe are in far better shape than in the US.

12 The standard source is World Bank, 1995. See also *The Economist*, 1996b, pp63–64 and Brown et al, 1996.

13 There is obviously some confusion, since the distribution data imply that the average urban household income must have been more than 10,000 Yuan.

14 The stifling Austro-Hungarian bureaucracy was well described by Franz Kafka, the Czech novelist. Even today, remnants of the old system can be found in Austria. Houses can only be painted in a few colors (mainly the ghastly 'Hapsburg yellow'); every chimney – used or not – must be cleaned bi-annually by a government-sanctioned chimney sweep, and so on. When I lived in Austria in the late 1980s, a single mother in Graz, trying to support herself, advertised her services as a caterer. She was sued by the local bakers' guild and fined 30,000 Austrian Schillings (about US$4000 at the time) for engaging in a restricted occupation.

Chapter 9

Economic Growth versus the Environment[1]

BACKGROUND

Before the beginning of the industrial revolution, human activities were generally compatible with a healthy and sustainable biosphere. The vast majority of humans lived and worked on farms. Land was the primary source of wealth. Horses and other animals, supplemented by windmills, sails and waterwheels, provided most of the power for plowing, milling, mining and transport.[2] The sun, either directly or through products of photosynthesis, provided virtually all energy for heating and cooking, as well as food and feed. Metals were smelted by means of charcoal, but their uses were very limited and almost exclusively ornamental (in the case of gold, silver, copper and tin) or mechanical (in the case of iron and bronze). Lead was used in Roman times for water pipes and wine jars, which undoubtedly had some toxic effects on the upper classes. Only arsenic, lead and mercury, with very low melting points, had any 'chemical' uses – mainly as pigments, medicinals and cosmetics. Recycling of most metals was normal and quite efficient.

In short, wealth was derived exclusively from the land, except for a few mines and fisheries. But at the end of the eighteenth century, thanks to increasing wealth, the population of England was growing exponentially. In 1798 the Reverend Thomas Malthus wrote a pamphlet entitled (in part) *An Essay on the Principle of Population as it Affects the Future Improvement of Society* in which he spelled out his thesis that population tends to increase up to the limits of its means of subsistence, being limited only by war, famine and pestilence. He believed that the means of subsistence could only grow arithmetically, whereas population growth tends to be exponential (Malthus, 1798).

As we approach the end of the twentieth century, humans are far more numerous and also wealthier (on average) than they were two centuries ago when Malthus wrote. In particular, those countries that industrialized first are now comparatively rich. Most people live in cities. Substantial accumulation of man-made capital (infrastructure, machines, knowledge) has occurred. Land is no longer the primary source of domestic wealth. Malthus is widely derided today by conservative economists and technological optimists for having misunderstood the miraculous generative powers of the capitalist economic system.[3]

However a key attribute of this rise to wealth by some countries is that it has been achieved by exploiting and depleting an endowment of natural capital, not only fossil fuels (as pointed out in Chapters 2 and 5) but also forests, fisheries, topsoil and minerals. For some material resources such as fossil fuels, technology can eventually offer viable substitutes – for instance, photovoltaic (PV) electricity and solar hydrogen.[4] Some of the scarcer elements, such as copper and tin, can be replaced for most uses, in time, by less scarce elements like glass or aluminum. For other resources in the natural endowment – notably topsoil, fresh water, clean air, equitable climate, and the biosphere and its many essential functions – no such technological substitute is likely.

If Malthus were alive today, he would undoubtedly revise his original thesis in light of more recent developments and information. He would have to acknowledge the demographic evidence that population growth has essentially stopped in Europe and is slowing down globally, thanks to gradually declining birth rates. But the fundamental problem he identified remains, though in a different guise. The neo-Malthusian thesis might be summarized more or less this way: the capitalist industrial system, as it functions today, tends to grow to the limits of its subsistence. Economic growth tends to be exponential. (In fact, since the industrial revolution it has been hyper-exponential, insofar as economic growth rates have accelerated.) On the other hand, notwithstanding substitution possibilities, the natural resource base is still finite. Although technological progress allows for some increase in the efficiency with which natural resources can be discovered, extracted, processed and utilized, the rate of increase of resource availability cannot be exponential in the long run. Thus there is a mismatch between exponential growth and the availability of natural resources to support it.

SUSTAINABILITY VERSUS UNSUSTAINABILITY

In 1985 the UN General Assembly created the World Commission on Environment and Development (WCED), more widely known as the Brundtland Commission after its Chairwoman, Prime Minister Gro Harlem Brundtland of Norway. The Commission labored for two years, met dozens of times in different cities, and listened to hundreds of experts. Its report was published in 1987 under the title *Our Common Future*. The theme of the Commission report was sustainable development, which was defined as economic growth which meets the needs of the people living today without compromising the ability of future generations to support their own needs. It recognized that there is a very real conflict between meeting the needs and desires of the five-and-a-half billion people now alive and the possibility of satisfying the ten to twelve billion people expected to be living on Earth by the middle of the next century.[5]

A large number of alternative definitions of 'sustainable development' have been proposed. The current interpretation of sustainable development from mainstream institutions like the World Bank is virtually indistinguishable from the notion of continuing economic growth as measured in the usual way, ie in terms of consumption of market-tradeable goods and services. The requirement of assuring future generations an equal chance is supposed to be met automatically by accumulating capital and (if necessary) substituting man-made capital for natural capital. In short, to address issues of sustainability, mainstream economics relies on the standard tools and assumptions of neo-classical growth theory. (See also Chapter 7 and Chapter 13.)

In contrast, what has been called the 'ecological' criterion for sustainability admits the likelihood that some of the important functions of the natural world cannot be replaced by man-made capital or human technology within any realistic time frame – if ever. In other words, man-made capital and engineering technology, no matter how sophisticated, cannot substitute for all of the essential services provided by natural capital, such as the hydrological cycle, or biological waste assimilation and detoxification. I think it is obvious that these environmental services, not to mention others including natural scenery and biodiversity, cannot be either recreated or replaced by man-made equivalents.

Nevertheless, I think it is a lot easier to identify unsustainable activities and trends than it is to define sustainability in a precise and operational manner. I use the word 'unsustainable' in the most literal sense; these trends cannot continue indefinitely (or even for very much longer, in some cases) without running into a natural limit. Here is a short list of unsustainable trends of truly global significance:

1) Damage to the stratospheric ozone layer caused by CFCs, allowing more short-wave ultra-violet radiation (UV–2) to reach the Earth's surface. This radiation has an adverse impact on many marine organisms that reproduce in shallow water (frogs, for example), not to mention causing skin cancer and eye damage in humans.
2) Buildup of greenhouse gases in the atmosphere with climate warming effects, resulting in shifts in precipitation patterns and storm tracks, increased probability of large storms, reduced snowpack at higher elevations, faster and earlier spring runoff with more damaging floods, increased probability of summer droughts and increased stress on forests and other natural ecosystems.
3) Sea level rise, a consequence of global warming, and a serious direct threat to low-lying coastal areas and estuaries, including the most fertile agricultural lands in the world (eg the Nile Delta, the Ganges-Brahmaputra Delta, the Mekong Delta).
4) Depletion of non-renewable natural resources, such as fossil fuels, fresh water, topsoil and some non-ferrous metals.
5) Acidification of the terrestrial environment and buildup of toxic elements and chemicals in soils and surface waters.
6) Increasing eutrophication of the Earth, due to sharply increasing the availability of certain bionutrients, especially nitrogen and sulfur. This is good for forest growth but very bad for coastal fisheries, for instance.
7) Loss of biodiversity as a storehouse of potentially valuable genetic information, especially for purposes of plant breeding for insect and disease resistance.

The above list of unsustainable trends is hardly exhaustive. But it is sufficient to make the essential point; sustainable growth may be hard to define, but unsustainability is visible all around us.

Population growth is also unsustainable. The slums of the world's mega-cities are holding zones for people who can no longer support themselves from the land and whom the cities can neither employ nor feed. It might be tempting to think of them (as Julian Simon does in *The Ultimate Resource* (1980)) as a potential source of bright ideas and a future market for goods. But, at the same time, one must recognize that slums breed crime and disease, not to mention social instability. Most other problems of the global environment cannot be solved if the world's population is not stabilized soon.

Technological optimists have unhesitatingly projected that early twentieth century rates of increase in agricultural productivity can and will continue into the indefinite future.[6] However, most agricultural experts are much less optimistic. The alarm has been raised once again, certainly on better grounds than in Malthus's time. Today there are no more new lands waiting for cultivation, and experts say that the potential increases in yield available from the use of chemical fertilizers and plant breeding have already been largely exhausted in the industrialized countries. The potential gains from wider application of traditional methods, for instance in China, are well worth seeking. But they are definitely limited. Erosion is carrying off topsoil four or five times faster than it is being created by natural processes, even in Europe and the US where soil conservation is practised. Elsewhere the problem is more acute. Moreover, non-renewable ground water (left over from the last glacial age) is already becoming seriously depleted or contaminated in many regions of the world – including the US Great Plains – where intensive irrigation cum chemical agriculture have been practised for a few decades.

The total cultivated area in the world has remained virtually constant for the last two decades. Some new lands are being cleared in a few places, but this is roughly compensated by the loss of formerly fertile land by erosion and desertification in other areas. Deforestation has now become an acute problem throughout the humid tropics, and most tropical forest soils are not very fertile to begin with. Once cleared, they are rapidly exhausted of nutrients by leaching as well as cropping. With regard to the possibility of continuing to increase the productivity of existing arable land, there is a continuing push to develop improved varieties and higher photosynthetic efficiencies. Biotechnology is now beginning to be harnessed to increase food production. There is optimistic talk of a second green revolution. But for some years past, global grain production per capita has actually been declining. Thus, significant incremental improvements in the productivity of the available farmland will be needed just to keep up with population growth.

Most environmentalists think in terms of localized ecosystems and regional biomes. The sum total of disturbances at this level is indeed a significant environmental problem, though individual cases tend to be geographically localized. However there are also global systems that are being dangerously disturbed by anthropogenic activity. Examples of global systems include the hydrological cycle and ocean currents.[7]

Two Dutch experts have prepared a summary table of quantifiable sustainability indicators (Table 9.1) that covers much of this ground in fairly simple fashion. (One need not accept every number in it as gospel; the authors acknowledge that it is a first attempt.) The notion of 'sustainable level' in regard to pollution, toxification, acidification, greenhouse gas buildup and so on is predicated on the idea that natural processes will compensate for some of the damage. For instance, natural weathering of rocks generates some alkaline materials that can neutralize acid. (Increased acidity will, however, increase the rate of weathering.) Similarly, it is assumed that some of the excess carbon dioxide produced by combustion processes may be absorbed in the oceans or taken up by accelerated photosynthetic activity in Northern forests. Some minerals (like aluminum and iron) can be mined more or less indefinitely, even though the highest quality ores will be exhausted first. Other mineral ores could be effectively exhausted, in the sense that recovery from minable ores would be too expensive to be worthwhile except for very specialized and limited uses. Copper might be an example of this kind, though not necessarily the best one.

Table 9.1 Sustainable Versus Expected Level of
Environmental Impact for Selected Indicators

Dimension/Indicator of Environmental Impact	Sustainable Level	Expected Level 2040	Desired Reduction	Scale
Depletion of Fossil Fuels				
• Oil	stock for 50 years	stock exhausted	85%	global
• Natural gas	stock for 50 years	stock exhausted	70%	global
• Coal	stock for 50 years	stock exhausted	20%	global
Depletion of Metals				
• Aluminum	stock for 50 years	stock for >50 years	none	global
• Copper	stock for 50 years	stock exhausted	80%	global
• Uranium	stock for 50 years	depends on use of nuclear energy	not quantifiable	global
Depletion of Renewable Resources				
Biomass	20% terrestrial animal biomass	50% terrestrial animal biomass	60%	global
	20% terrestrial primary production	50% terrestrial primary production	60%	global
Diversity of species	extinction of five species per year	365–65,000 species per year	99%	global
Pollution				
Emission of CO_2	2.6 gigatonnes carbon per year	13.0 gigatonnes carbon per year	80%	global
Acid deposition	400 acid equivalent per hectare per year	2400–3600 acid equivalent	85%	continental
Deposition nutrients	Phosphorus: 30 kg per hectare per year	No quantitative data	not quantifiable	national
	Nitrogen: 267 kg per hectare per year	No quantitative data	not quantifiable	national
Deposition of metals:				
• deposition of cadmium	2 tonnes per year	50 tonnes per year	95%	national
• deposition of copper	70 tonnes per year	830 tonnes per year	90%	national
• deposition of lead	58 tonnes per year	700 tonnes per year	90%	national
• deposition of zinc	215 tonnes per year	5190 tonnes per year	95%	national
Encroachment				
Impairment through dehydration	reference year 1950	no quantitative data	not quantifiable	national
Soil loss through erosion	9.3 billion tonnes per year	45–60 million tonnes per year	85%	global

Source: Weterings and Opschoor (1992) Table 6, p25

As regards renewable resources such as forests, fisheries and ground water, it has long been known that there is a level of exploitation that can be sustained indefinitely by scientific management, but that beyond that level harvesting pressures can drive populations down to the point where recovery may take decades, or may never occur at all. Many fisheries appear to be in this situation at present, notwithstanding the fact that sustainable levels are not very precisely known. Granted some uncertainty, it is nevertheless clear that sustainability would require significant reductions in current levels of consumption of some so-called renewables, including forests and fish taken from the oceans.

I have tried to make the point that technology as currently applied is taking us in the wrong direction. This is not to deny that increased dependence on human technological intervention will be necessary to achieve long-run eco-sustainability. For example, methods of artificially accelerating tree growth may compensate for some net decrease in the area devoted to plantation crops. Biotechnology has an important role to play in the future (despite some risks). Use of fertilizers and irrigation of the deserts of the world might do some harm but is unlikely to do more harm than good.

Having said this, in my view, eco-sustainability does *not* admit the acceptability of major climate changes, widespread desertification, deforestation of the tropics, accumulation of toxic heavy metals and non-biodegradable halogenated organics in soils and sediments, or sharp reductions in bio-diversity. Yet all of these changes are occurring, and they appear to be direct consequences of economic growth as it is occurring today and as it is conventionally defined. Unfortunately, the last point is arguable, which leads me to the next section.

THE ENVIRONMENT/DEVELOPMENT DILEMMA

The proposition has been set forth that economic growth, in general, is actually good for the environment. Proponents of this proposition assert that economic growth per se has been a significant factor in the improvements that have occurred in North America, Europe, and Japan over the past two decades. The empirical backing for this argument, as recently articulated,[8] is based on the 'inverted U' pattern that one sees if certain environmental pollution measures (such as smoke, sulfur dioxide, biological oxygen demand, chemical oxygen demand and contaminated water) are plotted on a scatter chart against GNP per capita. The poorest countries without any industrial base exhibit low levels of these types of pollution. The pollution level rises as more fuel and other resources are processed. As GNP per capita increases, the level of pollution also increases for a while because higher GNP is correlated with industrial development. However, as countries become still more prosperous, services begin to predominate over manufacturing, and the curves turn down again – hence the 'inverted U'. However, the empirical correlation between prosperity and environmental improvement at higher levels of GNP per capita only applies to a relatively small subset of indicators, notably the ones mentioned above. In some other cases (nitrogen oxides, chlorofluorocarbons) the relationship doesn't hold. For the majority of indicators (such as those listed in Table 9.1) there are no reliable data for most countries.

The inverted U argument is nevertheless taken seriously by many economists for a different reason, namely that environmental services such as clean air appear to be 'superior goods'. This means that as people get richer they will value the environment more and pay more to protect it better. People living in slums will drink contaminated water if they must choose between feeding their children and boiling their water. However, while this is doubtless true, it doesn't prove that economic growth is good for the environment.

I'd like also to mention another set of arguments by environmental 'contrarians' who still doubt (or claim to doubt) that there is a serious environmental problem that will not be solved by yet more economic growth. There are three primary assertions:

1) that the environment (in Western countries) is now in better shape than it was a few decades ago;
2) that environmental regulation costs more than it is worth; and
3) that continued growth, free markets and technological progress will automatically and painlessly solve any remaining problems.

The third contrarian assertion is the easiest to refute. It is sheer fantasy. I will discuss the problem of common property resources and the limitations of markets and market mechanisms more academically in the next section.

The second contrarian assertion is also easily contradicted by numerous economic analyses of the costs and benefits of specific regulatory programs. Admittedly, some of the improvements that have occurred could probably have been achieved far more efficiently by other means. For instance, if automobile manufacturers had been taxed on the basis of emissions from their vehicles, based on random tests, they would probably have developed a clean burning engine long ago that would have avoided the need for, and cost of, catalytic convertors.[9] Many economists believe that the last version of the US Clean Air Act (1990), if fully enforced, will cost much more than the value of any marginal benefits it could achieve. This is disputed, but in my opinion quite likely to be true.

Much could be done to rationalize and improve environmental regulation, using economic rather than legal instruments. The outstanding failure of environmental policy in the US to date, without doubt, has been the legislation known as CERCLA – the Comprehensive Environmental Response, Compensation and Liability Act, or Superfund – that was intended to finance the cleaning up of old toxic waste dumps. The idea behind it was to force those originally responsible, or their legal successors, to pay for the cleanup costs. There was no provision in the Act to compare the risk of leaving the site alone with the risk and cost of the cleanup.[10] Nor was there any mechanism for equitable allocation of costs. The law includes a provision known as 'joint and several responsibility' which means that anybody who ever used such a dump, or possibly even a bank that loaned money to somebody who used a dump, could be held liable – not just for their proportional share of the cost of cleanup, *but for all of it*. Needless to say, this legislative monstrosity has spawned a host of lawsuits and enriched many lawyers, while achieving very little. This particular environmental law, and a few others, do not satisfy any reasonable test of benefits versus costs. Yet the more influential environmental groups, for the most part, fiercely resist any modification of the Superfund legislation for fear that somehow it would open the floodgates to wholesale gutting of a whole range of other environmental protection measures that have been laboriously achieved.

As to the first of the above assertions, namely that the environment is in better shape thanks to economic growth but little thanks to regulation, here is the main evidence cited by the contrarians:

- forests are re-growing in parts of the Appalachians (Eastern US), where farmers and charcoal-burners once cut;

- eroded cotton plantations in the Southern US have given way to tree farms that feed the pulp and paper industry. The soil erosion has now all but stopped;
- most kinds of air pollution have decreased in the US. Lead pollution is the best example: it is down 90 per cent. Particulate emissions are also down significantly, along with carbon monoxide. Pittsburgh, Cleveland, Chicago and other industrial cities of the Midwest – and the same is true in Japan and Western Europe – are much less smoky than they once were; and
- the greatest environmental improvements since the 1960s have been in water pollution. The major rivers and lakes of North America, and also of Western Europe and Japan, are now much cleaner than they were two decades ago. Lake Erie is no longer a 'dead' lake, and there are fish – even salmon – once again in the Hudson, and the Thames.

The first success story was the regrowth of the Appalachian forests. It is true forests now cover the hills and that the deer population has exploded (because there are no more wolves or bobcats to prey on them). The same phenomena are visible, on a reduced scale, in Europe. This occurred mainly due to the substitution of iron for wood in shipbuilding and coal for charcoal in iron smelting, brick-making, and for other industrial purposes. The regrowth of the forests also occurred because the opening of transportation routes to the fertile Midwest made agriculture uneconomic in the hills.

The shift from cotton to tree plantations, and the consequent reduction in soil erosion, in the Southern states of the US occurred only because the original rich topsoil had been washed into the sea. Tree farms replaced cotton fields in Georgia, Alabama and Mississippi because the eroded land was – and is – literally worthless for other agricultural purposes. Monocultural tree farms are better than nothing, but they do not harbor diverse biological communities. I should add that reforestation is a local phenomenon. As regards the global picture, the World Wildlife Fund (WWF) has compiled the first detailed database. Global forest cover (defined as 40 per cent crown cover) has fallen from 50 per cent to 31 per cent, of which 10 per cent is tropical, 13 per cent is northern coniferous and 7 per cent is temperate broadleaved. Only 6 per cent of this total forested area is protected and the annual loss rate from deforestation is now 1 per cent per year. In the US, only 2 per cent of the original old growth forest remains uncut, and cutting has accelerated.

In the case of air pollution, the reduction in particulates and sulfur occurred partly as a consequence of the phasing out of coal as a fuel for domestic and most industrial purposes. Air pollution from automotive exhausts – except for lead – is only slightly lower in US cities than it was in 1970 and in most of the world it is much worse. The decline in lead pollution was entirely due to the federal ban on use of gasoline with tetraethyl lead by new passenger cars, which began in the early 1970s. However nitrogen oxide emissions have not fallen. Further progress was due to regulations, namely the Clean Air laws of the 1970s, which have been amended and tightened several times. In Europe, the availability of natural gas from the North Sea and from Russia has been the single biggest factor in reducing air pollution. Smoke control legislation, applied to electric power generating plants, comes second.

The improvement in water quality in North America came about for two reasons. First, government regulation forced communities to borrow large sums of money (subsidized by the federal authorities) to build sewage treatment plants. The story is similar in Europe and Japan, though salmon do not swim, as yet, in the Rhine or the

Elbe due to industrial and mine wastes. Second, government regulation forced industry to install water treatment facilities and/or to otherwise dispose of many wastes and pollutants that had formerly been dumped indiscriminately into rivers. In many cases, such as the chemical and metallurgical industries, the major change has been that pollutants formerly dumped without treatment are now concentrated into 'sludges' and buried in landfills. In a few cases industrial processes have been changed significantly to convert wastes into fuel or into salable by-products. The pulp and paper industry, once the most notorious of all polluters, is perhaps the best example of real progress in this area. Nowadays most of the so-called 'black liquor' (lignin waste) is burned to recover heat and chemicals. But this would not have happened without regulation. The banning of lead, DDT and other dangerously long-lived pesticides, polychlorinated biphenyls (PCBs) and CFCs was also entirely due to regulation or (to a lesser extent) voluntary changes by industry in the anticipation of future regulation.

To summarize: the favorable changes in our environment have occurred either because of regulation or because of technological developments (such as the avail-ability of natural gas and increasing electrification) that had no relation to environ-mental problems. I know of very few cases – if any – where totally unregulated competition in the private marketplace solved an environmental problem for its own sake. Technological alternatives sometimes emerge to solve environmental problems as a result of purely private responses, in *anticipation* of future regulatory or economic incentives imposed by government. Technology is not autonomous. It does not respond to social needs unless there is a customer, with cash in hand, willing to pay the price. In the case of environmental protection, the only paying customer (apart from a few foundations) is government itself or industry anticipating government regulation. That rule is unlikely to be repealed in the future.

To return to the question that was posed earlier: is economic development good for the environment? In brief, I think the answer is generally 'no'. Consider four stylized facts:

1) economic growth historically correlates closely with energy consumption (not to mention other resources), although the E/GDP ratio tends to decline in richer countries (see Fig. 10.1).
2) Most environmental problems, and many health problems, arise from pollution.
3) Harmful pollution is, for the most part, directly traceable to the use of fossil fuels and/or other materials, such as toxic heavy metals or chlorinated chemicals. In short, every material extracted from the environment is a potential waste, and it usually becomes an actual waste within months or a few years at most.
4) Most wastes that are disposed of in air or water are capable of causing harm to the environment, if not directly to human health.

Many environmentalists, and some environmental economists too, argue from these facts that sustainable development is a contradiction in terms. On the other hand, a large majority of business and political leaders appear to assume that the problems are real but minor and we should defer the serious cleanup efforts until our society is richer. According to this view, growth is the key to everything and minor changes in current technology and/or regulatory policy would suffice to overcome any known environmental threat. In fact, many environmentalists appear to believe that the most serious environmental threats we face are related to human health, viz contaminated water or food or skin cancer. Lesser or minor problems that get attention include forest die-back (*Waldsterben*), oil spills, dirty beaches, litter, haze, bad smells, noise, and so on. Few people worry about disturbances to the large scale bio-geochemical cycles, on the integrity of which the Earth's habitability rests.

In short, I don't fully agree with either of the standard positions with respect to sustainability. I don't think sustainable development is a contradiction in terms. Nor do I think it is a second-order problem that can be put off until we have more money. The major message of this book is that environmental protection is essential, not optional. But, at the same time, economic growth need not be antithetical to environmental protection. Ecologically sustainable growth is theoretically possible. But it is surely not what is happening; nor is it inevitable.

THE SHARP END: POLLUTION, DEPLETION, HEALTH AND WEALTH

People living in the wealthy and (relatively) under-populated OECD countries[11] haven't experienced the sharp end of environmental degradation. It is relatively easy, sitting in a window overlooking a well-tended park, to think that all these problems are being exaggerated by doomsayers. Besides, isn't nature perfectly able to recover from a little localized damage? There is another side of the story, however. People are dying of pollution now, in enormous numbers, just out of sight of the big new luxury hotels where the business elite gather. This phenomenon is being experienced today in many countries. In fact, it would be more accurate to say *most* countries.

This topic is more complicated than it seems just at first. The problem, in a nutshell, is that wealth for the few in developing countries is now being produced, in large part, not by any creative process but by adverse redistribution. To be specific, throughout the developing world natural wealth – such as rich agricultural land, ground water, mineral deposits and forests – is being appropriated (if not expropriated) by government agencies on behalf of the ruler's family and cronies and the MNCs, and the profits are being redistributed to the least deserving. Meanwhile, the dispossessed tribesmen and rural peasants – by the million – are being evicted, forced to work in mines or migrate to cities where they are unwanted and unfitted to work productively, starved, and exposed to air pollution and water contamination on a scale we in the West can scarcely imagine. The inequity of economic development has already been discussed at some length in the last chapter. The inequity of natural resource exploitation and environmental degradation deserves closer scrutiny.

I cannot summarize the environmental miseries of Afghanistan, Northeastern Brazil, Central America, China, Egypt, Haiti, India, Mexico, Nigeria, North Korea, Peru or the former USSR in a few paragraphs. I can only cite a few tell-tale statistics and try to make one overwhelmingly important point. The point is that apparent economic growth – even where it exists – is largely being paid for by degrading natural capital. This includes quantifiable components like minerals taken from the ground, virgin forests being cut and burned for charcoal or pulped into paper, topsoil being lost from farmland, and fisheries whose productivity has been depleted by over-fishing. To put it in domestic terms, the national account statistics assume that if you sell your furniture and your house, the proceeds are counted as part of current income. This is exactly what countries are doing.

All of these kinds of depletion can and should be accounted for in official national accounts statistics, but they are not (yet). As a consequence, GNP for many countries includes a large component of capital consumption – capital that is being depleted but not being replaced.[12] It means, of course, that GNP growth rates are being overstated by failing to allow for this depletion. Quantitative studies of the extent to which apparent GNP growth rates for some countries have been exaggerated by this omission have been carried out by Robert Repetto and his colleagues at the World Resources Institute in Washington DC, in collaboration with scholars in several countries. On the basis of a detailed quantitative analysis of Costa Rica, for instance, it was found that the asset value of forests and fisheries declined by US$4.1 billion (1985 Dollars) from 1970 to 1989, more than one year's GDP. Topsoil loss from erosion amounts to 13 per cent of the value added by livestock production, 17 per cent for annual crops and between 8 and 9 per cent for agricultural production overall. The traditional fishery has essentially been wiped out by over-fishing and pollution. Profits were negative in 1988, even valuing fishermen's time at the subsistence wage level. The Philippines and Indonesia exhibit similar phenomena. Depreciation of natural capital in Indonesia was in the neighborhood of 14 per cent of GDP in 1985, and rising steadily.[13] Recent studies suggest that depletion of forests, farm and grazing lands and water shortages amounted to between 5.5 and 9.5 per cent of China's GDP in 1990.[14]

But depletion of forests, fisheries and underground mineral resources is only a part of the problem; perhaps the least part. Another sort of depletion is occurring in those parts of the world where rapid industrialization is occurring without adequate environmental protection. To consider one example; people who live and work in heavily polluted air, as coal miners in Wales and West Virginia once did, and coal miners in the Northern Czech Republic, East Germany, Poland, the Donetz basin of Russia and coal mining regions of India and China still do, sacrifice years of potentially productive working life to silicosis and 'black lung' disease, not to mention bronchitis, emphysema, lung cancers and other debilitating illness. The economic cost in terms of lost working days is considerable. Workers in many coal mining regions of the world have an average life expectancy in the low 50s. Workers in some Chinese coal mines cannot work after the age of 36 (Smil, 1996).

While large new electric power plants nowadays generally incorporate electrostatic precipitators (ESPs) to remove the fly ash from the effluent stream, flue gas desulfurization is almost unknown in these countries. Yet all hydrocarbon fuels average 1–3 per cent sulfur by weight, and some of the coals in Southern China, for instance, average 4 per cent or more. Worse, most of this low-grade coal from local mines is not burned in large efficient electric power plants (which get the best quality coal), but in small factory boilers or household stoves which burn the fuel inefficiently and remove none of the ash or the sulfur. Thus several hundred million Chinese – not to mention Russians, Poles, Czechs, Indians, Turks and others – are constantly exposed to a dense pall of sulfurous smoke. It is very hard to attach realistic economic values to this, and other forms of pollution. However, based on very conservative valuations of hospital costs and lost work days by economically productive adults only, Smil has estimated the cost at between 1.7 and 2.5 per cent of GDP for China in 1990 (Smil, 1996). Estimating costs more liberally would increase these totals considerably. They also increase year by year.

THE ROLE OF MARKETS

The present economic system is institutionally unlikely to cure itself. Here I am taking direct issue with the assumption, shared by most business and financial writers and some conservative economists, that free competitive markets will automatically create the necessary incentives (via price signals) to end unsustainable practices. This touching faith arises from a central thesis of neoclassical economics, namely that, given the right incentives – prices – and enough time, technology is capable of finding a way to avoid essentially *any* physical resource bottleneck.

I am not denying that markets often function quite well within their domain. For instance, alarmists since Thomas Malthus have warned of the forthcoming exhaustion of natural resources, from land and water to minerals and fuels. Yet, with the sole exception of forest products (and land itself), prices of most classes of commodities and exhaustible natural resources have actually tended to decline continuously over the decades. This fact stands as a continuing reproach to those who underestimate the power of efficient markets to call forth innovative activity.

However the market is never *perfectly* competitive, nor does it encompass *all* of the environmental goods – or services – that need to be preserved. The last point is the crucial one. Consider the environmental services such as air, rainfall, the ozone layer or the carbon cycle. These services are essential to the continuation of all life on Earth. They are indivisible in that they cannot be subdivided into small pieces that can be individually owned or exchanged. They are common property. They cannot be bought or sold as such in any marketplace. Scarcity of these environmental services does not raise their prices because there are no prices, and hence does not inhibit demand. When demand exceeds capacity in the case of a common property resource, the result is degradation and destruction. This is the 'tragedy of the commons'.[15] In fact, when a common property resource is scarce, as is now the case for a number of fisheries as well as many of the large mammals such as great whales, tigers and rhinos, there is likely to be an intensified competition to capture the last few that remain.

For all these reasons, the standard economic model of market-driven resource allocation does not apply to environmental services. In principle, when market transactions result in damage losses to third parties external to the main transaction, those who suffer the damage should be compensated by those who gain by the transaction. The market price of whatever good is exchanged must be high enough to allow for such compensation, in addition to production costs and profits. The higher price would also inhibit the demand for such goods, creating economic incentives to minimize emissions or damages. This notion has become popularized as the polluter pays principle, or PPP. However, the principle would not have had to be formalized if it were built-in to the market system. In fact, PPP is an ideal, not an actuality.

For instance, a number of quantitative studies using a variety of methodologies have suggested that the real social (eg health) costs of using coal are several times higher than the current market price. The same is true for gasoline, in the US at least, and probably also in Europe. Hence the existing market price is far below what it should be to optimize the balance of benefits and damage costs from use. It is difficult to determine the right prices in cases like this where the market price does not reflect all the social and environmental costs of use. Practical difficulties abound. Damage costs are much greater in densely populated urban areas, for instance, than they are in rural areas. Worse, a number of governments – including Germany and China – actually subsidize the mining of coal rather than taxing it heavily, as they should to implement the PPP.[16] The reason, of course, is that the Chinese government wants to encourage industry and coal is the main source of energy for industry in China. In Germany, the coal miners' unions are politically powerful and they use their power to protect their own jobs regardless of all other considerations.

To summarize, it cannot be assumed technology will come to the rescue in the public domain of common property resources, where normal market mechanisms of profit and loss don't function effectively. It follows that, to achieve long-run eco-sustainability, governments will have to intervene much more vigorously to create the missing economic incentives and to correct the distortions that decades of growth-oriented policies have introduced into markets. However, I do not share the conclusions of some environmentalists that the only answer is an end to growth itself. In fact, it seems to me that a no-growth policy is a non-starter. It would be politically unacceptable to the developing world, even if the Americans, Europeans and Japanese could be persuaded to adopt it. However, as I have said, I am convinced that economic growth and a clean and healthy environment can be reconciled (see Chapter10.)

The point is that current economic and environmental trends, supported and encouraged by current tax and trade policies, are definitely antithetical to ecological sustainability. As far as trade is concerned, the first order effects of reducing barriers to trade are clear. They are: i) increasing goods traffic; and ii) continued exploitation of primary extractive activities in remote areas at the expense of secondary and recycling activities in the importing countries that might otherwise compete with them. Both of these effects, in turn, are antithetical to the environment.

To take one example, consider the impact of goods traffic. It is hard to believe (but true) that German potatoes are currently shipped, by truck, across the Alps to Italy for washing, and then shipped back to Germany for frying. Dutch pigs, fed on manioc and other feeds imported from Thailand, are also shipped in trucks across the Alps to Italy where they are slaughtered and processed into Parma ham, which is then sold all over the world. The biggest fishing port on the Adriatic coast of Italy is now totally dependent on imported fish brought by refrigerator ship from the South Pacific, the local fisheries having long since been depleted. Austrian attempts to restrict heavy truck traffic across the Brenner Pass – the only all-weather pass currently capable of carrying such traffic – because of local noise and pollution problems have been strongly opposed by the Germans and Italians as restraint of trade. One of the reasons the Swiss elected not to join the European Union was for fear of being forced by EU rules to allow more such trans-Alpine traffic, thus permitting heavy trucks to pollute their ecologically fragile high valleys. The Swiss are building a major new railway tunnel instead, to accommodate future north–south goods traffic.

As regards the second environmental effect of trade, one consequence of reducing trade barriers is that it is getting easier for rich countries to export their industrial (and other) wastes. This is a rapidly growing business, despite international agreements restricting it. Somewhat surprisingly, perhaps, the 'green' Germans are the world's biggest exporters of wastes, partly to Poland and other parts of Eastern Europe, and partly to more distant countries like Indonesia, where German packaging wastes, for instance, are sold as raw materials – thus undercutting local scavengers and reducing the incentives for German industry to develop uses for these materials, as was originally intended.

The lowering of trade barriers and transport costs has favored large centralized producers with good access to local raw materials and ocean shipping. By the same token, these factors have reduced the effectiveness of environmental protection laws and reduced incentives to develop efficient methods of re-use, repair, renovation, remanufacturing, and recycling materials in a local region. Obviously, environmental protection regulations are harder to enforce, and 'take back' legislation that encourages manufacturers to be responsible for the final disposal of their products is harder to justify when manufacturers are located far away. I will return to this point again in Chapter 10.

Economic development along standard lines is not good for the environment. The invisible hand of the market does not necessarily have a green thumb. On the contrary, increasing labor productivity as a response to perceived needs for increasing competitiveness means decreasing labor intensiveness by further increasing capital intensiveness, materials intensiveness and energy intensiveness. Increasing resource productivity, on the contrary, would imply a reverse of all of the above.

SUMMARY AND IMPLICATIONS

This chapter makes several important points. The first of them is that the natural environment provides essential services that cannot be replaced by man-made capital or technology. Critical environmental problems cannot be prevented or solved by technological intervention alone. True, technology can make a difference, mainly by reducing the rate at which we approach the point of planetary no return. Renewable energy technologies, such as photovoltaics, would help, and eliminating the use of fossil fuels would also help a lot in reducing the rates of acidification and toxification. But many of the projected environmental damages are irreversible – or, at least, very long lasting – and neither known nor imaginable technology can reverse them. There is no conceivable technology to lower the sea level once it has risen. No technology can restore the glaciers or the icecaps once they melt. There is no technology to remove greenhouse gases from the atmosphere, to manufacture ozone in the stratosphere, to detoxify soils or to replace fossil groundwater or eroded soils. Above all, extinct species cannot be recreated, except in Hollywood.

In short, technology is still a minor player, at best, in the area of environmental repair and rehabilitation. Even where we know technology can help (solar energy, for instance), it will not come to the rescue of the environment automatically. Established interests may well gang up to oppose and delay it. As always, the potential losers know who they are, and they have financial power and political clout. The potential winners are disorganized and do not know who they are. The contest is uneven. A technology like PV, that could be competitive very soon on a level economic playing field, may be delayed for many years by powerful forces that combine to tilt the playing field (called the 'free market') in their own favor.

A second major point is that environmental protection and economic growth along current trajectories are indeed antithetical. It is not true – as has been claimed by the World Bank, among others – that uninhibited growth is good for the environment. It is true that there have been some environmental gains in the last three decades, especially in the richest countries. But, on closer examination, there is no serious case for arguing that these environmental improvements occurred because of economic growth. In the US they are mainly the result of one of three things: the substitution of coal for wood as a fuel for industry in the nineteenth century; the increased availability of natural gas (to replace coal) as a domestic fuel in the postwar period; or direct regulation. The two technological substitutions in question may have contributed to economic growth, but they were not consequences of it. In developing countries like China, the relationship between economic growth and environmental damage is far more negative. Depreciation of natural capital, which ought to be deducted from GDP but is not, typically ranges from 3 to 10 per cent of GDP in many developing countries. Health costs, paid for by reduced life expectancy and lost working time, add to this total. These costs are directly related to industrialization without adequate attention to environmental protection.

The third important point is that unfettered market forces have not, and will not, create technology to solve environmental problems except by accident. It is hard to find any reason to think that 'painless' market-driven technological progress will eliminate greenhouse gases such as CO_2 unless some other non-polluting source of energy can be shown to be cheaper and more profitable. For instance, the oil industry is currently secure in its oligopolistic dominance. This is partly the result of the bounty of nature, partly a legacy of past and present subsidies to producers of oil and to users of motor vehicles[17] and partly a consequence of the sheer financial muscle of the combined oil and auto industries. These industries are well protected from potential competitors such as electric vehicles or photovoltaic hydrogen-powered fuel cells.

The oil industry expects to go on indefinitely, drilling more and deeper wells even in the last Arctic wilderness areas, the last tropical jungles and under the ice. The industry has no serious plans to develop technological substitutes for fossil fuels or fossil fuel burning vehicles. Its current strategy in fending off critics is to insist that any change would be enormously costly, and that no change is warranted, pending scientific proof of need. The energy industry is much more likely to resist and obstruct the introduction of promising new technologies, such as renewables and fuel cells, than to promote them. The most worrying possibility is that these fossil fuel giants will buy up the competition before it can get going.

NOTES

1   Most of this chapter has been taken from a paper originally written five years ago at IIASA and since modified several times, most recently for the UN University, where it has become the introductory chapter of a multi-author volume entitled *Eco-Restructuring*, of which I was the editor-in-chief and which should appear in 1997. Material herein is reproduced with permission.
2   This was true in Europe, at least. In China and India human muscles probably played a major role, though quantitative data are lacking.
3   This is a strange irony, because Malthus was on their side; his political target was the British Poor Law system, which provided indiscriminate doles to large families. Malthus condemned this system of bounties on the grounds that it tended to encourage excess births and thus to aggravate the very problems it was supposed to alleviate. The current right-wing Republican attack on welfare is based on precisely the same economic reasoning. To compound the irony, Malthus is credited with being the first to formulate the law of diminishing returns as applied to agriculture. Admittedly he did not call it by that name, and may not have fully realized its significance.

4 From electrolysis of water, using PV cells.
5 The impact of this report triggered the creation of a UN Commission on Environment and Development (UNCED), chaired by Maurice Strong of Canada. This finally culminated with a global environmental summit in Rio de Janeiro in June 1992 and produced many documents, including a global plan of action entitled *Agenda 21* (Strong, 1992).
6 For a super-optimistic view see Kahn et al, 1976; Kahn, 1984; and Simon et al, 1995.
7 Phosphorus is the other nutrient element that is required in amounts greater than the Earth's crust normally contains. It is not recycled biologically, however, but accumulates on the ocean floors where it is recycled by ocean currents and by tectonic action. If the Earth ever ceased to be geologically active, the land surface would eventually run out of phosphorus.
8 Notably in the 1992 World Bank *World Development Report* (World Bank, 1993).
9 Honda actually did avoid the use of convertors for some time with its CVCC engine in the 1970s. Ford and Peugeot had both invested hundreds of millions of dollars on an advanced clean-burn design that would have made convertors unnecessary. Greenpeace undermined this effort by a publicity campaign that forced Ford and Peugeot to put convertors on every car. Greenpeace hailed this (like Brent Spar) as a great environmental victory. It was actually a victory for the catalyst industry.
10 A notorious example is a site in Aspen, Colorado, a famous resort, where a number of houses had been built on land contaminated by mine spoils from an old lead mine. No health problems attributable to the mine wastes have ever been identified, nor was there any evidence that residents had higher lead concentrations in their blood than others. Yet, having been identified as a site, and over the strong objections of the residents, the county was forced to produce a plan for decontamination which would have involved moving the houses, digging up all the old mine waste, and shipping it to another site by truck, where it would be reburied 'safely'. It is quite obvious that the so-called decontamination and reburial, in this case, would expose a number of workers to dust and generally accomplish nothing useful at great cost. Unfortunately, the law contains no provision for a sensible compromise. Neither the EPA officials nor the local officials have any discretion in the matter. Nor is there any provision in the law under which a site, once on the list, can ever be removed from it.
11 Obviously this does not apply to Japan, nor to parts of Europe, especially the low countries, Western Germany and Northern Italy.
12 The UN Statistics Office and several national governments are working on a new system of green national accounts that is supposed to rectify some of the omissions in the existing statistics. Meanwhile, governments (and the World Bank) continue to use the old statistics and to judge their relative performance thereby.
13 Indonesia is a major oil and gas producer; these accounted for much of the country's income during the 1970s and 1980s. But the statistical problem is complicated by the fact that new discoveries are treated as additions to resource stocks – which they are not. In 1974 reported Indonesian oil reserves increased very sharply (apparently due to changes in US tax laws) resulting in a statistical 'blip'.
14 See Smil, 1996, and several other studies cited therein.
15 The reference is to a famous article by Garett Hardin (1968).
16 The first to suggest the use of taxes to correct market failures was the Cambridge economist, Cecil Pigou. Such taxes are often referred to as 'Pigovian' taxes.
17 Subsidies, direct and indirect, to automotive transportation have been conservatively estimated at US$300 billion in the US alone. They include direct subsidies extraction (the depletion allowance), subsidies to local and state road building and maintenance, military expenditures to protect the lifeline to Middle Eastern sources, costs of health care to uninsured road accident victims, free parking, health damage (and costs) due to air pollution. Other environmental damages are not included. See MacKenzie et al, 1992; also Roodman, 1996.

Chapter 10
Eco-restructuring for Sustainability

INTRODUCTION

In the last several chapters I have focused on unsustainable trends and looming crises. The dominant theme has been that economic growth (of the standard kind) is now being expected to solve the very problems that it has largely created. These problems are not independent; nor can they be solved independently; they are tightly interlinked. The prospect for business as usual is gloomy. But is our situation hopeless? The answer to this is 'no'. Eco-restructuring is needed, without doubt.[1] There will be many difficulties. But humans are an ingenious, adaptable race. We have the intelligence to analyze alternatives and the collective ability to look ahead. I see this as a time of opportunity. For the first time in history, it seems to me, we humans are beginning to develop the knowledge, institutions and policy instruments to enable us to take control of our own destiny. This is a grand generalization, admittedly. It needs a good deal of justification and many caveats. The knowledge and policy instruments I mention are far from fully developed. Nevertheless, I think we can begin the process of identifying feasible technological paths and, above all, least cost strategies – if not win–win strategies – for conversion to a sustainable path. This chapter and the next two focus not on problems as such, but on possible strategies for change.

ECO-RESTRUCTURING AS A STRATEGY

For all the reasons noted in Chapters 5–9, a completely new economic strategy is needed. For simplicity this strategy can be called 'radical dematerialization'. In more sober language, the new strategy must be a gradual but massive reverse substitution of human labor for fossil energy and physical substances extracted from the environment. We need more jobs and less waste. Fortunately, the radical dematerialization strategy is also the most effective possible long-term green strategy, since a radical cutback in material and energy inputs to economic processes is the only sure way of cutting back on wastes and pollutants that are beginning to overwhelm the assimilative capacity of the environment.

To recapitulate: the West, with under 20 per cent of the world's population, consumes 80 per cent of its resources. Given moderately optimistic assumptions about economic development and the spread of literacy and family planning, the world's current population (5.5 billion) is almost sure to double before finally stabilizing. The implications are uncomfortably clear. A middle class US or European standard of living for 9–11 billion people, given current technology, implies something like a tenfold increase in aggregate material and energy consumption.

Yet humans are already exploiting, if not fully utilizing, 40–50 per cent of the terrestrial biomass. Humans are already mobilizing other natural resources at an unnatural and unsustainable rate. It is difficult to avoid the conclusion that a ten-fold increase would push the limits of resilience of the biosphere far beyond prudent bounds. Already we see ominous indications that global balances are being disturbed: acids and toxic chemicals are accumulating in the soil; the stratospheric ozone layer is under attack; climate warming from greenhouse gases in the atmosphere is more and more apparent; the sea level is rising; parts of the Antarctic ice are cracking; tropical deforestation is accelerating and deserts are spreading. In short, continued economic development is essential. Yet continued economic development along present lines is ecologically unaffordable.

This means that sustainability implies radical change. To put it in a nutshell, to allow some room for increased per capita use of the world's material/energy resources in the poorer countries, the rich industrialized countries will have to cut back aggregate use of these resources drastically. To express this imperative as a single round number: the industrialized world may have to cut its material consumption per unit of GDP by as much as 90 per cent – a factor of ten – over the next two generations. This implies either a reduced standard of living or a truly radical change in the structure of demand and a sharp increase in the productivity of materials and energy.

I am sure that this is not an impossible goal, at least from the technical perspective. But the goal cannot be met by incrementalism, still less by business as usual. It will require a major effort (in which government must take a leading role) to close the materials cycle. The cowboy economy, in which resources were cheap and labor was scarce, is a thing of the past. We must shift very quickly to a 'spaceship economy' in which resources are used again and again.[2] Most primary materials extraction and processing industries will have to be phased out because the Earth cannot tolerate the quantities of mining, industrial and post-consumer waste that a ten-fold expansion of our present rate of throughput would entail. Instead, materials-intensive products will have to be redesigned for repair, re-use, renovation and upgrading, remanufacturing and – as a last resort – recycling. Dissipative uses of many materials will have to be phased out.

The sustainable economy of the next century will have to be almost entirely based on services. This is not to say that material goods – especially capital goods and durables – will no longer be needed. It means, however, that firms will no longer be able to sell products to final consumers. Instead, they will sell the services of those products, while retaining the ownership (and long-term responsibility) for the product itself. Product responsibility and take back laws will become universal. Eventually, leasing and remanufacturing will become the norm for durables.

The basic reason for this long-term imperative is that in no other way can profit incentives – which are essential for economic efficiency – be consistent with long-term eco-sustainability. A firm that sells material products is motivated to sell as much as possible to keep its factories busy. Under present conditions manufacturers' profits are maximized when throughput is maximized. This is a consequence of economies of scale. It is also an essential part of the growth paradigm. On the other hand, a firm that makes its profit by selling immaterial services (no matter that the services are partly or wholly produced by machines and equipment) is highly motivated to minimize costs by designing its machines and equipment for long life, easy repairability and easy remanufacturability. Ergo, firms must learn, or be induced, to sell services, not products as such.

Let me reiterate that I believe that a tenfold increase in resource productivity at the aggregate (national) level is certainly possible via the service strategy. But it will not be achieved painlessly. There will be losers, as well as winners. And the likely losers know exactly who they are, whereas the future winners do not. Those who are threatened will resist change. Some of them will have to be compensated. It is the social, economic, and political challenge that is much more serious and more difficult. It will require unprecedented collaboration between business and government. In both cases, a new and more sophisticated awareness of the nature of the problems (and opportunities) is also needed.

NARROWING THE ISSUES

A number of supplementary questions deserve comment. For example: are there any feasible strategies, and implementable means, of bringing global population growth to an end without a crash? Can it be done without undue sacrifice of civil liberty, government coercion, war or epidemic? Which of the approaches that have been suggested would involve the least economic cost and/or the least conflict with deeply held religious beliefs? Having raised the question, however, I propose to avoid any attempt to answer directly. It is enough to point out that this particular issue is primary: unless the population problem is solved, none of the other problems can be solved. Luckily, there are indications that global birthrates are already falling.

Another important set of issues is the technical question: how is the postulated tenfold increase in resource productivity to be achieved? What are the technological possibilities that would be compatible with long-run economic and ecological sustainability? Is it important, now, to delineate a plausible set of technological fixes? The viewpoint of the business and government establishment, of course, is that current technologies (including nuclear power) are not causing irreparable harm in the first place and will therefore suffice for the foreseeable future. I strongly disagree. Yet, I equally disagree with the opposite implication: that technological solutions are impossible. This conclusion has been strongly and somewhat dogmatically asserted in the past by some environmentalists of the 'no growth' school. What may be new, here, is my assertion that current technologies cannot satisfy the requirements of eco-sustainability, but that there are feasible alternatives that may do so.

Standard economic growth theory tends to assume that the technologies in use represent the optimal choices (see Chapter 13). This would be true if the economy were in a static equilibrium. Standard economic theory also tends to assume that technological progress is automatic, exogenous and cost-free and that it drives economic growth in that hypothetical equilibrium state. In contrast, one could argue that the economy is not in, or very close to, static equilibrium and that there are many unexploited win–win opportunities to combine profit with dematerialization and reduced pressure on the environment.[3] However, it is also important to reiterate that technological solutions will not necessarily emerge automatically under current policies and conditions. Market mechanisms do not function in domains where there is no private property and no profit potential. Where protection of common property resources is concerned, public policy must intervene.

Market mechanisms can be effectively harnessed by public policy; indeed, one way in which they may already be operating, although thus far the effects have not been seen as generally applicable, is the changing legal concept of product liability. Until the 1950s the burden of proof was squarely on the consumer. In several landmark cases the California Supreme Court effectively shifted the burden. The caveat emptor doctrine that formerly laid the burden entirely on the buyer has now been largely abandoned. It is no longer necessary to establish that the manufacturer was wilfully negligent. It is widely accepted that if a consumer is injured by a faulty product, or even one that is misused because of inadequate protection or labeling, the manufacturer will have to pay.

Thus far, product liability has been used in the US as a means of recovering civil damages against firms that have produced or marketed unsafe products. The threat of product liability litigation has become a significant deterrent to radical innovation in some fields, but it has also undoubtedly forced manufacturers to be much more careful about manufacturing and labeling.

A subtler change in legal doctrine began with the class action suits against asbestos manufacturers and others whose manufacturing process, or product, might have caused health problems to employees, even if the extent of the risk was not known at the time. Lawsuits against manufacturers of silicone breast implants have extended the realm of potential liability. Firms that have sold the products are now being forced to pay enormous sums into trust funds. The legal doctrine embodied in the US Superfund law extends potential liability in another way. Under this law, firms that dumped toxic or hazardous wastes in the past, in ways that were perfectly legal at the time, may be retroactively forced to pay the costs of cleanup. Indeed, they may be forced to pay costs on behalf of others who bore greater responsibility but who are no longer identifiable or accessible.

The point I am making here is that a firm may be held liable in the future for actions that are legal and acceptable under current law. It may also (as under CERCLA) be held liable for the actions of others. It is therefore not beyond the bounds of imagination to suppose that, in the future, firms may be held liable for environmental damage caused by its suppliers. I can certainly imagine future class action suits against, for example, food processors who sell canned tuna fish caught by environmentally unacceptable means. In short, any product is not only a potential waste but also a potential legal liability. The best way to avoid such liabilities in the long run is to produce and sell only services, retaining products as capital assets. Firms will be increasingly pushed into thinking along these lines by their legal counsel, insurance carriers, and also by their accountants and auditors. Accountants are increasingly being forced to allow for potential future liabilities in calculating net worth, for instance.

LIMITS TO RECYCLING?

The next question might be: is there any fundamental technological limit (other than the second law of thermodynamics) to the energy and materials productivities that can be achieved in the long run? Is there any fundamental limit to the long-run efficiency of materials recycling? It seems to me that the latter question can best be addressed theoretically by putting it in the negative sense: are there any fixed minimum materials/ energy requirements to produce useful goods and services for humans? Or, are there fundamental limits to the amount of service (or welfare) that can be generated from a given energy and/or material input? If there is no fixed relationship between primary energy or materials requirements and GDP, then there is no such limit. In this case, one would have to conclude that energy (exergy) intensities and materials intensities can presumably be reduced without any fixed limit. In this case it follows that there is, in principle, no theoretical maximum to the quantity of final services – that is, economic welfare in the traditional sense – that can be produced within the market framework from a given physical resource input. It follows, too, that there is no physical limit (except that imposed by the second law of thermodynamics) to the theoretical potential for energy conservation and materials recycling.

This restatement is quite critical to the fundamental case for optimism today. However, it is not a mainstream view among engineers, business leaders, or even economists, at present. In common with the World Commission on Environment and Development (WCED), virtually all of these groups regard continuing economic growth as both necessary and possible. However, the implication that economic growth can and must be permanently delinked from energy and materials use is far from generally accepted among engineers, business leaders and government leaders, despite its near-universal acceptance among economic theorists.

This is still an area of sharp disagreement. The politically powerful extractive industry and its legion of acolytes argue strongly for linkage. They insist that economic growth is impossible without increasing supplies of natural resources (especially fossil fuels). For instance, the following quote is taken from a Mobil Corp public service advertisement:

> *No doubt about it, we all need to be careful of the amount of energy we use. But as long as this nation's economy needs to grow, we are going to need energy to fuel that growth. ... For the foreseeable future, there are no viable alternatives to petroleum as the major source of energy ... Simply put, America is going to need more energy for all its people*
>
> Source: *New York Times*, April, 1991.

In short, a lot of interest groups are taking positions that are internally inconsistent. It means they have not thought through the logical consequences of their assumptions. In fact, I think something like an existence proof is needed to demonstrate that there are feasible technologies which, if adopted, could end our current dependence on fossil fuels and substantially close the materials cycle. The next section takes a closer look.

ENERGY CONSERVATION: ARE THERE LIMITS?

In principle, any such fixed relationship between energy/materials use and economic activity would be quite inconsistent with fundamental axioms of neoclassical economic theory. Economists generally argue for, and assume, general substitutability of all factors of production. Economists who have been quick to attack neo-Malthusians for

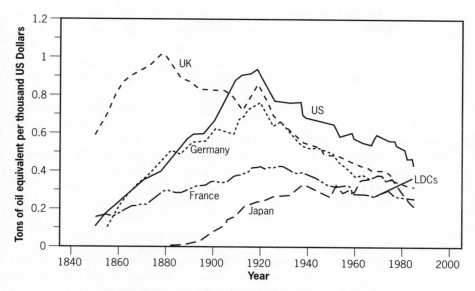

Figure 10.1 Long-Term Trends in Energy Intensity

unjustified worry about natural resource scarcity should be equally optimistic about the potential for energy savings by increased conservation and technological substitution. Unfortunately, this has not been the case up to now.

Optimism in regard to the potential for energy/materials conservation – or increasing energy/materials productivity – is also justified by recent history. The energy intensity of GNP (E/GNP ratio) has been declining more or less continuously for many decades in the case of the advanced industrialized countries (Figure 10.1). Past experience suggests that this ratio tends to increase for countries that are in the early stages of industrialization, only to reach a peak and decrease later. This is the inverted-U phenomenon mentioned earlier. Moreover, countries industrializing later have lower peaks than countries that industrialized earlier. Lower energy intensity reflects the shift from heavy industry to high-tech and services. The trend would almost certainly continue in any case. It can probably be accelerated significantly by appropriate policy changes.

The E/GNP ratio is partly related to the thermodynamic efficiency with which the economy uses energy. For this purpose, it is convenient to define the 'second law' efficiency – or, in European parlance, the exergy efficiency – with which energy is converted from primary sources to final services.[4] Electricity is currently generated and delivered to homes with an overall efficiency of about 34 per cent in the US. This figure has increased only slightly in recent years. Efficiency in less developed countries (LDCs) is significantly lower, implying greater room for improvement. Energy experts generally agree that by the year 2050 this might increase to something like 55 per cent – 60 per cent for steam-electric plants, taking advantage of higher temperature (ceramic) turbines, combined cycles, co-generation, and so on. Energy is currently used very inefficiently to create final consumer services, as compared to the first stage of energy conversion and distribution. The problem is that energy is lost and wasted at each step of the chain of successive conversions, from crude fuels to intermediates, to finished goods, to final services. For instance, conventional incandescent lights (converting electricity to white light) are only 7 per cent efficient, in the sense that only 7 per cent of the electricity goes into producing visible light; the rest is wasted in the form of useless heat. The new compact fluorescent lights are about fivefold better, or 35 per cent efficient. But they are not yet widely deployed, partly because they are still rather bulky and expensive, even though they produce light very economically. There is still some way to go.[5] Moreover, lighting fixtures are typically deployed very inefficiently, in the sense that most of the light does not illuminate anything that contributes to human comfort or well-being.

Taking the argument a bit further, most light fixtures provide too little illumination where it is really wanted (say on the page of the book you are reading). Overall, the efficiency of producing electric light where it is wanted is pretty low, probably less than 1 per cent in terms of the electric power consumed. If pure 'cold' light was provided precisely where and as needed for comfort, the amount of power needed would be about one-hundredth of the amount now used. Of course, the generation of electricity itself is only about 34 per cent efficient on average.

Based on arguments along these lines, I have estimated that the overall efficiency of energy use by the US in 1970 was somewhere in the range 2.5–3 per cent, and that it had risen to perhaps 3–3.5 per cent by the early 1980s.[6] This means that the final services provided by the economy (heat, light, transport, cooking, entertainment, and so on) are currently obtained by the expenditure of 30–40 times as much energy as would theoretically be necessary to achieve the same results in the most efficient possible way. Western Europe and Japan are both a little bit more efficient (in the sense defined above) than the US, but still very inefficient. Eastern Europe, the former USSR, and China, on the other hand, are considerably less efficient than the US.[7] For the world as a whole, it is likely that the overall efficiency with which fuel energy (exergy) is converted into final services is extremely low – probably below 3 per cent.

This being so, there is no fundamental technical or economic reason why end-use efficiency could not be doubled, tripled or even quadrupled in the course of the next half century or so. If end use efficiency were tripled, the world would still be using energy with an overall efficiency of less than 10 per cent, which is hardly an upper limit. And it is important to remember that I have postulated *no* change in the mix of final services demanded by consumers. In reality, of course, there is every likelihood that the mix will change. Current trends suggest that low-energy entertainment and communications services (based on computers and information technology, or IT) will substitute for at least some of the materials- and energy-intensive products and services currently being consumed.

While a comprehensive discussion of the technological alternatives cannot be attempted in a book such as this, I believe that many technologically and economically feasible possibilities really do exist.[8] Consider personal automobiles. One of the main reasons the US uses more energy than Europe or Japan is that Americans own more cars and use their cars more. This is partly because of greater distances, spread-out cities and low population density. It is also partly because of lack of alternative modes of transport. And finally, it is because of very low gasoline prices. If the average car were slightly smaller and considerably lighter, with a different engine, more efficient transmission, better tires and better aerodynamics, fleet average fuel economy could easily be doubled (or more) without significant sacrifice of comfort, safety or performance. This would cut overall fuel consumption per vehicle-km by

50 per cent. This is a comparatively modest improvement. In fact, a super-efficient lightweight 'hypercar' has been proposed that would be capable of increasing fuel economy by over fivefold as compared to the current US fleet average, with no reduction in performance, safety or comfort.[9]

The average US car travels about 15,000 miles (25,000 km) per year, carrying an average of 1.2 passengers. Postulate a combination of improvements in alternative modes of transport, 'piggy-backing' of cars by trucks or trains over densely travelled network links, strong encouragement of car pooling and ride sharing, restrictions on road use during rush hours by single-occupancy vehicles, and so on. Given a combination of these modest innovations, one can imagine that each passenger car travels only 7500 miles (12,500 km) per year carrying 1.8 passengers. Taken together, all the above changes in usage patterns would cut fuel consumption per car by three-quarters (75 per cent) and fuel consumption per passenger-km by five-sixths (83 per cent). Suppose, in addition, that just one third of the vehicles – the urban fraction – were electrified and that they consumed neither fossil fuel nor electric power from fossil fuels. This would bring the overall saving in fossil fuels up to eight-ninths (89 per cent). In other words, the combination of several modest technological changes and innovative transportation policies *could* reduce fossil fuel consumption by private cars ninefold to just 11 per cent of the current level. Nor is that by any means an upper limit to the potential for savings. The 'hypercar' would go much further. All of these changes except electrification have been or are being implemented already in various places around the world. None is extraordinarily radical. Even the electrification of urban vehicles is being considered very seriously in France, among other countries.

The extent of opportunities for energy/materials conservation is generally underestimated. This happens because narrowly focused energy analysts have only calculated the thermodynamic efficiency of producing finished materials or final forms of energy, such as electric power or mechanical work (applied to an automobile drive shaft, for instance). This is very misleading. It neglects opportunities for savings and efficiency gains in the production of final services, such as personal transportation from power at the drive shaft, or lighting from electricity provided to the light bulb. These opportunities are now probably much greater than the opportunities for efficiency gains in the energy conversion process per se. Combining the two types of efficiency gains it can be seen that the potential is still very great.

WHAT ABOUT THE AUTOMOBILE?

It is important to raise a final but crucial question: among the technological fixes postulated above, is there one (or more) trajectory that is also inexpensive to consumers, and/or even profitable to producers and service providers? Can the needed technology, together with the needed institutional changes, be harnessed at modest, or even negative, cost? In short, are there any convincing win–win or double dividend opportunities that might induce industry to make the needed eco-restructuring without coercion by government? I don't want to hazard a definite yes or no answer on this point because the answer depends on the application and on many other factors. Probably the alternative urban automotive transport system I have postulated in the foregoing paragraphs would not be profitable for private enterprise in the US given the present institutional structure, including the existing pattern of taxes and subsidies. For instance, gasoline is very lightly taxed in the US as compared to most other (non-oil producing) countries. Also, road and highway travel is heavily subsidized in the US, mostly in ways that are not very obvious. – for example, public financing of most road construction and road maintenance and provision of police and traffic safety services out of general tax funds. It has been estimated by the World Resources Institute that effective annual subsidies to automotive transportation in the US amount to US$300 billion, give or take a few billion.[10] Clearly, if the direct subsidies were eliminated, if parking charges and insurance costs were increased, and if car ownership, fuel and road use were more heavily taxed to reflect the true social costs of pollution and congestion, then alternative modes of transport would automatically be more attractive and auto usage would decline somewhat. This would obviously create profitable opportunities for alternative modes and combinations that do not exist now.

One line of reasoning suggests that in the long run, privately owned cars will largely disappear from the urban scene. Cars will still exist, of course. But automotive transportation could be provided as a service, like bus, rail and air transportation. Private ownership may gradually become less and less attractive as the cars themselves become more standardized and indistinguishable. The costs of parking and insurance are rising rapidly.[11] The psychological utility of private ownership as opposed to service on an as-needed basis will continue to fade. Leasing by the month or year is already becoming a popular alternative that reduces some of the responsibility and potential legal liability associated with ownership. Leasing firms may find ways to make leasing contracts much more attractive by including insurance and maintenance, for instance. Electronic identification and satellite-based geographic location systems, already available at modest cost, make this extended service more realistic. Indeed, Mercedes-Benz together with the Swiss watch company Swatch are rumored to be planning to offer such a service in the near future.

Cars in 2050 may (indeed, should) be integrated into a comprehensive transportation network. In this case cars would merely be the local pickup and distribution elements of the larger system. The transportation provider(s) would have – or coordinate with – a variety of larger vehicles, including aircraft, and also some dedicated high speed links with piggy-back capabilities for bridges, tunnels and high-speed inter-city travel. The distinction between chauffeur-driven cars (i.e. taxis) and self-driven cars may gradually fade as dispatching computers and roads themselves take over more and more of the guidance functions.

In 2050 you will choose the service provider and the class of travel and pay for service as you use it. The annual or per km costs of travel by car will not differ radically from costs we pay (in Europe) today. The big difference will be that the costs of travel will be allocated to specific trips and conditions, and thus will be much more visible. Consumers and business travellers will be able to be more discriminating in their choices. Congestion charges will induce people, and businesses, to make more efficient use of roads and to use other options more frequently. All this means that fewer vehicles (used more efficiently) will be needed to provide the service. Fewer vehicles, in turn, mean less congestion, which will benefit public mass transport and further cut the demand for individual cars on major routes.

The transport service providers may or may not be the manufacturers. But the key point is that all the equipment will be owned and maintained by the service providers. The providers will have every incentive to minimize energy consumption and utilize equipment efficiently. They will have incentives to assure efficient use of their equipment, to assure that it will be properly maintained, returned to the manufacturer for scheduled maintenance, refurbishing, upgrading and eventually returned for remanufacturing/recycling. This is in sharp contrast to the present situation where manufacturers maximize profits by selling products, not services, and take no responsibility for how those products are used, maintained and eventually disposed of when their useful lives are over.

DOUBLE DIVIDENDS

From the macro-economic perspective, the final critical question is: can continued economic growth be achieved in the coming decades simultaneously with environmental improvement by increasing resource productivity without significantly decreasing labor and capital productivity? To put it another way, is it feasible to find ways to increase *all* factor productivities simultaneously? Opportunities of this kind are sometimes called 'double dividends'.

It is interesting to note that affirmative answers to these questions imply a high degree of technological optimism. As I have noted earlier, mainstream economics tends to adopt an extremely optimistic stance in regard to questions of resource availability. That is, it is an article of faith that, if any one material becomes scarce, another can be found to take its place at little if any increase in cost.[12] But, surprisingly and inconsistently, many of the same people who are optimistic about resource availability and cost become pessimists when it comes to whether there are technological opportunities to grow the economy and reduce environmental stress at the same time. The standard argument is phrased like this: 'If such opportunities really did exist, some entrepreneur would soon come along and take advantage of the opportunity to make money'.

As I have noted previously, economic theory assumes that the economic system is very efficient at finding and exploiting such opportunities. When a scientist or engineer identifies an opportunity to save energy or reduce pollution while simultaneously reducing costs, some skeptic with economics training is likely to say that the opportunity is illusory, thanks to hidden costs that the scientist or engineer failed to take into account.

The counter-argument is simple. It is possible to cite literally hundreds of specific cases where investments in energy conservation (or clean technology) have yielded impressive returns on investment. Sometimes these savings, which go straight to the bottom line (i.e. profits) turn out to be far beyond the average return obtained by the average firm.[13] The usual response by a skeptic is to argue that, no matter how many examples are cited, they are all 'special' and 'exceptional' cases. The existence of a few exceptional cases does not prove a general proposition. There is no way to resolve the argument on this basis.

There is, however, a stronger argument. It is this: if the economy were really in, or very near, some static equilibrium there would be no opportunity for innovation or risky but high-return investments (or for investment advisors). There would also be no unemployment. It follows that there couldn't be any exceptional profit opportunities of any kind. All investments would necessarily yield roughly the same rate of return which would be essentially the same as the average growth of the economy and the average bank interest rate. Clearly nobody would borrow money to invest. The latter argument for disequilibrium seems to me to be quite conclusive.

The hypothetical transportation system described above involves radical changes indeed. It is hard to imagine the auto industry taking the lead in such a radical set of innovations. Because of its size, wealth and power, the automobile manufacturing industry will be one of the last to change its strategy. It will probably not do so unless government intervention changes the rules of the game in some important way. Are there other industries that could more plausibly lead the way? I think there are some. For instance, consider the case of Rank Xerox, the European manufacturer and distributor of xerographic copying machines. Starting in 1987, Rank Xerox embarked on a bold strategy to protect its market position against a new threat: that older Xerox equipment taken in trade for new equipment would be reconditioned by unauthorized local firms and offered in competition. This possibility was seen as threatening because the local reconditioners would not have either the technology or the quality standards to assure good performance in the field. Rank Xerox feared for its reputation.

The new program was known as 'asset recovery'. Rank Xerox created a new, wholly owned subsidiary to acquire old copying machines – from any manufacturer – from local distributors. The distributors are paid for the machines. The shipping costs to a central location in The Netherlands are also paid. There, the returned Xerox equipment is classified by age and condition, then disassembled into subassemblies. Subassemblies in good condition are cleaned, tested and reconditioned by replacement of worn parts, repainting or recoating as necessary. This is normally done by the original supplier, as compensation for lost sales of new subassemblies. The reconditioned subassemblies are then sold to the parent company (Rank Xerox) for use in remanufactured machines, which are labelled and sold to distributors as such. They compete with new equipment and carry the same warranties, but bear a lower price tag. Returns of other firms' equipment are disassembled and the parts are sent to materials recycling.

Subassemblies in less good condition are further disassembled to the component level, cleaned, reconditioned and tested. Components that meet the standard specifications are sold back to the parent company for use in remanufacturing. Substandard components may be sold to others. (For instance, substandard ball bearings are sold to a manufacturer of yachts for use in applications where some looseness is actually desirable.) Most substandard components go on to the materials recycling section. Recycled materials, such as aluminum alloys with exact composition specifications, can go directly to component manufacturers. Plastics are mostly recycled within the company. Each component thus has at least four lives, first in a subassembly of a new machine, second in the same subassembly in a remanufactured machine, third, in a remanufactured subassembly in a remanufactured machine, and fourth, as recycled material. Some subassemblies (such as electric motors) can be reconditioned and re-used several times.

After eight years in operation, the scheme is surprisingly profitable. The asset recovery operation itself is a financial break even, by design. But the parent company saves very considerably (around US$70 million in 1996) on purchased materials. Moreover, new jobs have actually been created in the asset recovery operation. To be sure, some of these new jobs are at the expense of jobs in upstream suppliers. But it is evident that human labor is being substituted for materials in this case. Rank Xerox cuts its materials costs sharply, at no reduction in quality, by clever use of labor. This is a good omen for the future.

The scheme I have described above is truly radical in an unexpected sense. Although Rank Xerox does not retain ownership of its products over their lifetime, it effectively internalizes the products that it takes back, just as if the product had never been sold. This means that Rank Xerox is no longer really selling material products at all. Rather, it is selling the services of those products. (Reflecting this new orientation, Xerox calls itself 'The Document Company'.) Having internalized the product, Xerox now has all the incentives to maximize profits by minimizing new materials use, that is, keeping existing parts and materials in service as long as possible, while still allowing for constant upgrading and improvement of the product.

On the basis of this and a number of other such examples, I am personally quite optimistic with regard to finding profitable solutions to the employment cum growth problem and the environment problem at the same time. After all, simple intellectual consistency would seem to require that people who see no problem of resource scarcity should also admit the likely existence of many unexploited technological opportunities for profitable resource conservation – double dividends. But, in all candor, I don't think the number of double dividend opportunities available today, under current political–institutional conditions, is enough to take us where we need to go. Governments will have to create stronger incentives to move industry as a whole in the right direction. In short it will be necessary to change some of the rules of the game. I discuss this in the next chapter.

SUMMARY AND IMPLICATIONS

This chapter has five important implications. First, that population growth and economic catchup by developing countries would require a tenfold increase in materials and energy throughput by the middle of the next century. Second, that this level of materials/energy throughput is unsustainable because it would vastly overload the Earth's waste assimilation capacity, even if there were no resource availability crisis. It follows that sustainability requires a major eco-restructuring and radical dematerialization. Incremental changes will not suffice.

The third key conclusion is that a tenfold dematerialization is technically feasible, bearing in mind that there are significantly greater opportunities for energy and materials conservation in the production of final services than there are in the processing and production of finished materials, electric power or mechanical work. However, the fourth and most important conclusion is that the incentives operating in our decentralized economic system do not promote conservation or efficiency. This is mainly because economies of scale favor maximizing capacity utilization (ie throughput maximization) as long as the manufacturer has no responsibility for the operation, maintenance or final disposal of the product. It follows that the only way to reconcile the incentive structure that operates at the firm level with the imperatives of global dematerialization is for firms to learn or be induced to sell only services to final consumers, while retaining full ownership and responsibility for the material products themselves. Only under such a restructured economic system will firms have the incentives to maximize opportunities for operating efficiency and opportunities for recovery, re-use, reconditioning, remanufacturing and recycling of durables.

The fifth point concerns the extent to which firms might move towards a service orientation with full product internalization without government coercion. This depends on the extent and scope of double dividends to be found in the current system. I believe that there are actually far more such opportunities than standard economic doctrine would admit. I also believe that the gradually broadening doctrine of legal liability will increasingly force firms to recognize that not only is every product a potential waste, but it is also a potential future liability. To minimize such liabilities it makes sense to begin to sell services, rather than products, and to treat products as capital assets. Lawyers, insurers and accountants will begin to force firms to think along these lines.

However, at the end of the day, there is little doubt that governments will have to intervene to accelerate the eco-restructuring process. This is the subject of the next chapter.

NOTES

1   The reference is to Ayres et al, 1998.
2   The useful distinction between cowboy and spaceship economies is Kenneth Boulding's (1966).
3   This has become known as the Porter Hypothesis after Michael Porter, the Harvard Business School professor who first enunciated a version of it (Porter, 1991). A number of economists have taken issue with the Hypothesis, and it is a fairly hot topic at the moment.
4   The 'second law' efficiency of any process is defined as the ratio of the minimum amount of energy theoretically needed for the process to the energy actually used. It can be defined consistently, in principle, for any process (given a suitable convention on the treatment of co-inputs and by-products), although actual numerical determination can be difficult in some cases. It must be pointed out that there is another widely used definition of efficiency, namely the ratio of 'useful' energy outputs to total energy inputs. In some cases, such as electric power generation, the two definitions are equivalent. However in other cases (such as heating units) there is a very big difference. Gas furnaces are often advertised as having 'efficiencies' up to 90 per cent, which merely means that 90 per cent of the heat is 'useful' and only 10 per cent is lost with the combustion products. However, it often happens that the same amount of final heating effect could have been achieved with much less energy expenditure (eg by means of a heat pump). In this sense, most heating systems are actually very inefficient.
5   The most efficient possible lighting system would utilize light-emitting diodes (LEDs) operating in the visible range. These are the devices that are used for flat computer display terminals, for instance.
6   See Ayres, 1989b.
7   Note that efficiency of use is quite independent of the amount of use. The US uses by far more energy per capita than India, for instance, because it receives more energy services. But many energy-using activities in India, from electric power generation to cooking, nevertheless tend to be considerably less efficient than their Western counterparts.
8   See, for instance, the latest report to the Club of Rome by von Weizsäcker et al in German (1994), and in English translation (1997).

9 The basic reason why such large gains are possible is that the thermodynamic efficiency with which fuel energy is converted into mechanical work by a standard US car is about 9 per cent (Carnahan et al, 1975). The average auto at the time weighed about 2500 lb (1200 kg) whereas 1.5 passengers and luggage (assuming average occupancy) weighed less than 250 lb or 120 kg, so the payload efficiency was only 10 per cent. Combining the two, the overall efficiency of personal transport service by auto was less than 1 per cent. Thus, a threefold reduction in vehicle weight has the effect of increasing overall efficiency by the same factor. The hypercar would achieve this by using ultra-light composite materials and construction technologies from the aerospace industry. It would also gain another factor of two (more or less) by using a small hybrid electric drive system (a small engine, optimized for constant speed, driving an alternator with electric motors in the wheels). The hypercar proposal, which includes a complete design, comes from the Rocky Mountain Institute, Old Snowmass, Colorado. See, for example, Lovins et al, 1996.

10 See note 17, Chapter 10.

11 In Tokyo, a car cannot be registered unless the owner has a permanent parking place within 700 meters of his/her residence.

12 The most widely-cited paper on this issue is by Goeller and Weinberg (1976)

13 See Ayres, 1994.

Chapter 11
The Government Role

INTRODUCTION

In this chapter I shift the focus to government policy. However I refuse to be inhibited in my proposals by premature considerations of political feasibility. Let's talk about what makes sense first, and then let the professionals figure out how to get from here to there.

Herewith I offer some policy ideas that might be worthy of more extended public discussion. In all cases, I am concerned with their direct or indirect impact on dematerialization and the conversion of firms from the production and sale of products to final consumers, to selling services only and treating products as assets. Employment is also a continuing concern.

OPTIMAL TAXES

Many people consider tax policy to be the key to eco-restructuring. It is certainly one of the major determinants of the business environment. Here is a list of some attributes of an optimal tax system relative to the present system:

- the optimal tax system would be efficient. It would encourage entrepreneurial activity, risk taking, technological innovation, saving (accumulation of capital) and the investment of capital in productive activity. By contrast, it would discourage the accumulation of unproductive assets (eg gold, collectibles, land held for speculative purposes).
- The optimal tax system would encourage workers to sell their labor; similarly, it would encourage employers to buy labor, and especially to create new jobs.
- The optimal tax system would discourage socially harmful activities such as the abuse of firearms, alcohol, tobacco or drugs, the premature exhaustion of limited and irreplaceable natural resources and the dispersion of hazardous wastes and harmful pollutants into the environment.[1]
- The optimal tax system would be equitable. This implies equal treatment of those in similar circumstances. It implies progressiveness with respect to income distribution. (That is, higher-income people would pay more than lower-income people.) It also implies some attention to inter-generational issues. How much future

wealth are we justified in sacrificing for the sake of increasing consumption in the present? It would be neutral with respect to international competitiveness.

- The optimal tax system would be transparent and (relatively) simple to compute and enforce, thus reducing the heavy accounting and record-keeping burden, especially on small businesses.

The appropriate weights to put on these attributes cannot be determined altogether objectively, insofar as they depend somewhat on personal values. Individuals might attach quite different weights to the five criteria, and it is not clear that simple averaging is the most appropriate mechanism for arriving at a compromise. Moreover, what is appropriate at a given time depends on circumstances. For instance, the importance of discouraging the accumulation of economically unproductive assets depends on the extent to which investable funds are being diverted into such assets. Art may be regarded as unproductive by some people, but not by others – including me. On the whole, countries that have invested heavily in art (like France and Italy) also offer a higher level of quality of life to their citizens than countries that neglect it. So art in the environment contributes to national welfare.

The importance of equity, transparency and administrative simplicity in tax reform also depends on the circumstances. Equity is a much more important issue today than it was 20 or 30 years ago precisely because it has been decreasing. Transparency and simplicity are less important in relatively law abiding countries than in countries with a long tradition of widespread tax evasion. However, excessive inequity and/or complexity will almost certainly convert a law abiding country into a tax-evading country, over time. I think this is happening now in the US. Simplicity and transparency are the basic appeal of the flat tax espoused by Jerry Brown in the 1991–1992 Democratic Presidential Primary elections and by Steve Forbes in the 1995–1996 Republican Primaries. Unfortunately, the flat tax fails the equity test unless it includes a fairly hefty personal exemption.[2]

The importance of taxing 'bads' (environmental or other) depends partly on the amount of damage they are doing. It may be counterproductive to tax bads for the sake of revenue, since the government would then become reliant upon that revenue and consequently inhibited from doing anything to reduce the revenue stream. (This is a very real problem in Russia where much of the government's revenue – especially after 1989 – is from taxes on vodka sales.) In Europe and Japan, high taxes on gasoline and motor fuel have been in place for many years, and this contributes significantly to government revenues. This could be a contributory factor behind the rather pro-motorist policies of Germany and France (high speed limits, minimal enforcement of speed limits, generous deductibility of personal automobile commuting costs from income tax, etc). It has been argued that the best long-term strategy for resource conservation would be to raise resource (eg energy) prices slowly over a long period through gradually increasing taxation (for example, von Weizsäcker and Jesinghaus, 1992). This is probably true. Yet there would also be some risk in becoming too dependent on an energy tax, or a resource tax, for exactly the same reason – it would tempt governments to do things that would maximize the revenue. This might well lead to policies indirectly encouraging energy use and undermining the purpose of the tax. However, for economists the primary point of interest with respect to tax systems is the extent to which they encourage or discourage savings, investment, risk-taking innovation, and employment.

A quick survey of the existing tax structure, in terms of the above criteria, quickly indicates how counter-productive it really is in virtually all countries. In the 12 of the countries constituting the European Union, taxes of all kinds swallowed up 41.28 per cent of GNP in 1992. Of this amount, direct taxes on labor, including social security, accounted for 23.44 per cent of GNP and taxes on consumption (VAT) accounted for 10.86 per cent, while fuel and automobile ownership taxes were only 2.37 per cent. Taxes on capital (mostly indirect) accounted for 6.98 per cent of GNP. In the US, by contrast, consumption taxes were lower (although variable from state to state) while taxes on capital – mainly real property – were somewhat higher, but the overall tax burden was closer to 31 per cent of GNP than to 41 per cent.

The progressive income tax is an effective tool for redistributing (ie equalizing) incomes. It is less burdensome on the very poor. However, it is comparatively counter-productive in terms of economic growth, insofar as growth is influenced by savings. It inhibits saving and it punishes investment. The savings tax and VAT are comparatively regressive, but they are much less counter-productive from a savings/investment perspective. It should be noted that while VAT seems, to consumers, to be a sort of sales tax, it is effectively a tax on payments to employed labor (ie on wages). The VAT paid on a consumer item and collected by the shopkeeper is actually a tax on markup, that is, labor value added by the shop. The value added by a shop (or any other business) is exactly the gross revenues less non-labor expenses, which is mostly labor. VAT is also paid at each prior stage of the production process, again based on value added. In this sense, VAT is directly comparable to the Social Security tax in the US, except that the latter is earmarked for a particular purpose.[3] However, the VAT is collected at source and is therefore 'invisible', whereas the social security tax is collected partly from individuals. To the extent it is collected from employers it is like VAT. Both are indirect costs of labor employment.

The Social Security tax, as it operates in the US, is just about the most counter-productive tax imaginable. Not only is it a direct tax on the employment of labor, it is the most regressive of all taxes. Low-income workers actually pay a higher rate than higher-income workers, because of the income cutoff. There is no such cutoff in Europe, where the tax rate is also considerably higher. This peculiar US structure is justified on the basis that the tax is really a form of insurance, with benefits – retirement income and Medicare – that are distributed more or less in proportion to contributions. In reality, the benefits bear little or no relationship to contributions.

Taxes on labor help make the real cost of employing a worker much higher than the actual wages paid. The 'overhead' burden on employers in the early 1990s was as follows:

- Italy – 51.7 per cent
- France – 47.5 per cent
- Germany – 46.4 per cent
- EU average – 40.5 per cent
- UK – 30.1 per cent
- US – 27.9 per cent

Everywhere this additional burden translates into higher costs and prices of goods, but differentially from one country to another. The burden eventually falls on labor, however, in the sense that employers make hiring decisions based on both the total cost of compensation and the cost of laying off excess workers if business conditions require cutbacks. The greater the total cost of labor, the more employers will seek to save on direct labor costs by automation, or use of part-timers or 'out-sourcing' to countries with low labor costs. In other words, the greater the cost of labor, the less of it employers will buy. And when they do buy, they try hard to get the labor without paying the social overhead costs. It is not optimal to tax labor heavily and resource use lightly, given that our objective should be to use more labor and less resources. Shifting the tax burden from one category to the other would change the relative price levels and, consequently, relative utilization rates.

TAX/SUBSIDY REFORM

Many of the problems with slow economic growth, growing inequity, unemployment and environmental degradation in the Western world could be eased just by restructuring the tax system. The fundamental causes of under-employment in Europe are dual. On the one hand, labor has become too productive, mostly as a result of substituting machines and energy for human labor. On the other hand, it has become too inflexible. The underlying basic idea of the change would be to reduce the tax burden on labor, so as to reduce its market price relative to capital and resources, and thus encourage more employment of labor vis-à-vis capital, fossil fuels and other resources. The problem of inflexibility should be tackled simultaneously by modifying some of the regulations.

If there is any implication of neoclassical economics that seems to be beyond challenge it is that shifting the relative prices of factors of production (ie labor, capital, resources) will eventually induce the economy to substitute the cheaper factor for the more expensive one. In the past, heavily-taxed labor has become increasingly costly and therefore unattractive to employers in comparison with less heavily-taxed capital or untaxed resources. Consequence: the economy has substituted capital and resources for labor. By the same logic, to reverse this unfortunate trend it will be necessary to cut the tax burden on labor and increase the tax burden on resources and activities that damage the social or natural environment. This would not only induce employers to use more labor and less resources; it would also discourage some anti-social and anti-environment activities at the same time.[4] Among the activities that damage the social environment of Europe and the US by increasing unemployment, the export of capital and the import of products made by low-wage labor are the most important.[5] I do not regard deliberate exclusion of imports by means of either tariffs (old style) or by means of regulatory and administrative barriers (Japanese style) as an attractive or efficient means of solving this problem. But I do not think that denial of the existence of the problem is an appropriate response either. I come back to this issue later in connection with trade.

Activities that damage the natural environment are multifarious. But one major category is the extraction and conversion of non-renewable resources from the Earth's crust, especially those non-renewable resources that are eventually converted by production and consumption processes into electric power, fuels, material products and finally into toxic substances, pollution and wastes. This change would have to be gradual, so as to avoid unnecessary disruption. But it should also be signaled well in advance, so that taxpayers and firms know what to expect in the future and can begin to plan their investments and lifestyles in response.

So much for generalities. What taxes should be reduced? In both the US and Europe, the first priority target for reduction in my opinion should be social security taxes, with corporate income taxes next on the list, followed by personal income and capital gains taxes.[6] These taxes account for almost all central government revenues in the US and perhaps half in Europe (the remainder being VAT and motor fuel taxes, for the most part). In principle I would like to see the overhead costs of hired labor cut to as near zero as possible.

The question is, how can such cuts be financed? The alternatives are straightforward: cut government spending, or tax something else. Take the spending side first. Again, there are two possibilities. The first is to reduce spending by operating more efficiently. Politicians have talked so much about eliminating 'waste and fraud' in government that most people imagine that these are major potential sources of savings. There is a lot of waste, to be sure, but outright embezzlement and cheating accounts for very little of it. Mostly it is of two kinds. The first is excessive bureaucracy, mandated by legislatures to monitor and regulate, that is, to ensure that government programs are carried out as intended (ie without waste and fraud). The second kind of waste is far greater, but harder to eliminate: it consists of unnecessary subsidies to the politically well-connected. Here, virtually everybody except the beneficiaries themselves agree that something should be done. However, the one thing most people think could save a lot of money is welfare. There is a widespread mythology of 'welfare cheats' living comfortably off the public purse. How much money is actually involved? The answer is that welfare expenditures of all kinds (in the US) amounted to around 1 per cent of GNP circa 1990. Relatively few of the beneficiaries are cheats. The recent US welfare reform is actually a sharp cut in support for poor families, especially those with children. By the year 2000 changes in the rules will certainly cut the outlays still further, knocking many people off the rolls who are not dishonest, merely unfortunate. There is not very much scope for savings here, at least in the US case. In Europe the scope for savings is somewhat larger, of course, and governments hard-pressed for cash are beginning to crack down on some of the more blatant boondoggles.

The government procurement system, in the US, Europe and Japan, is absolutely perverse. It does not encourage efficiency. The inefficiency of the US health system is particularly egregious. But more legislative mandates to audit, second-guess, renegotiate and unilaterally reduce allowable overheads will only add further to the indirect but real costs. It is estimated that in the US, government mandated paperwork of all kinds now accounts for about 1 per cent of the GDP. This money supports an army of essentially unproductive clerical staff, tax accountants, auditors, and lawyers. This overhead cost is a large number in absolute terms, and well worth reducing if possible. But the only way to cut such costs would be to give government program managers the same kind of discretionary authority that private sector program managers have and expect. But the US public, and its elected legislators, do not trust the civil service, so this solution seems remote.[7]

The alternative route to efficiency is through privatization of as many government functions as possible, not excluding parts of law enforcement and education. Privatization is the current fashion, so it need not be discussed at length, except to say that I support the idea in general, provided it does not leave the poor unprotected. However, as regards specific application to social welfare itself, see below.

So much for reducing waste and fraud. Consider the second category of waste, namely subsidies to the well-connected. I mean subsidies to tobacco farmers, peanut farmers, dairy farmers, people who don't farm for not farming, irrigation, grazers and loggers on public lands, mining and mineral depletion, drivers on public roads, drivers who are uninsured, free parking, real estate developers and vacation homes... the list is very long. The highest priority for reduction would (in principle) be the elimination of existing subsidies to activities that also contribute to social pathology or environmental degradation. Examples of the first kind include tax subsidies to induce industry to move jobs away from one region to another, or subsidies that encourage road building and suburban sprawl which encourage the deterioration of central cities. Examples of the second kind include subsidies to mining, subsidies to energy use, subsidies to mechanized chemical-intensive farming, and – again – road-building. These subsidies are considerably larger than most people imagine. For instance, a significant part of the cost of maintaining the US Navy is openly and explicitly justified by the need to protect ocean shipping routes to and from the Persian Gulf, which is the world's major source of exportable petroleum. This subsidy to energy use alone is of the order of several tens of billions of dollars per year. Other subsidies to automotive transportation include free parking for employees and customers, urban and rural non-freeway road construction, maintenance and law enforcement paid from the public treasury, accident costs caused by uninsured drivers, and so forth.[8]

Having eliminated as many subsidies as possible, and cut spending to the limit through various reforms, it is appropriate to reconsider taxation. I pointed out already that an optimal tax system would discourage undesirable social and economic activities and encourage desirable ones.[9] I am willing to assert that the extraction of nonrenewable raw materials from the Earth's crust should be reduced dramatically. This should be done both for the sake of preserving some resources for future generations and to minimize the stress on the environment that results from industrial pollution and final consumption wastes. (Every ton of raw material extracted from the Earth is a future waste. The time lag is seldom more than a few months.) This environmental stress is a 'bad' that should be taxed, if only as a way to force those who cause the stress and damage to pay the full costs of the damage they do. This is the principle, widely advertised but normally ignored in practice, known as the polluter pays principle or PPP.

Two kinds of bads need to be considered here. The first arises from the use of tradeable goods and services with more or less well-established past or present markets, but of which society disapproves the use. In most cases, this disapproval is due to social problems and costs attributable to the use of the product or service. For instance, the high rate of use of handguns in criminal activity in the US is certainly traceable to the wide distribution and relatively unrestricted sale and purchase of handguns. Both law enforcement agencies and sociologists agree on this; in countries where handguns are not allowed, as in Europe and Japan, violent crimes are far rarer. The use of addictive recreational drugs is also a major cause of robberies and burglaries to obtain money for the needed 'fix'. Similarly, relatively wide use of alcoholic beverages causes a relatively large number of automobile accidents.

The second category of bads consists of social disservices arising directly from externalities due to market failures. A market failure is an impact, from an economic transaction, on someone who was not actually a party to the transaction and who has no influence on the price of the commodity or service being exchanged between the buyer and seller. These are called market failures (or externalities) because, in a theoretically perfect market, no such third party effects would occur. Pollution, noise, congestion and litter are all examples of externalities resulting from market failures. In this connection I would add the consequences of market failures in labor markets and international trade. These include economic inequity, unemployment and social pathology. As I remarked earlier, the export of capital and the import of products made by cheap labor (not to mention child labor and slave labor) have contributed to unemployment in the West. I do not think a ban would be appropriate or efficient. I think, however, that taxation of international monetary flows (which would cover both capital exports and payment for imports) could be a useful approach. The tax rate need not be very high – perhaps only 1 per cent – and it could be waived for small transactions such as credit card purchases by tourists. There could also be a quasi-market solution along the lines of tradeable import permits, discussed later.

As regards 'bads' that are taxable in principle, the obvious candidates are tradeable goods or commodities such as tobacco products or firearms. A less obvious, but real, candidate is money itself. Consider undesirable commodities first. If societal disapproval is wide enough and if the trade is hard to keep secret, a simple ban may be effective. The slave trade is perhaps the clearest case. Whaling might be another.[10] The use of lead in gasoline, or the use of DDT, PCBs or CFCs might be other examples. However, where the disapproval is widespread but the commodity is compact and the trade is easy to conduct in secrecy, a ban will not suffice. We know this very well in the case of heroin or cocaine; it is also true for child pornography, plutonium (and other nuclear weapons technology), plastic explosives, automatic weapons, elephant tusks, rhinoceros horns, tropical bird feathers, and so on. The ban strategy will be even less effective where the disapprobation is not even shared by an overwhelming majority of the population, as is the case for abortion, prostitution, alcoholic beverages, tobacco, marijuana or personal handguns. To discourage the use of commodities and services that society disapproves of but which are difficult to ban effectively, a sales tax may be the most effective means. To collect the tax, of course, the trade must be carried out openly and legally. Legalizing trade permits the government to collect revenues that would otherwise be collected by organized crime. These revenues can be used for socially useful purposes, including financing the medical and other social costs associated with the antisocial commodity. Tobacco products, alcoholic beverages and certain emission permits might be candidates.

Enforcement is a critical issue, of course. Prohibition failed in the 1920s, despite its considerable popularity, because it could not be effectively enforced in a society that did not universally share the values of the temperance activists. However, the government was able to prosecute many criminals for non-payment of taxes, in part because convictions did not depend on the testimony of witnesses who could be intimidated by threats of violence. A tax can only be regarded as an effective instrument of social policy if its enforcement mechanism is sufficiently reliable and cost-effective. This is a particular problem for (hypothetical) taxes and charges on pollution and waste disposal.

The technical problems of taxing airborne and waterborne pollution emissions directly are greatly magnified by the inherent difficulty of attributing downstream emissions to their sources. While modern technology does offer possibilities of identifying sources – in some cases – by means of their optical or chemical fingerprints, the requirements for legal proof are not easy to satisfy. Moreover, the use of lawsuits and courts as an enforcement mechanism (as advocated by libertarians) is somewhat impractical, given the costs involved. However, in cases where the polluter is also the final consumer, there is a convenient alternative to taxing the polluter directly. It is to impose the tax on the input material (eg fuel). The carbon tax, widely discussed in connection with the problem of climate warming, exemplifies this approach. A carbon tax would be a tax on fossil fuels proportional to their carbon content, and consequently their potential for generating CO_2 when burned. The tax could be collected from the coal mine or the oil and gas producer, the fuel processor or the importer.[11] There are a variety of estimates of the degree of reduction in fuel use that such a tax would cause, depending on various estimates of the responsiveness of consumers to look for alternatives, and the costs of such alternatives (such as using photovoltaic cells to generate electricity). A tax of $75 per ton of carbon is often discussed.[12] In the US this would add US$43.87 per ton of (average) coal, US$.02 per kilowatt hour (kWh) to the price of electricity and US$0.22 per gallon of gasoline. For a typical US household, using 100 million BTU of natural gas, 6000 kWh of electricity and 500 gallons of gasoline per year, the tax burden would be US$350.

Assuming this average family (with 1.5 wage earners, more or less) has an earned income of around US$35,000 per year, the household is paying at least US$2500 into the social security fund. It is easy to see that, if the carbon tax were paid directly into the social security fund, and if personal contributions were reduced correspondingly, the family would be no worse off than before. In fact, even if the carbon tax were raised by a factor of five, to US$350 per ton of carbon, the annual indirect carbon tax burden on this family would be US$1750. In that case, assuming no reduction in energy use at all, its social security tax bill would simply be reduced by this amount and the family would still be just as well off as before.

But, quite obviously, consumers would be able to reduce their carbon tax burden considerably in various ways. They could do so by driving more fuel-efficient vehicles, combining trips to drive fewer miles, adding thermal insulation to the walls and roof, and so on. Upstream industrial users of energy would also confront greater costs, giving them greater incentives to conserve. The suggested carbon tax, at the modest rate of US$75 per ton, would generate around US$110 billion per year in the US at 1990 fuel consumption levels, and less to the extent that consumption was reduced. At this level of tax, the ultimate reduction in fuel use over a ten-year period would be relatively modest – perhaps 25 per cent below the baseline case. The average family described above would still be paying the same total tax bill (carbon plus social security), but it would be saving money on its energy bill.

Greater reductions in fuel use would require higher carbon taxes.[13] The US motor transport sector alone consumed 133 billion gallons of fuel (gasoline and diesel) in 1992, at prices around US$1.20 per gallon, or about US$150 billion worth. Federal taxes only accounted for about 11 per cent of this, or US$0.13 per gallon. Taxes on motor fuel alone in the US at European or Japanese levels (roughly US$3 per gallon) would have produced nearly US$400 billion at the same level of consumption, or US$300 billion in case of a plausible 25 per cent reduction in motor fuel usage. In any event, this tax alone would have been enough to finance a large fraction of US social security taxes (roughly US$414 billion in 1992). Taxes on other carbon-based fuels at the same level would generate comparable revenues. Taxes at higher levels, and/or taxes on other non-renewables and extractive resources, would make it possible to take a big bite out of corporate and personal income taxes as well. In fact,

I suspect that resource taxes could, in time, replace all social security and some income taxes.

I mentioned the danger of the government becoming so dependent on these revenues that it loses sight of the main purpose of the tax, which should be to discourage excessive consumption of natural resources and resulting wastes and pollution. This danger is not entirely hypothetical. In Europe, tax revenues from motor fuel go into the central treasury and (unlike social security taxes) are not earmarked for anything in particular. The consequence is that finance ministers in Europe (and probably Japan) are extremely reluctant to contemplate serious action to reduce motor vehicle usage, because it would cut into one of the more reliable revenue streams. In fact, they are rather more inclined to support new highway construction programs.

Another difficulty with resource taxation to reduce resource consumption is that it would be seen to penalize domestic manufacturers in comparison to foreign manufacturers, unless accompanied by equivalent taxes on the resource-content of imported goods. Direct taxes on imported fuels and natural resources would obviously be objectionable to natural resource exporters (such as the Middle East and many African countries). Assuming the import taxes were also applied to the materials content of the goods, such taxes would also be opposed by foreign exporters of manufactured goods. At the very least, mechanisms would have to be developed to ensure that such taxes did not discriminate against foreign producers in favor of domestic producers. Ideally, a world-wide coordination and equalization mechanism should be agreed upon. Given the history of GATT/WTO, that would be a major diplomatic undertaking. The clerical and computational problems would also be formidable. Nevertheless, it should be tried.

WELFARE REFORM AND EXCHANGEABLE QUOTAS

When government spending has been cut as much as possible by eliminating waste, fraud and inappropriate subsidies, and when taxes have been shifted as far as possible from labor and capital to resource extraction and use, we are still left with some of the most intractable social and environmental problems. Social security (including income support for the poorest) and health care are two of the major challenges. Environmental degradation resulting from excess consumption and waste constitutes a third. (I doubt that taxes alone will bring about the needed restructuring of business.) This brings me to the question of welfare reform.

The best way to cut spending on welfare and income support, without doubt, would be to increase productive employment and thereby reduce some of the social pressures that breed crime, social pathologies and health problems. However, government has not been very good at delivering economic growth that creates jobs. Besides, no conceivable economic fix in the job arena could possibly work quickly enough to have a short-term positive impact on central government budgets. So I move on to consider policies with a potentially more immediate payoff.

Since political pragmatism has been ruled out as a consideration here, let me go the whole hog. Why not privatize social welfare, at least partially? A presidential commission is now considering a variety of possibilities along these lines, including ways to convert 'defined benefits' into 'defined contributions' and giving individuals individual retirement accounts (IRAs). Since most Americans get more from the social security system than they put into it, any such conversion scheme would also tend to reduce actual benefits. But many people would probably accept this in exchange for having more direct control over their retirement funds. Sadly, not everyone is competent to administer his/her own retirement account. Given control over their savings, many financially unsophisticated people would use them to gamble or fall victim to fraudulent 'get rich quick' schemes, of which there are all too many examples in Eastern Europe at the present time. How could these people be protected without excessive government intrusion? Nobody has a convincing answer, so far as I know.

A new source of income for the disabled, unemployed, impoverished or retired would be needed to supplement cuts in federally guaranteed social security benefits. One possibility (not the one I prefer, however) is that all other existing welfare programs except health, from food stamps to unemployment compensation to aid to dependent children (ADC), should be replaced by what has been called a 'negative income tax'. This simply means that every adult, regardless of other income, would be entitled to receive a direct tax-free cash stipend from the government at roughly the poverty level, ie more or less equivalent to welfare payments (including non-case benefits) today.[14] All additional income could then be subject to a flat or graduated tax, without personal (or any other) exemptions. The logic is compelling because the present system is so perverse. The way the current system works is that if any amount of income is earned by a welfare recipient (in the US, at least) the welfare payment is simply reduced by a dollar for every dollar earned, until the payment reaches zero. In other words, the effective tax rate for earned income among the poorest welfare recipients is 100 per cent! Even if earnings are twice as much as the welfare payment, the effective tax rate is still 50 per cent. Needless to say, this arrangement is a considerable disincentive for people to take very low-paying jobs. No wonder there are some welfare cheats. The indirect tax on welfare income should be ended. To pay for the proposed negative income tax, or to provide an equivalent from some other source, another source of tax revenues or private revenues must be found. I have a suggestion along these lines, which I discuss in more detail below.

The health care system is next on the list for reform. In Chapter 3, I pointed out that costs in all Western countries are rising steadily for several reasons that need not be recapitulated here. One point is worth emphasis, however: US health care costs are the world's highest, by a considerable margin, despite the fact that the US system is also the most privatized. This is not because the health care being provided in the US is extraordinarily good; on the contrary, except for some frontier areas of outstanding expertise, US health care is mediocre. Privatization on the US model is not necessarily the mechanism for maximizing efficiency of health care delivery. To oversimplify a bit here, I would advocate a publicly financed basic system – similar to that in Canada, the UK, France, or Germany but with less paperwork – with the service itself to be provided by private health maintenance organizations (HMOs) contractually bound to accept a standard fee for standard service. A privately financed 'premium' care system would be permitted to operate in parallel for those prepared to pay more. The basic system would be financed by fee-for-service, with a major medical insurance component for the indigent financed by the government (from taxes, of course). The paperwork reduction could be accomplished by issuing each individual who is covered by the system a special health credit card with an imprinted code specifying the insurer and allowing certain pre-approved services up to a specified limit. Further services could be approved by designated institutions such as hospitals. Most of the record-keeping and auditing could be computerized.

There is a possible approach to welfare reform that is particularly attractive because it doubles as a direct inducement to dematerialization. The scheme I have in mind is to allocate equal (class A) consumption quotas for *all* natural resources – starting with fossil fuels – to all legal adult residents of a country, plus children of school age. These quotas should be exchangeable. The idea would be to permit under-consumers of resources (such as students, the incapacitated, the poor and elderly) to sell their unused quotas to others who are willing to pay a price for additional consumption shares. The inclusion of pre-school children is problematic; it would be a mistake to allow the quota system to become an inducement for poor families or single parents to have more children as a source of income. One possible way out of this impasse would be to award non-exchangeable (class B) quotas to young children, exercisable by parents, but not assignable to third parties. These class B quotas could also be adjusted to a lower level of consumption. The trades could be carried out through banks or via a computer-assisted auction, similar to the operation of some stock markets. Total consumption at the national level would be set to keep base prices moderate for a certain standard entitlement. But there would also be an incremental downward adjustment year by year to enable people to adjust gradually to lower levels of aggregate material commodity use.

Supply and demand would determine the value of consumption quotas. By selling under-used quotas, bicycle commuters would receive an income supplement from long-distance automobile commuters (who are currently being subsidized indirectly in a number of ways). People living in small, energy-efficient homes or apartments would be subsidized by people living in large inefficient show-places. Similarly, hikers and walkers would be subsidized by drivers of vans, RVs and power-boats. The use of tradeable consumption quotas would partially answer the usual criticism of direct consumption taxes as an instrument of demand reduction, namely that they tend to be regressive and to hurt the lower income groups most. Actually, it would constitute a very straightforward income redistribution scheme involving neither taxes nor bureaucracy. The only role of the government would be to set the annual individual quota for carbon (or any other non-renewable commodity) and to supervise the trading process. The rest is distribution and monitoring. There are probably several ways to accomplish all this, using currently available technology. However, for the benefit of skeptics, I will describe just one such mechanism briefly, using fuel as an example.

The main problem is to devise a foolproof means of assuring that each individual receives his or her proper fuel entitlement, each month, and to inhibit fraud. For adults this could be done with magnetized and coded credit cards that draw upon a numbered account kept in a local commercial bank, using the individual's social security number for identification. The fuel credit account in the bank would be replenished automatically on a monthly basis. The cards themselves could only be used after manual verification of the code number in a magnetic card reader. This system, now widely implemented in France, virtually eliminates the problem of card theft, since a thief would not know the personalized code number. At intervals, any account holder with a surplus fuel credit could sell it (probably through the bank) at the posted price of the day. The monetary value received for the sale of fuel entitlement would then be deposited automatically in the seller's deposit account. Similarly, any account holder needing more fuel credit could buy it in the same way, also through the bank, the cost being automatically debited to his/her current deposit account.[15]

The rationing (tradeable quota) scheme may not be applicable to all kinds of bads, but where it is immediately applicable – for instance, to the use of fossil fuels – it has the great advantage of being implementable within any country, without causing massive cross-border trade distortions. It would also, in all likelihood, reduce fossil fuel use more effectively than taxation alone. Finally, of course, it has the very considerable advantage of partially (if not wholly) privatizing the social welfare system, by providing an automatic source of cash income to people who are willing (and able) to consume less material-intensive and energy-intensive goods and services than others. This money would, of course, be paid by those who do use such goods and services, by passing the government and its bureaucracy.

The idea can be applied quite generally. For instance, it could be applied to pollutant emissions, as well as to resource consumption. Sulfur dioxide emissions quotas are already exchanged among electric utilities in a quasi-market in the US. The system has achieved acceptance with significant increases in economic efficiency. Why not try it in the case of motor vehicle emissions? Moralists and lawyers will object, citing the old 'license to pollute' argument. But suppose the Environmental Protection Agency were able to specify a total aggregate amount of each automotive pollutant that is to be tolerated for the coming year, for each region. For instance, take NO_X. At present all manufacturers are obliged to meet a standard emission level for new cars, and states are supposed to enforce the same standards for older vehicles. The standards themselves are uniform everywhere, even though the pollution problem is essentially non-existent in rural areas and particularly serious in cities, especially those at high altitudes or in areas where atmospheric inversions are common.

There are a number of implementation possibilities, but here is one. Suppose each adult received an annual NO_X quota. Suppose each vehicle were to cost 'quota points' in accordance with its average emission of NO_X, times an adjustment multiplier based on its location and mode of use (as defined for insurance purposes). Thus a vehicle registered in a highly-urbanized county and used for commuting or local delivery would require a lot of quota points, as compared to a vehicle registered in a rural county. People living in areas with a NO_X problem would have a choice of buying a non-polluting (eg electric) or low-polluting vehicle, or buying extra quota points through the sort of auction system described above. The sellers – mostly rural people, or people who do not own cars – would receive the money as an income supplement.

TRADE REFORM

The basic exchangeable quota scheme could also be applied, I believe, to the problem of trade imbalances. As I have noted in Chapter 6, trade deficits have adverse social consequences that should be weighed in the balance with any economic benefits to consumers or importers. Social costs, which do exist, should therefore be borne by the beneficiaries. This could be done through a traditional tax (tariff). Or it could be accomplished by some equivalent scheme, such as tradeable quotas. The tariff option is undesirable because it is too open to political manipulation (as we have seen repeatedly in the past), apart from being discouraged by agreed international trade rules. I propose the quota approach.

Up to now, we Westerners have blinded ourselves to reality by assuming that opening foreign markets will take care of the trade deficit problem. The US is discovering just how difficult it will be to persuade the Japanese, Koreans and Chinese to play the trade game by Western rules. Their whole system is geared to keeping foreign products out of their markets, and they will not allow foreigners to dictate to them how they should run their society. (Why should they?) They cannot reasonably complain, however, if we in the West decide that enormous and increasing trade deficits are intolerable for employment reasons and that we must take steps – within the rules – to ameliorate that situation. The scheme I propose is the following:

- announce a firm policy of balancing imports and exports (or at least restricting the magnitude of any trade deficit to a preset limit);
- state clearly that importers must expect to pay the social costs of unemployment associated with trade deficits;
- set policy requiring explicit import (ie foreign exchange) licenses, purchasable on the open market;
- set trade deficit reduction targets in quantitative (monetary) terms;
- award exchange rights to exporters, dollar for dollar. Allow exporters to use or sell these rights to importers;
- if (and only if) import licence requests exceed available exchange from exports – resulting in a projected trade deficit for the next period – additional import licences should be auctioned to the highest bidder (just as licences for off-shore drilling are auctioned). The government should set a minimum price for the rights, based on expected unemployment and other costs. Such auctions could be computerized.

The surplus revenues from the periodic licence auction could be earmarked for the unemployment insurance and/or social security trust funds. But an even more radical solution is possible that would restrict the government's role to setting overall policy on deficit reduction. The scheme I have in mind is to allocate tradeable foreign exchange 'rights' equally to every adult in the country. These rights would be deposited in a special account, more or less like gasoline consumption quotas, mentioned earlier. For instance, the 200 million adults in the US might each receive an annual foreign exchange rights allocation of US$2000, corresponding to total foreign currency allocation of US$400 billion. (To be absolutely clear, to receive a right to buy foreign currency for trading purposes is not the same as receiving the money itself. But the rights would have a market value.) Most individuals would not use their full foreign exchange allocation directly unless they take a vacation abroad. The same is true of exporters. Unused allocations could then be pooled for sale, through the banks, to importing businesses. If the total national demand for foreign exchange (to pay for imports) exceeded the national allocation, importers would have to bid for additional exchange rights in an auction market. In effect, they would have to pay a surcharge for the right to buy foreign currency to purchase goods or services abroad. The surcharge would be paid, *not* to the government, but to exporters and citizens with unused exchange rights.

The economic impact of this scheme – apart from tending to balance the international payments accounts – would be twofold: first, it would tend to increase exporters' profits, thus increasing capital creation in the export sector; second, it would tend to raise effective prices for imported goods, thus reducing their relative attractiveness.

For instance, petroleum prices might be driven up (depending on the overall trade balance), resulting in some decrease in final demand for petroleum products. This, in turn, would help the domestic energy producers and the industries producing capital goods for energy conservation. Similarly, domestic food prices might fall, thanks to cross subsidies by exporters. Prices of goods produced domestically would, in general, be slightly lower while prices for imported goods would, in general, be slightly higher.

Obviously if there is no trade deficit there would be no auction revenues and no need for them. In this case, the monetary value of foreign exchange rights would be zero. However, in the case of the US, with its large and persistent trade imbalance, such rights would probably have a significant market value. This money value, divided between exporters and ordinary citizens, would constitute a second source of income for low-income consumers, and an indirect tax on high-income consumers of imported goods. It would have the same effect on imports as a tariff, but without the same potential for abuse by inefficient, but politically well-connected, domestic producers.

REGULATORY REFORM

There are cases where economic instruments will not work as effectively as regulation. For instance, it is economically attractive to impose costs for waste disposal, both to raise needed revenue and to encourage materials recovery and recycling. The most straightforward way to do this is to tax consumers directly for waste disposal services. However, this has two serious drawbacks, apart from the large amount of information processing involved: firstly, the consumers bearing the costs have little or no influence on upstream product design and technology choice decisions, so the consumer's only choice is to buy or not to buy. Impact on materials re-use will be minimal. Secondly, if the costs of disposal become non-negligible, there will be incentives for compaction and 'midnight' disposal, such as illicit roadside dumping. This can be worse than the common system of waste disposal paid for by local communities. The overall effect of such charges, in some cases, at least, could well be counterproductive.

There are potentially more effective ways to include the cost of waste disposal in the price of goods. One is to implement a universal returnable deposit scheme to encourage users of re-usable or remanufacturable products to return them to the store (and ultimately to the manufacturer) before getting a replacement. This would apply quite well not only to soft drink bottles, but to cars, batteries, tires, light bulbs, TVs, printer cartridges and so on. Its major benefit (from a waste disposal perspective) is that manufacturers are encouraged to design their products for both easy re-use and remanufacturability, but also to create the logistic systems necessary for implementation.

The returnable deposit idea has already been implemented in various places, in a variety of forms, mainly for bottles and cans. Until recently, packagers and retailers lobbied fiercely, and usually successfully, against such laws. But they are effective. Michigan is getting return rates approaching 100 per cent of sales on cans and bottles, doubtless including contributions from neighboring Ohio, Indiana and Canada. Sweden has achieved more than 90 per cent returns on aluminum cans.

The German 'green dot' (*Duallesysteme*) program, now fully operational for several years, is a variant on the deposit-return scheme. The deposit is paid, not directly by consumers, but by manufacturers and packagers who pay for the privilege of putting a green dot on the package. Retailers are paid to provide facilities for collecting returns. The central fund also pays for the collection of waste packaging from the retailers and (in principle) for developing technologies and markets for recycling. In practice, however, much of the collected packaging material has been shipped out of the country (eg to Indonesia) because local recyclers have been slow to establish themselves.

A system such as 'green dot' could easily be extended to other recyclables, such as motor oil. Motor oil is relatively easy to re-refine and re-refined oil is almost as good as new oil. There would surely be a market at some appropriately discounted price. Yet waste motor oil is currently burned for fuel (with significant emissions of impurities such as lead), used for dust control on dirt roads, or simply dumped. Much of it finds its way into rivers and streams. This market would probably have developed spontaneously, except for opposition by the oil refiners who essentially control the distribution of motor oil through their retail outlets. Re-refined motor oil would obviously compete with the new product, which happens to be very profitable. A deposit (or tax) on new motor oil could be used to pay dealers to provide suitable collection facilities for used oil.

Tires offer a major opportunity. Used tires collected in bulk have no value, even though some of them could be retreaded, because the sorting and logistics make it uneconomic. However a deposit return scheme, payable if and only if tires are returned in condition to be retreaded, could be effective. The funds would pay for collection. A still more effective system would be to create tire service companies such as currently operate successfully for heavy trucks and airlines. The service company retains ownership and responsibility for the tire, which is rotated and returned on a regular basis. At present the system works only where there are a lot of tires at one location. However, a decentralized version could operate through local service stations or dealerships, under a system requiring regular inspections and exchanges. Effective tire life could be extended several-fold, while cost to consumers could be reduced at the same time. (The large tire companies would, of course, be losers.)

The Netherlands has now established a national deposit return system for automobiles. Each new car purchaser pays about US$250 into the system, to be returned when the car is scrapped. This fund has financed a major effort to upgrade the capabilities of scrap dealers around the country, develop more sophisticated dismantling and disassembly capabilities, and develop new markets for parts and components. A more radical approach along the same lines would be to keep actual ownership and life-cycle responsibility for product disposal with the original manufacturer, or a designated service provider. This approach was once the norm for telephones, computers and Xerox machines. It was discarded, mainly, for anti-trust reasons. However, some compromise may be possible between the anti-trust problems that would arise from a return to this scheme, and the waste disposal problems that are literally piling up today.

An important element of regulatory reform, then, is to reduce existing administrative barriers to resource recovery, re-use and remanufacturing. Restrictions on the movement of waste materials fall into this category. Manufacturers who would cheerfully recycle or remanufacture their own worn out equipment constantly complain of legal restrictions (eg on shipping hazardous materials across state lines) that make such activities uneconomic or illegal. Why should it be more difficult to ship a truck-load of used batteries to a recycling plant than a load of uranium fuel rods, sulfuric acid, chlorine gas, or pesticides? Why, to take another case, should it be illegal for a pharmaceutical firm that cultures specialized organisms – such as antibiotics – to use wastes from these cultures to grow mushrooms or to feed fish? (Hard to believe, but true.) These are examples of the unfortunate consequences of ill-conceived laws and regulations. Surely reasonable men and women can devise more reasonable rules. One of the principles I would advocate is that companies should be responsible for the products they sell and the wastes they dispose of, but that internal operations, including transportation from one site to another, should be exempt from regulation except as regards safety. Safety rules for goods transport should be consistent, not favoring one type of good over another.

SCIENCE AND TECHNOLOGY

An extended discussion of specific needs and opportunities in the area of science and technology seems unnecessary at this point. However, it is important to bear in mind that the government does have a significant role to play. In the first place, there is a fundamental argument for government subsidy to science and technology. To put it in a nutshell, private firms cannot recover all of the benefits of knowledge they develop. The more fundamental the knowledge, the less of the potential benefits can be captured by a private sector sponsor of the research. Moreover, if a private enterprise does try to maximize its private return by keeping important basic research results secret, it deprives others – the public – of benefits that might otherwise have been derived. Most of the gains will go to society as a whole. This is the basic reason why it makes sense for governments to sponsor fundamental research. As research becomes more and more applied, of course, the private sector sponsor may be able to capture a larger proportion of the total benefits, such as they are. The larger the firm, the larger the fractional recovery. This is the reason large firms do more research than smaller ones.

In emerging fields like renewable energy technologies, much of the needed research is still fairly fundamental in nature. For instance, with regard to photovoltaic (PV) technology it is not yet clear whether amorphous silicon, polycrystalline silicon or thin films offer the most promising approach. There are a number of competing materials that might be used for thin films (and probably some that haven't yet been thought of). There are a number of possible routes to manufacturing. Thus even large firms are unlikely to gain much of an advantage from investing heavily in research at this stage. Small firms had best stay out of the game, unless they already possess some major (and scarce) expertise. There is also the problem of scale. The idea of putting PV cells on satellites, or on the moon, is potentially very attractive, but depends on the development of advanced aerospace capabilities that are far beyond the capability of any private firm today.

In short, the government is the research sponsor of last resort. Significant R&D support for new technologies at this stage could be extremely important in accelerating the inevitable shift away from fossil fuels (and, hopefully, not to nuclear power). It is very unfortunate and discouraging that budgetary problems are getting in the way at this critical time. The amount of money that could be productively used for developing PV technology (for instance) is trivial compared to the amounts that are being unproductively used by governments in other ways. But, for some reason, science and technology always seems like the easiest target for budget-cutters.

SUMMARY AND IMPLICATIONS

Under the heading of tax reform, I advocate, first, a serious and comprehensive attempt to eliminate obsolete subsidies (admittedly, this is hardly an original proposal, but it remains a vital first step). Second, we should consider a phased elimination of the social security tax, followed by reductions in corporate and personal income taxes. This should be accompanied by phased and equivalent increases in taxes on both renewable and non-renewable resource use. Other taxes on bads should also be introduced including taxes on road use (congestion taxes), pollution and waste disposal (where feasible), and international financial transfers.

Under the heading of welfare reform, I advocate a number of old ideas, including increased privatization and portability of pensions, universal health insurance coverage for major medical problems, and expanded use of health maintenance organizations (HMOs) for the rest. The major innovation proposed is the use of a system of tradeable consumption quotas for natural resources, allocated in the first instance to adult residents and children over some cutoff age. Sale of under-utilized quotas through computerized auction markets would provide a guaranteed minimum income for underconsumers. All firms would be required to purchase their consumption requirements in the market. The role of the government would be to set the annual quota and supervise the markets.

Under the heading of trade reform – to eliminate long-term trade deficits or surpluses – I propose the use of exchangeable import quotas, again based on an allocation and auction market permitting under-users to sell their surplus to importers. Exporters would receive import credits, which could be sold. The role of the government would be to set acceptable trade deficit (or surplus) levels, allocate the quotas and supervise the market.

Under the heading or regulatory policy reform, as regards the environment, I advocate reduced emphasis on direct regulation and greater use of economic instruments. The deposit return scheme – and other forms of take back legislation – for encouraging consumers to return used products (such as bottles, tires, batteries, etc) deserves much greater emphasis. One major area of needed reform is to modify the liability rules (eg CERCLA) pertaining to old waste dumps. Another is to eliminate unnecessary regulatory barriers to resource recovery, re-use and remanufacturing.

As regards science and technology policy, I can only emphasize the importance of continued – even expanded – government support for basic research, especially in areas such as photovoltaic power where the future technological development trajectory is not yet clear enough to attract high levels of private sector investment.

NOTES

1   Some libertarians will argue that, while some variants may be worse than others, all taxes are economically burdensome. Others (including me) argue that some taxable activities are inherently harmful to society and that taxation may be a more efficient way of discouraging those activities than outright prohibition. Such taxes have been labeled 'sin' taxes. There is a point of view that finds this idea repellant, on the grounds that to tax an activity is to give it an implicit license to exist, whereas truly sinful activities should not be licensed, and licit activities should not be taxed. However this perspective is too absolutist for my taste. It ignores both the need for obtaining revenue from some source and the practical difficulties of enforcement of an outright ban (prohibition) in cases where even a large minority of the population engages in the designated activity.

2   One revenue-neutral flat tax proposal, put forward by Stanford economists Robert Hall and Alvin Robushka, would leave the first US$25,000 of income for a family of four untaxed, with a 19 per cent rate on all other earned income. Of course, the flat tax would mean eliminating popular deductions such as the deduction for mortgage interest and the deduction for charitable donations.

3   This is misleading because social security funds are lumped in with other governmental revenues for budgetary purposes, and the present social security surplus is effectively being diverted to fund the federal deficit. Also, the system is still being falsely advertised as a kind of savings plan to provide for retirement. Many people have no other pension. In fact, retirement benefits are paid out of current revenues and individual contributions are nowhere near large enough to pay for expected future claims. The system can only be saved by cutting back on future benefits – most likely by postponing the age that benefits begin and cutting back on the indexation.

4   There is a school of economists who dispute this statement on the grounds that all taxes are ultimately paid by labor, hence the shift of taxes from labor to resources would be merely cosmetic. On closer scrutiny, however, this proposition can be seen to be derived from theorems based on extremely dubious assumptions and oversimplified models. In short, I think they are quite mistaken in concluding that tax policy can have no impact on employment.

5   The import of narcotics is a special case, which needs to be dealt with in other ways, beyond the scope of this book.

6   The corporate income tax is essentially a direct subtraction from funds potentially available for investment. Thus, if increased capital investment is the objective, this tax should be eliminated before the capital gains tax, which is levied on individuals and which should be levied, if at all, only on capital gains from investments in new stock issues.

7   Civil servants are still trusted by the public in Japan and Northern Europe. Unfortunately this trust is being undermined by spreading allegations of corruption.

8   See note 17, Chapter 9.

9   Many – indeed, most – academic experts in public finance (ie tax policy) insist that taxes should be neutral with respect to social policy in other spheres. That is, the sources and mechanisms of revenue generation should not influence social choices (though the ways in which revenue is allocated obviously do). The idea is that taxes should not be used as a tool for social engineering. Why not? The fact is that tax policy does strongly influence personal and social choices of all kinds. It is best to recognize this fact openly and discuss how this influence can be channeled in desirable directions, rather than in undesirable ones. Obviously such a discussion is and must be political.

10 It need hardly be pointed out that the slave trade (mostly for girls) still exists in many Arab countries, and in rural areas of India. However, it has largely disappeared from the West.

11 Such a tax should also be imposed on breweries, lime kilns and cement plants, because they also produce CO_2.

12 See NRDC, 1992.

13 For comparison, note that motor fuel costs in Europe and Japan are – and have been for many years – roughly four to five times higher than in the US. Gasoline in the US is one of the world's greatest bargains. Motor fuel use per capita in Europe and Japan is 40 to 50 per cent less than in the US. Evidently raising the cost of gasoline does not have an enormous impact on vehicle usage, once the vehicle is owned. However, it has some effect on car purchasing habits. Urban residents in Europe and Japan are considerably more likely than Americans to live without a car.

14 I don't know for sure who first suggested this idea; reputedly it was the conservative University of Chicago economist and Nobel laureate, Milton Friedman. Richard Nixon seriously proposed it as President. He was distracted by other events, unfortunately.

15 Admittedly there are some people who do not have current checking accounts in banks. However, assuming they have social security numbers, it should be possible to make comparable arrangements for them through other institutions, such as credit unions or the Post Office.

Chapter 12
International Development Issues

INTRODUCTION

Now I want to return to global economic issues. This is partly to anticipate an obvious criticism on the grounds that my view of the world is implicitly too Europe-centered or America-centered. The accusation could be made that I am taking a 'dog in the manger' position for the rich countries. It might be argued that my strategy – of slowing down the globalization process and cutting back sharply on consumption of manufactured goods by taxing resources and encouraging recovery, re-use, remanufacturing and recycling – would 'condemn several billion Asians and Africans to perpetual poverty'. The quotes are from a letter I received from one of the readers of an earlier draft of this manuscript, who shall remain nameless. So let's get these issues out into the open.

I would never seriously suggest that Asia or Africa should stop economic development (properly defined) to protect a privileged position for Europe or the US. On the other hand, I'm sure that my *soi disant* critic would not advocate trade policies that could literally destroy Western society and the global environment in the name of the Asian/African poor, lacking any assurance – except promises from the self-interested – of long-term amelioration of their poverty. I think the destruction of West, in its present liberal democratic form, is now a serious threat. I also have very grave doubts that what is going on in Asia deserves the name of economic development. Much of it is certainly not eco-sustainable. What is the point of repeating the mistakes (as we can see them retrospectively) of the West in places where the problems are worse and the resources to solve them are already significantly depleted?

WHAT CAN THE NORTH DO TO ASSIST THE SOUTH?

To put it in the crassest terms: does the West have a selfish interest in promoting economic development in the developing world? Obviously it does, if the word 'development' doesn't mean cutting the last tree and burning the last barrel of oil. We live on the same small globe, and it will not be possible to insulate ourselves indefinitely, either from global pollution, global warming, or from the problems arising from poverty, over-population and breakdown of civil order. Does this mean we should actively help in the economic development process? Yes, up to a point, I think it does.

It is wrong, and misleading, to suggest (or imagine) that economic development is a natural process that will occur anywhere in the world, if we only allow businessmen enough freedom to move money and goods around.

The lesson is: there is a lot we can and should do to help the less developed countries. There is also a lot we should *not* do. For instance, a great sin of the West – as future historians may see it – has been to export weapons and military technology to places like the Persian Gulf (especially in recent years) in exchange for raw materials, especially oil. Further sins include exporting dangerous technologies, such as toxic pesticides, that cannot be used safely in local conditions, and addictive and toxic consumer products like cigarettes. In fact, I think consumerism is one of the Western exports that the world doesn't need and can't afford. Airlines, modern multi-lane high speed highways and energy-intensive luxury consumption goods – like Mercedes-Benz cars – are only slightly less sinful. A free trader may argue that this is trade and that the consumer is always right. A great many economists and free traders, at least on the libertarian fringe, will argue that consumer sovereignty must be respected, that it is none of our business to prevent people from doing what they want to do. I think that is nonsense.

Conservatives say that consumers must be sovereign. But this would mean that producers must be free to supply the consumer's every desire regardless of social or environmental damage. This rule would have to apply to pornography, abortions, drugs, guns, nuclear weapons, and – why not? – even slavery. Conservatives who also strongly oppose at least some of those items (especially drugs, pornography and abortion) on 'moral' grounds clearly haven't accepted the consequences of their ideology. Similarly, conservatives in the Western business community argue that it is none of our business if sovereign governments trample on human rights, persecute and expel unwanted minorities, invade weaker neighbors (as India did with Goa, Bhutan, Sikkim and Kashmir, China did with Tibet, and Indonesia did with West Irian and East Timor), flout inconvenient agreements, steal intellectual property (as China does routinely) and destroy global environmental resources. I don't agree. If human rights abuses in China or Indonesia are not our business, then to protect our own workers and consumers is surely our obligation and none of their business. In short, sovereignty surely cuts both ways. Consumers can't have it all. Trading partners have to share responsibility. Otherwise it is too much of a dog-eat-dog world.

In my opinion (illiberal though it may be) we should *not* encourage economic development in Asia or Africa under the pure consumer sovereignty regime. We should not encourage Western automobile companies to invest in China (or India or Indonesia), knowing that the petroleum is running out and that highways and suburbs are being built on the best and most productive farmland. We should not buy products for sale in our own countries made with slave (or child) labor, or products made by clear-cutting tropical forests or fishing by methods which kill – and waste – far more fish (not to mention dolphins) than can be harvested. To be perfectly clear, I do *not* see any need for perfect symmetry in this matter, either. I don't oppose the use of DDT for malaria control in the tropics, even though it is banned in the US where malaria is not a problem. Nor do I agree with Greenpeace that the US should ban exports of toxic chemicals that cannot be used in the US, if there is reason to believe that production will simply move to other countries where environmental and safety regulations are more lax.[1]

I am perfectly happy to allow Western investors to export capital to invest in Asia to build factories, employing Western capital goods and Asian labor, to supply products primarily for the Asian market. If some are exported to world markets, C'est la vie. I am not at all happy for Western firms (like Nike) to use Asian factories under contract to produce products for the Western market, thus displacing their former Western workers. The notion that Western exports to the same low-wage countries will create enough jobs to compensate is sheer wishful thinking, as I said earlier (Chapter 6). If this is protectionism, I am a convinced and unapologetic protectionist.

A NEW APPROACH TO SUSTAINABLE DEVELOPMENT

My hypothetical critic may ask that I delineate my own strategy to feed the Asian and African poor. I'm not entirely sure there is one. Many will certainly starve, whatever we do.

However, to address the question (and ignore, as before, the obvious problem of political feasibility), any such interventionist development strategy would have five components:

1) a serious and effective universal (especially female) literacy program. This requires schools, teachers, laws, money and political will. But it has been discussed amply by others and I have nothing to add to what has been said elsewhere except with regard to the money (see below).
2) A serious population control program. In its objectives, at least, China is on the right track. In terms of human rights, I would prefer to use less coercion and more economic instruments (such as higher pensions for fewer children).[2] An interesting theoretical possibility would be to introduce exchangeable child-bearing rights.[3] However, again, such a program requires people, laws, money and political will.
3) An end to the arms trade, or at least an end to the sale of arms by the West to developing countries. A global agreement with enforcement would be required, but enforcement is easier for the very expensive and sophisticated weapons than for small arms. This is where I utterly reject consumer sovereignty arguments. The arms trade is as bad as the drug trade and Western democracies should not engage in it. Period. The rubric 'merchants of death' that was coined to describe the activities of Vickers-Armstrong in the days when it was selling arms to both sides of a bloody war between Greece and Turkey is no less applicable today.
4) Implementation of tradeable consumption quotas on an international level. The scheme I described in the last chapter for a single country could be extended to apply to groups of countries. In other words, over-consuming countries would have to buy consumption rights from under-consuming countries. There would have to be an international mechanism to decide and agree on global consumption levels for major resources and/or emission levels for major pollutants such as carbon dioxide. This is already being discussed under the rubric 'joint implementation'.

The funds transferred to the developing countries under the exchangeable consumption quota program should not be used to increase aggregate final consumption by individual consumers. Nor should they be used for consumer goods, weapons, or for 'developing' new sources of non-renewable raw materials for export. That would defeat the purpose. These funds should be reserved largely for investment in infrastructure and education (including both female literacy and family planning, as noted above).

The mechanisms for achieving this laudable, but practically difficult, objective cannot be fully spelled out here. However, I should say that I would rule out direct monetary transfers to governments.

Westerners don't have very many levers on the first two policies at present. Literacy requires schools and teachers, which are very scarce in the areas that need them. Unfortunately certain religious groups try to prevent us from doing even the little that would be feasible on the population front. Western business interests (not to mention governments in the developing world) would be likely to oppose either of the last two policies. But one can always hope for a miraculous conversion in the capitals of the West. A great visionary leader with charisma would help, but none is in sight.

One other lever is the World Bank. In my view, this institution is still on the wrong track, though it has recently made some useful changes in its policies. It should, however, be redesigned from top to bottom. It should stop acting as a cheerleader for conventional resource-based development. It should stop financing 'mega' projects, like giant dams and nuclear power plants, and especially projects to extract and process non-renewable raw materials, like metal ores and minerals, for export. This simply keeps the prices of raw materials artificially low, discourages re-use and recycling, and indirectly contributes to over-consumption and – as the night follows the day – excessive waste and pollution. Instead, the World Bank should act as a lender, regulator and backstop investor/insurer for local financial institutions – micro-credit banks – with access to local savings. These institutions should lend mainly to small farmers and small entrepreneurs under clearly articulated and environmentally sound rules. (For instance, agriculture should be encouraged to use integrated pest management; fishermen should agree to rules on allocation; loggers should be forced to replant not only harvested acreage but also 'waste' lands that were once productive; and so on.) The Bank should also finance projects to add value to local raw materials and – eventually – to convert them into products that can be consumed locally and in other markets in developing countries.

There is a good case for World Bank financing of infrastructure, such as roads, water and sewer projects and communications, and, not least, schools and birth control clinics. But if the Bank is to be in the infrastructure business, it had better be involved all the way, which includes national, regional and city planning. It is very poor policy to finance roads piecemeal, thus encouraging an auto-dependency, if a rail net would make more sense from a larger social and environmental perspective. Regional self-sufficiency should be promoted, not long-distance shipment of goods. Communications should get priority over goods transportation. Pipelines and river transport should and can be utilized much more efficiently. Highways should certainly *not* be built in densely populated countries unless no other mode will serve and there is also a built-in means of financing them via user charges, not only to cover the direct costs but also the (much larger) indirect long-term costs. Similarly, water supply projects should be integrated with sewer projects for entire watersheds, not individual communities. As far as possible they should be designed to be self-financing, at least in the long run, by a system of enforceable user charges and sanctions.

THE GLOBAL ENVIRONMENT

A few more words on the environment ought to be added here. I said at the beginning of the last section that my international sustainable development program would have five legs. Only four were listed. The fifth is the environment. Not all environmental problems are global. Most of the ones people worry about are not global. Environmental concerns in developing countries tend to be quite local; for example, clean water and sewage treatment. The one global problem that will affect the developing world *more* than the industrialized world is global warming and sea-level rise. Warming will affect disease vectors and pests. It may increase storminess. Low-lying areas like Bangladesh and the major river deltas of Southeast Asia are particularly vulnerable to sea-level rise. The potential impact of sea-level rise on coastal provinces of China has been considered in detail in a recent report prepared jointly by UNEP, the World Bank and China's National Environmental Protection Agency. Based on a scenario of continued carbon dioxide buildup and climate warming, an increase of 70cm in mean high tide level is envisioned off Shanghai and 60cm off the Pearl River delta (Canton) by the year 2050. A one meter rise in sea level would result in storm flooding and inundation of areas below the four meter contour line, which includes a number of major cities and 92,000 km^2 of fertile agricultural land with a projected population of 76 million people. These are the areas of China currently experiencing the most rapid economic growth. Protective dikes and river barrages are probably feasible to counter the threat via conventional engineering techniques such as the Dutch have developed (at great cost, however).

But the countries most seriously threatened by increased storminess and sea-level rise are the countless islands, estuaries and coastal zones of Southeast Asia, from Bangladesh, Indonesia, Indo China and the Philippines to Melanesia and Polynesia. These are areas that are still mostly rural and poor, but not necessarily unpopulated. While the Chinese coast may be protected, it is doubtful that tens of thousands of small islands can be protected. Since evacuation in advance of perceived and immediate need is highly unlikely, the people living in threatened locations are very much at risk. Similarly, the possibility of changing rainfall patterns is most threatening to densely populated tropical countries adapted to and dependent on the annual monsoon. By contrast, the potential beneficiaries of climate warming (if any) would be the unpopulated northern lands of Canada, Scandinavia and Siberia.

Clearly, the industrial world has a major responsibility here. It is the industrial countries that have emitted most of the carbon dioxide and other greenhouse gases in the past century. The polluter pays principle should be applied in this case. Those countries that want to continue to use fossil fuels on a large scale should pay for the privilege, since they are consuming a limited global resource, namely the ability of the oceans and the biosphere to absorb carbon dioxide. This would be an ideal application of the tradeable quota scheme described in the last chapter (for carbon, initially), but on the international level. National quotas must be set by an international agreement and allocated to nations on some agreed basis, but not necessarily in proportion to current population. Let the nations with excess needs or wants buy the unused quotas of others. Let the market set the price. It would be a worthwhile form of international income redistribution that would also contribute to long-run eco-sustainability.

The rest of the book is a discussion of economic doctrines and theories as they affect policy. It is slightly more technical than the chapters up to this point, although I have tried to make it accessible to thoughtful people who are not professional economists.

NOTES

1   People who claim this doesn't happen are ill-informed. Insiders know of plenty of examples. Montrose Chemical Co was the last DDT producer in the US. The plant was literally transported from California in 1983 to Bognor, near Jakarta, where it is a locally notorious polluter.

2   A program along these lines was proposed by economist Ronald Ridker and experimentally initiated by the US Agency for International Development in 1967 in some of the tea plantations of Southern India. In its first few years of operation, the program was apparently working fairly well. Unfortunately, such programs require long-term commitment, which is scarce among government programs.

3   This idea was advocated twenty years ago by Herman Daly (1977, revised 1991). I think it may have been suggested earlier. Of course, the problem is that it would be almost impossible to implement without the use of effective abortifacients. A suitable drug has been developed in France, but its use is bitterly opposed by organized anti-abortion groups.

Chapter 13
The Economic Growth Paradigm

BACKGROUND

The time has come to focus at last on economic growth from an economics perspective. What is it? How does it occur? Will it continue? Why do I speak of a paradigm? To begin with the last question, it is important to distinguish the paradigm of economic growth from two other aspects of the broader problem: the *physical possibility* of environmentally sustainable economic growth, and the *socio-political necessity* of continuing growth. The growth paradigm, strictly speaking, concerns our assumptions about the *definition and mechanism* of economic growth.

To be as clear as possible, I do not challenge the physical possibility of very long-term economic expansion, especially allowing for eventual conquest of space and colonization of other planets and planetoids of the Solar System. As to the socio-political necessity of continuing economic growth (in real terms), at least for many decades, I have no doubts at all. A world with so much inequity, poverty and destitution can afford nothing else. What I challenge is the necessity of continued growth narrowly based on substituting machines, chemicals and fossil fuels for human workers leaving unemployment, social malaise and environmental devastation in their wake. The use of ever-increasing amounts of non-renewable raw materials and energy, generating ever more pollution and waste, in order to put more people out of work is both immoral and unsustainable.

But the immediate problem is to understand the phenomenon of economic growth better, so as to be able to encourage it to continue more effectively and less destructively. It is too often forgotten that economic growth has been a relatively episodic phenomenon in human history. Modest periods of real growth occurred at various times in the more distant past, but growth that took a century in the late Middle Ages is now compressed into a decade, or even a single year. What has changed? Is the change irreversible?

According to economic historian Angus Maddison, economic growth between AD500 and AD1500 averaged 0.1 per cent per year or 10 per cent per century (Maddison, 1982).[1] From 1500 to 1700 growth in Western Europe accelerated four-fold; it accelerated even faster, to 0.5 per cent per year, in the eighteenth century. Great Britain achieved a growth rate of 1 per cent per year throughout the eighteenth century, becoming the richest country in the world as a result. By contrast, a number of countries have sustained growth rates in recent decades of more than 10 per cent per year. The US did it during World War II. Japan managed to keep it up through the 1960s and 1970s. Taiwan and Korea have done as well in the 1970s and 1980s. Most recently, China has grown at this rate throughout the 1990s. Can the recent surge of economic growth, which began two centuries ago (and is still accelerating in some parts of the world) continue indefinitely? To what do we owe this great leap forward?

Then again, other questions arise. Can the human race tolerate so much of this kind of success? What are the risks? Are there countervailing forces at work that could slow or stop the forward momentum? Is the train on the track? Can it be controlled?

The standard growth paradigm has two aspects. The first reflects a macro-perspective and the second reflects a micro-perspective. Surprisingly, perhaps, the two are not altogether consistent with each other. It is the macro-perspective, based on savings and investment, that I discuss first, below. The macro version of the growth paradigm is not dependent on detailed mechanisms. By contrast, the micro-perspective is mechanism-oriented. I discuss it subsequently.

THE STATE OF MACRO THEORY

Theories of economic growth (and, for that matter, theories of trade) are only one small part of neoclassical economics. But growth is such an important phenomenon that a good theory is a vital prerequisite of policy. Unfortunately, it must be said that if a 'good' theory is one that allows predictions with an accuracy significantly better than random, no such theory exists. Sadly, this fact has never stopped economists recommending policies, sometimes in the strongest possible terms. Sometimes these recommendations have been sensible and right. But, at other times, in the past, the recommended policies have turned out disastrously.[2]

There are, to be sure, many growth models consistent with the growth paradigm. The basic idea of the neoclassical paradigm is that the drivers of economic growth are labor and capital. The labor force is assumed to be (roughly) proportional to population. Beyond this, the relationship is seldom explored more deeply. Capital is driven by investment, which in turn comes from savings (ie gross output less consumption). It is usual to equate the two. Gross economic output (GNP or GDP), then, depends on factors of production, usually identified as labor, capital and land or resource inputs. The output is generated from inputs by a production function, which may or may not be given explicit mathematical form.[3] The models usually include other relationships (without which they would be under-specified), such as assumed models of the rate of labor force (ie population) growth, the rate of capital accumulation (ie investment less depreciation) and the rate of natural resource depletion.

One of the most important of the assumed relationships is that supply and demand remain in balance, thanks to automatic correction mechanisms in the competitive free market. The first explicit statement of this supposed balance was by Jean Baptiste Say, an early nineteenth century French economist. 'Say's Law' is usually stated as: 'supply creates its own demand'. The underlying idea is that if consumer demand temporarily exceeds supply, it will be reduced automatically as income is diverted into savings to finance new supply. Similarly, if consumer demand falls momentarily below supply, wages and output will fall until the balance is restored, presumably by spending money out of prior savings. (Say was never explicit about the details of the balancing mechanism.) The second half of this proposition was apparently contradicted by major slumps, even in the nineteenth century. But since there was an eventual recovery, Say's Law was assumed to have been responsible. It was regarded as axiomatic by orthodox *fin de siècle* economists like Alfred Marshall, and remained the basis of government policy advice in most Western countries until World War II.

The extended worldwide economic slump of the 1920s (except in the US) followed by an even deeper slump in the 1930s, appeared, to John Maynard Keynes in particular, as a clear violation of Say's Law. Keynes argued convincingly that supply and demand need not be balanced automatically in a free competitive market because of a vicious circle: declining demand would cause manufacturers to cut wages and/or lay off workers, thus reducing buying power and causing demand to fall still further. This seems rather obvious today. Keynes's policy recommendation was for governments to step in to fill the gap in demand (and employment) through deficit spending on public works.[4]

Formal growth models were introduced in the 1930s, beginning with Frank Ramsey's theory of optimal saving and capital accumulation in 1928. The so-called Harrod-Domar-Mahalanobis models were developed by Cambridge economists from 1936 to 1956 and more or less based on Keynes's ideas of multipliers and accelerators. They focused on the neoclassical aggregates, viz capital, labor and savings, with particular emphasis on capital formation. The operation of the market had almost no role in these models, since savings could be voluntary or government enforced. A key implication (which later turned out to be an artifact) was that growth was very sensitively dependent on the exact balance between capital and labor in different sectors. This gave rise to much talk of 'structural disequilibria' (bottlenecks) which was really a defense of central planning. These models were later used, mainly by Cambridge-trained economists, for economic policy and planning purposes in India and some other non-communist developing countries. The results were, to say the least, poor. In retrospect, it is probable that the central planning (socialist) bias did more to inhibit growth than to encourage it.

Incidentally, a significant part of the theoretical literature on economic growth concerns a very special and totally unrealistic mathematical model introduced by the Hungarian mathematician John von Neumann in 1932 (translated into English in 1945). Von Neumann's model has several interesting features. First of all, it postulates a closed set of products and processes in supply–demand equilibrium, as postulated in the nineteenth century by Leon Walras.[5] Each product of the model economy is essentially produced by a linear combination of others. The matrix of coefficients remains fixed, which means that there is no structural change over time. (The term for this kind of growth is 'homothetic'.) The virtue of the model to mathematical economists is that a growth solution, in which supply and demand remain in perpetual Walrasian equilibrium, actually exists. This model was the first of the breed that is now known as 'computable general equilibrium' (CGE) models, about which I have more to say later. Unfortunately the main virtue of such models is computability, not realism. Admittedly, realism of assumptions is not necessarily a requirement, as long as the model has explanatory power. The argument, eloquently set forth many years ago by Milton Friedman (1953), is that it is enough for a model to work 'as if' it were a true reflection of reality. However I have a serious problem with one of the neoclassical assumptions, namely the notion (legitimized, in effect, by von Neumann) of growth-in-equilibrium. I will return to this.

Modern neoclassical growth theory really began in the 1950s. The starting point was empirical work by Fabricant, Abramovitz, Schmookler and Kendrick, among others, which reconstructed long timeseries of labor, capital and GNP data for the US since 1870 and developed factor productivity indices (aggregate output divided by a weighted sum of inputs). The purpose was to estimate quantitatively, for the first time, the relative contributions of capital, labor and technical progress to output growth. From this work it became clear that capital accumulation per se could not account for very much of the per capita growth in the US economy. Fabricant's estimate of the capital contribution was only 10 per cent.

This shocking discovery contradicted received wisdom and raised new and interesting questions. In 1957 Robert Solow showed a way to characterize 'neutral technical progress' in an aggregate production function by introducing a multiplier that depends only on time.[6] He statistically confirmed the assumption of neutrality, meaning that the multiplier is independent of the capital-labor (K/L) ratio. Fitted to US timeseries data for 1909 through 1949, Solow's technical progress multiplier accounted for 87.5 per cent of per capita non-farm growth in the US. It grew annually at about 1 per cent per annum during the first half of the period and 2 per cent per year thereafter (Solow, 1957). Solow's seminal work (for which he was later awarded a Nobel prize in economics) also gave some empirical justification to a key prediction of the neoclassical growth theory, namely that aggregate output should demonstrate declining marginal returns to capital. This means that the rate of growth should decline as the economy becomes more and more capital intensive. It follows that growth must stop when marginal returns to capital are only enough to compensate for annual depreciation. To be specific, in his timeseries from 1909 through 1949 the capital employed per unit of labor (K/L) rose from US$2.06 to US$2.70 (in 1929 prices). His fitted functions suggested that the saturation point might be expected when the K/L level reached two or above, which appeared to be rather far in the future when the paper was written.

Solow also pointed out that zero net marginal capital productivity sets in when adding some capital adds only enough product to make good the depreciation of the capital increment itself. He then did a rough 'back of an envelope' estimation of the annual capital depreciation rate, which he put between 3 per cent and 5 per cent, based partly on the K/L ratio noted above. In other words, capital saturation would occur whenever the gross marginal product of capital falls to 0.03–0.05. After that, the only available growth mechanism (if it can be called that) would be technical progress – which the model did not pretend to explain.

A final point of some interest that Solow did not comment on, curiously, is that his method of estimating the marginal rate of capital depreciation suggests that the rate of depreciation itself was rising. That is, if it was 3 per cent in 1909 it had increased to 5 per cent by 1949. This increase may well have continued. In fact, I think there is a good explanation. The total physical capital stock consists of a mix of long-lived infrastructure, structures and shorter-lived machines and vehicles. At the beginning of the century, structures and railroads, for instance, constituted a large fraction of the capital stock. Since then the mix has shifted in the direction of shorter-lived equipment, such as trucks. Structures, too, are now designed for shorter useful lives. In recent years even shorter-lived computers and software have been increasingly important. So it is almost certain that if the marginal capital depreciation rate was 5 per cent per year in 1949, it must be greater today. I have made no attempt to estimate it quantitatively – I know of no such estimate in the literature – but 6–8 per cent per annum would not be a big surprise.

To summarize briefly, the neoclassical growth model as formalized by Solow and elaborated subsequently by others includes many simplifying assumptions, as is to be expected. But three of their implications are crucial. The first implication is that the contribution of capital investment to growth will slow and finally cease due to capital intensity saturation. The second follows: the only source of growth after saturation must be technological progress – which the model does not explain and treats as exogenous.[7] The third implication is that poorer countries (with less capital investment) will grow faster than rich ones, other factors remaining the same. This third implication follows from the others; namely, the law of diminishing returns to (man-made) capital.

PROBLEMS WITH THE THEORY

The basic problem is that the standard neoclassical macro theory has very little predictive or explanatory power. Thus the 'as if' argument for admitting unrealistic assumptions cannot hold. One problem is that Solow's growth theory, based on the neoclassical assumption of declining returns to investment, implies that growth should eventually slow down for the rich countries, as compared with the poorer ones. It hasn't. Specifically, the existing theory does not explain why the industrialized countries as a group have grown as fast as the poorer countries, or why growth has not slowed down – although the period of most rapid growth was 1950–1970 and there has been a significant slowdown since then.[8] To quote from *The Economist* (1996c): 'Do these theoretical predictions accord with the real world? The short answer is no'.

One weakness in growth theory, as formulated by Solow, arises from its failure to reflect known micro-economic growth mechanisms. In particular, I refer to the 'Salter cycle'.[9] This mechanism depends on two characteristics of production processes and consumption behavior that have no place in the neo-classical macro theory. They are: increasing returns to scale and experience or 'learning by doing' in production at the macro level; declining marginal utility of consumption. The first of these characteristics is difficult to reconcile with the standard macro-economic assumption of constant returns to scale. But it is undoubtedly a fact of life in industry. The second component of the Salter cycle, declining marginal utility of consumption, is fundamental in economics and not at all controversial. It has an important implication, namely that declining prices will generate increasing demand. The reason is simply that, if the next increment of supply of a given commodity or product has less value (utility) to a consumer than the last one, then the consumer will be willing to pay less for it. By the same argument in reverse, a lower price per unit of supply will generate a greater demand. In technical terms, the product has a negative price elasticity of demand.

In brief, the idea of the Salter cycle is quite simple. Economies of scale are normal in manufacturing. This means average unit costs tend to drop as volume increases. The underlying reason is that fixed costs (R&D, design, plant and equipment, etc) can be spread over more and more units. Thus profits are generally maximized when production is maximized (ie at the limit of capacity). It follows that manufacturers with fixed investments to amortize have a strong incentive to increase sales. This is the basic reason why it pays to advertise. It also turns out that price cutting is usually effective, which is why advertising campaigns so often feature price reductions. The price reductions are not always permanent. (Prices can, and do, tend to rise whenever market demand exceeds current capacity.) But, as I have said, price reductions normally generate additional sales. This happens because even a slightly lower price can bring in marginal customers who couldn't quite afford to buy at the higher price. There is a lot of tactical game playing in marketing, since manufacturers want to sell as much as they can at the highest possible price. In other words, they try to 'skim the cream' before cutting prices. But when the cream has been skimmed, the only way to increase sales further is to cut prices.

The virtuous circle now appears. The increased demand generated by a price cut justifies a larger scale of production. The larger scale of production, together with the learning that has taken place, causes costs to fall. Decreasing costs justify further price cuts, which generate increased demand, which results in greater economies of scale... and so on. What all this amounts to is that growth itself begets more growth. The process continues in each market until it reaches a state of complete saturation. At this point the price elasticity approaches zero.

In fact, returns to scale (via the Salter cycle) have apparently accounted for a significant part of the economic growth experienced by advanced countries since World War II. For the period 1948–1976, Edward Denison at Brookings Institution estimated that 18 per cent of total US economic growth could be attributed to economies of scale – and presumably experience – in manufacturing (Denison, 1979). Not surprisingly, the contribution of scale economies was apparently much larger for Germany and Japan. This is because their economies were much smaller in the early postwar years, and manufacturing accounts for a much larger percentage of total output in both cases. For Japan, Denison estimated that scale effects accounted for 44.4 per cent of total growth from 1953 to 1971. This seems to have increased still further to 54 per cent during the 1970s (Usui, 1988, Table B–6). It should be said that economies of scale and experience in manufacturing are not the only drivers of long-term economic growth. Other factors considered by Denison (op cit) include 'structural change' (the growth of services), urbanization, investment in infrastructure, investment in plant and equipment, technological progress and investment in human resources (ie education).

It should also be noted, again, that the Salter cycle is inconsistent with the neoclassical macro theory described above in two fundamental ways. First, it is based on increasing returns to scale (the higher the better), which don't exist in the neoclassical theory. And second, it depends on profits being a function of scale. This is problematic because the neoclassical theory assumes growth in equilibrium. But in a competitive Walrasian static equilibrium, as is well known, prices must fall to marginal costs of production. There can be no profits in such a case, which is why neoclassical economic theory puts so much emphasis on saving as the only possible source of investment. However, without profits – returns to capital – or dividends, there is no economic incentive for individuals to save or invest.[10]

Something called 'new growth theory' (see Romer, 1986, 1987, 1990, 1994) has been getting attention for suggesting a new wrinkle that might solve the first of these problems, viz the notion that human capital (skills, education and knowledge) is unlike man-made capital in that it need not be subject to the law of diminishing returns to capital investment. If this is so, the assumption can be discarded and the capital saturation problem may go away. Then economic growth can theoretically continue indefinitely and need not depend only on exogenous technical progress. However, notwithstanding Solow, it must be emphasized that growth does not occur in competitive equilibrium and (related to this) technological change is not exogenous. Still less is it automatic. This point is elementary, but it has been almost universally neglected in growth theory until recently. This assumption is analytically convenient for constructing mathematical growth models employing aggregate production functions. In all fairness, economic theorists are aware of the deficiency and there now is a significant body of research, kicked off by Romer's work, on ways of 'endogenizing' technological progress into the standard theory. To do so convincingly, however, it is necessary to discard several of the other classical simplifying assumptions of that theory, namely the assumption of 'perfect information' and the related assumption that the economy grows in equilibrium. In fact, if the economy were in equilibrium there would be no investment opportunities yielding abnormal returns, and hence no innovation.

SOURCES OF TECHNOLOGICAL PROGRESS

The reason technological progress has seemed to be exogenous (the 'as if' argument, cited above) is that it follows from multiple and diverse sources. One of them is simply experience or 'learning by doing'. It seems that learning is a collective phenomenon, in that the hours of human labor required to produce a given product, whether cigars or airplanes, continue to decline more or less indefinitely as a function of the cumulative number of those items produced since the beginning of production.[11] But the rate of improvement is not a fixed law of nature. Workers do not all learn at the same rate. Old workers learn slower than young ones. Illiterate or semi-literate workers learn much slower than well-educated ones. Under-nourished or unhealthy workers don't learn as fast as well-fed healthy ones. Unmotivated workers don't learn at all. So human resource policies, especially education, are enormously important. On the other hand, such policies take a long time to be effective. Today's highly motivated, disciplined and well-educated German workforce is the product of culture, policies and institutions long in the building.

Another source of technological progress is prior investment in R&D. In the past, before R&D was institutionalized, there was often a long lag between invention or discovery and successful application. But the most likely beneficiaries were the inventor himself, and/or his colleagues, financial backers or local rivals. Until recently, technology diffused around the world rather slowly. The first beneficiaries were the innovators themselves and the local people in the city or region where large-scale production began. Today the situation is very different. Diffusion of knowledge is faster because communication is much faster. Countries lagging in the technological sweepstakes have learned that some kinds of technology can be imported and adapted as easily – or more easily – than it can be developed. However, this merely means that if a wealthy country is to stay wealthy, it is more important than ever before to maintain a technological lead over poorer and hungrier rivals. This requires effort.

The reality is that government investment in education, institution building and R&D plays an enormously important – probably dominant – role in the creation of new technology. But there is more. Economic benefits do not necessarily accrue to the creators of technology. They accrue to the entrepreneurial innovators who create products, services and markets. The greatest asset a country can have is a literate and numerate workforce, a strong scientific establishment backed up by good engineering schools, and an entrepreneurial, innovative climate in which new small enterprises can grow into giants. Very deep social, political and cultural forces are involved. Economic growth theory does not (and probably cannot) account for all these factors.

Nevertheless, economists have not totally neglected the problem of innovation. Joseph Schumpeter called attention to the importance of 'radical innovation' as a driver of economic change and growth as early as 1912 in his book *The Theory of Economic Development*. Schumpeter did not treat innovation as exogenous (as Keynes did). On the contrary, he pointed out that innovation in a non-equilibrium world permits innovators to gain temporary but significant monopoly profits, until the rest of the world catches up with the innovator. (Patents are legal monopolies awarded to inventors precisely for the purpose of rewarding and thus encouraging innovation.) These profits provide the incentives that are absent in the equilibrium theory.[12]

The key point I must emphasize again is that marginalist equilibrium growth theory, like classical theory, concludes that economic growth must be driven by private consumer savings because – in equilibrium – there would be no profits! Yet the empirical evidence (discussed previously) shows clearly and unmistakably that this is not true and never has been true. To recall an earlier comment, the contribution of capital to per capita growth in the US economy, at least prior to 1950, was estimated by Fabricant to be 10 per cent and by Solow (using a different methodology) to be 12.5 per cent. The rest was attributed to technical progress. Moreover, it is misleading to lump all savings and investment together. An accounting balance (discussed later) indicates clearly that it is not private savings but overwhelmingly business profits (including allowable depreciation) that finance business capital formation. Household savings are channelled into the purchase of durable goods, housing, and financial institutions (insurance and savings banks) that – in turn – largely buy government bonds. As a practical matter, lower consumer savings would correspond to a slow-down in housing starts, not a slowdown in business investment.

RESOURCES AS FACTORS OF PRODUCTION

Still another weakness of the standard neoclassical theory of growth, in my view, is its failure to reflect the role of energy and natural resources. The standard model treats these as 'intermediates', meaning they are produced by capital and labor. Yet this rather casual assumption can only be defended by making an 'as if' argument of some sort; it makes no sense a priori. It is (physical) capital that is, in fact, produced by human activity, whereas natural resources are truly a gift of nature. Labor and capital may be used in the process of discovering, extracting and finding resources. But they do not create the resources. This is not merely a semantic point. As much labor and capital are needed to dig an oil or gas well whether or not hydrocarbons are found. Nor is this weakness – better say omission – of the growth models irrelevant to current policy concerns. The reason it is important is that Solow's approach – taking labor and capital as factors – has led to the conclusion that growth is primarily driven by autonomous technical progress, defined as a residual. But the model neither explains technical progress nor does it properly reflect the role that increasing availability of cheap fossil energy – notably coal, then oil, now natural gas – has had in driving the substitution of machines for human labor over the last 200 years. If this particular substitution process were explicitly reflected by the growth model, then one might have a far more realistic idea of the role of technical progress as distinct from the role of cheap energy.

The argument for neglecting resource inputs in today's economy is worth addressing explicitly. Some historical context is helpful. At the beginning of the industrial revolution, when most economic product was created by agriculture, labor on the land was extremely scarce at certain critical times, especially during plowing, planting and harvest. In this context, historians have emphasized the importance of such things as the sixth-century invention of the moldboard plow, pulled by a team of oxen. This was followed in the ninth century by the invention of special harnesses that allowed the use of horses and doubled the effective rate of plowing. These innovations, in turn, permitted more intensive use of the land, and the characteristic three-field crop rotation in Western Europe (White, 1967). The result was a significant increase in the application of animal muscle power to agriculture. In effect, they amplified the available human muscle power. Obviously later introduction of machines to perform these tasks was a further amplification. While machines, such as tractors, were direct replacements for horses, they also substituted the use of fossil fuels for animal feeds. These machines greatly increased the speed of plowing and harvesting, thus allowing a given number of agricultural workers to handle a much larger land area. The fact that agricultural land formerly devoted to the production of animal feeds such as oats (for horses) could be diverted to producing corn and wheat for human consumption amounted to a further increase in the effective productivity of the human workers and of the land.

The importance of machines and processes utilizing fossil energy in later industrial development can hardly be doubted. The smelting of metals, for instance, now depends almost entirely on fossil fuels or electricity. Electric power, which became available in a few locations only a century ago, is needed for almost every industrial operation – not to mention consumer services. It is largely obtained from steam turbines using fossil fuels. The glass, brick, ceramic clay and cement industries are equally based on high temperature combustion processes. The entire petrochemical industry is directly dependent on fossil fuels. And, of course, the transportation sector that ties the rest together is almost entirely based on the use of hydrocarbon liquids, notably gasoline, diesel fuel and kerosine.

Notwithstanding the foregoing, some growth theorists will continue to argue that fossil energy is not a significant factor of production, based on the empirical argument that the apparent cost of natural resource inputs to the economy has been declining for many decades and is now very small – only a few per cent.[13] There are two problems with this line of argument. First, it will be recalled from earlier discussion that the conventional GDP measure makes no allowance for resource depletion. In particular, it treats the sale of natural resources as income, without making any corresponding subtraction for the depreciation of natural resource capital stock. I discussed this problem in the context of failing to allow for the depreciation of environmental resources, such as forests and fisheries, in calculating GDP (Chapter 10). But that criticism applies equally well to mineral depletion, which also ought to be subtracted from GDP for the same reason.

Surely the cost of replacement of those resources should be taken into account somehow. In fact, unlike man-made capital, natural capital cannot necessarily be replaced at the same cost as locating and exploiting the original resource. A marginal barrel of oil pumped from Saudi Arabia today may have cost US$10 (or less) in terms of current dollars. But the future replacement barrel of oil, from deep in the Gulf of Mexico or from northern Siberia, might cost US$30 or more to find and extract. And replacement costs keep rising. Obviously, one can obtain liquid hydrocarbon fuels from other primary resources – natural gas, coal or shale – at some price. But once again, the replacement is significantly more costly than the original. It seems clear that valuing exhaustible resources at their current market prices is seriously misleading for this reason alone.[14]

There is another problem, however. The use of fossil hydrocarbons generates combustion wastes, including carbon dioxide and nitrogen and sulfur oxides. Carbon dioxide contributes to global warming. Fuel-bound sulfur and nitrogen oxides produced in high temperature combustion processes both contribute to acid rain. Economists consistently argue that when the use of a resource causes harm, the damage cost should be reflected in the price of that resource, but they are currently *not* included. In the case of hydrocarbon fuels (and many other resources, such as heavy metals) the environmental damages resulting from use may outweigh the market prices of those resources several fold. It is difficult to be authoritative about such estimates, of course, but it is hardly legitimate to set the damages arbitrarily at zero.[15]

As applied to feasible replacement alternatives, the two sources of under-estimation must be combined. For instance, the likely 'backstop' technology for petroleum is to extract liquid hydrocarbons from shale or coal. The cost of doing so is probably at least US$50 per barrel, or 2.5 times the current price (US$20). Since the efficiency of the liquefaction process is unlikely to exceed 50 per cent, the environmental damages associated with such an extraction process would also be roughly double the damage associated with the use of petroleum per se. So if the environmental damage cost associated with a barrel of petroleum is US$30, the corresponding cost for a barrel of 'synthetic' petroleum would be at least US$60. Whereas current statistics suggest a value of US$20 for a barrel of petroleum, based on current markets, the more appropriate valuation taking into account depletion and environmental damage might easily be US$110 per barrel. Again, the numbers are purely illustrative, and I am only making the point that, in principle, damage costs should be internalized, and that they might be quite large.

In short, resource costs are undervalued by a significant amount – possibly a factor of five or even an order of magnitude – for both of the reasons noted above. What all this implies to me is that fossil energy is, indeed, as much a factor of production as physical capital. Both are produced by human labor, together with capital and energy. In short, labor, capital and energy are co-factors. The technical detail of correctly accounting for the energy share of production is not something that needs to be discussed further here. Suffice it to say that the problem needs to be addressed more seriously than it has been to date.

THEORY VERSUS CURRENT POLICY PROPOSALS

The conservative (Republican) theory of economic growth is a particular variant of the classical macro-paradigm, based on Say's Law. In effect, this theory is roughly based on the economic orthodoxy of the 1920s; that savings are the first priority, that savings will create investment and that investment will increase productivity and wealth. The increased wealth, in turn, will generate increased demand for goods and services that will somehow produce new jobs. It also assumes that tax cuts for the wealthy will result in increased savings, on the grounds that the wealthy do most of the saving. These savings then (by assumption) flow into increased investment, thence increased productivity, increased output (GNP) and finally, increased income and welfare for all. Here is the summary version of a proposal by *Business Week* (1996) timed to appear just before the Republican National Convention. It consisted of three major points:

1) **Balance the (federal) budget**. Argument: 'balancing the budget will cut the cost of capital to business. Interest rates would fall by almost two percentage points, igniting a much needed investment boom.'
2) **Overhaul taxes**. Argument: 'A simpler clearer tax system can cut the cost of compliance... Rates can be cut back... by eliminating industry-specific tax breaks and overgrown personal deductions. The result: funds will flow to the most economically sound investments.'
3) **Privatize social security**. Argument: 'Today's pay as you go retirement system is a drain on savings – and is headed for breakdown. Diverting part of the payroll tax into private retirement accounts will create a healthy mix... the payoff will be higher savings and faster growth.'

I can agree with much of this program, so far as it goes. But the emphasis is exclusively on taxes and private savings. No other growth mechanism is even mentioned in the plan. Unfortunately, while private retirement accounts would permit investment in stocks and bonds, more such investment might just drive up stock prices and a lot would just flow into the pockets of Wall Street brokers and mutual fund managers.[16] There is no direct link between money flowing into Wall Street and money flowing into real job-creating investments. The problem is that other important factors of long-term growth, especially technological progress including education and R&D, are likely to be cut back even further in the effort to balance the government budget 'painlessly'.

A variant doctrine, known as 'supply-side' economics to some (and 'voodoo economics' to others), holds that tax cuts from present levels will stimulate enough growth to create more revenue than is lost by the cuts. This occurred once, briefly, during the Kennedy years. Proponents claim that tax cuts in 1982 were the cause of the so-called Reagan boom, forgetting the enormous deficits that tripled the national debt during those same years. Yet the Republican fascination with tax cuts as a painless mechanism to secure both growth and government revenues at the same time continued with the Dole presidential campaign of 1996 and was partially adopted by the Democrats. The Democratic (demand-side) theory – largely shared by both conservatives and social democrats in Europe – depends somewhat more on stimulating investment (and savings) indirectly, by neo-Keynesian demand management. Although not well articulated in recent years, the traditional Democratic theory starts with the imperative for increased consumer demand (to be partially financed by debt, if necessary) and assumes that private investment and growth will then follow.

Both theories largely depend on the same set of axioms, with one exception. Republicans also assume that increased savings will automatically produce increased domestic investment and stronger export performance. This is why so many financial writers assume that the strong currencies of Japan and Germany can be explained simply in terms of comparative national savings rates. For them, it is not necessary to look below the surface at other national policies with respect to trade, investment and capital flows.[17] For them, tax policy should emphasize savings; since it is the higher-income groups that provide all the savings, it is they who need to be encouraged to save more. On the other hand, Democrats (in the US) and Social Democrats (in Europe) generally believe the first half of Say's Law; that demand for goods and services will generate the necessary investment to create its own supply. Since it is the lower-income groups that have the most unsatisfied wants and needs, it is they who should receive the most relief. I lean toward this view.

Both Republicans and Democrats seem to have misunderstood an important point about taxes, however. Consider the relationship between private savings, private sector capital investment and productivity. An accounting identity is derived in Appendix 1. One of its implications can be stated as follows:

{Net new domestic business capital formation}

equals

{net financial inflows to the business sector

minus net financial outflows from the business sector}

equals

{domestic revenues from final sales to consumers

plus sales of goods and services to government

plus exports of goods and services

**plus royalties and repatriation of profits on
existing foreign investments**

plus new capital investment from household savings}

**minus {wages, salaries, rents, royalties and dividends paid by
business to individuals**

plus imports of goods and services

plus new capital exports for new foreign investment plus business taxes}

Domestic intermediate purchases and sales within the business sector itself are omitted from both sides of the above equation because they cancel each other exactly. Domestic final sales of goods and services to consumers are equal to personal consumption expenditure (PCE) less household purchases of government services and spending by tourists traveling abroad. The items in the second set of curly brackets in the above expression can be equated to total revenues on sales, plus foreign royalties and repatriated earnings on foreign investments. Similarly, the items in the third set of brackets can be equated to the cost of production plus capital exports. Thus the expression can be rewritten:

{Net new domestic business capital formation}

equals

**{gross profits for the domestic business sector plus
new capital investment from households}**

minus

**{business taxes plus dividends plus capital exports for
new foreign investment}**

Gross profit, as used in the above identity, includes allowable depreciation; that is, the part of gross profits that is exempted from taxation as replacement of capital. Net profit is, of course, gross profit less depreciation, less taxes. The contribution from household savings can only be available to businesses through equity sales of new shares to the public or through new bank loans for expansion. Data on these flows are scarce but they do not appear to be large. The fact is that most household savings (in the US) are invested in housing.

It follows that profits retained after business taxes and dividends – including allowable depreciation – are the primary source of new capital creation in the private business sector. The capital thus created can be allocated either to domestic business, or to investments in foreign countries. In point of fact, gross personal saving in the third quarter of 1995 (the latest data I have) at seasonally adjusted annual rates was US$221 billion; gross business saving was US$843 billion, of which undistributed profits contributed US$161 billion and depreciation (technically, capital consumption) contributed US$682 billion.

It is worthwhile to note here that exports of foods and services contribute to gross business profit, while imports reduce it. In other words, net exports add to capital creation, while net imports have the opposite effect. This fact alone probably accounts for the high investment and rapid growth rate enjoyed by Japan (until the early 1990s, at least) and other East Asian countries with their high and persistent trade surplus. The same fact partially explains the slowdown in investment and growth in the US since the 1970s. Incidentally, it might appear that the best way to increase both profits and productivity is to cut wages. Firms have been accelerating this process for the last decade or so. But at the aggregate level, this strategy is a double-edged sword. Cutting wages means reducing personal income, and therefore reducing PCE, which is also the main source of domestic revenue for the business sector.

The major government policy levers affecting after-tax business profits – hence private business investment – are depreciation allowances and business tax rates. In fact, virtually all other policies are second order in importance, at best. The much touted US personal capital gains tax, for instance, is unlikely to have any significant impact at the aggregate level, one way or the other. It is true that both new private and new public credit needs to compete with new investment in business, but only indirectly and to second order. It is equally true that interest and dividend income from existing debt (of all kinds, including government) contributes directly to corporate profits and therefore to capital formation. But one direct effect of the US trade deficit is loss of manufacturing jobs. Not only are jobs being lost, but competition from low-wage countries is keeping wages down and suppressing income growth in the West.

This is good for the short-term profits of firms with existing markets, so it is actually releasing more investable funds. But where, and in what, are they being invested?

Meanwhile, wage restraint, coupled with increasing unemployment (partly due to the impact of IT and partly because manufacturing jobs are being exported), has an automatic restraining effect on aggregate domestic demand. Trade theorists will say that this loss is compensated by demand generated by the return flow of dollars coming back as investments, since the total number of dollars in the system at one instant is more or less constant (actually the money supply increases, but slowly). But, as I have noted earlier and will point out again in the next chapter, the return flow need not go into productive investment. If attractive brick and mortar investment opportunities are lacking – as is currently the case in the West – this money can simply drive speculation in currencies, real estate, commodities, joint ventures with foreign partners or stocks. In any case, in the short run it would seem that demand – not savings – is the key to driving investment and thus growth. This conclusion directly contradicts the main assumption underlying the conservative Republican theory of growth, which stresses personal savings as the point of departure.

The Democratic theory of growth partially avoids this problem, first by depending less on private savings and second by putting more stress on public goods, such as infrastructure, education and R&D. But the Democratic theory also depends more on bureaucratic choices of investment. Unfortunately, as a practical matter, the latter almost inevitably become politicized 'pork barrel' projects. Moreover, investment in services provided by the public sector can lead to disastrous consequences if key labor unions are in a position to shut down the whole economy, as truck drivers and air controllers have tried – and luckily failed – to do in the US, and as the same unions (along with railway workers) have twice succeeded in doing during the last four years alone in France.

In addition, the Democratic theory of growth is built on the same insecure foundation that the Republican theory is built upon; namely that increasing labor productivity within a country is, at bottom, the key to wealth creation within the same country. This idea is a reasonable interpretation of what happened in the industrial world during the two centuries between 1780 and 1980 or so, but the future will almost certainly be different. I think that preoccupation with labor productivity is a very poor guide at best, and probably a major mistake for the future. But the notion is so widely held and so seldom challenged that it will take more than this little book to change the prevalent assumptions. Still, as has often been said, the longest journey starts with a single step.

IN CONCLUSION

That first step, I suggest, is to recognize an important fact; namely that the West now has a long-term and growing labor surplus. Officially measured unemployment in the OECD countries, taken together, reached the 35 million mark around 1990, and is probably over 40 million today, having increased erratically since the 1960s (see Figure 7.1). The official figures are certainly too low. In fact, the classifications used to measure unemployment have been repeatedly changed for various 'technical' reasons, but somehow they always seem to make the official figures look smaller.

Virtually everyone can identify one or two or three (or more) people who are essentially unemployed but who are not counted in the official statistics or receiving welfare assistance. These include people employed part time, students living at home with parents into their 30s, and early retirees who would work if they could find any. No wonder that selling drugs is a popular form of employment for inner city children. In any case, averages are deceptive. Unemployment among the young, especially boys and minorities, is already at socially dangerous and probably intolerable levels, especially in Europe.

In the circumstances, I think it no longer makes sense to seek increased productivity by investing capital in labor-saving technology. Investment in labor-saving capital equipment generates unemployment, but the money saved by employers is creating too few new jobs, at least in the West. What must be done instead (call it the new paradigm) is to increase the *value* of the outputs and reduce the physical resource – material and energy – inputs. To a certain extent, past policies of substituting machines powered by fossil fuels for human labor must actually be reversed. This must be done not only to create more employment opportunities for the young and unskilled, but also to reduce the environmental burden, including the greenhouse effect and global warming, that has been created by excessive emissions of the products of combustion of fossil fuels.

I believe that the theory underlying the (old) growth paradigm as a whole is inadequate, to say the least. Both the Republican and Democratic variants are faulty. The paradigm has at least four major technical faults. First, the standard paradigm emphasizes private savings and capital investment to increase labor productivity in the private sector, underestimating the role of other factors of production (notably natural and environmental resources) and the role of government investment (in infrastructure, education and R&D). It also neglects the role of environmental regulation in protecting those neglected factors of production. The assumed causal link between private household savings and investment and productivity is inappropriate and faulty. Business capital formation in a static economy is entirely derived from business profits. Even in a growing economy it is not clear that greater personal savings would find their way into additional business investment, unless directed by government. It is far from clear to what extent technological progress depends on business or private investment. Investment is necessary for growth, as noted above, but it is by no means clear that private savings would finance investment in the areas (such as human capital) where it is really needed.

Second, the paradigm treats technological progress only as a multiplier or accelerator of the other factors of production (labor and capital). It fallaciously treats technological progress and productivity gains as 'free goods'. But doctrinaire free marketeers continue to ignore the obvious implication of endogenizing technological progress; namely that if productivity growth is not an exogenous phenomenon it must be largely the result of government intervention. It is first and foremost a consequence of the government's role in financing most education at all levels,[18] basic science and much applied R&D, as well as promoting and supporting entrepreneurial activity, restraining monopolies and encouraging competition. Technological progress has a cost side. But the assumption of automatic increases in productivity stemming from exogenous technological improvements also ignores the fact that technological change today (especially IT) is having a perverse effect; IT is drastically cutting the useful life of both products and productive capital, including human capital.[19] In effect,

IT has accelerated the rate of depreciation of capital. This implies that investment (properly defined) must be accelerated to achieve a given rate of economic growth. I have discussed these points in Chapter 5.

Third, the paradigm fails to reflect the fact that cheap natural resources, especially fossil fuels, have contributed enormously in the past to what is so glibly called 'technical progress'. Only when resource inputs are explicitly treated as a factor of production can the contribution of technical progress be properly evaluated and understood.

The fourth and last deficiency of the standard paradigm is that it provides no assurance that increased output will necessarily find its way back to the average worker/citizen in terms of higher real income, still less greater welfare. The benefits, such as they are, are now being distributed more and more inequitably, as I noted in Chapter 9. The standard paradigm assumes that increasing welfare is the fruit of economic growth as conventionally measured and that this benefit will automatically accrue to all of the citizens of the country, or at least most of them. In other words, it is assumed that more money in circulation buys more social welfare. Without this assumption there would be no reason to grow.

It is this aspect of the growth paradigm especially that I feel needs to be challenged. I am now convinced that conventional economic growth has little to do with welfare, and that welfare in the US, at least, has actually been declining for the last two decades. It is also now declining in the UK and some of the other countries of Northwestern Europe. Japan is in the process of catching up to the West in this respect, too. The old paradigm fallaciously assumes that aggregate economic growth necessarily increases social welfare, while totally neglecting the role of social welfare as an implicit factor of production.

The new growth paradigm must emphasize increasing value added, via new technology or better quality, and increasing resource (as well as labor) productivity. Finally, it must focus more explicitly on measuring and promoting welfare, not mere activity.

NOTES

1   Admittedly, there were major ups and downs that distorted the figures. The thirteenth century was relatively prosperous, whereas the fourteenth – which encompassed the Black Death and the Hundred Years War – was an economic disaster. Growth accelerated for a while thereafter, in part because depopulation of the countryside created labor shortages and raised wages. This, however, led to peasants' rebellions that, in turn, triggered both religious turmoil (including the rise of Protestantism) and social/religious reaction. Serfdom was gradually relaxed in Western Europe, which subsequently began to industrialize slowly, starting in the fifteenth century. On the other hand, serfdom was reimposed harshly in the eastern part of Europe and emancipation did not occur until the nineteenth century.

2   It should not be necessary to document this statement in detail, since this has been done perfectly well by economists themselves (in criticizing their colleagues). The literature is full of half-baked ideas that have confidently been advanced as a basis for policy shortly before being proven wrong or inadequate. In this context, one might mention Say's Law (the basis of economic orthodoxy before Keynes), Keynesian theory itself, the quantity theory of money, the Phillips Curve, the 'natural rate' of unemployment, the Laffer Curve, and 'rational expectations' (the argument that government policy cannot influence

markets). A recent conspicuous example of theory-based policy that backfired was the newly-elected Thatcher administration's attempt to control inflation by following Milton Friedman's dictum of 'monetary discipline' (controlling the money supply) while simultaneously doubling the VAT and allowing large increases in public sector wages (Ormerod, 1994, p95).

3 The most modern models are known as KLEM, because they incorporate four factors: capital (K), labor (L), energy (E) and materials or mass (M). Production functions are generally expressed as separable functions of these variables. The earliest and simplest growth models used Cobb-Douglas production functions, which were simple fractional powers of the factor inputs, subject to the assumption that the sum of the (two, three or four) exponents must equal unity. This constraint expresses the mathematically convenient – and plausible – assumption that the economic system as a whole is characterized by constant (ie neither declining nor increasing) returns to scale.

4 To be sure, Keynes also proposed that, in times of full employment, governments should compensate for their deficits by increasing tax revenues and running budgetary surpluses. The latter half of the Keynesian formula has seldom been implemented. It must be said, however, that Keynes was concerned with full employment, rather than with growth per se.

5 Walrasian equilibrium is actually a static concept. The notion that such an equilibrium can co-exist with growth is somewhat strange and contradictory, since all known micro-economic mechanisms for growth involve some departure from equilibrium.

6 Solow was careful to say that he used the phrase 'technical progress' as shorthand for any shift in the production function, whether from slowdowns, speed-ups, educational improvements or whatever.

7 Economists tend toward the assumption that technological change is exogenous, despite much empirical evidence to the contrary. One cannot help but wonder whether this tendency is related to the fact that, if technological change were assumed to be endogenous (ie a consequence rather than a cause), the equations of growth models would be immensely complex and non-linear— and most models would be insoluble by known techniques.

8 As it happens, these two predictions of the standard theory are not confirmed by observation. In the first place, the 16 richest countries grew much faster in the 1950–1970 period (3.7 per cent per year) than they did in the prior 80 years, when growth averaged about 1.3 per cent per year. Even after the slowdown in the early 1970s, growth continued at around 2.1 per cent per year, which is slower than 1950–1970 but faster than the long-term average. In the second place, plotting growth versus GDP for 118 countries shows no detectable correlation between the two variables, though the theory implies that countries with higher GDP should have lower growth. See Barro and Sala-I-Martin, 1995. My own interpretation of the long-term record is quite different, however. I doubt that the composite record of 16 countries over the period 1870–1950 is particularly relevant to post-World War II experience for several reasons, including the fact that it aggregates countries whose growth peaked earlier (such as the UK) with countries that peaked or accelerated during the period. The record since 1950, on the other hand, shows a consistent decline in growth rates among the major countries, including Japan.

9 This mechanism is sometimes attributed to the Cambridge economist, Arthur Salter, although it was not described as such in Salter's book (1960). However Salter did draw attention to the importance of scale and learning effects.

10 This, in turn, was the reason Marxists concluded that an efficient system would need no capitalist entrepreneurs, and investment should be the responsibility of government in accordance with centralized planning.

11 This observation was first quantified in the case of aircraft assembly (Wright, 1936). It has subsequently been verified for many other commodity products, including cigars and semi-conductor chips.

12 'Evolutionary' theorists, such as Richard Nelson, Sidney Winter, Stanley Metcalfe, Geoffrey Hodgson, Giovanni Dosi and Gerald Silverberg, have been working on explicit models of the innovation process since the early 1980s. See for example Nelson, 1995.

13 See, in particular, the landmark study by Resources For The Future Inc (Barnett and Morse, 1962).

14 H Boone Pickens, a successful oilman and one of the earliest corporate raiders, was motivated by the fact that the proven reserves of most petroleum companies were not adequately reflected in their share prices. Pickens concluded that the shares were much too cheap because they attributed values to current oil reserves far lower than the cost of replacing those reserves by new discoveries. Pickens put it succinctly (and quotably) by saying 'the cheapest oil is on Wall Street'. Based on this insight he led a hostile takeover attempt aimed at Gulf Oil Co, which made a lot of money for him, though Gulf resisted and eventually merged with Chevron.

15 One set of German studies put the environmental damages associated with electric power production by coal burning roughly equal to the cost of the electricity itself (Hohmeyer, 1989; Hohmeyer and Ottinger, 1991); a counter-study taking a more conservative view set the damages at between 3 and 17 per cent of the cost of the electricity (Friedrich et al, 1989; Friedrich and Voss, 1993). Similarly, one US study set the 'true' cost of Appalachian coal at ten times the market price of coal (ie about US$200 per ton) (Cullen, 1993, 1994). However, a conservative counter-estimate – predicated on the assumption that damage costs had already been largely internalized by regulation – set the damage costs for a newly built coal burning plant using best available technology at a negligible level (Trisko, 1994). In these cases the protagonists and antagonists are not really discussing the same thing. However, it is fair to say that the numbers are disputed.

16 This is a serious point. During the past 15 years real incomes of average New Yorkers have risen by just 3 per cent, while incomes of Wall Streeters have risen 47 per cent.

17 Until quite recently Japanese citizens were not permitted to invest their savings abroad; they had to invest through low-interest post office savings accounts or Japanese banks, which in turn provided the capital for (Japanese) industrial expansion. Japanese trade policy, coordinated by the powerful government agency MITI, effectively excludes imported goods from all except luxury markets, with minor exceptions resulting from long and painfully detailed negotiation with trading partners. The details of this policy have been thoroughly described by a number of authors. Germany relies less on government coordinated policy than on close cooperative relationships between a few large banks, industry and unions. German banks are the controlling stockholders in most German companies, and representatives of the unions sit on their management boards. Financial buccaneering on the Wall Street model is rare in Germany. Thus German managers essentially shared the economic interests of German citizens and workers. German companies have not routinely downsized as US firms have done, nor did they routinely transfer domestic production abroad to cut labor costs. To remain competitive internationally, Germans have, for many years, focused on engineering and quality. Germany also excels in applied research and training. Apart from these virtuous policies, Germany also restricts imports in a number of areas by explicit 'buy German' policies in the public sector and national monopolies such as railways and telecommunications. However, all of this is now changing.

18 The basic need for government financing of most education arises from the fact that the benefits accrue to individuals and to society as a whole, and cannot be appropriated by firms operating in a competitive environment. (The same fundamental argument for government funding applies to basic scientific research, as economists have long recognized.) However, government financing need not imply government management. There are very strong theoretical arguments for privatizing the school system – subject to regulation to prevent racial or religious discrimination – and financing it through education credits allocated directly to individuals of school age, but spendable only on tuition. This approach, which I endorse in principle, has been recommended by a number of conservatives.

19 Here I must note that the so-called 'new' growth theory (which has received a lot of attention by theorists) was stimulated by what has been called a 'seminal' suggestion by Paul Romer. Romer argued in an article in 1986 that the law of diminishing returns may not apply to capital if the definition is extended to include human capital. For instance, the accumulation of physical capital might somehow stimulate a firm to learn to use it more efficiently, or to be more innovative. This line of argument has been used to suggest that the modified standard theory is not inconsistent with the observed increase in growth rates among the rich countries. For reasons mentioned in Note 7 above, I do not fully agree. As I have said in several places, especially Chapter 5, I think that IT is now actually increasing the depreciation rate of both human and physical capital, although this effect is mostly quite recent and hard to confirm from historical data.

Chapter 14
The Free Trade Paradigm

BACKGROUND

In several places in earlier chapters I promised a more detailed discussion of trade theory and its relevance to the suite of economic problems faced (but not fully recognized) by the West. Let me begin by saying that, beyond doubt, free trade is a worthy ideal in an ideal world. The question that I have raised repeatedly is whether accelerated globalization driven by an alliance of profit-driven multinational firms and financial interests and given intellectual support by academics is really in the best interests of Western society in this imperfect world at this point in time. I don't mean to claim that trade is a zero-sum game, nor would I deny that the trade concessions that strengthened the Asian Tigers have had other important benefits over the past four decades. Nor do I have any problem with the notion that neighboring Mexico should now be given trade concessions by the US or that neighboring Eastern Europe should be similarly treated by Western Europe. The socio-political argument for doing so is good, even if the economic argument is shaky. However, I draw the line – if a line must be drawn – at China.

In the public policy arena, what should be a serious debate has been caricatured as a simple-minded conflict between progressives (waving a banner misleadingly labelled 'freedom') versus reactionary protectionists who are either racist or parochial. Because the assumptions underlying the standard theory are less than transparent, the weaknesses of the theory – and their implications as regards its relevance – are not obvious to the public. In short, trade theory has not been used to clarify the issues, but more often as a weapon in this rather one-sided conflict.

If capital, labor and resources stayed at home while goods (and services) were traded freely without any restriction, free trade in an unchanging world would ensure that every good and service would be produced as cheaply and efficiently as possible. Thus maximum possible aggregate output would be achieved at the minimum aggregate cost. Since overall goods availability would be maximized and prices minimized, it follows that each country would maximize its static welfare, *ceteris paribus*. Given the validity of the assumptions, the conclusion follows. I do not argue that point; it is mathematically provable. I do argue, below, that some of the core assumptions are so unrealistic that the major conclusions do not hold in the real world.

This chapter is intended to explain why the protectionists may have a much better economic case than their academic opponents have acknowledged. I confess to some embarrassment over the likelihood of being seen as a defender or ally of H Ross Perot or the late Sir James Goldsmith. I do not admire either their works or their words nor would I defend their over-simplifications or their narrow-minded xenophobia. Nevertheless, I think they are more nearly right than wrong on this ticklish issue.

THE IMPLICATIONS OF STANDARD THEORY

The conventional theory of free trade in its basic form says that free trade increases the efficiency of the economy and therefore increases the size of the economic 'pie', which is ipso facto good for everybody. Free trade advocates go so far as to assert that a country that opens its markets to all comers will benefit even if its trading partners do not reciprocate. The beneficiaries, in this case, are mainly consumers, of course. The free trade theory also qualifies as a paradigm. It embraces many and diverse models, but all of them share certain common features and omit others. The basic notion is simple and quite long in the tooth. Trade theory is really a theory to explain the benefits of specialization based on 'factor endowments'. Its theoretical development began two centuries ago, more or less, with Adam Smith, David Hume and David Ricardo. Ricardo is famous for his observation that, based on natural endowments and 'comparative advantage', the English should manufacture cotton cloth for export to Portugal and the Portuguese should produce wine for export to England. Adam Smith made similar comments with respect to France. The basic argument was, and still is, that if each country specialized in producing and exporting the product or service it produces most efficiently, while importing the rest of its needs from other producers, then all countries would be more prosperous than otherwise. In other words, economic interdependence is more efficient than autarchy.

It is true that Ricardo's insight about comparative advantage is sometimes misunderstood by non-economists, who often tend to confuse it with competitive advantage. The differences are important. I discuss the two concepts in detail later in this chapter. Economists – and *The Economist* – tend to get upset when those outside the charmed circle of professionals use the terms carelessly. Ricardo meant that the Portuguese produced wine more efficiently than cloth, while the English produced cloth more efficiently than wine. Therefore, he argued, each country should specialize in what it does best. Exchange rates are then supposed to adjust themselves automatically to assure that England can sell enough cloth abroad to pay for what it needs to buy (including wine). However, it clearly follows that, in a Ricardian world, the English would not import cloth and the Portuguese would not import wine.

Modern trade theory stems from a set of mathematical models elaborating the original Ricardian notion of specialization. These models were formalized half a century ago, and have been considerably augmented since. The heart of trade theory is the Hecksher-Ohlin (H-O) model and several derived theorems, namely the H-O theorem, the Samuelson factor–price equalization theorem and the Hecksher-Ohlin-Vanek (H-O-V) theorem. The H-O theorem states that countries with the same technologies that produce the same commodities will export products based on abundant factors of production and will import products based on scarce factors. The H-O-V theorem is a generalization of the H-O theorem to factor services. It implies, for instance, that a capital-abundant country will export capital services. The Samuelson theorem states that, under some additional conditions, factor prices – namely wages and interest rates – will equalize across countries even if labor and capital are not mobile.

Assuming labor and capital to be the only two factors of production (an assumption I disputed in Chapter 13), and assuming that all trading countries make the same products and have access to the same technologies, it follows from the H-O-V theorem that industrialized countries should specialize in capital-intensive products while low-wage countries should specialize in labor-intensive products. Given a broader definition of what constitutes a factor of production (see Chapter 13), a wider range of specializations is indicated. For instance, if natural resources are considered to be factors of production, then countries with petroleum reserves should produce petrochemicals, mineral-rich countries should process and export mineral products, and tropical countries should produce oranges, bananas, chocolate, coffee, tea and sugar. If environmental waste assimilative capacity is a factor of production, then 'underpolluted' countries should also attract 'dirty' industries.[1]

The standard theory makes one unambiguous – and seemingly paradoxical – prediction: that trade liberalization will cause the prices of abundant factors of production to rise and the prices of scarce factors to fall. This is because, in a less protectionist environment, countries should increasingly specialize in the products where they have the greatest comparative advantage. These are the products utilizing their most abundant factors of production. It follows that land rents in countries with abundant land should rise and wage rates should fall. Conversely, land rents should fall and wages should rise in countries with scarce land and plenty of surplus labor. And wages should fall in countries where labor is scarcer, that is, in countries with full or nearly full employment. It is fairly obvious that these predictions do not correspond with the facts.

Naturally, economists have attempted to modify the theory so as to explain the observed facts. One modification involves disaggregation. Nowadays, economists distinguish between skilled and unskilled labor, or even between highly skilled/educated labor, medium-skilled labor with basic education, and unskilled (uneducated, illiterate) labor. Here again, as trade barriers fall, the price of skilled labor should rise (relative to the price of medium-skilled or unskilled labor) in countries where skilled labor is relatively abundant and conversely. In short, disaggregated trade theory predicts that globalization will induce international wage rates for unskilled labor to converge. But since the theory predicts that the prices of relatively abundant factors will rise, it also predicts that wages for skilled labor will rise in Japan, Europe and the US; that farmland rents will rise in the US, Canada and Australia; that petroleum and gas rents will rise in the Persian Gulf; that forest rents will rise in Scandinavia, Canada and Siberia; and that tropical plantation product rents will rise in tropical countries. Finally, the theory also predicts that the returns (ie rents) on capital will rise in the industrial countries where capital is most abundant.

The first prediction with respect to unskilled labor seems to be roughly in accordance with the facts. Real wages for unskilled labor in the US are indeed declining, no doubt because of competition from still lower-cost labor in developing countries.[2] Ditto the last prediction, with respect to returns on capital. These have indeed been rising, mainly, it would appear, at the expense of labor. The other predictions, however, are generally not confirmed by casual observation. I do not believe detailed econometric studies would show a trend of rising profits for Persian Gulf producers, or rising land rents in the US grainbelt, Northern forests or tropical plantations. Indeed, the latter trend, if true, would be totally inconsistent with the well-documented complaints of poor developing countries that the terms of trade – that is, the prices of their exports in relation to the prices of the industrial goods they import – have been increasingly unfavorable over many years.

Though wages for unskilled labor have declined, the predicted rise in wages for skilled labor in the industrialized world has also not occurred. Ironically, trade advocates (see, for instance, Krugman and Lawrence, 1994) have used this failure of the theory to make a fairly convincing case that the decline in real wages for unskilled manufacturing workers in the US since 1973 is not primarily attributable to the effects of trade at all. They point the finger instead at technology as the job-destroying villain. The main argument here was briefly summarized in Chapter 5. However, a more complete explanation seems appropriate at this time. In effect, they rely on the fact that trade liberalization – other factors being equal – should tend to raise the wages of highly skilled workers in rich countries, where such skills are abundant. Thus, it is argued that if competition with low-wage countries had been the cause of the decline in jobs in the industrialized countries, then two other things should also follow. First, the US should be preferentially importing goods from those countries in sectors with a high percentage of unskilled labor. At the same time, it should be exporting more goods from sectors requiring a high percentage of skilled labor. (This implication follows from the so-called accounting balance, discussed later.) In a free and flexible labor market, of which the US is a reasonable approximation, this should increase the wage differential between skilled and unskilled workers. It should push the wages of unskilled workers in the US down and the wages of skilled American workers up.

In response, employers should then find ways of using fewer skilled workers and more unskilled workers to redress the balance. Nevertheless, the net result of trade-driven competition should be a small increase in the wage differential. In addition, other factors being equal, the ratio of skilled to unskilled workers should decline in all sectors, but the employment in more skill-intensive (exporting) sectors should have increased due to increased exports.

Contrary to this implication of the standard theory, however, it seems that the employment of skilled workers actually increased more or less equally across the board, and employment in the more skill-intensive sectors increased scarcely at all. This is taken by some leading theorists to be evidence that US trade with low-wage countries had little if any impact on wages, at least through 1993. Krugman and Lawrence have pronounced, rather magisterially: 'We have examined the case for the havoc supposedly wrought by foreign competition and found it wanting'. The majority of trade theorists and economists seem to agree with them.[3] However a significant minority of economists, starting from different theoretical perspectives, have come to different conclusions. Using different models and assumptions it is possible to explain increasing income inequality in other ways. For instance, George Borjas and Valerie Ramey point out that most US imports are autos or other goods that are produced by highly concentrated industries that have had extraordinarily high rents, which allowed them to pay unusually high wages to low-skilled workers while also making large profits. In effect, the monopoly rents are divided between workers and owners. Competition from imports cuts into these monopoly profits and, accordingly, into the workers' share, thus reducing the average wages of low-skilled workers. (It should be noted that US exports such as aircraft are also largely from concentrated industries.) On the other hand, Adrian Wood attributes declining relative wages of low-skilled workers partly to lower trade barriers and partly to increased basic education in the South. Still other interpretations are possible. For instance, US exports of industries with high-skill labor may have failed to rise because they lack competitive advantage, despite having comparative advantages. Or it could be that skill levels and productivity in (some) developing countries are increasing so fast that there was no increased demand for imports from these sectors. In other words, the downward pressure on wages in the US and Europe may not be limited to the low-skill sectors after all; it may simply hit them hardest.[4]

In short, I am by no means persuaded that future downward pressure on wages resulting from radical increases in the scale of trade, especially with China, can be dismissed as easily as free traders like Krugman and Lawrence do. I am equally unpersuaded that, even with perfectly free trade, manufacturing wages in China would ever rise to near Western levels. There are simply too many available workers for the number of manufacturing jobs that could conceivably be created. Certainly, the fact that the globalization of trade hasn't been the major cause of declining wages for the unskilled workers of the US – so far – is not much of an argument for more trade liberalization.

In fact, apart from the two general predictions about globalization noted earlier with respect to declining wages for unskilled labor and increasing returns on capital, the H-O-V theorem is a very poor predictor of actual trade relationships. In fact, the correlation of the theorem's predictions with empirical data is almost exactly 50 per cent; the same as the probability that a coin toss will yield 'heads'. Until a few months ago, however, no alternative theory had been formulated that fitted the real data better and also yielded economically plausible parameters.[5] This lack of correlation of the basic theory with outcomes should be reason enough to go slow in pushing policies based on such crude models. For instance, President Clinton's economic advisors predicted that the conclusion of the Uruguay Round of the GATT negotiations would increase gross world product by US$5 trillion – a piece of 'pie in the sky'. Unfortunately, this basic precautionary principle has been ignored.

I should acknowledge here that there is some new trade theory that overcomes at least one of the major weaknesses of the standard theory. The new theory admits the possibility of increasing returns to scale and the possibility that under some conditions increasing returns would justify protectionism. Mainstream trade theorists counter by arguing that increasing returns actually increase the potential efficiency gains of free trade in general, and that the special conditions needed to justify protection are too rare to bother about. I disagree with the latter argument, however, for reasons noted at several places in this book.

COMPARATIVE ADVANTAGE VERSUS COMPETITIVE ADVANTAGE

Comparative advantage, as explained above, refers to what a country produces most efficiently within its own borders. Competitive advantage, of course, refers to cross-border comparisons. Comparative advantage may be a necessary condition for competitive advantage, but it is certainly not a sufficient condition. The two frequently do not coincide.

To clarify this point, let me review some economic history. In the eighteenth century Britain had a domestic comparative advantage in spinning and weaving wool cloth, due to skilled labor and access to raw materials. It had no international competitive advantage with respect to Flanders, however, because the Flemish had already partially industrialized their weaving industry and still produced higher-quality woolens. Some clever inventions in the eighteenth century extended the British comparative advantage in woolen cloth to include cotton yarn. But, again, the British had no competitive advantage in respect to cotton cloth. In fact, the British imported high-quality muslins and calicos from India. It took five to six decades of invention and protection for British cotton weavers to match Indian quality and prices. Indeed, as late as the 1770s the only significant competitive advantages of Britain in world markets were in the areas of finance, merchant shipping and naval combat. This gave Britain control over seaborne trade – from which much else ultimately followed. Toward the end of the eighteenth century Britain also pioneered steam power and became the world's low-cost iron producer and machinery manufacturer.

Reverting to Ricardo, however, no one could argue with the statement that England is not a promising location for wine production, certainly in comparison with Portugal. However, in a free trade situation, Portugal, as a low-wage country relative to Britain, should have been a better place in David Ricardo's time to produce both port wine and cotton cloth, given only the necessary capital investment. That is hypothetical. But it is not hypothetical that India had both a comparative advantage and a competitive advantage in producing cotton cloth, given that it was already a cotton producer, with better access to raw materials, more skilled labor and lower labor costs than Britain. All it lacked was independent access to European markets.

Did free trade make Britain rich? Not a bit. In the eighteenth century Britain wanted to import cotton cloth and tea, as well as indigo dye and spices, from India, but it had no significant trade goods to export in return. Indian merchant exporters insisted on payment in gold. The days of Queen Elizabeth I, when British privateers (with or without letters of marque from the Crown) simply stole gold from Spanish merchantmen, had passed. To obtain the needed gold, the British parliament introduced the policy of 'mercantilism' which forced all British merchant traders dealing with markets other than India (such as the American colonies) to exchange British manufactured goods for gold bullion and raw materials. No manufactured products were to be imported from colonies, except from India. To enforce this policy, the British actively suppressed local industry in New England. They also imposed and collected both import and export taxes. But this one-sided policy of exploitation was most strongly resisted by the colonies with nascent manufacturing industries. The American colonies eventually revolted (and incidentally developed their own navy and merchant fleet to bypass British ports).

Britain started the nineteenth century with a comparative advantage in the cotton textile sector, but not a competitive advantage. Ricardo merely pointed out that England could make cotton cloth more efficiently than wine. Undeniably, in 1820 or so, England could make cotton cloth more efficiently than it could produce anything else except, perhaps, iron and ships. But the same (as regards cotton cloth) was also true for India. Moreover, India – with its own cotton supply, cheaper and more skilled labor – could make cotton cloth cheaper and better than England. So, according to the H-O-V theorem mentioned in the last section, India should have specialized in cotton cloth and undercut the British in world markets. In an ideal Ricardian world, it probably would have. In the real world, having lost the built-in trade surplus (in gold) with their former American colonies, a new sort of protectionist policy was initiated by the

British. The British East India Company – using its competitive advantage in military technology – simply destroyed the Bengali cotton clothmaking industry (source of muslins and calicos) to open the Indian market to machine-produced cloth from Manchester. It also invested in tea plantations to by-pass the local merchants. This brutal coup made the British East India Company self-supporting, in that the export profits of trade paid for the costs of maintaining a private army. (Later, of course, after the suppression of the mutiny in 1859, India became a crown colony and the costs of local administration were paid by tariffs on imports.)

By the middle of the nineteenth century, the British were low-cost producers for a whole range of manufactured products. What gave Britain its competitive advantages in world trade? The answer was obvious to every industrialist. The British benefited from economies of scale, and learning by doing, or experience (as the new trade theory would presumably acknowledge). Competitive advantage in manufacturing generally lies with the largest and most experienced producers, ie the current market leaders. This is the fundamental reason why the most industrialized countries – led by their exporters (and cheered on by some importers) – tend to embrace the doctrine of free trade, but only after becoming industrially dominant. The British became official free traders in the mid–nineteenth century, and the US followed suit after World War II. Doubtless the Japanese will also promote free trade in every sector where they have become competitive – and no others.

Free trade in manufactured goods generally favors the largest and most dominant producers of each type of goods. Thus AT&T, Boeing, Caterpillar, Dupont, Exxon, Ford, GE, GM, IBM, Intel, Kodak, Merck, Mobil, Motorola and so on will be favored against most of their smaller competitors. This advantage will be increased if they are allowed to produce anywhere in the world and ship their products anywhere else. Many less powerful firms with hitherto profitable national markets will soon fall by the wayside. Competition in many products and services will ultimately be reduced to a few major brands, as is already the case for many products.[6] The rich – namely the managers and owners of the giant firms – will, as usual, get still richer at the expense of their smaller competitors, customers and workers – ie everybody else. Meanwhile, the large multinational firms become increasingly independent of national origin. A few have actually changed nationality to exploit technological skills, market access or other advantages.[7] Many, if not most, multinationals routinely pit one host country against another to minimize taxes, regulation, union power and threats of nationalization. Even new trade theorists have never really tried to come to grips with this set of problems.

Agriculture, forestry and mining are the only areas where competitive advantage is inherently based on location. In these cases the resources are fixed to locations and firms own the resources, such as gold mines. So except where the resource industries have been nationalized, it is still specific firms that have, or lack, a competitive advantage based on natural resource ownership. Agriculture is the exception. But there is no international free trade in agricultural products, for a simple political reason. The US is the world's most efficient producer and major exporter of many key crops, including wheat, corn and soya beans, not to mention meat and dairy products. Many governments, especially in Europe and Japan, are unwilling to expose their own politically powerful farmers to US competition.

In short: global free trade is certainly good for the dominant international producers, almost all of which grew up in large markets. But it is equally tough on the little people in small markets. Trade theorists mostly shed no tears, arguing that efficiency gains are good for all. Perhaps they have a small point. But the key point is that compara-tive advantage in trade is attributed to relative abundance of factors of production. This has little to do with competitive advantage in manufacturing. The single dominant advantage in manufacturing is market share, as many management consultants have emphasized in recent decades. Market share can be regarded, at least in the short run, as a factor endowment no less than technology, labor or resources. But it has not yet been incorporated explicitly in any trade theory, as far as I know.

The basic concept of comparative advantage is much better suited to interpreting trade patterns than to predicting them. As an example of the difficulties, remember that in the 1940s labor and capital were considered to be the only factors of production. In the 1950s and 1960s the US had very high labor costs relative to other countries, while capital was cheap. Thus capital was relatively more abundant than labor. Yet the US was a net exporter of labor-intensive manufactured products like aircraft, and a net importer of more capital-intensive manufactured products like cars. After this odd fact was observed by Wassily Leontief (1954), economists reconsidered the theory in order to explain the paradox. The current view is that it wasn't a paradox after all (when the appropriate redefinitions of labor and capital had been introduced) and anyhow, the once-thought-to-be paradox has disappeared from the data for the past 20 years. Perhaps so, but then how relevant are the current data?

I think most economists, at least those not professionally defending trade theory, would probably explain US exports of large commercial aircraft in terms of competitive advantage due to market dominance and scale, not technology. In fact the successful challenge to US dominance by Airbus, the European consortium, would seem to prove that technology was not the critical factor. Nor can the Japanese and Korean success in commodity semiconductor manufacturing be attributed to abundance of the relevant factors of production. On the contrary, in fact, both Japan and Korea started their investments in semiconductor manufacturing despite acute shortages of qualified engineering personnel. China is now doing the same thing, with Japanese help.

The Economist had a lot of editorial fun sneering at President Bush when he went to Tokyo with the presidents of the three big US car companies to challenge the Japanese to open their markets. According to the editors of that magazine the Japanese have a comparative advantage in making cars – except BMWs – and presum-ably also in steel, ships, consumer electronics, cameras and machine tools. Therefore, according to *The Economist's* interpretation of free trade theory, the Japanese cannot be expected to import these things.

What should the Japanese import? It is clear that in a Ricardian world they would import all of their food, fuels, steel, petrochemicals, plastics, wood products, paper, aluminum, supercomputers and airplanes. Of course, in the real world the Japanese produce most of these things themselves under a protected regime; they virtually refuse to import many products including rice, oranges, apples, beef, paper, plastics, aluminum or even supercomputers, all of which they can (or once could) get at lower prices from the US or elsewhere. The rice import ban broke down only last year, due to an extreme shortage. In practice, the Japanese import raw logs to make lumber and paper, copper concentrate to make copper, bauxite to make aluminum and crude oil to make petrochemicals and plastics.

And what is the US's comparative advantage; that is, what does the US produce best and most efficiently? *The Economist* notwithstanding, cars are probably on the list. Indeed, it is reasonable to assume that competitive advantage presupposes comparative advantage. In this case beef, movies, electronic computers, airplanes and many of the same things the Japanese consistently refuse to import also belong on the list of things the US should export. Japanese protectionism has been extensively documented. But in its zeal to castigate the US for losing its enthusiasm for free trade by asking for reciprocity, all this evidence is lightly dismissed as exceptional. *The Economist* has openly supported the Japanese assertions that Japanese markets are really open!

TRADE DEFICITS AND THE ACCOUNTING BALANCE

The leading trade theorist of today is probably Paul Krugman of Stanford or MIT. Krugman is particularly impatient with people like me who worry about trade imbalances and capital exports to build factories in low-wage countries. Krugman insists that this is no problem because no country can simultaneously be a capital importer and have a surplus in its current trade account.[8] This assertion follows not from the theory discussed above, but from an 'accounting identity' (savings minus investment equals exports minus imports), which holds as long as all monetary flows must be classified as consumption or capital investment. A more complete version of this accounting identity is described in Appendix 1. Thus, according to the standard theory, if a country has a surplus in trade it must have a deficit in capital flows, and conversely. However, this assertion is a bit too simplistic, as will be seen below.

In particular, the accounting balance implies that US dollars that flow out of the US must eventually come back to the US, except for temporary accumulations or draw-downs, known in accounting circles as 'inventory adjustment'. Similarly, it implies that the dollars that flow into country X must eventually flow back out again. An individual can exchange dollars for the currency of X, but that merely changes the ownership of the dollars. It does not reduce their number. If the dollars don't flow out of country X in payment for goods and services, they must flow out in some other way. Japan and Germany, with large trade surpluses, must also export capital.

For the ordinary observer, however, Krugman's argument seems, at first glance, to be contrary to some widely publicized facts regarding both the US and China. (I discussed the Chinese case in Chapter 4.) On the one hand, the US has a large and well publicized trade deficit in manufactured goods exceeding US$153 billion in 1995, of which over US$60 billion was with Japan and US$35 billion with China. (For the 12 months ending in July 1996, the negative trade balance was US$170 billion.) Taking into account trade in services, flows of factor income and transfer payments, the deficit for 1995 was US$1,487 billion.[9] On the other hand, US business is known to be a large capital exporter. The US Commerce Department says that US-based businesses invested US$44 billion abroad during 1994 and US$33 billion in the first six months of 1995 alone. US firms invested US$40 billion in China alone during 1966. Thus it appears at first glance that the US must have had a deficit in both accounts at the same time. To satisfy the accounting balance, well over US$200 billion in hidden reverse flows must have existed in 1995, and even more in 1996. This inflow of dollars consists of foreign investments in the US over and above US investments abroad. Much of this, including foreign investment in US businesses, isn't readily monitored and it certainly isn't publicized as much as the trade deficit.

Financial writers and conservative politicians (citing the accounting balance mentioned above) often suggest that the major portion of this return flow is used to purchase US government bonds, to help cover the annual federal deficit.[10] The deficit was US$164 billion in fiscal year (FY) 1995; it was about US$115 billion in FY 1996, sharply down from the FY 1990–1992 deficits of US$230 billion, US$270 billion, and US$290 billion, or about US$1400 billion for FY 1990 through FY 1995. (Unfortunately, the decline appears likely to end in 1997.) The deficit is financed by the sale of treasury bonds. How much of this is financed by foreigners? Again referring to the *Economic Report of the President* (CEA, 1996), some US$848 billion of the US$4,965 trillion US federal debt was owed to foreigners as of September 1995, up from US$656 billion one year earlier. Thus in fiscal year 1995 foreigners purchased (net) US$192 billion in bonds, rather neatly accounting for the deficit in payments. However, the foreign-owned share of US federal debt has been rising more rapidly in recent years. The increase from 1994 to 1995 roughly equalled the increase from 1990 to 1994. For the six-year period 1990–1995 (fiscal years) during which the cumulative federal deficit was US$1400 billion, the foreign-owned share increased by about US$400 billion, or about 38 per cent of the gross federal budget deficit. Over half of the cumulative payments deficit – which was about US$850 billion over the same six-year period – must therefore have gone somewhere else.

The possibilities to account for the gap include direct investments by foreigners in US assets, including securities. The value of foreign private sector holdings in the US (at cost) increased from US$1942 billion in 1990 to US$2613 billion in 1994 (five years), for a net inflow of US$670 billion over that period. It is likely that the inflow continued in 1995. On the other hand, US direct investment abroad must be subtracted. During the same five-year period US private assets abroad (valued at cost) grew from US$1800 billion to US$2233 billion, for a total increase of US$423 billion. Thus the net influx of private capital into the US was US$337 billion over the five years 1990–1994. There is still a significant discrepancy. A major 'leak' in the accounting balance is that a significant part of the money never returns at all. Instead, it is deposited in offshore banks as dollar accounts (eg 'Eurodollars'). Or it is circulated as paper money in countries where inflation is rapid.

The Bank for International Settlements (BIS) in Switzerland is the monitor of official monetary reserves. It reported that global official international reserves at the end of 1995 were US$1.35 trillion. Of this total, dollars accounted for 65 per cent or US$882 billion. Not only that, the official dollar reserves grew by US$168 billion in 1995 alone.[11] (Arguably this period was exceptional, due to massive buying of dollars by central banks around the world in spring 1995 to support the dollar against the Japanese yen and the German Deutschmark.) However, considering the 12 months ending in July 1996, Japanese reserves alone increased by US$52 billion (to US$207 billion), while Italy and Spain increased their reserves by US$15.6 billion and US$14.8 billion respectively. In this period official currency reserves of other OECD countries, not including the US itself, increased by roughly US$80 billion (data from *The Economist*, 1996d). Including the fast-growing countries of East Asia, the overall increase in reserves would have been significantly larger. Hence, it is likely that increased dollar currency reserves, on average, account for a significant share of the continuing negative US trade balance.

Unofficial paper dollar reserves held by individuals in cash (eg in Russia and Latin America) would add to this 'leak'. (Some of the money used to import drugs like cocaine falls into this category.) It is estimated, for instance, that US$20 billion in

US dollars – mostly in US$100 bills – is in circulation in Russia alone. The global total is probably several times that much. It rises annually by several billion dollars. In Russia and a number of other former communist countries, as well as parts of Latin America, paper dollars are the only 'hard' currency. An unknown amount of money also resides in private dollar-denominated deposits in offshore banks in places like the Bahamas and the Channel Islands. Such deposits can be used as collateral for loans in other currencies that can be reinvested outside the US.

I think it is obvious that the 'circular flow' argument based on the accounting balance is too over-simplified. It seems to take the bare fact of an accounting balance, by itself, to be a sufficient proof that free trade is 'benign' (Krugman's word). According to this view, reducing trade barriers isn't, and can't be, harmful to the interests of workers in high-wage countries, taken generally. Theorists apparently believe that the compensating inflow of money through the financial system necessarily and automatically creates an equal number of new jobs in the high-wage country. I cannot agree with that line of reasoning. Indeed, it seems likely that, in the case of the US, less than half of the trade deficit (on average) is used to purchase US government securities, while another third consists of (net) direct investment. The remainder goes to increase foreign currency reserves of various sorts. Of the net direct investment, much – or most – goes into the stock market, where it drives prices up. Much of the rest is used to buy existing productive assets (which result in increased personal income or capital gains to well-to-do individuals), or it goes into speculative markets for unproductive assets such as empty land. There is little or nothing to compensate for the primary direct effect of a US trade deficit, which is the loss of US manufacturing jobs.

A secondary, but still direct, effect of a trade deficit – as I noted in the last chapter – is to increase the investable gross profits of foreign producers, while reducing the gross profits of domestic producers. This means domestic capital creation is reduced by the amount of the trade deficit, while capital creation in foreign countries is increased by the same amount. (This statement, too, is an accounting identity, at least for a static economic system.) In short, the downstream effects of the US trade deficit are five-fold:

1) the loss of well-paid manufacturing jobs – admittedly the return flows finance some investments that create some new jobs, but not as many (or as well-paid) as were lost;
2) it contributes to capital creation in foreign countries while reducing capital creation in the US;[12]
3) it finances government debt, which tends to increase the government share of the economy;
4) it finances speculation in US real estate, stocks, commodities, collectibles, derivatives and currencies; and
5) it accumulates in the vaults of foreign central banks as reserves.

There can be little question, it seems to me, that currency reserves and unproductive investments account for much of the return flow from US trade deficits since the early 1980s. It will take more than theory-based assertions by academic economists, however respected, to convince me that trade deficits are benign.

TRADE AND ECONOMIC GROWTH

Apart from the problem of deficits, the free trade paradigm has another implication that I find implausible. The advocates of global free trade normally assert that increasing global trade (a predictable consequence of decreasing trade barriers) contributes importantly to the economic growth of all trading countries, regardless of whether they play by the free trade rules. A recent *Economist* article on the status of negotiations at the WTO ended by scolding the Americans for insisting on reciprocity in telecommunications. It asked rhetorically, 'When will America learn that free trade benefits the liberalizer whether or not others open up?' My rhetorical response is: 'Why should we learn it if it isn't true?' In other words, the free trade paradigm glorifies trade per se as an engine of economic growth. How could this happen? The supposed mechanism is quite straightforward: increased trade implies bigger markets, hence greater demand and greater production volume. Economies of scale, in turn, enable volume producers to cut prices. Lower prices increase demand still further, and so on. This cycle was described in the last chapter, on the growth paradigm. It operates, normally, within the borders of a single country. The contribution of reducing barriers to international trade, then, would only be to expand markets beyond national borders. This has been done in Europe, with moderate success, although the greatest beneficiary has probably been Germany, the most successful exporter in the region and, by some measures, in the world.

Steadfast German support for European economic integration, at least up to now, arises from exactly this fact. The creation of a free trade area in Europe has been extremely beneficial to German industry. This, in turn, has benefited German workers, thanks to the ever-increasing strength of the Deutschmark and the generous social services afforded by prosperity. German-based manufacturers dominate not only the domestic German market, but the entire West European market, and now the growing East European market as well. The bigger the free trade area became, the more beneficial it has been for German manufacturing firms. The past financial success of German multinationals does not necessarily bode well for German workers in the future, however. Although German firms were slow to move production outside their home territory – as compared to US, UK and other MNCs – they have now started to do so in earnest. Ireland and Spain were early beneficiaries of German capital exports. Now the Czech Republic, Hungary and Poland are being increasingly used as low-wage export platforms for German firms.

However, Europe is homogeneous compared to the world as a whole. What worked in the US 200 years ago and appears to be working (albeit slowly) in Europe need not necessarily work on a global scale.

THE ABSENT TIME DIMENSION

Standard trade theory is still essentially static. It does not take account of phenomena with a time dimension. Hence, it fails to reflect the fact that comparative advantages can and do change over time, as natural resources are depleted, wages rise or fall, capital resources accumulate or depreciate, and human resources gain knowledge and experience, or are wasted. Moreover, technology, experience, scale and market share are really attributes of firms, not countries. I would argue that trade theory must be substantially revised to take these facts into account.

I noted previously that the British did not achieve trade dominance in cotton textiles by relying on the doctrine of comparative advantage. In a Ricardian world, India would have taken that role. Nor would the British have become the world's low cost iron producer (and later, steel-maker) without protection. During most of the eighteenth century Sweden was the low-cost producer in Europe. If the British had simply imported their iron and steel, they could not have developed their own industry. By the same token, the American colonies were actively restrained by the British from developing a domestic industrial base. Only after the British were expelled (and then distracted for three decades by the French Revolution and the Napoleonic wars) did the newly United States become an independent seafaring, trading and manufacturing power. The British attempt to reassert control over the breakaway Americans in 1812 was defeated rather easily, despite the short-lived British occupation of Washington DC and the burning of the White House.[13]

Now consider Asia. According to standard trade theory, the Japanese (indeed, everyone in the world) should have maximized short-term consumer benefits and imported their computer chips from the US companies that were low-cost producers in the 1970s. Instead, the Japanese blocked imports, restricted foreign direct investment, and built their own computer chip manufacturing – and exporting – industry. The South Koreans and the Taiwanese have since followed exactly the same scenario with many other products they wanted to learn how to manufacture. Would the average Japanese have been better off today by maximizing consumer welfare in the short run, as standard Anglo Saxon trade theory recommends? Hardly. If the Japanese leadership had followed the advice of academic free traders in 1955, Japan would probably still be a weak and struggling country, instead of the global power it is today. The protectionist policies of Japan have been extremely effective, and profitable, for Japanese industry. Indirectly, the Japanese consumer has also gained enormously from these protectionist policies (at least until 1990 or so). This has occurred, however, not through domestic price competition from imported goods, but thanks to continuing low domestic interest rates, modestly rising incomes in Yen terms, and above all, a gradually but continuously rising Yen. These phenomena are real (and predictable, within limits) but they lie outside the domain of the standard trade theory.

Standard trade theory is basically a theory of static optimization. It does not reflect possibilities for sacrificing present benefits for future advantage. Nor does it reflect the advantages of scale or 'experience' in manufacturing. If competitive advantage rests on market share, scale and experience, and if free trade were rigorously practised according to the precepts of the standard theory, many small countries and a number of large ones would be virtually condemned to unfavorable terms of trade and perpetual poverty, because they have no comparative advantage except cheap unskilled labor. Only by practising Japanese-style protectionism to build up domestic manufacturing capabilities and exploit returns to scale and experience across the board, without any requirement for reciprocity, have such countries any hope of developing rapidly. Since most of the leaders of the developing world are smart enough to know this, their adherence to the new WTO is essentially hypocritical. They all hope the US will be forced by world opinion and its own academic doctrines to play by the rules and continue to allow virtually unlimited imports. Formerly free-trade Hong Kong will, of course, gradually adopt the trade policies of China. The other Asian Tigers (except for the entrepot Singapore) have absolutely no intention of changing their own protectionist policies, which are modeled on those of Japan.

There are many ways to pervert free trade. Tariffs are only the simplest. Distorted exchange rates are the favorite of centrally planned economies like China. Industrial policy is another. Japan's MITI is the exemplar, but others have followed the example. For instance, in the 1970s Brazil forced the three US light aircraft manufacturers (Cessna, Piper and Beech) to compete among themselves for the opportunity to build and equip a production facility in Brazil, with complete technology transfer and a five-year contract for spare parts. In other words, the contract was to create a viable competitor (Embraer), not only in Brazil but also in export markets. This ploy was successful because the Brazilian government was a monopoly buyer (actually a monopsonist), whereas the US firms were prohibited by US anti-trust law from joining forces to resist the Brazilian demand.

The Communist regimes of Eastern Europe used a similar strategy to induce Fiat to build and equip several complete automobile production plants in Poland, Yugoslavia and the USSR. In all of these cases, of course, the newly created competitor was a monopoly operating in a protected market. None exported successfully to the West, but that was a consequence of other failures in the Soviet system. The Japanese exploited the monopoly strategy much more cleverly, by using MITI as a single agent to negotiate all licencing and investment terms with foreign firms. MITI was able to obtain licenses for most of the important computer and semi-conductor patents – not to mention other technologies – from US and other Western firms under very favorable conditions, but without giving up the internal benefits of competition among Japanese firms.

Frankly, most developing countries would be foolish to open their markets, notwith-standing the advice of *The Economist*. Scale effects strongly color international trade relations. Because of scale effects a country with a small open market, even with the advantage of cheap labor, may be unable to compete on even terms with larger, stronger economies.[14] The realistic choice for a poor country may be to become totally dependent on imports from a foreign MNC that is, in reality, an oligopoly or to protect the market for inefficient but locally based firms. The latter choice may be disadvantageous to consumers in the short run, but the former could be disastrous if the MNC decides to move its operations elsewhere.

Some less developed countries – notably OPEC members, Russia, Kazakhstan, South Africa, Zaire and Zimbabwe and a few countries that still have virgin forests – can export natural resources, in exchange for manufactured products that could not be produced locally at competitive costs. But not all countries have significant exportable natural resources (consider for example, Bangladesh, Burundi, China, Egypt, Ethiopia, India, Kenya, Myanmar, North Korea, Pakistan, Sri Lanka, Ruanda and Uganda). According to conventional international trade theory, resource-poor developing countries must specialize in labor-intensive products, especially those involving manual assembly. The classic examples are shoes and apparel, toys, and more recently electrical goods.

There are some obvious examples where this strategy has worked. Japan and Hong Kong began with apparel (and special access to the US and British markets respectively). Specialized offshore assembly operations in East Asia and Mexico have also developed for certain electronic products. Unfortunately for most developing countries, however, the total world demand for products that have a sufficiently high labor-content to be worth transporting over long distances is not nearly large enough to offer a universal path to robust economic development. The sad fact is that low cost, unskilled labor is no longer a significant advantage, at least in manufacturing and infor-mation-based service industries that produce exportable products. This fact has a nasty implication; it means that because of scale effects and 'lockout', global free trade dominated by the MNCs would probably condemn the 50 or so least developed countries to very long-term, if not perpetual, poverty. With economies of scale on their side, not to mention technology, advanced countries now have an overwhelming competitive advantage against producers in poor countries with undeveloped domestic markets, unstable governments and primitive infrastructure. Those countries are unstable (because of their poverty), unattractive as export platforms, unable to compete in world markets and therefore unable to attract private investment. Nobody invests in places with no physical or institutional infrastructure. Even Russia, with all its resources, will not attract significant foreign investment until it stabilizes and creates new institutions. This may take decades.

CONCLUDING COMMENTS

Despite its failure to reflect or predict reality, adherence to free trade orthodoxy of the *Wall Street Journal* or *Economist* sort is akin to charismatic religion. It puts faith and doctrinal purity above reason or evidence. The propaganda barrage in favor of free trade and against protectionism has been unbelievably persistent – and surpris-ingly successful. Protectionism is blamed for the Great Depression, World War II and poverty in the developing world. As Fred Iklé noted (1995), it is worse to be called a protectionist than to be called a racist.

The conventional wisdom of free trade is also increasingly at odds with the impera-tives of environmental protection. Free trade advocates are beginning to see environ-mentalists as the enemy, because it is impossible to enforce international agreements to ban environmentally damaging practices such as clear-cutting tropical forests or packaging in non-returnable packages unless the US and Europe can refuse to import products produced by illicit and environmentally destructive means. Yet the GATT/WTO tries hard to prevent this sort of trade discrimination (or any other) and fiercely resists any watering down of the rules.

I am not opposed to real free trade among economic and technological equals, or near equals. In this respect (but not some others) I agree with Sir James Goldsmith.[15] Unlike him, I even think that the single European market is probably beneficial to all its member states. (The Euroskeptics who bemoan loss of national sovereignty are dreaming of a world that no longer exists, if it ever did.) A larger free trade zone encompassing Europe and North America would also make sense to me, if the tricky problems of agricultural subsidies could be resolved. Such a free trade zone could afford to open its markets conditionally, without full immediate reciprocity, to a few near neighbors with common borders, such as Mexico or the countries of Eastern Europe. As these countries are fully absorbed into the free trade zone, the borders could be further enlarged in stages to admit the next group of neighboring countries, and so on. However, it is time to acknowledge that the West cannot afford to enter a one-sided global free trade agreement that allows all the Asian countries open access to Western markets without insisting on reciprocal access to Asian markets. Economic growth simply cannot be export-led everywhere. On the other hand, global free trade – according to the Anglo Saxon prescription – is not in the short- or intermediate-term interest of developing countries in Asia or elsewhere, as their leaders are perfectly well aware. The developing countries of East Asia (except for Japan, Hong Kong and Singapore) cannot afford to open their markets to imports without restriction, because foreign companies have so many advantages of scale, experience and market dominance.

Thus the new WTO is an anomaly. At one level, it represents the victory of an academic theory over common sense. But academic theory is only the window dressing. In practice, NAFTA and the WTO are supported by a powerful lobby of special interests. These are multinational corporations and financial institutions, along with their political outriders. But, in my opinion, the emperor is not wearing any clothes; the selfish interests of the people who run these institutions are *not* coincident with the long-term interests of their own workers or their fellow citizens.

I realize that lower prices for imported goods is an attraction to consumers in the short run. But, when the domestic producers are driven out of business – as happened in the case of TVs, VCRs and cameras, for example – and the dollar declines sharply against the Yen, the result is a sharp increase in the prices of these same goods. The Yen has appreciated by 250 per cent in the last decade and a half and, despite a recent pause, it will probably appreciate more. This amounts to a price increase of the same order of magnitude for goods imported from Japan. It is very unlikely that domestically produced goods would have risen in price quite so fast. So, in the long run, it is the Japanese consumer who has gained, not the US consumer. It is true that Latin American and Indian-style protectionism (import substitution) did not work as planned. This was because it tends to reward inefficiency and political connections. But, to me, this failure does not justify elimination of all protection for domestic industry, either in the West or in the developing world. The sensible solution is for developing countries to permit foreign equity investment in domestic production for the home market – in preference to imports – with free entry (to ensure competition) and free repatriation of profits. Regional free-trading blocs should be encouraged to allow for economies of scale and intra-regional specialization.

Trade between regions is another matter. The particular abuse that must be stopped is the transplantation of production facilities from Western countries to export platforms, simply to exploit cheap labor and lax environmental regulation. Whereas intra-regional trade is mutually beneficial, inter-regional trade should be minimized for several reasons. In fact, there are strong environmental arguments for high tariffs and/or export taxes on some commodities, especially raw materials and fuels. The industrialized countries are using far too much of both, and excessive consumption must be curbed for the sake of the environment and for the sake of future generations.

A final word on theory and evidence; my skepticism about the supposed benefits of free trade has two sources. One is the fact that, in practice, US workers have suffered from discriminatory trade practices by other countries, mainly to the benefit of rich foreign factory owners and the well-to-do owners of domestic US financial assets. Trickle down has been minimal. The second is its unfulfilled promise of accelerated economic growth. The expected benefits of NAFTA and WTO to the industrialized countries and their citizens have been grossly exaggerated, while the costs to workers have been glossed over or simply ignored. The chief beneficiaries are a much smaller group, consisting mainly of the owners and top managers of large firms, and the financial community.

Paul Krugman insists that the notion of international competitiveness between nations is an illusion, and that international trade is generally benign.[16] I think, on the other hand, that the supposed benefits are largely illusory and that international trade in manufactured goods – at least between grossly unequal partners – is only benign in the sense that a tumor may be benign; that is, it doesn't do much harm as long as it is relatively small in scale. In particular, large trade imbalances with large countries are potentially very dangerous and very destabilizing (notwithstanding the circular flow of funds). When the scale of global trade grows too fast, the side effects are likely to prove very unpleasant.

NOTES

1   This is not a particularly new idea, but it received worldwide attention as a result of a leaked memo in December, 1991, by Lawrence Summers, then Vice President and Chief Economist of the World Bank. Summers pointed out that economic logic suggests exactly such an outcome.

2   A similar trend occurred in the years between 1895 and 1914, when international trade increased sharply due to a fall in transport costs. In particular, there was a strong convergence of wages of unskilled labor in the UK, Ireland, Germany and Sweden during those years (British and Irish wages actually fell). This appears to be roughly in accordance with the predictions of standard trade theory. However, whereas before 1895 European wages were gradually closing the (large) gap with US wage rates, as the theory predicts, the gap increased again between 1895 and 1914. The ratio of wage rates to land rents in Europe did increase significantly from 1870 to 1914, while the wage to rent ratio declined equally sharply in the US and Australia. These shifts were consistent with the theory. See *The Economist*, 1996e.

3   The quote is from Krugman and Lawrence, 1994.

4   All authors quoted in this paragraph are fully cited in Burtless, 1995.

5   A paper published by Daniel Trefler in the prestigious journal *American Economic Review* (1995) appears to have solved the puzzle, at least partially. Trefler began by noting that the deviations from randomness are actually systematic. After testing a variety of different modifications to the basic H-O-V model, he finds that significantly better correlations with real outcomes are obtained by introducing a multi-parameter, semi-empirical model incorporating two major modifications of the standard theory: a measurable bias in every country toward buying products produced domestically, and allowing for technological differences (ie productivity differences) between countries. It is noteworthy that the H-O and H-O-V theorems assumed that each trading country makes the same products and has access to the same technologies. Obviously these assumptions are highly unrealistic.

6   It is interesting to note that most of the big, powerful firms of today became big and powerful thanks to protection of their national markets. This is certainly true of most of the Japanese firms (except Sony), and all of the Korean firms. Many of them have grown to be giants partly at the expense of formerly large US firms (such as RCA and Xerox). Airbus was created from scratch by massive government subsidies, with the explicit objective of overtaking Boeing and McDonnell-Douglas. Virtually every big firm in France and Italy is kept alive by either direct subsidies or massive injections of government money as capital, not to mention purchases by other government-owned firms or the government itself.

7 One of the best known is Syntex, the pharmaceutical firm that grew large on sales of birth control hormones ('the pill'). It began in Mexico, selling pharmaceutical raw materials based on Mexican yams. When the firm's chemists (mainly US citizens working part time) learned how to synthesize its products, it moved to Palo Alto, California, in order to be close to Stanford University. Some firms, like Nestlé, Philips and ABB, are already virtually stateless.

8 See Krugman, 1995. Krugman's article is a complaint that many people who write about international economic issues – including Kennedy, Lester Thurow, Robert Reich, Jeffrey Garten, Clyde Prestowitz, Edward Luttwak, Ira Magaziner and Mark Patinkin, and The World Economic Forum – have views that are 'startlingly crude and uninformed' and are guilty of 'failure to understand even the simplest economic facts and concepts' [ibid]. The main examples of such misunderstanding cited by Krugman are failure to distinguish between comparative advantage and competitive advantage, the idea that wages should reflect national productivity rather than marginal productivity at the plant level, and failure to understand the 'accounting identity' (viz, savings minus investment equals exports minus imports).

9 CEA, 1996. A more complete picture, not counting investment flows (referring to the third quarter of 1995, at seasonally adjusted annual rates) including trade in services, factor income (dividends and interest) and transfer payments, shows a deficit of US$148.7 billion. This deficit is accounted for by the Department of Commerce as net foreign investment in the US. However, it is an accounting residual.

10 For many years there has been a strong lobby arguing that the best – perhaps the only – way to increase domestic business investment is to balance the federal budget. The underlying assumption, which I find somewhat implausible, is that money not used to purchase government bonds will be invested in plant and equipment instead. Chapter 13 discussed this argument in more detail.

11 Based on International Monetary Fund (IMF) definitions of reserves (excluding gold). Data from the 1995 annual report of the Bank of International Settlements (BIS), in Basel.

12 Here I must disagree with Krugman's argument that countries do not compete.

13 This is a fact well-known to American schoolchildren and virtually unknown to the British.

14 Obviously a small country may happen to be home to some large multinational firms that grew up from national beginnings. This is the case for several of the small countries of Western Europe. Thus, Switzerland (for instance) can export watches and pharmaceuticals to the world, while importing all its cars. Finland can export paper products and paper-making machinery, and cellular telephones.

15 Goldsmith, 1994. Paul Krugman says that this is 'a terrible book; its economic argument is nothing but the classic "pauper labor" fallacy... mixed in with a thorough ignorance of the basic facts'. Krugman has only one good thing to say about Goldsmith's book; 'that it has the courage of its convictions', viz that it is frankly opposed to free trade except among countries with similar wage levels. In contrast, another review of the book in *The National Interest* by Fred Iklé (1995), another former MIT professor (of political science) who later became an Under Secretary of Defense in the Reagan administration, arrived at the opposite conclusion. This is not the place for a review of the reviews, but Goldsmith should not be dismissed quite so lightly.

16 See above, note 8.

Chapter 15

National Debt and National Wealth

BACKGROUND

In the last two chapters I have reviewed the growth and free trade paradigms in some detail, though hopefully in language simple enough to permit interested non-economists to follow the arguments. My personal contribution in those areas is essentially synthetic and critical, rather than original research. This chapter serves a similar function, but also introduces some new, previously unpublished, research results.

I remind the reader that wealth is usually measured independently in terms of the market value of tradeable assets. But, since income, to an economist, is taken to be a product of labor and capital, wealth can also be thought of as the capitalized value of expected future income. In fact, the current efforts to measure natural capital, discussed previously in Chapter 9, are based on this way of looking at wealth. The main purpose of this chapter is to provide perspective and a common framework for thinking about, and evaluating, all forms of wealth – both human-made and natural.

THE INADEQUACY OF MARKET MEASURES OF WEALTH

Wealth in the distant past was generally supposed to consist of: arable land; domesticated animals; commodities like grain, oil or wine; hides and furs; metals like copper, tin, silver and gold; precious gems; spices, medicinals and dyes. Until the late middle ages, land was still thought to be the ultimate source of wealth. The growing importance of manufacturing (especially of textiles) and of banking and trade, starting in Renaissance Italy, undermined that notion. Credit created new forms of money to supplement the use of metal coins. Money, itself, became a form of wealth. The technological advances that made formerly worthless substances like coal, petroleum, natural gas and various metal ores into valuable natural resources introduced another new form of wealth. But, while the older definitions are clearly incomplete, society has yet to come to grips with the true source of all wealth other than gifts of nature, namely human capital (ie knowledge and skills).

As applied to an individual, wealth in modern terms seems, at first glance, to be easy to measure. It consists of so-called real property (land and structures), other tangible assets (eg vehicles, furniture, clothing, jewelry, etc) and financial assets. The latter consists of money in bank accounts, stocks, bond, mortgages and shares in unincorporated businesses. Debts must be subtracted from assets, of course. We think we know how to value land and financial assets via markets. We speak of market value, meaning the amount of money a tradeable asset would fetch in an efficient auction where all interested bidders could participate. (This definition does not apply to non-tradeable assets such as public goods, for which other, less objective, methods of valuation are needed.) But economists also regard the value of a productive asset, such as a mine or farm or a bond or a share of stock, as the present value of the expected future income stream from that mine or farm or bond or share. Though most economists think that the value assigned by competitive markets is not only valid, but the only legitimate method of valuation, there are two serious problems with this interpretation. One is that market values are inherently marginal. They equate value with prices actually paid, even though only a few assets are actually changing ownership. The other is that a very heavy burden falls on the innocent little word 'expected'. The point is that present value is a function of current expectations about the future.

Recall the earlier discussion of Japan's bubble economy and Tokyo land prices. One of the lessons is that the *real* value of Tokyo land surely did not change much from 1989 to 1995. What changed was the *expected* value. And the expected value of Tokyo did not change because of a change in the expected value of future revenues from that land. It changed because the Japanese Ministry of Finance raised interest rates and introduced lending controls in 1989 to puncture the bubble economy of the late 1980s. In other words, the government made it clear by its action that prices were too high and would have to fall. Before 1989 Japanese real estate buyers (and banks) expected that rising prices would give them an automatic profit. People took out 50-year and 100-year mortgages in the confidence that prices would never fall. After 1991, of course, they stopped believing. A great many people and banks lost their equity or were bankrupted. Expectations changed because land prices themselves stopped rising. This phenomenon is hardly new. There have been a number of well documented speculative bubbles in history, including the famous Dutch tulip mania of the early seventeenth century, the Mississippi scheme of John Law (1718–1720), the South Sea Bubble of 1720, the California and Yukon gold rushes, and the Wall Street stock market frenzy of 1928–1929. There was also a brief silver bubble as recently as 1980. In all of these cases prices went up not because underlying values were rising, but simply because people expected prices to keep on rising.

Apart from the psychological bubble problem, to what extent is it realistic to assume that marginal prices (eg for stocks or farmland) can safely be interpreted as true average values? This is an important issue as I write (1997); the US stock market is breaking records almost daily. Analysts are never at a loss to account for such phenomena, but the only coherent explanation I have heard recently is that people are pouring cash into mutual funds and therefore mutual funds have to buy stocks. In other words, the market is going up because people are buying. The deeper question here is: to what extent do financial assets increase (or decrease) in value because of national euphoria or its dysphoric – not to mention dyspeptic – after effects? Can we eliminate the speculative element from national wealth estimates? For the moment, unfortunately, I doubt that one can do more than call attention to the problem.

There is a further constraint on the use of markets for valuation. It is the implicit condition that not too many similar properties or shares are up for auction at the same time (as occurs when a bubble collapses). When everybody wants to sell, prices fall sharply, even though underlying values – whatever they are – remain unchanged. Conversely, when everybody wants to buy, prices rise. As already noted, market value is a marginal concept. And yet we are interested in the aggregate value of all property, not the marginal value of property that is actually being bought and sold. We have to ask ourselves; is aggregate wealth equal to the sum total of all marginal wealth? The answer, as will be seen hereafter, is emphatically no.

It is deceptively straightforward to extrapolate the marginal approach to the national level. This extrapolation was, until recently, done annually by the Council of Economic Advisors to the President of the United States and published in the *Annual Economic Report of the President*. I do not present the figures at this point because they were inconsistent and therefore seriously misleading. They were inconsistent not only because they are sums over extrapolations based on marginal values, but because they omit the two most important components of wealth, human capital and natural capital. The section on national wealth has been omitted from the 1996 Report.

Tangible reproducible wealth and financial assets are not the whole story, by any means. Reproducible wealth is created by people via work, saving and investment, discovery or invention. The ability to create reproducible wealth is, itself, another sort of wealth. Only a small part of this is captured in tradeable financial assets, which essentially measures the discounted present value of expected future returns on capital investment. Profit-making firms in the US, where employees are especially mobile, invest relatively little in human capital for the simple reason that they cannot appropriate or exchange this form of capital.[1] The only owners of human capital are individuals themselves. The necessary investment is primarily made by government.

It is tempting, at first, to argue that the value of human resources to the economy is already taken into account through financial markets. Thus stock prices might reasonably be presumed to reflect the perceived quality of a firm's workers. This argument would seem to apply, in particular, to sports and entertainment, fashion designers, biotechnology and computer software firms whose future income is entirely dependent on the quality of their leadership and the creativity of their employees. But this argument is misleading for two reasons. In the first place, the financial markets focus narrowly on marginal values which means (in this case) the value of marginal employees. In the second place, stock markets obviously attach no value at all to the present or future labor of individuals not employed in the private sector. In Europe, this category of labor accounts for 40 per cent of the work force, and the fraction is close to a third in the US. I return to this point below.

Consider the first point. The financial market *in principle* should attach non-zero positive value to aggregate employment, if only because employees are necessary to production and unemployed people are not significant consumers. Market indexes, in recent years at least, seem to react favorably to increasing unemployment, because the Federal Reserve Board (which fears inflation more than unemployment) will be less likely to raise interest rates. For instance, a front page newspaper headline recently announced 'Wall Street Plunges 3 per cent on Strong Jobs Data' (*International Herald Tribune*, 1996a). This is by no means an isolated instance.

In fact, more often than not financial markets attach *negative* marginal value to human resources (ie employees) in the case of large companies. This assertion is easily verified; typically the financial markets attach higher values to the shares of firms immediately after they have announced that they will lay off large numbers of employees. AT&T stock rose sharply the day after it announced that 40,000 of its employees would be let go to cut costs. GE and IBM both cut employment sharply and were rewarded by dramatic increases in share prices. The recently announced merger of Swiss drug makers Sandoz and Ciba-Geigy (to create Novartis), which is expected to result in layoffs of 12,000 workers, caused the prices of both stocks to rise; Sandoz shares rose 22 per cent and Ciba shares rose 45 per cent on the news. Perhaps there were other reasons, but expected lower labor costs were clearly a factor.

The danger of extrapolating from marginal values is clearly illustrated by the following observation. Evidently the financial market 'thinks' that most large firms have too many employees, even though the firms may be profitable. Yet if all firms reduced employment to zero, the economy would evidently collapse. Since the marginal value of labor – as determined by financial markets – is negative for most firms, it follows that the market value of traded securities cannot be assumed to include the average value of human resource capital utilized by those firms. It further follows that too much of the firm's profits is thus attributed to capital investment, rather than to labor. Consistent with the above, human capital is assumed to have zero value for corporate accounting purposes. The book value of a company is based only on original cost (depreciated according to a schedule allowed by the Internal Revenue Service) or appraised market values of hard assets that are exchangeable, such as land, buildings, machinery and inventories. If there is any difference between stock market valuation or price actually paid by one company for another, it is attributed for accounting purposes to 'goodwill'. The latter cannot be depreciated as capital for tax purposes.

The second objection to the assumption that financial market values automatically include human resources is that, by this measure, workers in the public sector have no value at all, either as consumers or as producers. This assumption may appeal to some extremely doctrinaire libertarians, but to most people it is obviously nonsense. The fact that many essential public services are performed by government, or by not-for-profit organizations (including the educational system), should suffice to make the point that workers in the public sector both *create* value, and also *embody* value, just as workers in the private sector do. The fact that some government agencies may be over-manned[2] is no more relevant to the valuation of human capital than the fact that some private firms have too many employees.

The problem of measurement arises from the fact that neither people, nor their knowledge and skills, can be bought or sold by auction *as such*. Knowledge and skills can only be acquired by personal effort and learning over a period of time. Teaching assistance can be purchased (and sold), as a service. But teaching does not automatically assure learning. Attendance at school does not assure that either education or training actually occurs. Similarly, the possession of knowledge and skills on the part of the teachers does not guarantee transfer to the student. Both talent and dedication on the part of the student are also required. In short, knowledge and skills are transferable between people, but the process is time consuming and personal. They are not exchangeable through an auction process like barrels of oil or bushels of wheat. It is true that computers and information technology are beginning to disembody some kinds of knowledge and skills, making them more easily transferable (via other computers) and thus more like standard commodities. For instance, some machinists' skills are now embodied in commercially available computer programs for programmable machine tools, although higher order skills are needed to create those programs. This devalues human machine operators to some extent. Similarly, computational and accounting skills are now embodied in commercially available computer programs, reducing the need for certain kinds of human skills (such as book-keepers) and increasing the need for others higher level skills (such as accountants). Word processing has reduced the need for typists, but not the need for (or value of) secretaries with organizing skills. So far, at least, the process of disembodiment of knowledge and skills has displaced humans from certain routine tasks. But to the extent that some jobs have been lost, others have been created. Up to the present, it seems, IT has not significantly reduced the need for, and the economic value of, human labor per se.

There are reasons to fear that the marginal job losses that have occurred so far are only the beginning, and that future job losses resulting from encroachment by IT on the formerly human domain will be far greater. The long-term implications of these trends should be taken very seriously, as I pointed out in Chapter 5. For the purposes of this discussion, however, I assume that uniquely human skills and capabilities – suitably educated and trained – will continue to have market value in the foreseeable future. More specifically, I assume for purposes of analysis (below) that those now employed will, on average, continue to be gainfully employed for the rest of their normal working lives.

It is now commonplace for economists to talk about skills and technical information as forms of human capital, in contrast to other forms of capital. Evidently, marketable skills and knowledge must be embodied, either in people, or in capital equipment of some sort (including software). The chief problem, as I have already implied, is that of ownership and exchangeability. In a society that does not permit slavery, human resources (ie future labor) cannot be bought and sold as such. The resource itself can only be the property of individuals, with a few exceptions (see Note 2). Many others work on a contractual basis, receiving payment only for work actually performed. But the principle is clear; future paid work has current value, both to the workers themselves and to those who have products to sell, even though there is no well-developed market process for ascertaining that value. In short, human capital is also a form of wealth.

Confirmation is all around us. Consider the fact that students are willing to borrow large sums to get a college education, and the higher the reputation of the college, the more they are willing to pay. They borrow even larger sums to get a medical degree, a law degree or an MBA. Why? Because these credentials enable the possessor to earn much more money in the future than the average person. News magazines routinely report economic calculations of the extra value (in earning ability) of a college degree vis-à-vis a high school diploma. Engineering degrees are valued more than arts degrees. Ivy League colleges are worth more than lesser schools. Oxbridge is worth more than redbrick. A Masters degree or PhD also has computable economic value. An MBA or a professional qualification in law or medicine is worth even more. Again, an MBA from Harvard, Stanford or INSEAD is worth more than one from Podunk University. In some states of the US a divorced wife who has helped finance her husband's law degree or medical degree can justifiably claim part of the future income stream from that degree. Divorce courts are increasingly sympathetic to such arguments.

Similarly, banks and credit card companies routinely consider future earning capacity in making personal loans. They are even willing, nowadays, to offer significant amounts of credit to individuals with no current income at all, based entirely on the expectation of future earnings. There is nothing necessarily imprudent about this. It is now standard business practice in most Western countries, though it was not the case even three decades ago. Until credit cards became widespread, unsecured consumer credit was a relatively small and specialized field. Unsecured loans were the province of department stores (who gave credit only to well-established customers) and small loan companies. Today, unsecured credit card debt alone is a significant fraction of total private debt in the US and, by the same token, the asset (from the lender's viewpoint) is a significant fraction of the corporate equity of lenders and creditors.

MEASURING HUMAN CAPITAL

Economists assert that the market value of a share in a business is effectively the present value of expected future net earnings of that firm, per share. Financial institutions are willing to treat a part of this value as security for loans (which is the basis for the practice of buying stocks 'on margin'). Stock prices are volatile, so the maximum borrowing potential on a share is only a fraction of the market value. The difference can be regarded as the risk premium. It is a straightforward extension of the same logic to assert that the unsecured borrowing power of an individual is proportional to that individual's expected future earning power. Borrowing power is, by extension, part of his/her personal assets. It is, at least partially, fungible. Individuals can exchange borrowing power easily for cash or other forms of wealth, either tangible assets like clothes and furniture or financial assets. At least a few successful business enterprises have been started on the basis of personal credit cards alone.

This new practice has an interesting consequence for corporate accounts, balance sheets and wealth statistics. Unsecured lenders must count loans outstanding as if they were 'hard' financial assets, with an adjustment for statistical risk. Otherwise such lenders would be automatically bankrupt. But national wealth – as it has been routinely calculated in the *Annual Economic Report of the President* – is a mixed bag. It is not a straightforward generalization of individual net worth, due to the peculiar role of the government. Nor is it simply the sum total of the financial net worths of individuals. Individuals count holdings of government bonds as assets and credit card debts as liabilities. The conventional method of accounting for national wealth does exactly the opposite. It counts government debt only as a liability, while treating unsecured personal debt as an asset. Thus, the conventional method is both fundamentally inconsistent and incomplete.

At one time it might have been reasonable to define the sum of all human wealth as the sum total of reproducible tangible wealth, plus land, animals and forest resources but excluding labor. However, this is no longer adequate, if only because so much economic effort (and wealth) is expended nowadays on increasing the raw value of human labor by adding skills and knowledge that are not genetic endowments. The source of value added to human capital is the diffusion of transferable skills and existing knowledge by on-the-job training or via specialized teaching institutions such as schools and universities. On-the-job training through formal apprenticeships was probably the most important single source of human capital creation in the middle ages and well into the nineteenth century. More formal compulsory education in schools, beginning early in the nineteenth century, has since become nearly universal throughout the world. Education is clearly the essential first step in economic development. An important further aspect of the human capital of a nation is collective and social. It relates to social organization, inter-generational relationships and obligations (eg whether parents feel an obligation to educate and support their children, or whether they feel entitled to be supported by their children), attitudes to work (eg the work ethic), attitudes to learning, attitudes to science and religion and so on. These things are obviously of the utmost importance. They probably account for most of the differences in economic performance and well-being of countries – far more so than differences in market openness and relative tax burden. However, direct measurement remains a problem, and these aspects of intangible national wealth are not considered further in this book.

However, it is possible to outline a straightforward (if approximate) fix for the first of the measurement problems, which is the omission of personal future earning power from wealth statistics. While accountants will certainly want to argue the details, the general outlines of a consistent scheme can be set forth as indicated below. The results, as will be seen, permit one to draw some useful conclusions about the relationship between investment, growth, trade and wealth.

A more precise name for human capital would be expected future personal labor surplus or EFPLS. The word 'expected' is important since it provides the link between future and present. Apart from other reasons for including this term, there is a dominant one. The standard accounting methodology counts unsecured personal debt as a financial asset for businesses. But the standard accounting system does *not* recognize the comparable form of implicit personal wealth from which this debt should be deducted. Corporate debt is a claim on future (gross) earnings. Thus unsecured corporate debt (eg bonds), *ceteris paribus*, subtracts from stockholder equity while unsecured personal debt is counted as a corporate – hence stockholder – asset. It is inconsistent to treat unsecured corporate debt differently from unsecured personal debt. To present the problem in a slightly different way, stockholder equity can be regarded as the net present value of expected future returns to capital. But there is no corresponding category in the standard accounting methodology for representing the net present value of expected future returns to labor. Yet personal debts, including credit card debts (but excluding mortgages and car loans secured by tangible property), are obviously claims on the value of expected future personal income (net of costs) which is another form of wealth.

It is equally inconsistent to subtract unsecured government debt from total national wealth – as has been done for the US (eg in the annual *Economic Report of the President)* – without including any allowance for the future income streams against which these forms of unsecured debt are claims. Evidently, government debt is secured by expected future revenues. These are mostly derived by direct transfer (taxation) from either the business or the personal sectors. Government revenues are invariably redistributed to the other two sectors, either through wages and income transfers (such as pensions and subsidies) or by purchases of goods and services. However, some tangible government assets, held in common, are not included in either the personal or business category. These must be counted separately.

US national wealth, as it was formerly calculated, consisted of four categories of items, namely: private tangible reproducible wealth (US$7.76 trillion in 1992); private financial wealth (US$9.948 trillion in 1992); tangible reproducible government assets

(US$2.587 trillion in 1992); and government financial assets (US$2.59 trillion in 1992). The total was US$17.7 trillion, all in 1987 dollars. So-called 'tangible repro-ducible assets' consist mainly of structures (including infrastructure) and equipment. More detailed data are available for 1989. The gross value of such assets in the US in 1989 was US$23.8 trillion. Of this, structures accounted for US$14.77 trillion and equipment accounted for the rest. The net stock (essentially, book value) of private tangible assets was US$8.18 trillion, while the net stock of tangible assets owned by government was US$2.65 trillion. The gross value of consumer durables (included in the total) was valued at US$1.934 trillion in the same year (STATAB, 1991, Table 762).

Net depreciated values, cited above, take into account standard depreciation schedules, determined for tax purposes by the Internal Revenue Service. The usual depreciation accounting method – called 'straight-line' – is to deduct a simple fraction (1/N) from the initial value of the investment each year until the residual (depreciated) value is zero. The number N allowed by the IRS may vary from 5 years to 40 years.[3] Clearly, in the case of many long-lived assets such as highways, bridges and dams, this depreciation schedule (which is determined for tax purposes, not to provide realistic estimates of value) is too fast. While most business structures and virtually all equipment really do lose their value over 40 years, this is by no means true of residential houses or infrastructure. Many of these assets actually appreciate over time. For this reason, a third measure – replacement value – is probably more appropriate for some kinds of assets, especially water and sewer systems, roads and bridges, rail lines, tunnels and harbors.[4] Evidently their replacement value would be significantly greater than their depreciated value, and greater in many cases than the original cost. It therefore seems reasonable (for present purposes) to value structures at gross levels (about US$14.8 trillion) and equipment at net depreciated levels (about US$4 billion), for a total of US$18.8 trillion.

Private financial wealth reflects, in part, the market value of equity capital. It is clearly a function of expected future profits, and thus, indirectly, a function of expected economic growth. Implicitly, the market's estimate of value reflects the market's evaluation of growth prospects. If the market expects higher growth in the next few years, equities tend to rise in value, *ceteris paribus*, and conversely.

Net US government financial assets are negative; there is a net federal government debt which was US$2.59 trillion in 1992 in 1987 dollars, and was US$4.96 trillion at the end of the third quarter of 1995 in current dollars. But of course government bonds are assets on the books of the private financial institutions and foreign governments that hold them. US government debt held by domestic US lenders does not in any way subtract from national wealth, although the calculation is usually presented in such a way as to make it appear to do so. (The foreign debt is a different matter; however so far only about 17 per cent of US federal debt was held by foreigners at the end of the third quarter of 1995. About half of that was held by Japan (CEA, 1996, tables B-83 and B-85).)

By the same token, unfunded future entitlements of social security, pensions and Medicare/Medicaid payments from the federal government to individuals substantially exceed the federal government debt. They amounted to US$14.4 trillion at the end of FY 1991 by one calculation, compared to a federal debt of US$3.66 trillion at the time. If these entitlements are honored they will merely be a transfer from future taxpayers to retirees and the poor. In other words, money will go from one pocket of the body politic to another. It is important to emphasize once again that government debt does not simply reduce total national wealth, as current official calculations misleadingly suggest. In the first place, government debt is a financial asset to bond-holders, and is thus counted as financial wealth. It has been said, correctly, that government bonds are debts 'we owe to ourselves'.[5] The debit on the government side of the ledger is counterbalanced by an asset held by financial institutions. Government debt only affects EFPLS insofar as it creates an obligation on the part of citizens to pay taxes for future government debt service. In effect, it subtracts from future personal labor surplus – reducing disposable future income – by the compound interest charges on US$2.59 trillion (1987 dollars) at about 3 per cent per annum on the principal in real terms or 142 per cent over an assumed 25-year period.[6] This adjustment reduces undiscounted EFPLS by $3.68 trillion, leaving the principal unpaid of course. On the other hand, when EFPLS is discounted, as shown in Table 15.1, the present value to current workers of the future tax payments dedicated to payment of interest on national debt is considerably smaller, viz US$1.59 trillion at an 8 per cent discount rate, or US$1.35 trillion at a 10 per cent discount rate. These figures are to be compared to the US$2.59 trillion value of government bonds in private hands, which are current assets.[7]

However, as I have noted in Chapter 3, the implied burden of unfunded entitlements on future taxpayers cannot be shrugged off so lightly. Indeed, there is already a serious problem of excessive government spending – especially in Europe – and the demographic projections of an aging population are ominous. Taxes are a subtraction from current income of taxpayers. To the extent that taxes are used to redistribute national income, consumption is not reduced – in fact it is increased. So redistribution necessarily cuts into savings and therefore constitutes a drag on investment. Up to a point this is tolerable, and socially necessary. But governments have deferred too much of the tax-driven redistribution into future periods. Thus, continuing economic growth – and painlessly growing future government tax revenues – can no longer be taken for granted. For this reason I have estimated the present value (c1992) of EFPLS after allowing for irreducible subsistence costs and other fixed obligations, including taxation to pay debt service on government debts plus income transfers at a level sufficient to subsidize non-workers at the subsistence level. Taking into account two discount rates and three expected growth assumptions and subtracting the unsecured US$0.9 trillion credit card debt from the discounted totals yields the estimates in Table 15.1.[8]

Table 15.1 Discounted EFPLS in $ Trillions, 1992 (1987 $)

Expected Grown Rate	Assumed Discount Rate for EFPLS	
	0.08	0.1
0%	13.36	11.22
1%	19.15	16.13
2%	25.8	21.78

These numbers are obviously very sensitive both to expected growth rates and discount rates, especially the former. Even under zero expected growth assumptions, the present value of personal future labor income is by far the most important single component of national wealth at any time. Assuming a 10 per cent discount rate and

2 per cent expected growth, the discounted present value of EFPLS is nearly US$21.8 trillion. If one assumes that only 1 per cent per annum average growth rate for real earned income can be expected, the discounted 1992 value of EFPLS would be US$5.56 trillion less, or US$16.13 trillion. Assuming zero growth, the discounted value of EFPLS becomes US$11.22 trillion, nearly US$5 trillion less again. For the 8 per cent discount case the totals are slightly higher, but the impact of declining growth expectations is also slightly higher, albeit comparable. No doubt the above calculations are somewhat crude. They can surely be improved upon. But I have no doubt that the general conclusion is approximately right.

For purposes of comparison, the World Bank has recently published its own preliminary estimates of national wealth for 192 countries, which includes both human and natural capital.[9] This is not the place to describe or assess the World Bank methodology, except to say that all figures were imputed from GDP and GDP growth data, assuming all output to be a function of three types of capital assets: produced capital, natural capital and human resources. For the US, the world bank calculated the human resource component (c1990) to be US$62 billion, compared to US$17 trillion in produced assets. The latter figure is reasonably close to the US data I have used, but the former is obviously far larger. This difference is largely due to the fact that the World Bank considered human capital as a factor of production (based on a production function model using GDP as the output measure) but did not distinguish private intangible wealth as potential personal borrowing power against future personal income. It also did not make any allowance for future taxes to finance income redistribution as a subtraction from this borrowing power. The World Bank methodology also does not explicitly reflect the functional dependence of human capital on alternative future economic growth rates. The importance of these assumptions is obviously very great.

IMPLICATIONS OF INCREASING INEQUITY

The dependence of EFPLS on personal income growth has a very important implication. It means that, insofar as the economy shifts more money into corporate profits by increasing returns on capital at the expense of reduced payments for personal income from labor, the increased contribution to financial wealth of stockholders is probably more than compensated for by decreasing the (discounted) value of EFPLS. In other words, gains to owners of financial wealth that result from increasing profits (achieved by depressing wages) are not automatic win–win opportunities or free lunches for capitalists. Wage depression at the national level is not necessarily a zero-sum game in which gains to one player are losses to another (or others). It is more likely a negative-sum game, in which wage-earners whose wages are lower than they might be lose much more potential wealth than financial winners gain.

The extraordinary records still being set on the stock markets of the Western world (into mid-1997) are increasing apparent financial wealth by trillions of dollars. This is good for mutual fund owners and pensioners, as long as it lasts, although it is probably cutting into personal savings. But, to the extent that this is being done by reducing wage gains, or actually forcing down wages – and thus the expected value of future wages – it is cutting personal wealth in the form of EFPLS by even more trillions. Worse, the gains in financial wealth are entirely appropriated by the top 20 per cent of income earners – mainly by the top 5 per cent – who possess most of the financial wealth in the first place. The same group has also enjoyed accelerated gains in personal income and, by implication, in EFPLS. The losses are spread over the rest of the population, with the biggest percentage losses being suffered by the poorest people in the population.

Twenty years ago (1975), despite a recession, people in the bottom 20 per cent of wage-earners had enjoyed steady if unspectacular gains in real income for two decades. At that time, this group of people could reasonably expect to enjoy similar gains in the future. It has not happened like that. Today the poorest Americans are significantly worse off than they were before. This decline in actual status must surely be reflected in deteriorating expectations. Lower expectations, in turn, make people begin to feel poorer and spend less, thus cutting aggregate demand (the 'wealth effect' in reverse). There is no way to prove it, but I strongly believe that most Americans *feel* significantly poorer now than they (or their counterparts) did 20 years ago.

ENVIRONMENTAL WEALTH

I mentioned above that the official US figures make no allowance for the value of natural resources in the ground, or environmental resources. Estimates of monetizable natural capital were derived by the World Bank (see Serageldin, 1995; World Bank, 1995) from four categories, viz: land, fresh water, standing forest, and subsoil minerals. Land was valued in proportion to GDP per capita, but the proportionality constant was not given. However, cropland was given a basic valuation index of 2.0, forest an index of 1.75, pasture an index of 0.75 and 'other' land an index of 0.25. Further adjustments were made, such as a 50 per cent premium for prime (very fertile, irrigated) cropland or protected land. Steep slopes, high mountains, desert and tundra were valued at zero. Fresh water was valued at US$0.01 per gallon, while standing timber was valued (beyond the land value) at 50 per cent of the world market price. Underground minerals were also valued at 50 per cent of the prevailing world market price. For the US, the World Bank estimated the total value of monetizable natural resources (c1990) at US$26 trillion.

The non-monetizable component of environmental resources remains unquantifiable. The problem is measurement. Human life depends absolutely on the existence of a benign climate, large scale photosynthesis to produce oxygen and absorb carbon dioxide, a diverse biosphere to produce harvestable food and other biological products and to recycle biological wastes and restrain epidemic outbreaks of diseases or pests – among other environmental services. It follows that there could be no economic system on a dead planet. Destruction of the environment would be catastrophic and irreversible. No finite value can be put on such a loss.

Yet, we are faced with a seemingly less stark question. The problem is, apparently, to put a monetary value on small incremental changes, such as a 1°C climate warming or a 1 per cent loss of arable land due to erosion. Even though a 50 per cent change in either of these variables would be catastrophic, a 1 per cent change is evidently tolerable. How shall we proceed? There are three obvious candidates. The first approach is the most common but least justifiable: it is to ignore the problem. In effect (but never explicitly) this approach sets the value of unquantifiable environmental damages at zero. Regrettably, it is the approach adopted by most macro-economists.

The second possibility is known as contingent valuation (CV). The method is to conduct surveys of willingness to pay (WTP) for environmental protection or willingness to accept (WTA) compensation for environmental damages. This approach is currently favored among some environmental economists and lawyers. Indeed, some of the practitioners make a good living as expert witnesses in court cases. The problem, of course, is that the survey results are highly sensitive to the wording of the questions, which are, in turn, readily manipulated to obtain a desired result. Even if the survey questions are carefully formulated and the surveys are carried out by experienced experts, the problem remains that very few people can answer such a survey question honestly given that most of the situations described are distant and hypothetical.

For instance, consider the question: 'how much would you be willing to pay to reduce acid rain by 50 per cent?' Confronted with such a question, and knowing nothing about the causes or effects of acid rain, many people would answer 'nothing'. Told that acid rain might kill the old oak tree in their own front yard and asked 'how much would you pay to protect that old oak tree?' some people would name figures up to several hundred dollars. Told that acid rain results from sulfur dioxide emissions by electric power plants and that the cost of protection would be paid by the electric utilities, much higher damage estimates would result. The basic problems with the method are that people don't necessarily behave in the real world as they say they would in hypothetical situations, and that most people have very little knowledge of the real economic implications of environmental damage. Among other things, they don't realize that the utility will most likely pass its higher costs along to the consumer. The conventional neoclassical economist's assumption of 'perfect information' in the marketplace is especially inappropriate in cases where even the experts are uncertain.

The third possible approach, adopted mainly by environmentalists (but also some economists), is to argue that in the absence of reliable data on environmental damages, the cost of preventing or repairing the damages is a reasonable surrogate for the value of the damages themselves. This approach is very sensible and reasonable if we are talking about irreversible damages leading to potentially catastrophic consequences. The reason is that, if the damage is potentially catastrophic (as in the case of a 10–15 meter sea level rise, for instance), the cost of prevention is likely to be less than the damage would be. On the other hand, in the case of small or reversible damages, intuition suggests that the cost of prevention/repair may actually be much greater than the actual damage. Acid rain and biodiversity are good examples, and climate warming could be another (although I personally doubt it). A small increase in acidity or warming or a small decrease in biodiversity may not be particularly harmful. At least it is difficult to assess the harm, provided the changes are small. But any of these phenomena would be extremely expensive to prevent (albeit impossible to reverse). In these cases, a reasonable person would probably decide to suffer the consequences at first, rather than pay the costs of prevention. This decision is virtually assured by the conventional practice of discounting future costs and benefits.

The problem with this wait and see approach, of course, is that an accumulation of small and tolerable damages eventually and imperceptibly leads to large, intolerable, and irreversible ones. There is no objective global way to decide *a priori* when the first situation will turn into the second. What we need is a way of continuously assessing marginal damage costs of incremental increases in environmental acidity and incremental decreases in biodiversity and/or warming. These marginal costs certainly increase as a function of acidity, warming and lost biodiversity, respectively. When the marginal cost of acidity equals the marginal cost of prevention, the wait and see strategy would presumably shift to a prevention strategy.

In the real world, things are even less neat. For one thing, the costs of prevention aren't borne by the same people who suffer the damages. For instance, the direct costs of preventing climate warming through accelerated investment in alternative energy technologies would fall largely on the industrialized countries, while the most immediate victims of warming would be the dwellers of densely populated low-lying coastal areas of very poor countries like Bangladesh, China, Egypt, Indonesia and Vietnam, where rising sea levels and increased storm ferocity will exact their greatest tolls. Another difficulty is that any prevention strategy is likely to be quite capital-intensive and therefore impossible to implement quickly. Full implementation of an alternative energy system, not based on greenhouse-gas-emitting fossil hydrocarbons, will take a half century to achieve. Hence it will be necessary to begin to implement the prevention strategy decades before the actual marginal damages reach unacceptable levels. (In my opinion, we are already at the point where the preventive action is imperative.)

There is no need to discuss the complexities of environmental damages and protection strategy further, here. The point is that they certainly do have an impact on national and global wealth. It is only realistic to assume that society has (in effect) adopted the wait and see approach, which means that significant environmental damages in certain domains have accumulated already, without triggering fully compensating countermeasures. In other words, the roughly 2 per cent of GDP currently devoted to environmental protection – mainly health related – is insufficient to protect the nation against the cumulative damages from acidity, climate warming, and loss of biodiversity. Further countermeasures will therefore have to be adopted in the future, as the accumulated damages reach unacceptable levels.

The impact on economic growth is disputed. Most mainstream macro-economists argue that since the economy is now in (or near) an equilibrium condition with respect to technological choice, any changes induced by regulation will necessarily reduce economic growth. The results of typical calculations suggest that, to control carbon dioxide emissions (the prime cause of climate warming), economic growth could be reduced by something like 0.1 per cent per annum. As indicated in the discussion of expected future labor surplus (EFLS), even so small a reduction in expected economic growth would have a magnified effect on present national wealth.

My own view on this is heterodox. I do *not* believe the economy is in or near equilibrium. I believe it always operates well below its potential, due to a large number of inhibitory factors, most notably the tendency of large established mature industries and firms with obsolescent technologies to use economies of scale and political connections to protect themselves from competition by newer and smaller rivals. This being so, it is quite likely that strict environmental regulation (properly applied to performance and not to technology per se) can induce more rapid technological change and, as a consequence, more rapid economic growth, than laissez faire. I believe, in fact, that environmental regulation, if carefully designed and honestly implemented, can be economically beneficial by inducing firms to seek and find technical and organizational solutions they never would have found by doing business as usual.

CONCLUSIONS

To summarize: a fundamental difficulty in measuring national wealth relates to the treatment of human capital and unsecured personal debt. Individuals count government debt instruments (bonds) as assets and components of personal wealth. On the other hand, national accounts treat government debt as liabilities with no corresponding underlying assets. However, the national accounting approach is inherently inconsistent with the standard treatment of financial assets.

National accounts can only be made self-consistent by including human capital in some form, preferably by introducing a measure of potential borrowing power. This, in turn, is related to expected surplus earned income, above and beyond subsistence needs and future taxes to finance government debt and entitlements. Such a measure, called Expected Future Labor Surplus (EFLS), is introduced and estimated for several different growth scenarios and discount rates. However, even on the basis of rather conservative assumptions, this term is comparable to, or larger than, either tangible reproducible capital or financial wealth.

A further omission from the standard definition of wealth is the absence of any allowance for monetizable natural resources, not to mention environmental assets that are not exchangeable in any market and hence continue to be unpriced. It appears from World Bank estimates that the monetizable items alone are comparable in magnitude to the other components of wealth. Also, there are plausible arguments to suggest that the non-monetizable and unquantifiable components could become even larger – perhaps dominant – in the future.

NOTES

1   There are some exceptions to this statement, mainly athletes and entertainers, who contract to provide services for a fixed periods of time. These contracts are, to some extent, exchangeable.
2. The identity of such government agencies can be very controversial. Some people think the Internal Revenue Service should be abolished, even though the evidence is clear that increased manpower for monitoring and inspection would sharply increase revenues and cut the deficit. Many people think the military is over-manned; others want to increase its funding while eliminating social services.
3   The Commerce Department defines gross (private) assets as the sum total of private capital formation, assuming retirement of the asset at the end of a period that is 85 per cent of the 'service life' allowed for tax purposes by IRS Bulletin F. Net capital assets are calculated by straight-line depreciation at standard rates over the service life.
4   In this context, the US Army Corps of Engineers has estimated that US$1.5 trillion in repairs is needed on aging infrastructure. This figure is out of scale with the nominal US$2.65 trillion net value assigned by government accounting methodology to such assets.
5   Except for that 15 per cent or so that is held by foreigners.
6   Bonds are issued over varying periods, with varying interest rates, usually paid quarterly. Each individual bond is eventually repaid, but new ones are issued continuously. Thus the compounding scheme is essentially equivalent to what actually occurs (provided interest rates do not change, on average) and it makes the calculation easier.

7   All of this implies that, far from subtracting from national wealth, government debt actually *increases* aggregate national wealth! This is because the discounted present value of the taxpayers' share of future government debt is considerably less than the present value of the debt instruments to creditors. In other words, because the government can borrow money so much more cheaply than individuals can (3 per cent to 4 per cent in real terms as compared to 6 per cent or so for ordinary folks), it is financially beneficial to all citizens for the government to finance services that citizens would otherwise have to borrow money to pay for directly. (Health services and education are plausible examples.) The benefits of governmental borrowing would disappear, of course, if everybody could borrow money at a 3 per cent rate of interest, without providing security.

8   The details are too complicated to present in full here, but a complete derivation is available from INSEAD (Ayres, 1993).

9   Details are to be found in Serageldin, 1995; World Bank, 1995. The Serageldin paper, which provides the most detail, is clearly marked 'preliminary draft for discussion only' and readers are further warned to note that the work in question was not based on the same level of detail as typical World Bank country studies.

Appendix: Monetary Flows and Conservation of Money

Money normally obeys a short-run (weak) conservation law. However, the conservation law for money is not quite absolute. Whereas the quantity of energy or mass in a physical system can never change at all, the quantity of money can change gradually in a controlled manner. However, most of the implications of absolute money conservation hold approximately for the weak version of the law. The best way to approach this issue systematically and rigorously is via a 'flow of funds' matrix, shown schematically below.

Sector	1) Households	2) Business	3) Government	4) Finance	5) Rest of the World
1) Households					
2) Business					
3) Government					
4) Finance					
5) Rest of the world					

Figure A.1 National Flow of Funds Matrix

The elements of this matrix A_{ij} represent money flows *from* the sector indexed by i *to* the sector indexed by j. Matrix elements with the same index (i=j) represent monetary flows within the same sector. The intersectoral flows are as follows:

A_{12}: domestic personal consumption expenditure
A_{13}: personal taxes on income and property
A_{14}: interest payments on personal debt + net new savings
A_{15}: personal consumption expenditure in foreign countries (tourism) + remittances to relatives living abroad
A_{21}: wages, salaries, rents, royalties and dividends from business
A_{23}: taxes on sales, profits and value added
A_{24}: dividends and interest on stocks and bonds held by financial institutions
A_{25}: payments for imported goods and services + dividends and royalties to foreigners

A_{31}:   transfer payments (social security, pensions, subsidies) + wages to government employees

A_{32}:   Government payments to business for purchased goods and services + subsidies

A_{34}:   interest payments on debt to financial institutions

A_{35}:   direct foreign aid + payments to international agencies

A_{41}:   interest on personal savings + new consumer credit

A_{42}:   new business capital creation (debt or equity)

A_{43}:   new credit to government (deficit financing)

A_{45}:   capital exports

A_{51}:   remittances from foreigners to residents + funds brought by immigrants

A_{52}:   payments for exports of goods and services + royalties and repatriation of profits from foreign investments

A_{53}:   repayments of foreign debts to government + foreign purchases of government bonds

A_{54}:   capital imports for investment in the domestic business sector

A number of these flows are quite minor, and can be neglected in practice for the US, though not necessarily for other countries. (For instance, remittances from abroad are very important for Israel and the countries of Central America.)

An important aspect of the monetary system is that money is conserved absolutely by all sectors except the government. Only the government can create new money through its central bank.[1] But even the government cannot create money arbitrarily without igniting a self-defeating inflation. Effectively, if the economy grows at R per cent the government can (and must) increase the money supply by R per cent.

However, for analytical purposes, it is convenient to consider first the no-growth case R=0. Subsequently, the adjustment for R>0 can be made without difficulty. There is also another important simplification, namely that there are no changes in stocks of money in any sector, from year to year. This is not an onerous restriction, since it applies effectively only to paper money in private hands, of which there is very little.[2] Money in the form of bank accounts and credit instruments is automatically recycled through the financial system, almost by definition.

In the no-growth, constant money supply case, the total amount of money (eg dollars) in circulation is fixed. This implies that the monetary inflows and outflows to and from each sector must balance exactly. This is an accounting identity, not an approximation. It follows, immediately, that for the ith sector the column sum must equal the row sum. In other words, for all values of the index i:

1) $A_{i1} + A_{i2} + A_{i3} + A_{i4} + A_{i5} = A_{1i} + A_{2i} + A_{3i} + A_{4i} + A_{5i}$

where the diagonal elements A_{ii} appear on both sides, and thus cancel. (For instance, sales by domestic business units to other domestic business units must exactly equal purchases by domestic business units from other domestic business units.) This gives us five equations, of which four are independent.

Note that each off-diagonal term appears in two different identities. This yields two equations each for new private savings and new business capital. The first equation is the balance condition for households:

2)   **Net private savings** = total personal income – total personal outlays

= {wages + salaries + dividends received by individuals + interest on savings

+ rents and royalties + net transfers + remittances}

–{personal consumption expenditure (PCE) + remittances to foreigners

+ personal taxes + interest payments on existing consumer credit balance

+ new consumer credit}

Next, by applying the balance condition to the business sector, we have:

3a)   **Net new domestic business capital formation** =

net financial inflows (to the business sector)

– net financial outflows (from the business sector)

= {domestic revenues from *final* sales to consumers

+ sales of goods and services to government + exports of goods and services

+ royalties + repatriation of profits on existing foreign investments}

– {wages, salaries, rents, royalties, dividends paid by business to individuals

+ imports + capital exports for new foreign investment + business taxes}

where domestic intermediate purchases and sales are omitted from the above equation because they appear with both signs and cancel exactly. Domestic final sales of goods and services to consumers are equal to PCE less purchases of government services and spending by tourists travelling abroad. 'Exports' at the end of the first set of brackets includes final sales to foreign visitors and tourists. Note that the items in the first set of brackets in 3a can be equated to total revenues on sales, plus foreign royalties and repatriated earnings on foreign investments. Similarly, the items in the second set of brackets can be equated to the cost of production plus dividends and capital exports. Thus 3a can be rewritten:

3b)   **Net new domestic business capital formation** =

{gross profit less business taxes} – {dividends + capital exports}

It must be pointed out here that gross profit, as defined above, includes allowable depreciation (ie the part of gross earnings exempted from taxation as replacement of capital). It is also worth noting that profit — hence capital formation — is directly dependent on exports less imports. Thus a large positive trade balance (such as Japan enjoys) contributes directly to capital formation in Japan. Conversely, a negative trade balance (such as the US has) is a direct subtraction from capital formation.

For the financial sector the balance condition implies:

4)   **Net new domestic business capital formation** =

net inflows (to financial sector) – net outflows (from financial sector)

= {net private savings

+ interest payments on existing consumer, business and government debt

+ dividends received by institutional stockholders + foreign capital imports}

– {interest paid to individual savers + capital exports + new consumer credit

+ new government credit}

In the second expression with brackets, 'new government credit' is, of course, the net current deficit of the public sector including all levels of government, after payment of debt service. Evidently, both consumer deficits (new consumer credit) and government deficits also subtract directly from private sector capital formation.

However, it must also be pointed out that both categories of unsecured credit growth may, in fact, be financing various forms of investment. For instance, personal loans may be used to finance advanced education, while government debt may help finance infrastructure development, R&D and a variety of government human resource programs, including education and public health. Unfortunately, government budgets do not distinguish between developmental investments, other service functions (eg defense, police, courts, post office, air traffic control, etc.) and income redistribution (social security, Medicare, Medicaid, welfare assistance etc).

For completeness, the government sector balance condition can also be written, viz:

5)   **Deficit** = Expenditures – Revenues

= {wages + redistribution + purchases + interest on debt} – {tax revenues}

This condition states the obvious; it contains no surprising new insights.

The foregoing relationships 1–5 do not change significantly in the case $R > 0$. As long as the money supply is increased gradually and continuously, all other flows simply grow at the rate R. In other words, the entire system simply expands, leaving all the basic relationships unchanged.

NOTES

1   The money-creating mechanism is credit extended from the central bank (the Federal Reserve Bank) to other commercial banks belonging to the Federal Reserve system. The borrowed funds can then be reloaned to other customers. Obviously the FRB controls the supply of new money, both through credit restrictions and via the interest rates it charges other banks.

2   Admittedly there is a significant amount of US paper currency in permanent circulation outside the US, where it serves in some countries as a pseudo-currency and monetary reserve for individuals and businesses. The change from year to year is relatively small, however. In fact, it is too small to monitor accurately.

Bibliography

Abernathy, William J, *The Productivity Dilemma*, Johns Hopkins University Press, Baltimore, 1978

Abramovitz, Moses, 'Economics of Growth', in Haley (ed), *A Survey of Contemporary Economics*, Richard D Irwin Inc, New York, 1952 (for the American Economic Society)

Abramovitz, Moses, 'Resources and Output Trends in the United States Since 1870', *American Economic Review* 46, May 1956

Afheldt, H, *Wohlstand für niemand?*, Kunstmann, Munich, 1994

Anderson, Victor, *Alternative Economic Indicators*, Routledge, New York, 1991

Arthur, W Brian, 'Competing Technologies: An Overview', in Dosi, Giovanni, Christopher Freeman, Richard Nelson, Gerald Silverberg and Luc Soete (eds), *Technical Change and Economic Theory*, Pinter, London, 1988

Asimov, Isaac, *Foundation*, Panther Books, London, 1951

Ayres, Robert U, *Resources, Environment and Economics: Applications of the Materials/Energy Balance Principle*, John Wiley and Sons, New York, 1978

Ayres, Robert U, *Uncertain Futures: Challenge for Decision-Makers*, John Wiley and Sons, New York, 1979

Ayres, Robert U, *Energy Inefficiency in the US Economy: A New Case for Conservatism*, Research Report (RR-89-12), International Institute for Applied Systems Analysis, Laxenburg, November 1989a

Ayres, Robert U, 'Industrial Metabolism', in Ausubel, Jesse and Hedy Sladovich (eds), *Technology and Environment*, National Academy Press, Washington DC, 1989.

Ayres, Robert U, *Computer Integrated Manufacturing: Revolution in Progress* (Series: IIASA CIM Project), Chapman and Hall, London, 1991

Ayres, Robert U, *On National Wealth*, Working Paper (93/14/EPS), INSEAD, Fontainebleau, January 30, 1993

Ayres, Robert U, 'On Economic Disequilibrium and Free Lunch', *Environmental and Resource Economics* 4, 1994

Ayres, Robert U, Roman Dobrinsky, William Haywood, Kimio Uno and Ehud Zuscovitch (eds), *Computer Integrated Manufacturing: Economic and Social Impacts*, (Series: IIASA CIM Project) Chapman and Hall, London, 1991a.

Ayres, Robert U, William Haywood, M Eugene Merchant, Jukka-Pekka Ranta and H-J Warnecke (eds), *Computer Integrated Manufacturing Systems and Technology: The Past, the Present and the Future*, (Series: IIASA CIM Project) Chapman and Hall, London, 1991b.

Ayres, Robert U, William Haywood and Yuri Tchijov (eds), *The Diffusion of Computer Integrated Manufacturing Technologies: Models, Case Studies and Forecasts*, (Series: IIASA CIM Project) Chapman and Hall, London, 1991c

Ayres, Robert U and Paul Weaver (eds), *Eco-restructuring*, United Nations University Press, Tokyo, in press

Ayres, Robert U and Allan V Kneese, 'Production, Consumption and Externalities', *American Economic Review*, June 1969

Ayres, Robert U and Allen V Kneese. 'Externalities: Economics and Thermodynamics', in Archibugi and Nijkamp (eds), *Economy and Ecology: Towards Sustainable Development*, Kluwer Academic Publishers, Netherlands, 1989

Barlett, Donald L and James B Steele, *America: What Went Wrong?* Andrews and McMeel, Kansas City MO, 1992

Barnett, Harold J and Chandler Morse, *Scarcity and Growth: The Economics of Resource Scarcity*, Johns Hopkins University Press, Baltimore, 1962

Barro, R J and Sala-I-Martin, X, *Economic Growth*, McGraw-Hill, New York, 1995

Baumol, William J, *Speech*, Annual Meeting, American Philosophical Society, May 1993

Beckerman, Wilfred, *In Defense of Economic Growth*, Cape, London, 1974

Beckerman, Wilfred, *Small is Stupid*, Gerald Duckworth and Company, Ltd, London, 1995

Boulding, Kenneth E, *The Meaning of the Twentieth Century*, Harper and Row, New York, 1964

Boulding, Kenneth E, 'Environmental Quality in a Growing Economy', in Henry Jarrett (ed), *Essays from the Sixth RFF Forum*, Johns Hopkins University Press, Baltimore, 1966

Brown, Lester R, *Who Will Feed China? Wake-Up Call for a Small Planet*, Earthscan, London, 1995

Brown, Lester R, Christopher Flavin and Hal Kane, *Vital Signs 1996*, Earthscan, London, 1996.

Brundtland, Gro H (ed), *Our Common Future*, Oxford University Press, New York, 1987

Burtless, Gary, 'International Trade and the Rise of Earnings Inequality', *Journal of Economic Literature* xxxiii, June 1995

Business Week, July 8, 1996

Carnahan, Walter, Kenneth W Ford, Andrea Prosperetti, Gene I Rochlin, Arthur H Rosenfeld, Marc H Ross, Joseph E Rothberg, George M Seidel and Robert H Socolow, *Efficient Use of Energy: A Physics Perspective*, Study Report (399), American Physical Society, New York, January 1975

Cassidy, John, 'Who Killed the Middle Class?', *The New Yorker*, October 16, 1995

Council of Economic Advisors, *Economic Report of the President Together with the Annual Report of the Council of Economic Advisors*, United States Government Printing Office, Washington DC, February 1996

Coates, Joseph F, 'Reworking Work: Tough Times Ahead', *Annals of the American Academy of Political and Social Sciences* 544, March 1996

Cobb, Clifford W and John B Cobb Jr, *The Green National Product: A Proposed Index of Sustainable Economic Welfare*, University Press of America, Lanham, MD, 1994

Cole, H S D, Christopher Freeman, Marie Jahoda and K L R Pavitt (eds), *Models of Doom: A Critique of the Limits to Growth*, Universe Books, New York, 1973

Cruz, Wilfrido and Robert Repetto, *The Environmental Effects of Stabilization and Structural Adjustment Programs: The Philippines Case*, World Resources Institute, Washington DC, September 1992

Commoner, Barry, *The Closing Circle*, Alfred Knopf, New York, 1971

Commoner, Barry, *The Poverty of Power*, Bantam Books, New York, 1976

Cullen, R, 'The True Cost of Coal', *Atlantic Monthly* 272(6), 1993

Cullen, R, 'The Cost of Coal', *Atlantic Monthly* 273(5), 1994

Daly, Herman E, *Toward a Steady State Economy*, W H Freeman and Company, San Francisco, 1973

Daly, Herman E, *Steady-State Economics*, Island Press, Washington DC, 1977, revised 1991

Daly, Herman E and John Cobb, *For the Common Good*, Beacon Press, Boston, 1989

Denison, Edward F, *Accounting for Slower Growth*, Brookings Institution, Washington DC, 1979.

Douthwaite, Richard, *The Growth Illusion: How Economic Growth Has Enriched the Few, Impoverished the Many, and Endangered the Planet*, Council Oak Books, Tulsa OK, 1993

The Economist, August 14, 1993

The Economist, November 5, 1994

The Economist, 'Technology and Employment', February 11, 1995

The Economist, 'Le Défi Américain, again', July 13, 1996a

The Economist, April 13, 1996b

The Economist, May 25, 1996c

The Economist, July 20, 1996d

The Economist, 'Economics focus: factor prices', April 20, 1996e, p78

Feshbach, Murray, *Medical Situation in the Former USSR: Priority Regions and Cities*, Report to the World Bank, Washington DC, 1994

Feshbach, Murray, *Ecological Disaster: Cleaning Up the Hidden Legacy of the Soviet Regime* The Twentieth Century Fund Press, New York 1995a.

Feshbach, Murray, *Environmental and Health Atlas of Russia*, PAIMS Publishing House, Moscow, 1995b.

Feshbach, Murray and Alfred Friendly Jr, *Ecocide in Russia: Health and Nature Under Siege*, Basic Books, New York, 1992

Figgie, Harry and Gerald J Swanson, *Bankruptcy 1995: The Coming Collapse of America and How to Stop It*, 1992

Financial Times, September 21, 1995

Forrester, Jay W, *World Dynamics*, Wright-Allen, Cambridge MA, 1971

Forrester, Jay W, Gilbert W Low and Nathaniel J Mass, 'The Debate on "World Dynamics": A Response to Nordhaus', *Policy Sciences* 5, 1974

Friedman, Milton, *Essays in Positive Economics*, University of Chicago Press, Chicago, 1953

Friedrich, R, U Kallenbach, E Thone, A Voss, Hans-Holger Rogner and D Karl, *Externe Kosten der Stromerzeugung*, VWEW-Verlag, Frankfurt am Main, 1989

Friedrich, R and A Voss, 'External Costs of Electricity Generation', *Energy Policy* 21, 1993

Galbraith, John Kenneth, *The New Industrial State*, Houghton Mifflin, Boston, 1968

Gardels, Nathan, column in *The Washington Post*, April 12, 1993

Georgescu-Roegen, Nicholas, *The Entropy Law and the Economic Process*, Harvard University Press, Cambridge MA, 1971

Gilfillan, S Colum, 'The Prediction of Inventions', in Ogburn, William F et al (eds), *Technological Trends and National Policy, Including the Social Implications of New Inventions*, National Research Council/National Academy of Sciences National Resources Committee, Washington DC, 1937

Goeller, Harold and Alvin Weinberg, 'The Age of Substitutability', *Science* 191, February 1976

Goldsmith, Sir James, *The Trap*, Carroll and Graf, New York, 1994

Hardin, Garett, 'The Tragedy of the Commons', *Science* 162, 1968

Heilig, Gerhard, 'Neglected dimensions of global land use changes: reflections and data' *Population and Development Review* 20(4), December 1994

Hobsbawm, Eric, *Age of Extremes: The Short Twentieth Century, 1914–1991*, Abacus, London, 1994.

Hohmeyer, O, *Social Costs of Energy Consumption*, Springer-Verlag, Berlin, 1989

Hohmeyer, O and R L Ottinger, *External Environmental Costs of Electric Power*, Springer-Verlag, Berlin, 1991

Hueting, Rofie, *New Scarcity and Economic Growth: More Welfare through Less Production?*, North Holland, Amsterdam, 1980

Huntington, Samuel, 'The Clash of Civilizations', *Foreign Affairs*, Summer 1993

Huntington, Samuel, *The Clash of Civilizations and the Remaking of World Order*, Simon and Schuster, New York, 1996

Iklé, Fred, 'Book Review', *The National Interest*, Summer 1995

International Herald Tribune, July 25, 1995

International Herald Tribune, 'Wall Street Plunges 3 per cent on Strong Jobs Data', March 9–10, 1996a

International Herald Tribune, June 24, 1996a

International Herald Tribune, March 14, 1996c

Jackson, Tim and Nick Marks, *Measuring Sustainable Economic Welfare – A Pilot Index: 1950-1990*, Stockholm Environmental Institute, Stockholm, 1994

Kahn, Herman (with Julian Simon) (ed), *The Resourceful Earth*, 1984

Kahn, Herman, William Brown and L Martel, *The Next 200 Years – A Scenario for America and the World*, William Morrow, New York, 1976

Keyfitz, Nathan, 'Accuracy and Usefulness of the GDP', *Statistical Journal of the United Nations*, ECE 10, 1993

Kondratieff, N D, 'Die Langen Wellen der Konjunktur', *Archiv fur Sozialwissenschaft und Sozialpolitik* 56, 1926

Kondratieff, N D, 'Die Preisdynamik der Industriellen und Landwirtschaftlichen Waren', *Archiv fur Sozialwissenschaft und Sozialpolitik* 60, 1928 (English translation in *Review of Economics and Statistics* 17, 1978)

Krugman, Paul, 'The Illusion of Conflict in International Trade', *Peace Economics, Peace Science and Public Policy* 2(2), 1995

Krugman, Paul and Robert Z Lawrence, 'Trade, Jobs and Wages', *Scientific American* 270(4), April 1994

Kuznets, Simon, *Secular Movements in Production and Prices – Their Nature and Bearing on Cyclical Fluctuations*, Houghton Mifflin, Boston, 1930

Kuznets, Simon, *Economic Change – Selected Essays in Business Cycles, National Income and Economic Growth*, W W Norton and Company, New York, 1953

Leontief, Wassily W, 'Domestic production and foreign trade: the American capital position re-examined', *Economics International 7*, February 1954

Lewis, Michael, *Liar's Poker*, Hodder and Stoughton Ltd, London, 1989

Lovins, Amory B, Michael M Brylawski, David R Cramer and Timothy C Moore, *Hypercars: Materials, Manufacturing, and Policy Implications*, The Hypercar Center, Rocky Mountain Institute, Snowmass CO, Proprietary Strategic Study, March 1996

MacKenzie, James Jr, Roger C Dower and Donald D J Chen, *The Going Rate: What it Really Costs To Drive*, World Resources Institute, Washington DC, 1992

Maddison, Angus, *Phases of Capitalist Development*, Oxford University Press, Oxford, 1982

Malthus, Thomas Robert, 'An Essay on the Principle of Population as it Affects the Future Improvement of Society', in Abbott, Leonard Dalton (ed), *Masterworks of Economics: Digest of Ten Great Classics*, Doubleday and Company, Inc, New York, 1946 (first published 1798)

McRae, Hamish, *The World in 2020; Power, Culture and Prosperity: A Vision of the Future*, Harper Collins Publishers, London, 1994

Meadows, Donella H, Dennis L Meadows, Jorgen Randers and William W Behrens III, *The Limits to Growth: A Report for the Club of Rome's Project on the Predicament of Mankind*, Universe Books, New York, 1972

Mensch, Gerhard, *Das Technologische Patt: Innovation uberwinden die Depression* (Series: Stalemate in Technology: Innovations Overcome the Depression), Umschau, Frankfurt, 1975 (english translation: Ballinger, Cambridge MA, 1979)

Mishan, E J, *The Costs of Economic Growth*, Staples Press, London, 1967

Mishan, E J, *The Costs of Economic Growth*, Weidenfeld and Nicolson, London, 1993 (revised edition)

Murphy, R Taggart, *The Weight of the Yen*, 1994

Myers, David G and Ed Diener, 'The Pursuit of Happiness', *Scientific American* 274(3), May 1996

Nelson, Richard R, 'Recent Evolutionary Theorizing about Economic Change', *Journal of Economic Literature* XXXIII(1), March 1995

Nelson, Toni, 'Russia's Population Sink', *Worldwatch* 9(1), January/February 1996

New York Times, January 23, 1995

Nordhaus, William D, 'World Dynamics: Measurement without Data', *Economic Journal*, December 1973

Nordhaus, William D, *Managing the Global Commons: The Economics of Climate Change*, MIT Press, Cambridge MA, 1994

Nordhaus, William D and James Tobin (eds), *Economic Growth*, Columbia University Press, New York, 1972

Novak, Michael, *First Things*, American Enterprise Institute, Washington DC, 1995

Natural Resources Defense Council, Union of Concerned Scientists and the Alliance to Save Energy, *America's Energy Choices*, Washington DC, 1992

Organization for Economic Cooperation and Development, *Technology and the Economy: The Key Relationships*, OECD, Paris, 1992

Organization for Economic Cooperation and Development, *The OECD Jobs Study: Evidence and Explanations*, OECD, Paris, 1994

Ormerod, Paul, *The Death of Economics*, Faber and Faber, London, 1994

Persson, Torsten and Guido Tabellini, *American Economic Review*, June 1994

Peterson, Peter G, *Facing Up: How to Rescue the Economy from the Burden of Crushing Debt and Restore the American Dream*, 1993.

Pfaff, William, Column in *International Herald Tribune*, December 15, 1995

Pigou, A C, *The Economics of Welfare*, Macmillan, London, 1920

Porter, Michael, 'America's Competitiveness Strategy', *Scientific American*, April 1991

Prosterman, Roy L, Tim Hanstad and Li Ping, 'Can China Feed Itself?', *Scientific American* 275(5), November 1996

Rector, Robert, in Simon, Julian E, Calvin Beisner and John Phelps (eds), *The State of Humanity*, Blackwell Publishers Ltd, Cambridge MA, 1995

Repetto, Robert, *Natural Resource Accounting in a Resource-Based Economy: An Indonesian Case Study*, 3rd Environmental Accounting Workshop, UNEP and World Bank, Paris, 1985

Repetto, Robert, 'Accounting for Environmental Assets', *Scientific American*, June 1992

Rifkin, Jeremy, *The End of Work*, G P Putnam and Sons, New York, 1994

Robertson, James, *Future Wealth*, Cassell, London 1990

Romer, Paul M, 'Increasing Returns and Long-Run Growth', *Journal of Political Economy* 94(5), October 1986

Romer, Paul M, 'Growth Based on Increasing Returns Due to Specialization', *American Economic Review* 77(2), May 1987

Romer, Paul M, 'Endogenous Technological Change', *Journal of Political Economy* 98(5), October 1990

Romer, Paul M, 'The Origins of Endogenous Growth', *Journal of Economic Perspectives* 8(1), Winter 1994

Roodman, D M, *Paying the Piper: Subsidies, Politics and the Environment*, Worldwatch Paper (133), Worldwatch Institute, Washington DC, 1996

Salter, W E G, *Productivity and Technical Change*, Cambridge University Press, New York, 1960

Schumacher, E F, *Small Is Beautiful: Economics as Though People Mattered*, Harper Colophon, New York, 1973

Schumpeter, Joseph A, *Theorie der Wirtschaftlichen Entwicklungen*, Duncker and Humboldt, Leipzig, 1912

Schumpeter, Joseph A, *Theory of Economic Development*, Harvard University Press, Cambridge MA, 1934

Schumpeter, Joseph A, *Business Cycles: A Theoretical, Historical and Statistical Analysis of the Capitalist Process*, McGraw-Hill, New York, 1939

Serageldin, Ismail, *Sustainability and the Wealth of Nations: First Steps in an Ongoing Journey*, Third Annual World Bank Conference on Environmentally Sustainable Development, International Bank for Reconstruction and Development, Washington DC, September 30, 1995

Shambaugh, David, article in *International Herald Tribune*, April 10, 1995

Simon, Julian, *The Ultimate Resource*, Princeton University Press, Princeton NJ, 1980

Simon, Julian E, Calvin Beisner and John Phelps (eds), *The State of Humanity*, Blackwell Publishers Ltd, Cambridge MA, 1995

Smil, Vaclav, *Environmental Change as a Source of Conflict and Economic Losses in China*, American Academy of Arts and Sciences, Cambridge MA, 1992

Smil, Vaclav, *China's Environmental Crisis: An Inquiry into the Limits of National Development*, M E Sharpe, Armonk NY, 1993

Smil, Vaclav, 'Who Will Feed China?', *China Quarterly* (143), September 1995

Smil, Vaclav, *Environmental Problems in China: Estimates of Economic Costs*, East-West Center Special Report (5), East-West Center, Honolulu HA, April 1996

Solórzano, Raúl, Ronnie de Camino, Richard Woodward, Joseph Tosi, Vicente Watson, Alexis Vásquez, Carlos Vallalobos, Jorge Jiménez, Robert Repetto and Wilfrido Cruz, *Accounts Overdue: Natural Resource Depreciation in Costa Rica*, World Resources Institute, Washington DC, Tropical Science Center, San José, Costa Rica and WRI, December 1991

Solow, Robert M, 'A Contribution to the Theory of Economic Growth', *Quarterly Journal of Economics* 70, 1956

Solow, Robert M, 'Technical Change and the Aggregate Production Function', *Review of Economics and Statistics*, August 1957

Speth, James Gustave, 'Commentary', *New Perspectives Quarterly*, Summer 1996

Steinhard, Carol E and John S Steinhard, 'Energy Use in the US Food System', *Science* (184), April 19 1974, p312

United States Bureau of the Census, *Statistical Abstract of the United States: 1991*, United States Government Printing Office, Washington DC, 1991

Strong, Maurice, *Agenda 21*, United Nations Commission on Environment and Development, Rio de Janeiro, 1992

Tawney, R H, *Equality*, Capricorn Books, New York, 1952

Tobin, James and William Nordhaus, 'Is Growth Obsolete?', in *Economic Growth*, Nordhaus and Tobin (eds), Columbia University Press, New York, 1972

Trefler, Daniel, 'The Case of The Missing Trade and Other Mysteries', *American Economic Review* 85(5), December 1995

Trisko, E M, 'The Cost of Coal', *Atlantic Monthly* 273(5), 1994

Tyler, Patrick, 'China's Water is Drying Up', *New York Times*, December 1993

Tyson, Laura, 'Managing Trade and Competition in the Semiconductor Industry', in: *Who's Bashing Whom?*, Institute for International Economics, Washington DC, 1992

Uchilelle, Louis and Kleinfeld, NR, The New York Times News Service, March 6, 1996

Usui, Mikoto, *Managing Technological Change and Industrial Development in Japan*, Discussion Paper Series (380), Institute of Socio-Economic Planning, Japan, August 1988

von Neumann, John, 'A Model of General Economic Equilibrium', *Review of Economic Studies* 13, 1945 :1–9.

von Weizsäcker, Ernst Ulrich, Amory B Lovins and L Hunter Lovins, *Faktor Vier*, Droemer Knaur, Munich, 1994

von Weizsäcker, Ernst Ulrich, Amory B Lovins and L Hunter Lovins, *Factor Four: Doubling Wealth, Halving Resource Use*, Earthscan, London, 1997

von Weizsäcker, Ernst Ulrich and Jochen Jesinghaus, *Ecological Tax Reform: A Policy Proposal for Sustained Development*, Zed Books, London, 1992

Ward, Barbara, *Spaceship Earth*, Columbia University Press, New York, 1966

Weiner, Herbert, *Perturbing the Organism: The Biology of Stressful Experiences*, University of Chicago Press, Chicago, 1992

Weterings, R and J B Opschoor, *The Ecocapacity as a Challenge to Technological Development*, Advisory Council for Research on Nature and Environment (RMNO), Rijswijk, Netherlands, April 1992

White, Lynn Jr, 'Technology in the Middle Ages', in: Kranzberg, Melvin and Carroll W Pursell Jr (eds), *Technology and Western Civilization, Volume I*, Oxford University Press, New York, 1967

World Bank, *World Development Report 1992*, Oxford University Press, New York, 1993

World Bank, *Social Indicators of Development*, International Bank for Reconstruction and Development, Washington DC, 1995

World Bank, *World Development Report 1995*, Oxford University Press, New York, 1996

World Resources Institute, *World Resources 1993–94*, Oxford University Press, New York, in collaboration with UNEP and UNDP, 1993

World Resources Institute, *World Resources 1996–97*, Oxford University Press, New York, in collaboration with UNEP, UNDP and the World Bank, 1996

Wright, T P, 'Factors Affecting the Cost of Airplanes', *Journal of Aeronautical Sciences* 3, 1936

Zinsser, Hans *Rats, Lice and History: The Biography of a Bacillus*, Atlantic Monthly Press, Boston, 1963

Index

Numbers in **bold** refer to figures.